Faith
in the
Unseen

RASHID SEYAL

iUniverse, Inc.
New York   Bloomington

Faith in the Unseen

iUniverse books may be ordered through booksellers or by contacting:

iUniverse
1663 Liberty Drive
Bloomington, IN 47403
www.iuniverse.com
1-800-Authors (1-800-288-4677)

ISBN: 978-1-4401-7813-9 (sc)
ISBN: 978-1-4401-7811-5 (hc)
ISBN: 978-1-4401-7812-2 (ebook)

Printed in the United States of America

iUniverse rev. date: 7/7/2010

Committed
for
compassion with care and conciliation
for
all castes, creeds, colors, and cultures.

Faith

A Good Faith is at its best when the line
Between
The **Truth** and **Belief** is not discernable

And that's the Faith of:
Abraham [AS] Moses [AS] Jesus [AS] and Muhammad [PBUH1]
Asserted in all the Holy Scriptures

Cloisters, churches, oratories 'n' mosques in pace
An' like of the place
Where name of The Lord oft cited in Grace
Certainly would've been ravaged in trace
(If Lord wouldn't have assuaged in pace)
Surely!
Lord ease 'n' appease to brace
One who assist (Him) to assert
Indeed! Lord is for all to comfort
Lord, so
Impressive, Invincible in concert
(Al Qur'an 22:40)

And the *truth* lies in the deepest profundity of core
And Who,
Endowed the *truth* to abide in the veer of core
Wouldn't you discern to learn the answer in lore?
Once again concerning the sapience in lore.

---

1   "AS" is used for the Arabic word and "PBU" for the same text in English,
     meaning "Peace be upon ..."

Al Qur'an

Not all men and clan of the Book *are alike*
Some trend to faith *in abide*

And affirm to beseech *then assert to recite*
Verses of Lord, all through the night
And ardor and adore Lord, prone *in plight* (03:113)

They trust in Lord and the Day in Dictate
Bid in sane and deter evil *in base*
They determine not to practice *in ills*
And practice dictum of truth *in wills*
As they spin in sway good *to obey*
They're with the discipline of virtuous *in stay* (03:114)

They wouldn't be declined of good *in grace*
Lord!
Discerns all who fear (Him) *in trace*
And abide virtuosity *in pace* (03:115)

Those in verity of faith
And those of the Jewish affirming in faith
And of the Sabians and Christians *in stride*
Whoso trust in Lord and The Day[2] *to decide*
And those complying virtuous deeds *in pace*
For them,
There's no dread, nor sorrow *in place* (05:69)

All religions are basically alike as
They are incidental in comparison to great enduring
Truth,
On which the religions unite.

2   Doomsday—These verses elucidate the difference between the cynics, the
     nonbelievers, and men of the Book.

Faith and Religion

I believe almost all religions are divine institutions, unlike Karen Armstrong, who views religions as:

> ... human establishments that make serious mistakes because these were conceived by someone of our status that with certain gifted attributes.[3]

But my firm conviction is that virtually all the religions are divine institutions that have been distorted by human interpretations.

Therefore, the concept of religion is not interdicted to one faith but instead has been embellished to a common belief in His Almighty Deity. You may call Him Allah, God, or Bhagwan.

"A Single Deity, Who is the focus of all worship, would integrate society as well as the individual."[4]

---

3   Armstrong, *A History of God*.
4   Ibid.

Faith and Science

The Holy Scriptures Examined in the Light of Modern Knowledge
"The association between the Qur'an and science is a preference, not a surprise, especially since it is going to be one of harmony and not of discord."

—Dr. Maurice Bucaille in *The Bible, the Qur'an and Science.*
"Science without religion is lame and religion without science is blind."

—Albert Einstein
"There can be no conflict between science and religion."

—George Sine in *Introduction to the History of Science.*
"Science and Faith are in commensurable and there is no antithesis between them."

—Arthur Thomas in *Introduction to Science.*

Forbearance

The Qur'an very clearly declares:

For this purpose 'n' precept in relate
We commanded progeny of Israel in dictate
Not to slay in slight a man in state
Unless for settling of scores in plight
Or if it was a state of combat in fray
For if some inclined to kill a man in span
It would be a hideous of course in plan
As if killing of all the men 'n' clan
If one was to save the life of a man
It's like saving (the life) all humanity in span
There're Our messengers for them to advise
With Our distinct Signs 'n' Symbols to aside
Even so they didn't bother to allure
But stowed to dissipation in score
(5:32)

The philosophy of Jihad is not to kill the innocents. *It's only the discipline of faith* that can win over others, not the spiteful activities that have eventually distorted the image of faith.

Islam, the word, is derived from *s-l-m*, which means peace.

A faith of amity and accord, serenity and submission, it never counsels to instigate aggressive retaliation.

The Muslims' code of ethics prescribed in the Qur'an recommends conciliation and pacification, not hostilities or clashes in conflict.

A Sermon of Prophet Muhammad ^{PBUH}
(at the final Hajj)

Prophet Muhammad's Last Sermon

Date delivered: 632 AC, ninth day of Dhul al Hijjah, 10 AH in the 'Uranah valley of Mount Arafat.

After praising and thanking God, he said: O People! Listen well to my words, for I do not know whether, after this year, I shall ever be amongst you again. Therefore listen to what I am saying to you very carefully and take these words to those who could not be present here today.

The Equivalence of the Human Race:
All mankind is from Adam and Eve, so you have common ancestors. An Arab has no superiority over a non-Arab, nor a non-Arab has any superiority over an Arab; also neither a white has superiority over a black, nor the black have any superiority over the white except by piety and good action. Learn that every Muslim is a brother to every Muslim and that the Muslims constitute one brotherhood. Nothing shall be legitimate to a Muslim, which belongs to a fellow Muslim, unless it was given freely and willingly. Do not, therefore, do injustice to yourselves.

Women's Rights:
O People! It is true that you have certain rights over your women, but they also have rights over you. Remember that you have taken them as your wives only under God's trust and with His permission. If they abide by your right then to them belongs the right to be fed and clothed in kindness. Treat your women well and be kind to them, for they are your partners and committed helpers. It is your right and they do not make friends with anyone of whom you do not approve, as well as never to be unchaste.
Every right arising out of homicide in pre-Islamic days is henceforth renounced.

O People!

Listen to me in earnest: Worship One Allah (The Only Creator of the Universe), perform your five daily prayers (*Salaat*), Fast during the month of Ramadan, and give your financial obligation (*Zakaat*) of your wealth. Perform *Hajj* if you can afford to. Remember, one day you will appear before God (The Creator) and you will answer for your deeds. So beware, do not stray from the path of righteousness after I am gone.

O People!

No prophet or messenger will come after me and no new faith will be born. Reason well, therefore, O People, and understand words, which I convey to you. I am leaving you with the Book of God (the QUR'AN) and my SUNNAH [the life style and the behavioral mode of the Prophet] if you follow them you will never go astray.

All those who listen to me shall pass on my words to others and those to others again; and may the last ones understand my words better than those who listen to me directly.
Be my witness O God, that I have conveyed your message to your people.

The Charter of the UN

We the Peoples of the United Nations determined: to reaffirm faith in fundamental human rights, in the dignity and worth of the human person, in the equal rights of men and women and of nations large and small, and to save succeeding generations from the scourge of war, which twice in our lifetime has brought untold sorrow to mankind, and to establish conditions under which justice and respect for the obligations arising from treaties and other sources of international law can be maintained, and to promote social progress and better standards of life in larger freedom. And for these ends: to practice tolerance and live together in peace with one another as good neighbors, and to unite our strength to maintain international peace and security, and to ensure, by the acceptance of principles and the institution of methods that armed force shall not be used, save in the common interest, and to employ international machinery for the promotion of the economic and social advancement of all peoples, Have resolved to combine our efforts to accomplish these aims: Accordingly, our respective Governments, through representatives assembled in the city of San Francisco, who have exhibited their full powers found to be in good and due form, have agreed to the present Charter of the United Nations and do hereby establish an international organization to be known as the United Nations.

Contents

Foreword

He is the original exponent and leading authority in the world on the influences of synthetic blends in garments on various body systems, particularly the cardiovascular system. He elucidated the effects, which include hyperventilation syndrome, psychosomatic cardiovascular disorders, heart rate, blood pressure, cardiac arrhythmias, vasospastic angina, sudden unexplained death, and the wearing of such garments as a coronary risk factor. For his excellent work in this area, he was awarded a PhD and DSc.

In 1986, he was invited to speak on the influences of synthetic blends in garments on cardiac rhythm and blood pressure in Dallas, Texas, at the Man and Environments Conference.

In Lubbock, Texas, in 1988, at the American Society of Nuclear Physics Conference, Dr. Seyal delivered a keynote address on the mode of action of synthetic blends in garments in sudden cardiac death. Three Noble Laureates, Dr. Cormak, Dr. Fowler, and Dr. Wilson, attended the meeting. Dr Seyal was the only speaker from outside the USA.

He has also spoken on the subject at various international forums in several countries, including India, Egypt, Germany, Canada, and the United States.

He has many international publications to his credit and has been researching the subject since 1981.

I've been associated with him in the research of blends in garments for more than twenty-five years and have found him to be a person dedicated to the cause of humanity.

After the catastrophe of September 11, 2001, he turned his attention towards the study of all the possible means of bringing the world and people of all casts, creeds, colors, and cultures under the shawl of sorority and serenity with patience and peace.

His study of the Holy Qur'an is absolutely in the new direction of science and philosophy. It is to communicate to the West that Islam is a faith of pacification with order and accord, serenity and composure. We as a human folk should discern the true message of the Qur'an in the overall interest of universal reconciliation.

I wonder how one could write the detailed elucidation of Surah Al Noor, Verse 35, without the bestowal of Allah Almighty. Similarly, his writings on the Adam of Science and the Adam of Qur'an are really fascinating to comprehend in the light of Holy Scripture. Man still remains dazed to discern the fate of the grand universe as he cannot perceive as to how this gigantic model of an ever-expanding grand universe could behave as a closed model, and Qur'an very rightly points out the lower sky, surrounding the grand universe like a football cover, the limit of its expansion when the ever-expanding (around 300,000 km/sec) grand universe, with myriad stellar bodies, would smash against the lower sky leading to a series of big crunches and eventually forming the basis for the next creation. Similarly, the scientific assertion of *Me'raaj* is the first-time elucidation of Prophet Muhammad's indeterminate journey of the cosmic order. Similarly, his communication of *fate and fortune* is fascinating, and I believe he has interpreted this most complicated subject of faith in a very convincing way.

I wouldn't be surprised if the scientists one day come to digest the philosophy of the Holy Scripture and appreciate its wisdom at its core.

The cadence and course of Dr. Seyal's writing on the poetic stance of the Holy Scripture besides its philosophical and scientific discernment looks very imposing and inspiring within the folds of the true message of the text.

However, one thing is conspicuous and convincing, that Lord Almighty has given him the essential essence of this noble job to achieve. He seems to be motivated in the perpetuation of this most prudent and prodigious work for the drill and direction of people living in the developed world, who can affirm and embrace any ideology based on logic and intellect.

Professor Hayat M. Awan, PhD (Toronto)
Visiting Professor, University of Wisconsin, USA
Vice Chancellor BZU

A Reader's Report

In recent years, the debate over science, reason, and religion has reached a peak (or a high plateau, depending on your perception of time scales) of intensity, breadth, and confrontational vigor. Hundreds of Web sites, blogs, and forums have sprung up, enabling the debate to rage day-to-day. But people will always want points of view to be encapsulated in portable form: books. This has meant big business for publishers. On one side, we have Dawkins, Hitchens, Shermer, Harris, and others arguing that the breach between religion on the one hand and science and reason on the other is absolute. On the other side of the debate are writers and polemicists such as Dinesh D'Souza, Shmuley Boteach, John Cornwell, and Alister McGrath, who claim either that science and religious faith are compatible or (in the case of some individuals) that religion and reason go together, and science is simply wrong. This side is probably the more catholic (in the general sense), in that it comprises a range of opinions from fundamentalist creationism to "intelligent design" proponents and even some deistically inclined scientists.

Faith in the Unseen is a contribution to the debate. Its author, who is a consultant cardiologist with numerous books on (variously) cardiology and religion under his belt, approaches the debate on the "faith" side as a religious man (he is a Muslim) with a strong background in science. The title of his manuscript places the emphasis on the key issue that stands between the scientific atheist side and the faith side: evidence, and the absence thereof. For fundamentalist believers, evidence (other than what is written in holy books) is simply not an issue. However, for the rational religious believer, it is a pivotal point and must be rationalized.

One approach, which has been adopted by most theologians, is of "non-overlapping magisteria" (NOMA, for short) of naturalist and supernaturalist areas of thought. This is a position to which even some atheist scientists subscribe (for example, the paleontologist Stephen Jay Gould, who coined the term). What it means is that science and religion deal with fundamentally different things—the material and the spiritual—and should not attempt to intrude in each other's territory. The author of *Faith in the Unseen* is not a subscriber to NOMA. He is of the unifying school that believes that science and religious belief can complement and harmonize with each other, in other words, that there is no fundamental contradiction between the two.

The manuscript is a substantial and thoughtfully laid out package, as one would expect from an experienced author. This book is a work of scientific assertion in the light of Holy Scripture with a formal introduction, a short chapter in which the author discusses his premise.

> I find the men of all cast, color, creed, and culture of the modern era in an exceptionally vivacious stage, which immediately demands an attempt to reconcile religion with reason. I firmly believe that the day is not far off when the religion and science will discover mutual harmonies.
>
> … An attempt to siphon off the insight of The Holy Scripture needs deep knowledge of modern science in its all districts and domains, besides having the true discernment of philosophy and the veridical knowledge of the Scripture.

Thus, he sets out not only his philosophical premise but his qualification to build upon it. Although he is deeply committed to Islam (for instance, he uses the fastidious "pbuh" suffix whenever he mentions the Prophet) and approaches his subject primarily through the lens of Islam, he seeks to give an all-embracing perspective on religion, taking in not only the Abrahamic religions but also others, such as Hinduism.

It is a very substantial work, and I cannot hope to engage fully with it in this brief appraisal. The manuscript is divided into substantial chapters, each dealing with a major subject of faith and/or reason, and each chapter is subdivided into sections, which discuss various detailed aspects or examples. Some of the major subjects are: death and the afterlife; the philosophy of life; the notion of fate; religious and scientific ideas about origins and creation; Qur'anic vision and wisdom; and religious and scientific notions of time, ontology, and medicine. Of these individually large areas, probably the most substantial and comprehensively covered are those where *religion and science are usually most inclined to clash*: creation and time—in other words, biology and physics, each of which provides a fundamental challenge to traditional religious thinking.

In each case, it is the religious (typically Qur'anic) perspective that takes precedence. For instance, the chapter on "Perfect Creation" provides a representative illustration of the author's philosophical approach. The chapter opens with an account of the Qur'anic version of the *origin of the cosmos*, which the author argues is a rational anticipation of current scientific hypotheses and therefore represents the truth. Thus, there is no conflict between faith and science, *because scientific knowledge and theory have already been prefigured in holy texts.* At each point, his summaries of current scientific thinking are spot-on (he is, after all, a professional man of science), and his weaving of science with scripture is, to say the least, fascinating and engaging.

Tone is important in books of this kind. Much of the friction in the science/religion debate has been attributed to the polemical tone of participants on both sides, who have been variously described as "shrill," "strident," and "intemperate." None of these epithets apply to the author of *Faith in the Unseen.* He is measured, temperate, and good-humored throughout, undoubtedly reflecting his personal good nature and perhaps also his supreme confidence in his thesis. He is also very readable, with a flair for introducing accessible and pertinent examples.

In conclusion, *Faith in the Unseen* is challenging (in the intellectual sense, not the stylistically abrasive sense) and fascinating. An intriguing contribution to the debate on science and religion, it provides a remarkable insight into scriptural close reading and the "rationalization" of religious faith.

Austin Kehoe

Preamble

Science and faith have so far stood apart, and there seems to be no reconciliation to bring these two to some reasonable terms, because most modern scientists and other writers like Dan Brown assert:

> Every faith in the world is based on fabrication. That's the definition of faith—acceptance of that which we imagine to be true that which cannot prove. Every religion describes God through metaphor, allegory and from early Egyptians through modern Sunday schools. The metaphors are a way to help our minds process the incomprehensible. The problem arises when we begin to believe in our own metaphors. Religion allegory has become a part of the fabric of reality. And living in that reality helps millions of people to cope and be better people.

But if we can discern the basic truth of faith, in the light of modern-day scientific convictions, that forms the basis of all monotheistic religions, with assertions like faith in the unseen, the Adam of science and the Adam of religion are one not two, the creation of the universe and its ultimate fate, travel back in time, the theory of relativity and wormhole theories, along with quite a few others, we can create conformity between the two (i.e., science and faith). When we affirm the truth of faith as a reality in the light of scientific philosophy, we settle that faith is not a fabrication based on allegory but in reality a true discipline that will lead the new generation in the proper direction and not leave them in frenzied confusion.

Dan Brown seems to be convinced of his contentions because he asserts that the modern church is not passing a word of discipline but instead performing a few ceremonial rituals in our routine life.

The belief or faith is often distorted in the modern trends that have insinuated themselves into the minds of the young generation, for example, that there's no life in the hereafter, so one should cherish each moment of life in preeminent fashion. It's better if there's some discipline, for otherwise, there's no need to live a well-ordered life.

Dan Brown also affirms:

Unbiased science could not possibly be performed by a man, who possessed faith in God. Nor did faith have any need for physical confirmation of its belief.

Today, the young generation finds itself in a similar dilemma, thrown at the crossroads, bewildered and perplexed. Those who profess to accept this duality of thinking in their challenging experience of pursuing scientific convictions while still preserving religious faith are in fact split-up personalities with little prospect of finding the right path, for faith cannot take root in a divided mind. We shall have to philosophically evolve a way to scientifically prove the fundamental principals of faith without squashing the old, deeply insinuated beliefs.

In the writing of this book, I have tried my best to avoid any religious bias and sincerely endeavored to pass the word of faith in the light of modern-day scientific achievements.

As you read the text of the Holy Qur'an, at many places, without a proper scientific background, it becomes very difficult to figure out the true temperament of the message. This book is intended to discuss the most critical subjects intriguing the scientific mind of today.

Why couldn't creation take place without a "creator"? There's a mathematical affirmation besides scientific and philosophical assertions.

Faith in the hereafter and the philosophy of death: where are we destined to go after demise and is there life after death? The genetic code dispersed as dust and soot after demise and stored in the earth (hard disc) will be called back like the computer codes and bits stored in the silicon hard disc.

I have also endeavored to discuss certain other topics.

Perfection in creation and the fate of the universe are very lucidly elucidated in the light of the Holy Scripture: the initial big bang to follow the event of the big smash, affirming boundary conditions, like the lower sky is the limit, and ultimately eventuating in a series of big crunches, once again, a singularity providing a seedling for the next creation (54:1; 21:104; 29:53; 82:1–4; 21:104; 30:11).

The Adam of science and the Adam of Qur'an are one, not two. This goes beyond saying that gradual evolution alone could not conceive life with all the marvels of nature. Indeed, it was evolution but as determined by the Lord Almighty.

I created the man in elegant design
Gradually grow from mud *so refine*

An' then from the drop of sperm *in prime*
(30:30; 38:75; 40:67; 35:11; 23:14; 71:17; 24:45)

Integrity is intelligence, and immorality is ignorance. If one knows the virtuosity, he necessarily tries to seek the truth; if one hunts for something wrong, it can only be because he is trailing for the obvious—in other words, because he is unaware of what is in actuality moral or righteous. My reason for writing this book is to pass the word to treasure a definite certitude in belief after gaining full awareness of faith in the light of modern-day science.

Faith has no evinced certainty or substantiated expediency in and of itself but is the essential attribute of he who treasures the truth. These two concepts (i.e., faith and science) are associated to specific symbolic uniqueness of adjustment and should be defined correctly, yet the scientific and philosophical literature is fraught with examples of speckled uses of "faith" when referring either to the discipline of wisdom or discernment.

There is, of course, no faith without the truth of discipline. It is quite possible that personal experience can provide the basis for abstract representations having a wide application. The concepts we possess are thus dependent upon changes conceived or perceived by each one of us. I put it precisely: *discipline is discernible, but faith is not.*

I have already dealt with quite a few subjects in the introduction of the *Poetic Stance of the Holy Qur'an, Divine Philosophy and Modern Day Science,* and *Faith in the Scientific Philosophy of the Religion,* but one needs a few more of the details to rationally assert the truth elucidated in the Holy Scripture in the light of modern-day scientific achievements.

It was expedient to include certain passages from *A Brief History of Time,* because they formed the scientific basis for the Qur'anic affirmations.

This work is actually a comprehensive illumination of the fate of the grand universe and the evolution of life with a scientific discussion in the light of the Qur'an affirming that the Adam of science and the Adam of the Qur'an are one, not two. These subjects are figured out with scrupulous consideration without squashing the old, deeply insinuated convictions of faith. I emphasize if ever man would have sought direction from the Holy Book regarding different notions of scientific concern, he would not have been striving to figure out the secret of many facts prefigured in the Holy Text.

The Perfect Creation

Wheresoever you look around, you don't find a break or a breach. This entire stupendous job is so refined and meticulously harmonized and planned that even the slightest change in the mass, volume, or speed of any of the cosmic objects that are flowing in billions of trillions could have resulted in chaotic collision. But there is a word for the ultimate crash of the cosmic order into the lower skies. It was a *smash* that would eventually lead into a series of big crunches and the final *boundary conditions* providing a seedling for the next creation.

Philosophy of Life

What are we composed of? How will we be brought back to life in the hereafter, and how will our hands and feet assert for our doings of this life? We will also discuss the philosophy of the soul or the efflux and the intelligence, a bestowal of the Lord Almighty, for what we're ordained to conduct in this life, to ultimately cherish the boons in the hereafter.

The Purpose of Creation

There could be so many for the men of all casts, creeds, cultures, and colors to cherish the bliss of everlasting life in the hereafter (23:14–15).

The Reality of Fate and Fortune

Fate is destined through genetic array, but the fruits of fortune are through intelligence, for what we are responsible to perform in this vale and so to cherish the award and reward in the Hereafter.

Divine Perception of Time and Travel Back in Time

What about the theory of relativity, wormhole theory, and time travel concepts? If we can, somehow, prove that the Prophet Muhammad ᴾᴮᵁᴴ traveled much faster than the speed of light (thirty billion times the speed of light) (32:4–5; 70:4) through wormhole-like passages (23:17; 70:3) through different strata of the multiverses and the skies and came back through moving wormholes (51:7), we can scientifically prove the journey of *Me'raaj* (23:17; 70:3, and 51:7). That's actually a travel back in time or living in the present while traveling in a loop, with one mouth and two throats (i.e., future and past). People often cannot reconcile with the speed the Prophet Muhammad ᴾᴮᵁᴴ traveled in the Cosmic Sway during *Me'raaj*, but have you ever thought of traveling in the Cosmic Order while abiding on Earth?

We on Earth are spinning around its axis with a speed of 1,670 kilometers per hour and with it, around its orbit (around the sun) at the speed of 108,000 kilometers per hour, and with the planet as a part of the solar system around the Milky Way Galaxy at the speed of 720,000 kilometers per hour. And again, with the Milky Way, we are swaying with a speed of 950,000 kilometers per hour in its (the Milky Way's) universe, which is spinning in the multiverses with an unknown speed. The multiverses are also swaying with an unknown speed in the strata of parallel universes. The parallel universes are spinning around with an unknown speed in the cosmic order, and all is drifting away with a speed of about 300,000 kilometers per second from the core of the big bang or *Kun*, when it started to be *Fa Ÿa Koon*, and we don't even feel dizzy traveling with such a stupendous speed in the cosmic order.

You will find answers to these questions in quite a different design and will indeed cherish the wisdom of the Qur'an.

Rashid Seyal

One thing that never dies:
The glory of exalted perception and prolific accomplishment

Introduction

We find the men of all casts, creeds, colors, and cultures of the modern era in an exceptionally vivacious stage, which immediately demands an attempt to reconcile religion with reason. I firmly believe that the day is not far off when religion and science will discover mutual harmonies. I plan to evolve a physiologically less annoying and psychologically more appropriate way for a particular type of scientific or religious mind to reconcile religion with reason.

My efforts at rationalizing faith are not actually interdicted to one faith or belief but are for the whole of human society. My sincere hope is to scrub and swab the presumptuously miscalculated premise that has insinuated the minds of Western society and set them against Islam. It really has to be dealt with quite amiably in a mannerly way with a plan so that the religious bent and bias is no longer there and we as a human race can live in a complacent and composed fraternity.

My main purpose, at the same time, is not to admit the superiority of the philosophy of science over religion. I actually sincerely aspire to work in a new direction for the injunction and inclination of all thinkers of the modern century for their plea to the younger generation to be guided in the right direction.

In a cultural milieu permeated through and through with science, modern man has developed habits of concrete thought which render him less proficient and permitting of that type of inner experience on which religious faith ultimately reposes and remains because he suspects it to be "liable to illusion." And no one would hazard action on the basis of a doubtful principle of conduct. Religion stands in greater need of a rational foundation for its ultimate principles than the dogmas of science. In these circumstances, the demand for a scientific form of religious experience is quite natural. It was the fulfillment of this need that prompted me to reconstruct religious thought in Islam with due regard to the philosophical traditions of faith and the latest developments in various domains of human knowledge.

An attempt to siphon off the insight of the Holy Scripture requires a deep knowledge of modern science in its all districts and domains, in addition to a true discernment of philosophy and a veridical knowledge of the Scripture.

The subject is opening up a new perspective of research in this direction as the earl and count of assertion in diversified course and the conduct of scientific perspicacity in the world are joining hands to define the balance between scientific discernment, philosophy, and the message of discipline communicated in the Holy Text.

The subjects discussed in this book, if we go down into the details of the scientific affirmations in the light of the Holy Scripture, are not alien to the scientific mind but are really foreign to men of faith. The Qur'an very clearly elucidates quite a few subjects intriguing the scientific mind of today, and it might also discuss quite a few other subjects that we have not had the dexterity to realize or comprehend until today.

When I open the daily newspaper as part of my morning routine, I often see lengthy descriptions of conflicts between people over borders, possessions, or liberties. Today's news is often forgotten a few days later. But when one opens ancient texts that have appealed to a broad audience over a longer period of time, such as the Holy Scriptures, what does one often find in them? One finds a discussion of how the constituents of the universe— light, stars, life—were created, along with many other words of wisdom and truth. Although humans are often caught up in mundane problems, they are curious about the big picture. As citizens of the universe, we cannot help but wonder how the first sources of light formed, how life came into existence, and whether we are alone as intelligent beings in this vast space. Astronomers in the twenty-first century are uniquely positioned to answer these big questions.

Much of the attention in cosmology over the past several years has been focused on the cosmic microwave background radiation, which provides a snapshot of the universe at an age of four hundred thousand years. But between this moment and the appearance of the first galaxies was a period of almost total darkness, unbroken by so much as a glimmer of starlight. Hidden in the shadows of this era are the secrets of how galaxies took shape.

Clearly, it is hard to probe a period that is by its very nature practically invisible. The key is to look for the feeble radio waves emitted by electrically neutral hydrogen gas as it interacts with the background radiation. Observers are now starting to do that.

The result should be an even more interesting map than that of the microwave background. It will be fully three-dimensional and will show, step-by-step, how form emerged from formlessness.

The human mind could never know the real nature or the attributes of God; it could only agree with faith in affirming a spiritual power as the foundation of all reality. Similarly, for certain schools of thought, it seemed fatal to human morality and enterprise to believe, as orthodoxy did, in the complete predestination of all events by God and the arbitrary election, from all eternity, of the saved or damned (details discussed in "Fate and Fortune").

During the early days of Islam, there was lot of research going on to reveal the secrets of nature with hundreds of variations on this theme. The Mutazilites' doctrines spread rapidly under the rule of al Mansur, Harun-al Rashid, and al Ma'mun. Al Ma'mun, who was fascinated by this fledgling flight of reason, defended it. It was probably as a consequence that there appeared to Al Ma'mun (198–218H/813–33) in a dream, a man with a fair, ruddy complexion; a broad forehead; joined eyebrows; a bald head; light blue eyes; and a pleasing appearance, who was sitting on a couch.

Filled with awe, the commander of the faith asked, "Who are you?"

"Aristotle," was the reply.

Delighted with the answer and having been granted permission to ask further questions, he asked, "What is good?"

"That which is good in your mind," replied Aristotle.

"And what comes next?"

"That which is good in law."

"Then what?"

"That which is considered good by the people."

Finally, Aristotle advised Al Ma'mun that he should treat as gold whoever advised him about gold (alchemy) and should hold to the doctrine of *Tawhid* or the "oneness of God."

As a consequence of his dream, Al Ma'mun determined to seek the books of ancient philosophers and have them translated into Arabic, appropriating ancient knowledge.

The fable goes on to link Al Ma'mun's official support for the Mutazilites, who insisted on the primary role of reason in the matters of religious dogma, with well-known efforts to disseminate the science of the Greeks among the Muslims. The Mutazilites were called the *ahl-at-tawhid*, "the upholders of the doctrine of the oneness of God," because of their particular stand on the issue of God's attributes. Their position became epitomized in the doctrine of the createdness of the Qur'an as the word of God, which Al Ma'mun sought to force upon unsympathetic traditionalists and legists, thus initiating the inquisition. In time, his successor, al Mutassum (218–28H/833–42) led the persecution of Ahmad ibn Hambal, the highly esteemed traditionalist and founder of strict legal rational argumentation.

Tradition has it that al Mansur (138–9) and ar Rashid (170–94/786–809) laid the foundation of a government-supported library in Baghdad, which quickly became the center for the translation of texts into Arabic, but it was in the reign of al Ma'mun that the library—under the name of Bayt-ul-Hikma or the "Institution of Science"—reached its highest point. Greek scientific and philosophical books, which he had ordered, were translated. Another collection came from Cyprus. These collections were gathered from as far back as the end of the Umayyad period, when the process of translation had already begun.

It does appear, however, that the translation at Bayt-ul-Hikma, in the time of al Ma'mun, became a well-organized activity of unprecedented scope and vigor. This soon brought the bulk of Greek science and philosophy within the reach of a large number of Arabic-speaking scholars. And his personal interest in the translation activity may well have been connected with his sympathies with the Mutazilites or with his determination to find the logic behind the truth or the truth behind the logic. What those early Muslims did, however, was quite different and unexpected. Rather than suppressing the declining Greek intellectual traditions, they sought out their sources and encouraged their cultivation. Theirs was primarily an attitude of rejection or even of mere tolerance, but of protectiveness and active participation. The foreign sciences of the Greeks lived as long and developed as much as they did in Islam only because of continued interest and support. To characterize their status in Islamic civilization as marginal would merely serve to relieve us from the task of explaining their existence.

The paradox is heightened by the fact that the philosophical and scientific disciplines once essential for Islamic teachings in all teaching institutions or the Madrisas in the mosques are now kept out of these institutions of learning. Primarily, as we are discussing the period, the linguistic disciplines were necessary adjuncts to the Qur'anic studies along with learning the tradition and law.

It is an essential need of the time to once again cultivate such a tradition to bring the religious studies back to the glorious period of Islamic culture. Learning Qur'anic philosophy in the light of modern-day science is imperative to reason out the truth.

But with the text, we strive to find the answers to the following questions:

Where is the knowledge that is lost in communication?

- Where is the wisdom that is lost in the knowledge?
- And what wisdom is the faith going to offer to the world?

Nobody can for sure assert whether or not one religion is superior to the others because of their inherited traditions, which are deeply insinuated in the cultural heritages of the people. The unbiased study of this book might give an inkling toward the truth in the philosophy of faith ordained for the men of all eons.

I believe the basic philosophy of all the faiths is one and eternal: *the truth.*

If we can cultivate such a tradition in our social order, I'm sure we wouldn't be stranded in bewilderment, but we would understand faith in the true discernment of reason.

In the traditional times, it was assumed that the faith disclosed the ultimate nature of reality. In the sixteenth and seventeenth centuries, science began to cast doubts on that assumption; for the Scriptures only assert the truth, whereas controlled experiments can prove scientific hypotheses. After three centuries of confusion on the point, however, we now see that the proofs hold only for the empirical world. The worthless aspects of reality—its values, meanings, and purpose—will slip through the devices of science in the way that the sea slips through the nets of fishermen if we are not competent enough to devise a philosophy of reasoning to understand the truth of the Scripture.

But the logic of philosophy cannot ascertain the creation and the circumstances of the universe. Similarly, it has no means to reckon the genetic or galactic proscenium of the creation, and in like manner, it has no way to discern the myth of space-time. On the other hand, the scientific approach has no dexterity to discriminate the discernment of the efflux or the soul and life after death, nor does it have the cognition or the approach to interpret the inspiration of faith in the secluded or secret that His Almighty Lord directs to ordain us quite resolutely in the Holy Scriptures.

Where then shall we turn for counsel concerning the things that matter the most? Our realization is that science cannot help us reopen the door to look seriously again at what the wisdom tradition proposes. Not all of their contents are enduringly clear to our understanding, but a careful search for the truth probably lies within the scope of human discernment. Modern science has superseded these days, as it reflects the gender relations, class structures, and the like, and these must be reassessed in the light of changing times and the continuing struggle for the truth. But if we pass a strainer through the world's religions to lift out their conclusions about the reality and how life should be lived, those conclusions begin to look like the winnowed wisdom of humanity.

What is the specific truth of wisdom? The larger the island of knowledge is, the greater the shoreline of wonder.

So gathering a bit of historical background of reason in religion, we need to cultivate a reality of wisdom in faith to understand the modern trends in scientific achievements.

Perfect faith doesn't concern in strife
But!
Once it makes a preference in abide
Only if freed from hatred and adore
Indeed!
It reveals wisdom in the depth of core
When heavens and earth split in apart
A trillionth of an atto second in part
An atto second is,
Again a trillionth of a second in part
If you intend to cherish the bliss in eye
Don't have the urge, for or against to spy
Don't decide, your likes and dislikes in span
That's the depravity of your core in plan
The Faith is precise in perception to trust
For,
There's exquisite wisdom in the text

Like with the fate of the universe, scientists stand divided till today, but if we gather the details from the Holy Scripture, it very clearly gives an indication of the ultimate fate of the grand universe. Similarly, until today, the Adam of religion and the Adam of science stood apart, but when we study the Holy Scripture in the light of modern-day scientific convictions, it fairly elucidates the process of evolution, which is well determined under divine laws and the order of nature, unlike Darwinian theory.

Some scientists assert that our creation and the creation of the grand universe was occasioned *by chance*. As Max Tegmark, in "Parallel Universes" (a special issue of *Scientific American*) writes, our creation and the creation of all the universes is just a chance occurrence, as it may happen that one would receive a room in a hotel whose numbers are exactly as those of the person's date of birth. For example, a man who was born May 11 is assigned room number five on the eleventh floor of a hotel.

It may happen to be a once-in-a-lifetime occurrence, but if it happens exactly the same way the second time, he will be scared. And if it happens to be the same for the third time in a row, in some other hotel, upon finding himself assigned the same room number on the same floor, he will just stay back and ask the man behind the desk, "Who has arranged this room for me?"

If he receives the answer, "Nobody, it just turned out by chance," by nature, the man will stay back and say, "It cannot be chance, for I had the same room number on the same floor in Paris early this morning and in London this afternoon, and subsequently, when I arrived here in Toronto in the evening, I was asked to check into the same room number on the same floor. I cannot conceive of having the same room on the same floor as that of my date of birth just by chance all the time. Somebody must have arranged it for me. Please, be truthful, who did that?"

If he still gets the answer that it was just chance, he will not go to the same room because he will be scared of some real conspiracy behind the situation.

Only the cosmologist and the physicist of today could comprehend the discipline from an atom to the indeterminate cosmic order. All the stars, like the moon, earth, sun, and Milky Way galaxy, in which we are abiding, are all moving and drifting away from each other and also from the core of the big bang, in a definite order. This fascinating discipline was ordained from an indeterminate period of time. And how long from now they'll abide by the same order of discipline, we have no dexterity to comprehend.

Could it all be due to a stroke of chance?

How could one discern His order of discipline, until one looks into the details of each effect and equipage with an unbiased eye?

The question still remains to be answered: Who has arranged all these fascinating effects and this equipage for us?

If someone produces a new idea or a new thing, everyone appreciates his benevolent achievement, like a man who creates something for a better future for humanity. One should deliberate all these effects and the equipage of creation in this context.

Maybe I'm absolutely wide of the mark, but could it be?

The Lord Almighty wanted to settle many scores before the creation of *his real perfect design*: the life to cherish the bliss of everlasting life in the *hereafter*. Maybe we are unwittingly performing certain definite assignments without ever realizing the eventual purpose of their formation or impression. *And what's the source of knowledge?* Even people like Einstein affirmed that it's intuitive perception that opens new vistas of concern, and I myself stand a witness to that.

The ultimate nature of the assignment given to man is, at the least, not very clear to us, but in the Qur'an, the Lord Almighty asserts, "I've not created you [i.e., men of all castes, creeds, colors, and cultures] without any definite design in plan" (24:115). It very clearly affirms that the creation of all mankind, and not of the Muslim community alone, is planned with a definite reason.

What could that be?

Could it be something like the following?

A handful of genes that control the body's defenses during hard times can also dramatically improve health and prolong life in diverse organisms. Understanding how they work may reveal the keys to extending the human life span while banishing the diseases of old age (i.e., delaying dotage and relishing the boons of life experiences with senescence, for in the Hereafter there has to be life in prime condition with no dotage of decline).

But how could that be possible?

Genes that control an organism's ability to withstand adversity cause changes throughout the body that render it temporarily supercharged for survival.

Activated over the long term, this stress response prolongs the life span and forestalls disease in a wide range of organisms.

Sirtuins are a family of genes that may be the master regulators of the survival mechanisms.

Understanding how they produce health and longevity-enhancing effects could lead to disease treatment and ultimately longer, disease-free human life spans, for that's the life in the Hereafter with ever-flowing youth in profusion with no dotage in refuse.

The Qur'an is unfeigned supervision for the virtuous, who have determined a firm conviction to command the course of the Holy Scriptures and assert an assiduous faith in the unseen. They entreat and beseech to aver and affirm their agility, which is the award of sincerity in faith. They give due allowance and apportion of alms to the indigent and insolvent from whatever His Almighty has endowed them, and they also approve and endorse whatever has been given to them as guidance in the "Holy Scriptures" and also support and credit the Scriptures revealed to the earlier prophets. Over and above, they have a firm conviction of the Day of Judgment. Besides that, His Almighty asserts that these are the people who are on the right scent and spoor and track and trail of faith and such are the people who have dominant certitude in His Almighty with all His directives.

The Qur'an gives a detailed enunciation of faith, the truth, besides giving the fundamentals of the religion in a very articulate, eloquent, and effusive manner. The all-in-all discipline is realistically intended to teach the men of all cultures, casts, creeds, or colors and people of all ages and eons to adhere to a common belief and conviction that is insinuated deep in the human consciousness.

Accepting the deity that is flowering within him makes the man immaculate from the enticements of lust and spiteful pleasures, unscathed by any suffering, unbroken by any affront or insult, feeling no wrong and a fighter in the noblest cause. It makes him one who cannot be overpowered by any ardor or affection, enthusiasm or excitement, infatuation or indignation, who is dyed deep with truth in justice, accepting with all his soul that everything that happens is assigned to him as his segment and share from His Almighty. Imagine what another says or does or thinks, still without great necessity and for the general interest. For it is only what belongs to himself through the divine nature of embellishment with the assertions of the Holy Prophet. What he makes is the matter for his activity, and he constantly thinks of that which is allotted to him out of the sum total of things revealed in the Holy Scriptures. He makes his own acts fair, and he is convinced that his own morsel is wholesome. For the lot that is assigned to each man is carried along with him and carries him along with it. He who remembers the divine inspirations and indictment, illumination, incentive, edification, and enlightenment esteems that every rational animal is his kinsman and that to care for all men is according to man's nature. A man should hold on to the opinions not of all but only of those who live in a way worthy of confidence according to nature, but as to those who live not so, he always bears in mind what kind of men they are both at home and away from home, both by night and by day, and what they are and with what men they live an unworthy life. Accordingly, he does not value at all the praise that comes from such men, since they are not even contented and appeased, gratified and mollified with the boons, benedictions, and benevolence of His Almighty and not even with themselves.

Strive not to be disinclined or indisposed, nor without regard to the common appeal and advantage, nor without due consideration, nor with distraction, nor let deliberate adornment set off your thoughts. And be not either a man of many words or busy about too many things. And further, let the deity, who is the guardian of your instinctive being mainly at this age, escort you in the matter of all concerns. Be cheerful also, and do not lend ear to external help or the tranquility that others donate. A man then must stand upright in the shelter of the true discipline of faith ordained in the Holy Scripture, with agility and alacrity, nimbleness and liveliness, dexterity and devotion, submissiveness and spryness in the primacy of the Holy Prophet, and not be kept erect by others.

And you will find in the true faith everything better than justice, truth, temperance, and fortitude, for these are all a part of true faith, and in a word, anything better than your own mind's self-satisfaction. The things that enable you to do according to right reason and in the discernment that is assigned to you in the perception of true faith bestow unfeigned tranquility. If, I say, you see anything better than this, turn to it with all your soul and enjoy that which you have found to be the best in guidance, because this is the true follower of faith, who has accomplished true discipline of conviction as ordained in the Holy Scripture. But if nothing appears to be according to the deity, which is flowering in you, which has subjected to itself all your appetites, then carefully examine all the impressions, which have detached themselves from the persuasions of truth and been inclined to sensual and other delights, rather than submitting to the Lord Almighty for the care of mankind.

If you find anything else smaller and of less value than this, give place to nothing else, for if you once diverge and incline to it, you will no longer be able to give preference to the good. The thing that is in your proper possession and under your own control, the intelligence, indeed, is the real gift of Allah Almighty to escort you in the state of delusion.

But simply and freely choose the true discernment of faith in the light of the Holy Scriptures that is not only good for this vale but also for the everlasting life that we are sure to cherish after this temporary living and hold to it. That which is useful and proclaimed by His Almighty is the best. Well then, because it is not only useful to you as a rational being but also as an observant member of the society, keep to it. Take care that you make the inquisition by a sure method in the perception of the Holy Scriptures.

As already described, that intelligence is a real gift of His Almighty for His men and a part of that intelligence is true discernment, which is really yours. This is the perception of true discernment, which holds the intelligence to live in concurrence with the perpetuation of the nature of the order that is virtually to live according to the man's own true nature in the order of nature—true faith as ordained in the Holy Scriptures.

What shall be done to the man who never had the wit to be idle during his whole life but had been careless of what many care about: wealth and family interests, affluence, resources, profusion, property, and possessions? Reasoning that he was certainly an inordinately sincere, upright, and ingenuous man to follow in this way to live, he did not go where he could do no good to mankind but where he could do the greatest good privately to everyone and seek virtue and wisdom. He did not watch his sequestered approaches but cared for others before he looked to his personal interests, and this is the order, which he observes in all his actions. What shall be done to such a one?

There had been no deception but sincerity of the *cause in faith* that he faithfully ordained. When he leaves this vale, he desires earnestly to bestow upon him a blissful smile and suffer him not to perceive *Thy glorified, astral, and astounding glimpse* at that moment, as "You" once bestowed him with the elegant and imposing, sensational and spectacular exhilaration.

Kun: Fa ÿa Koon

By far way and away in place
Beyond the discipline of time and space
How could Nullity out of blue
Could sweep across the sway in blue
When Thou evinced in grace
With the interminable arrow of time in space
There was no notion of norm in around
Besides Thy Power glowing in abound
How could one have the lore in adore
To establish Thy Bounteous "Might" in score

Nullity or nihility,
Whatever the name we may adduce
It was all Thy Power in conclude
With the whisper of *Kun in grace*
There was the swizzle of initiation *in pace*

Fa ÿa Koon
Merging in eternity with notion *in swash*
It swept in sway quite grand *in dash*

There Thou,
Evinced three arrows of time
Thermodynamic, cosmological arrows of time
Besides the psychological arrow of time
Nature and discipline of Thy rule in sublime

The story of time and space
It's quite a bit vista in place
Now we don't have means and manners in hold
As to determine Thy seascape in whole

Thou will squeeze them once more in span
Into a bit of dot in plan
So none of the men and clan
Have the dexterity to comprehend in lore
The swizzle of initiation swaying in score
And when this all eventuate to smash
There'll be a big blow in dash
There then a series of big crunch in crash
Then again culminating in pace
Into a bit of seedling in trace
Waiting for another "*Kun*" in stance
Eventuating into another go in glow
That'll perpetuate forever in flow

O Allah

The moment I close my eyes in stance
Bestow **Thy** Gleam in Grace to glance

And then not to elude or slight in pace
From **Thy** Interminable Beauty in trance
Merging in the Stream of Eternity in place
Let,
I be a glimmer of **Thy** Elegance in Glow
Then as a shimmer perpetuating in flow

For all my beg and beseech in place
To anoint and asperse **Thy** Bounty in Grace

And so to applause and exalt in term
For **Thy** Munificent appease in return

O Lord!
I stay so reverent and meek in abide
And seek **Thy** clemency all in stride

O Lord!
Where to look around in surround
Where **Thou** don't evince in abound

And where not to,
Have glimpse of **Thy** Grandeur in sway
For all these captivating allures in array
Ardor and adore **Thy** Splendor in stay

O Allah!
Where to start my word in entreat
As I praise **Thy** Perfection in preach
Words defy me, whim of lore in treat

There's some around in span
Reciting Glorious Rhymes in Qur'an
Besides,
Captivating stance of "Allah" in enchant

Bewitched in lore in the veer of core
Words fail to glorify **Thy** Grandeur in adore

Me to cherish **Thy** rewards in swarm
That'd always been my notion in norm

Hither in place **Thy** Bounty to brace
Ever to cherish **Thy** Guidance in pace
And in the Hereafter **Thy** Glimpse in Grace

Well Some May Assert
(Inspired by Huston Smith)

I want to savor the honey in taste
But I don't want to be the honey in place
Because alluring adore is gracious in pace
The self will elude suggestions in trance
Even from one's "deepest self" in stance

But,
The God one loves is All Alone in Self
One, who insists to be oneness with Lord
If he deliberates for a while in sort

Can the flame scoff the flame in sear?
If the water could guzzle water in leer
Can the trees taste the fruit they bear?

He, who worships The Lord in pray
Must stand distinct from Him in stay

So only shall,
He knows the joyful love of the Lord
For if he insists that Lord and he are one
That joy, that love, shall instantly be gone
Pray one more for utter oneness with Lord

Where was,
Then the beauty to split in apart
If the jewel and setting were one
The heat and shade are two

If not,
Where was the love to pursue?
When after in friction they meet in hide
What joy they feel, the mother and child
Where's the joy if the two were one
Pray then not, for utter oneness with Lord

But!
He's all the true love you pursue
In His quest the love you allure
It's through the profundity in adore
That you cherish the semblance in core
When your body dwells in soul
Then becoming part of The Whole
Enchanting in adore His bliss in sway

As if,
You're a part of His Gleam in array
How'd you then stay a bit in away

Merging in state of eternity in calm
When He,
Created you of His Semblance in plan
Endowing His Efflux to you in span
So when you allure His notion in norm
O man!
Ardor and adore Him with sincerity in calm
Only then you have the taste of the fruit

When you with your soul swing in a loop
Becoming part of the Whole in swoop

If you tickle the perception in deep
You can treasure His Bliss in sweep
O Lord!
Forgive me all the ills in trance
That's,
Due to my nature built in stance
You're all and around in sway
But I worship You here in pray
You need not any praise in entreat
But I offer You the prayers in greet
O Lord!
Forgive my sins due to my ills in treat
(A word from the Sacred Hindu book Gita)
When goodness grows weak in pace
When evil increases in place
I make myself body in flow
In every age I return to bestow
To deliver the holy word in glow
To destroy the sin of ills in base
To establish virtuous backing with grace (Gita 1V:7–8)

He who does the task with pleasure
Dictated by duty to treasure
Caring nothing for self in stance
For the fruit of action in return
He is a true yogi in term (Gita V1:1)

One to me is loss again
One to me is fame or shame
One to me is pleasure in pain (Gita X!!)

Restless the mind is
So strongly shaken
In grip of senses all so broken
Truly I think
The mind is no wilder in token (Gita V1:34)

Only that yogi abound in grace
Whose joy is inward in pace
Inwards in peace
And his vision inward to please
Shall become Brahman in stance
And known Nirvana in glance
Without garments to cover in class
Clothing shed by the body in pass
Worn-out bodies in pray
Are shed by the dweller in fray (Gita 11:22)

The Lord Almighty made different religions to suit different aspirations, times, and societies. All doctrines are only so many paths, but a path is by no means God Almighty Himself, but cast no doubt on His discipline. Indeed, one can reach Him if one follows the true discipline of the path with whole-hearted devotion.

Someone asked Buddha, "Are you god?"

"No!" was the answer.

"An angel?"

"No."

"A saint?"

"No."

"Then what are you?"

Buddha answered, "I'm awake."

Lo!
As the blowing winds in swipe
So is the real moral of life
That's the grumble in gripe,
A swirling storm surround in life
Oh! It is the real sob in delight
It is only the real thing to pain
So let us allure the truth in pain

Like of the man,
We're born to delight,
That delight may adorn in pain
We're born in hope to remain
The hope once more dwindle in pain
We're born with flavor of love to allure
That love pitch to hate once again
And culminate in pain once more in score
And from pain,
Infinite agony perpetuate to sustain

We may give others pain as prime definition:
The right view; objective; discourse; behavior; occupation; right effort;
mind-fullness, and concentration.

We're born from the earth
Life isn't a journey in mirth

Universe is like an inn in sway
Passing years, struggle in stray
As though a closet of dust and dirt

Regard this phantom world in esteem
As a star at dawn, a bubble in stream

A flash of lightning in a summer cloud
Thundering rumble booming in aloud

Dwindling glow of the candle in dark
Flora and foliage perceived in adorn
He finds not, who seeks his own

The soul is lost that keeps in alone
By ourselves the evil is done

By ourselves, the pain we endure
By ourselves, we become so pure

No one saves us but ourselves in pray
No one can and no one may assuage in fray

We ourselves tread in faith
Discipline of faith escorts in pray

Morning Prayers

Far in there alluring and amiable resorts
Birds beseeching boon and bounty of Lord

Robin singing a sweet and seductive song
Cuckoo and catbird click a catching psalm

Drowsy cardinal chirps in seasoning sound
Prairie Philomel adds to the morning hymn

Honey guide and the scarlet bee
Adjuring appeasing swift and free

Swaying and swinging from dangling frill
In twilight tranquil with enticing thrill

Melodic surf of sweeping surge
Blooming silvery splash in merge

Ripples gleaming in reflective streaks
Mellowing entreat in seductive sweep

From snowy peaks in captivating reach
Could you discern their word in entreat
Melodious means and manner in beseech

Air so cool calm clear in drift
Emerald tinted spring in mist

Glistening water surge in swift
As if,
Mirror polished by the clouds in sweep
And,
Air humming with melodic waters in play
As snowmelt,
Waters drizzles down the creek
All in around charm in play

Below and beside slithering in glide
Glimmer of ripples seduce in slide
Therein nomadic clouds swing in sway
With sunrise breeze wandering in deep
Sailing in the sky in satiny sweep
Then get to merge swift in array

Eventually they cover the sky in swarm
Then subsequent to call held in command
Frighten and flinch dictum in demand

They blush to blaze flicker in glow
A deafening rumble boom in ado

Burst into snuffle like tears in swash
A sight of spatter, a sprinkle in dash
When torrent twirl swizzle in splash

Therein stance each dribble of rain
Ardor and adore Thy Bounty in claim

Therein,
The glow of shimmer of dawn
When it's early break of morn

Morning stillness evince in glow
Therein,
The depth of lake charisma in enchants
As heavens mirror deep in below
With,
Treasure of corals and marine plants

Dusted with wintry ash of snow
A timeworn cypress creeping in low

As though pleading clemency in prone
Therein the morn beseeching in alone

With,
Vibrant dapple in charismatic fawn
Birds then darting away in swarm

All beg to implore in melodic lore
As gliding waters lure in adore

While,
Breezy dawn ushers its beam in glow
There's,
A word of pray with a squeak of crow
In shimmering surge of dawning flow

Whispering sound of the rustling leaves
Flowers swinging in hustling breeze
Glittering rainbow on floral wreath

With scent, spoor and trailing perfume
Sobbing adjuring in blissful resume
All beg to brace Thy Mercy in bloom

Amiable gleaming sky in beaming dawn
With soothing swing of solacing psalms

Seyal with all implores, Almighty Lord
Dole me not out of Thy Exalted Rewards

Endow me Thy Gentle and Gracious Accord
Lest I slight,
Thy Boon Bounties and Benedictions Lord

Night Vigil

Pray,
Thee O Lord in prime faith in adore
We beg and beseech in resolute lore

It's five in times conforming in treat
But in semblance for some to entreat

Late night vigil so revering in beseech
When all are asleep some beg to plead

When stars set to sway and swing in slope
Then dip to decline and descend in probe

Some ardor in adore Lord to obey
Assert to affirm and conform in pray
Beg to beseech Lord in stay

Some part of the night
Others all through the night

If they ever swing to slip in slight
Then,
Beg to implore in drift of blight
For,
Lord discerns to concern all in plight

Converse and conclude all in sway
Extenuation of Lord humble in pray

Lord discerns your voice in resolute lore
For,
What you pray and plead, urge in implore

What a time to renounce snooze in sleep
Then beg to beseech and entreat in plead

Compassionate Lord we're "Thee" to allure
How'd we ever trend "Thy" love to secure

O Lord!
Thy term in tribute sure to grasp
That's course in conduct, all to clasp

O man!
Have ardor in adore in faith to brace
For it's the time of Divine Luminous Grace

Conceive ardor of soul for here in gleam
Benison of beseeching abound in esteem

His sanctity abound in norm
As surge in stream sway in swarm

For all His gifts and grants in grace
Pray and plead His pity to brace
Implore Thee O Lord all in pace

Seyal!
In supreme semblance of faith in lore
Begs to beseech so earnest in implore

Turning his looks to heavens in adore
In woe and ado from the veer of core

Supplicate submissive devout in relate
Sobbing adjuring in a blissful narrate

Appeal Thee O Lord! He pleads in state
Bestow me a gleam of elegance in grace
Lest I slight,
Thy Bounty in Boons to brace

Pray Thee, O Lord!
Seyal once more in stride
Cherish 'Thy' Bliss, me to aside

With,
Renditions of Qur'an in course to concern so clear
And accomplish Thy Benevolence as guide to steer

Seyal!
Not be a slave of self in soul
But as a humble servant in adore
With Bliss of Bounty, His love in core

Mind

Mind is like a mirror so bright
Take care to keep it clean in sight
Let not the dust or debris soot in slight

The core of mirror blurred in gleam
For it's through your vision in stream
Conviction of Faith escort in esteem

The darkness shawls the ills to spy
Where the logic is determined to doom and die
Glimmer of riddle flash in the eyes

My daily duties don't differ in part
Only I'm bound to conduct in accord

Renouncing not the passage in right
In all term in accord, the way in bright

Cutting woods or drawing water in deep
That's the Nature we adore in sweep

Tread with care and concern in stance
As the,
Footprint in sand don't evince in glance

Speak so well,
For the tongue even so slips in trance

Reckon so well,
That there's no counter in concealed
Cannot you abide with patience in reveal

Till your mud settles and the water is clear
Wouldn't you endure a breather in pace
Till the moment in bliss is there to steer

Nothing in the world in spread
So malleable and yielding to tread

So be a servant of Lord in stay
For,
None can conduct the course in way
In the bang of brittle world in fray
Other than the bliss of Lord in pray

The whole will perish, but ebullience and allegiance, clemency and compassion, seemliness and sincerity with the entirety of His Almighty will abide infinitely in His dictum to remain. We, therefore, must endure to live in order of acquiescence and amenability, subordination and servility, persistence and pertinacity, devotion and dedication, order and obedience to His decree in demand. That is the true concept of the philosophy of faith ordained in the Holy Scripture.

When we go through the composition of the Holy Scripture, at most of the places, we are adequately stranded, unable to conceive the real meaning of the text. We need still more defined and definite, befitting and becoming acquisition of the knowledge to accomplish and comprehend the discerning wisdom of the text of the Holy Scripture.

The Holy Scripture not only provides a clear elucidation of quite a few modern-day scientific concepts but also entices mankind to track and trail the truth of the actuality behind the philosophy of the creation of the universe and mankind.

I've tried to elaborate on the divine concept of time, the fate of the universe, and the creation of mankind with reference to modern-day scientific convictions, in addition to the theories of evolution and supersymmetry. Our concept of life is incomplete if we don't clearly understand the notion of death or the premise of life after death and what we the human beings are really composed of (i.e., the earthly pot, the divine endowment, the efflux, and the intelligence).

There could be some play on words in the explanation of these scientific notions, but I am sure the reader will not be confounded by these anomalies. To make things comprehensible for a common man, there had to be some vacillation.

I sincerely believe that the creation of the universe and mankind is for the *whole human race* as there is a definite design and plan behind the concept and creation of all the multiverses.

I cite Canadian scholar Wilfred Cantwell Smith, who wrote in the mid-twentieth century shortly before the Suez Crisis:

> We observed a healthy functioning Islam had for centuries helped Muslims cultivate decent values, which we in the West share, because they spring from a common tradition. Some Muslims have problems with the Western modernity. They have turned against the cultures of "People of the Book" and have even begun to Islamize their view of hatred of these sister Faiths that are powerfully endorsed by the Holy Qur'an. If Muslims have to meet the challenges of the day, they must learn to understand the Western traditions and institutions, because they are not going to disappear.

He also pointed out that Western society also has to recognize that they share the planet not with inferiors, but with equals.

> Unless Western Civilization intellectually and socially, politically and economically and the Christian Church theologically, can learn to treat the men of other faith with fundamental respect, these two in their turn will have failed to come to terms with the actuality of 21st century. The problems raised in this are of course, as profound as anything that Prophet Muhammad PBUH was confronted when he introduced the Discipline of faith.

As already mentioned, the discipline of faith is largely distorted by human interpretations, as the Catholic Church should instead be called the Constantine Church. The lineage of prophet-hood is the same in all the monotheistic faiths. The message of faith is deeply insinuated in the profundity of intelligence, whereas the discipline of faith is to make you a good human being and the best example of a person, as Karen Armstrong in her recent book, *Muhammad Prophet of Today,* writes:

> The brief history of 21st century shows that neither side has mastered these lessons. If we are to avoid catastrophe, the Muslims and the Western Worlds must learn not merely to tolerate but to appreciate one another. A good place to start with is with the personality of Prophet Muhammad a most sophisticated and complex figure in the history of humanity, who resists facile ideologically driven

categorization, who sometimes did things that were difficult or impossible to accept, but he had profound genius and led the faith a cultural tradition that was not based on sword but whose name is 'Islam' that signifies peace and reconciliation.

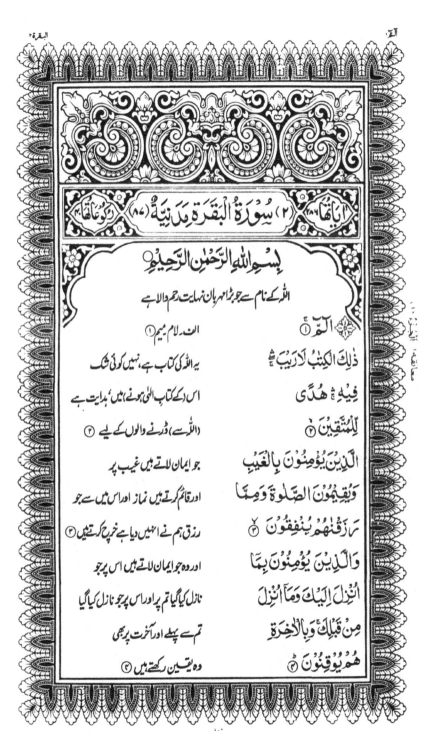

الٓمّ ۱

سُوْرَةُ الْبَقَرَةِ مَدَنِيَّةٌ (۸۶) اٰیَاتُهَا ۲۸۶ رُکُوْعَاتُهَا ۴۰

بِسْمِ اللهِ الرَّحْمٰنِ الرَّحِيْمِ

اللہ کے نام سے جو بڑا مہربان نہایت رحم والا ہے

الٓمّٓ ۱

الف۔لام۔میم ۱

ذٰلِكَ الْكِتٰبُ لَا رَيْبَ ۖ

یہ اللہ کی کتاب ہے، نہیں کوئی شک

فِيْهِ ۛ هُدًى

اس کے کتاب الٰہی ہونے میں، ہدایت ہے

لِّلْمُتَّقِيْنَ ۙ ۲

(اللہ سے) ڈرنے والوں کے لیے ۲

الَّذِيْنَ يُؤْمِنُوْنَ بِالْغَيْبِ

جو ایمان لاتے ہیں غیب پر

وَيُقِيْمُوْنَ الصَّلٰوةَ وَمِمَّا

اور قائم کرتے ہیں نماز اور اس میں سے جو

رَزَقْنٰهُمْ يُنْفِقُوْنَ ۙ ۳

رزق ہم نے انہیں دیا ہے خرچ کرتے ہیں ۳

وَالَّذِيْنَ يُؤْمِنُوْنَ بِمَا

اور وہ جو ایمان لاتے ہیں اس پر جو

اُنْزِلَ اِلَيْكَ وَمَآ اُنْزِلَ

نازل کیا گیا تم پر اور اس پر جو نازل کیا گیا

مِنْ قَبْلِكَ ۚ وَبِالْاٰخِرَةِ

تم سے پہلے اور آخرت پر بھی

هُمْ يُوْقِنُوْنَ ۙ ۴

وہ یقین رکھتے ہیں ۴

Faith in the Unseen

A'lif L'am M'im

This is the Scripture,
Whereof there's no doubt *to debate*
Guidance for the virtuous *in state*
Who assert and affirm, faith in unseen
And also abide prayers, *noble in esteem*
Dole out alms affirmed *in routine*
Out of Our Bestowal *in supreme* (2:1–4)

Assertion of faith in the unseen is the basis of Islam, but as a routine, scientists have refuted the discipline of faith in the unseen. When we open the second chapter of the Holy Scripture, it very clearly gives a true picture of the subject.

'*A'lif 'L'am 'M'im*—undoubtedly, there should not be any discrepancy or dissent, disavowal or dissension, disagreement or defiance in anybody's mind regarding the truth of discipline ordained in this book. Which book? The one which has been decreed and distinguished by His "A"lmighty "A"LLah and conferred through Gabrie"L," the archangel, to His Prophet "M"uhammad ᴾᴮᵁᴴ. The revelation pronounced by His Almighty Lord to His Prophet Muhammad ᴾᴮᵁᴴ through the Archangel Gabriel is perhaps the only Scripture that is preserved in its categorical conformation to stance and stanza of each word communicated by His Almighty and conveyed to His Prophet Muhammad ⁽ᴾᴮᵁᴴ⁾.

We recite the each venerable verse and each ornate word of the sanctified scripture in its glorious antediluvian configuration. When this concept prevails in the mind, it becomes exceptionally beseeching and bracing because these are the words uttered in their original pronunciation and position by the Lord Almighty, the Archangel Gabriel, and Muhammad ᴾᴮᵁᴴ, the Holy Prophet. When this perception deeply insinuates itself in the mind, that we are vocalizing the words, phrases, and verses that were primarily established by His Almighty, a state of serenity and satisfaction, blissfulness and beatitude prevails in the mind, body, and soul.

The Holy Scripture gives an account of all the instances, occurrences, and happenings when the things and the world itself had not actualized. Divine perception and vision commands all instances of how and when it would happen.

Has any book in this world ever made this challenge or pronouncement to defy its entirety and essence?

Perhaps none so far!

The Holy Scripture invites you to concentrate on the course and contents of the Scripture sagaciously and then look for any inconsistency, scruple, or suspense in the text, the slur or blur of its assertions and affirmations, proclamations and declarations.

It is guidance for the virtuous—precisely, it is the spring of erudition and edification, demeanor and deportment, injunction and inclination for mankind, but only those who strive to secure the convinced capabilities as enumerated below acquire virtuosity and vivacity, and they are blessed with benevolence in faith.

True faith has always endeavored to sense the softness and sweetness of the soul and determined diligence with fortitude and forbearance in the subjects who resolved after due forethought and with no vanity or vainglory in their minds, which men call exaltation or excellence. There should be an adamant faith of love with persistence, patience, and perseverance, and an ebullience to escort those who had anything to volunteer for the common weal of conviction. There is an everlasting firmness in giving to everyone according to the firm belief and the knowledge derived from the Holy Scripture that endows the experience of discernment and discretion, enlightenment and erudition, elegance and edification of special sophisticated subjects like modern-day science and philosophy, in addition to a bestowal of perception and prudence and discipline and direction in all walks of life.

The very first principle of perception as asserted in the Qur'an for the virtuous is to have *faith in the unseen.*

Is such a faith delusive and deceptive from a scientific point of view?

But when we concern the fundamental philosophy of the scientific convictions, for what they observe and assert is once again faith in the unseen, as Sir Arthur Eddington in his famous Cambridge lectures shows that all fundamental laws and constants of physics are deduced unambiguously from a prior consideration. These laws are very successful in explaining the objective world. So he concludes, in the age of reason, faith yet remains supreme, for reason is one of the articles of faith.

A few illustrations would make this point clearer.

Quantum physics starts with the assumption of a strange particle called a photon, which carries light energy. This particle does not have any dimension or charge. It does not have any property found in any physical object. Its rest mass is zero and moving mass is indeterminate. This scientific conviction has given birth to an idea that is considered to be one of the greatest achievements of human intellect.

De Brogue assumed that all microscopic particles could be associated with a wave when in motion. This is known as a *matter wave*. Since this is a complex wave, it does not have any physical parallelism and is purely abstract in nature. A wave is completely determined by measuring any two of the three parameters, namely, wavelength, frequency, and velocity. It is possible to measure all these parameters for the well-known electromagnetic and mechanical waves. But for the matter wave, no instrument can ever determine the wave frequency and wave velocity. A matter wave is a mathematical artifice, and its unique determination is inaccessible to observation. Yet believing in this matter wave solves complicated problems in atomic and nuclear physics. Thus, the matter wave is an article of faith in modern physics.

It is faith to believe that a moving particle behaves like a wave, and wave mechanics is based on this faith. Heisenberg's uncertainty principle states that the position and momentum of a particle cannot be accurately measured simultaneously and the product of the uncertainties in these measurements cannot be below a certain minimum. The existence of this lowest limit was initially an article of faith, namely that the smallest unit of action exists. This faith was verified experimentally, and the smallest unit was found to be $h = 6.63 \times 10^{34}$ joule/sec, known as Planck's constant.

In the theory of relativity, it has been possible to combine the effects dependent on time with space. But the theory in itself is a prior one. Scientists and mathematicians have not yet been able to remove the subjective effect of generic characteristics common to all observers. The theory of relativity again is another jubilant triumph of human intellectual activities in faith.

After all these scientific affirmations of a presumptuous, unseen particle like a photon that has no dimension or charge or any of the physical properties and at rest a mass of zero but while in motion assumes an indeterminate form, why don't we turn to concern the indeterminate cosmic order and try to discern the most fascinating and "mighty power" behind the effects and equipage of cosmic order—an unseen power that commands indeterminate control over all His creation?

In the Qur'an, the Almighty repeatedly reiterates:

What do you think all these Booms in Bloom are but just a rip and split, rend in trends and there is no Power behind this definite construct of intent in plan with immense effects and equipage.

Looking beyond the blinking lights and whirling gizmos, though, the new century is shaping up to be one of the most amazing periods in human history. The transitions we are undergoing define the scope of faith in the light of modern-day science. Max Tegmark in a *Scientific American* special issue on parallel universes asserts:

> Our creation and that of the universes is just a matter of chance, as we may happen to have room no: 5 in a hotel that turns out to be the same as our birth date i.e. room no: 5 on the floor eleven as our birth day of November 5th. The chance happens to be once in a while but not all the time. When you check in next time in another hotel and even so by chance you happen to have the same room # 5 on the floor eleven, you will be really concerned of the situation and when it would happen for the third time in a row, you'll be sure that someone is there to arrange all that. But why don't we consider of such a state of affair for the whole cosmic order where everything is most orderly organized in a fascinating manner, Could it all be by a stroke of chance or luck without any definite design?

Turn to the pages of perfect creation and you will be fascinated by the order of discipline in and around every object right from the core of an atom to the sprawling cosmic order where everything is moving with a tremendous speed in a definitely planned path—the orbit. The moon is moving around the earth, the earth is moving around the sun, the solar system is moving around the Milky Way Galaxy, and the Milky Way galaxy has its own way in the cosmic order.

(Do you know the speed of these objects? They are dashing away from each other in their orbits at a fascinating speed in a most orderly discipline. Read the text in "Perfect Creation."

Look at the most comprehensive order of arrangement. Do you find any flaw or fault in it? Nay, you cannot.

Turn your looks once again to sort out the situation. You might be able to discern some defiance in the discipline. But nay!

The Qur'an asserts:

> You are denied to find out any snare or snag and even a slightest bit of sway or swing in the order of cosmic discipline. (Surah Al Mulk)

We all accept the existence of things that we cannot see but could see if we moved to a different vantage point or merely waited, like people watching for ships to come to the horizon. Objects beyond the cosmic horizon have a similar status. The observable universe grows by a light-year every year as light from farther away has time to reach us. Infinity lies out there, waiting to be seen. You will probably die long before your alter egos come into view, but in principle and if cosmic expansion cooperates, your descendants could observe them through a sufficiently powerful telescope.

The idea of such an alter ego seems strange and implausible, but it looks as if we will just have to live with it, because it is supported by astronomical observations. The simplest and most popular cosmological model today predicts that you have a twin in a galaxy about 10×10^{28} meters from here. This distance is so large that it is beyond astronomical, but that does not make your *scientific assumption* any less real. The estimate is derived from elementary probability and does not even assume speculative modern physics, merely that space is infinite (or at least sufficiently large) in size and almost uniformly filled with matter, as observations indicate. In infinite space, even the most unlikely events must take place somewhere. There are probably infinitely many other inhabited planets, including not just one but infinitely many that have people with the same appearances, names, and memories as you, who play out every possible permutation of your life choices.

You will probably never see your other selves. The farthest you can observe is the distance that light has been able to travel during the past fourteen billion years since the big bang, or *Kun*, and the explosion initiated *Fa Ya Koon*. The expansion began. The most distant visible objects are now about 4×10^{26} meters away—a distance that defines our observable universe, also called our Hubble volume, our horizon volume, or simply our universe. Likewise, the universes of your other selves are spheres of the same size centered on their planets. They are the most straightforward example of parallel universes. Each universe is merely a small part of a large "multiverse." How congruent is the concept of modern science with the very first verse of the Holy Scripture where the Lord Almighty asserts, "All Praises for Lord of the Multiverses" (1:1).

By this very definition of "universe," one might expect the notion of a multiverse to be forever in the domain of metaphysics. Yet the borderline between physics and metaphysics is defined by whether a theory is experimentally testable, not by whether it is weird or involves unobservable entities. The frontiers of physics have gradually expanded to incorporate ever more abstract (and once metaphysical) concepts, such as a round earth, invisible electromagnetic fields, the slowing of time at high speeds, quantum superposition, curved space, and black holes. Over the past several years, the concept of multiverses has joined this list. It is grounded in well-tested theories such as relativity and quantum mechanics, and it fulfils both of the basic criteria of empirical science: it makes predictions, and it can be falsified. Scientists have discussed as many as four distinct strata of parallel multiverses. The key question is not whether the multiverses exist but rather how many levels they have.

One of the many implications of recent cosmological observations is that the concept of parallel universes is no mere metaphor. Space appears to be infinite in size. If so, then somewhere out there, everything that is possible becomes real, no matter how improbable it is. Beyond the range of our telescopes are other regions of space that are identical to ours. Those regions are a type of parallel universe. Scientists can even calculate how distant these universes are, on average.

And that is fairly solid physics. When cosmologists consider theories that are less well established, they conclude that other universes can have entirely different properties and laws of physics. The presence of those universes would explain various strange aspects of our own. It could even answer fundamental questions about the nature of time and the comprehensibility of the physical world. In the theory of relativity, it has been possible to combine the effects dependent on time with space. But the theory in itself is a prior one. Scientists and mathematicians have not yet been able to remove the subjective effects of generic characteristics common to all observers. The theory of relativity again is another jubilant triumph of human intellectual activities in faith.

After all these scientific affirmations of presumptuous unseen particles like the photon that has no dimension or charge or any of the physical properties and at rest a mass of zero but while in motion assumes indeterminate form, why don't we trend to concern the indeterminate cosmic order and try to discern the most fascinating and "mighty power" behind the effects and equipage of this cosmic order?

The role of faith is also discernible in the affirmations of Einstein, the greatest scientist of the modern age, with respect to the unified field theory. This great scientist spent the last thirty years of his life in search of a wider law covering both gravitation and electromagnetic fields. He firmly stuck to his faith to the last day of his life that such a law existed. Scientists, including Professor Abdus Salam, have been concerned with finding a grand unification theory (GUT) of interactions, namely the gravitational interaction, the electromagnetic interaction, the weak nuclear force, and the strong nuclear force.

Why should one attempt to unite the apparently disjointed interaction? After all, there is no difficulty in our understanding of nature even without the unification of these forces. The desire of physicists to unite these forces into a single one emanated from a faith, namely, that these forces are different manifestations of one and the same entity.

Salam's efforts and success in unifying the electromagnetic and the weak nuclear forces were understandably spurred by the vivacity of verses 3 and 4 of Surah 67 (Al-Mulk), which led him to an appropriate dignified faith in the order and equanimity of creation.

He created skies in series of seven
There's no want in slant in terms of creation
Most Amiable is Lord, *immense in initiation*
So trend your looks *once more to the heaven*
Can you discern a bit of slit *in generation*

Then trend and talent anew *in quest*
You're denied of flaw *in behest*
Not even perplexity or poop *in the rest*

Thus seeking patterns in laws itself implies faith in the grand proposition of the *Lord's creation*. In fact, there are hosts of other such matters in the scientific domain that are based on faith. All these discussions from the point of view of modern science tell us the role of faith in man's progress in knowledge. So faith in the unseen, as demanded by the Lord, is not illogical. For the unseen is beyond our comprehension due to our generic limitations. The above discussion points to the fact that faith in the unseen may not be inconsistent with the correct understanding of the materialistic world.

And what is faith in the unseen? The Lord Almighty is the creator of all the effects and equipage in the whole cosmic order and beyond; for though we don't have the means to comprehend His nature, the Qur'an gives a semblance of His Almighty, and besides that, we can otherwise derive mathematically and with philosophical interpretations that the creation could not have taken place without a creator. The next chapter discusses the details as to how the creation took place in this context and "who" is there behind all the cosmic sway.

Further to that, the next most important of all is "life after death." There has to be a logical philosophical discernment in this context, so that a man of average intelligence can well comprehend the life in the Hereafter to which Prophet Muhammad [PBUH] has attributed "Death is the final awakening."

Initial and Infinite

Agile Author Astral O Astute
Brilliant Beginner Bountiful O Beatitude
Conforming Creator in Care and Command

Once upon a no time when there was only the *precept of the principal with providence*[5] and when there was no perception of time or creation, there was not even a whippersnapper in actuality or the simile of a proposal in presentation of substantiality except for the bounty of the supreme principal, at that twinkling and trice the precept (ruling faculty) of the principal with providence (forethought) designed to devise the whole cosmic order with life into a reality of existence. And so He looked on the whims of surmise with a look of excellence, for nothing in actuality, not even the icon of initiation that is the source of all existence can bear the perfect manifestation of the Supreme Principal (Almighty Allah) with all the providence. Perhaps it was only nature that belonged to the basic framework of all the matter besides the precept of the principal with providence that governed the basic ingredients of matter, abounding the decree and deliberation of nature that directed the whole cosmic order.

If we see an object during daytime and not at night, it's because there's light during the day that helps us to see things. It supports the effect of light that assists us to see something. This consequence or the effect of light must have a source, (i.e., the sun). The sun did not conceive itself; there must be a discernable source behind the creation of this effect. We understand that each effect has a source and the source has a logic behind its creation. We invariably pronounce that source as nature. *A mighty nature* is behind the creation of the entire panorama with definite laws or the principles with forethought (providence).

All these effects and equipage to which I attribute the name Allah, some call it Bhagwan or Parmatma, and still others call it God, because nobody has refuted the word *nature*.

---

5   a mighty nature (principal) ruling (precept)

One cannot really comprehend His order of precept with providence in the whole universe from a microscopic speck of an electron, even to the extent of a photon that's not discernable even with the most powerful microscope, to the most ungraspable cosmic domain—the strata of multiverses. Only the lowest sky of that is decked with stellar sprawl in swarm. What could be His order of design and arrangements in the rest of the six skies, a desolate void of unlit cosmic sway.

The legend of modern science when combined with the philosophical inspirations invariably sorts out the labyrinth. The Qur'an has very clearly elucidated each notion. It is His Almighty Allah alone who dictates the decree of the universe, as we discern that each linguistic alphabet starts with the "A" of "Allah." The notion indicates the first numerical "one." A'llah Almighty is "one." Before "A," there is no word to substantiate any whim or notion of surmise, but before the first numerical one "1," there is zero "0," the nullity or nihility.

Now, we turn toward the perception of earlier initiation (i.e., the precept in the principle of providence concerning the cosmic order and all).

"A," Allah Almighty, besides there was singularity to say "one," but in materiality, it was nullity or the nihility "zero," for there was nothingness in physical being. According to the modern scientific conviction that substantiates that there was just one precept as a "principal" with providence, who commanded the "singularity" at the core that had virtually no order of discernment of any whim or inkling in turn of time (i.e., with no discernment of present, past, or future or time of term for matter before this prong and prick with the quirk of a unique feature).

Before proceeding, I would like to conclude on the subject that someone would ask, "Is there any letter before "A"?

The answer is, "How ridiculous!"

"And is there a number or numerical before one?"

Again, the answer is, "How it could be when the count starts from one?"

We have seen that nullity or the nihility is nothing but zero and it has no space to occupy and no physical features, so the nullity was nowhere there, then it possibly could be. And we have seen that the value of nullity or zero is just nothing without the figure "one"; otherwise, So we conclude that nullity was nothing but the indeterminate power in the might and command of Allah Almighty. He would evince His power and then conclude it once again to nullity, and the scientists believe that it would be the seedling for the next creation. This is a very interesting subject as the scientists still don't know how this ever-expanding model of the world is behaving like a closed model; the details in this context are given in "The Fate of the Universe."

9

When we turn to the earliest state of initiation, the Qur'an terms it as a smoke of inconclusive characteristic. Embracing the concept of "smoke" once again draws us close to the subject of discernment that initial matter had no contour or configuration to perceive as to what it could be like, as modern science turns to this notion as a "singularity" or the nihility of an inconclusive order of density and consequence eventuating from core to stellar sprawl with the decree and dictum of the precept of principal with providence.

We perceive the gleam of smoke with a stellar sprawl of about fifteen billion years before this time, and we cannot comprehend as to what it could be like before that instance of *Kun Fa Ya Koon*, as the Qur'an mentions, the earliest state of the multiverse manifest, as a smoke of inconclusive order observed today with our most sophisticated scientific endowments.

In the epoch of the sprawl of creation, the *big bang* or divine decree in dictate for this domain, *Kun*, when matter and time set out their travel and travail, *Fa Ya Koon*, from the nihility of singularity to an indeterminate order of imperceptible consequence, one must diligently try to deliberate as to where the modern scientific concept differs from Qur'anic philosophy at this most critical juncture of the creation of time and the matter of the cosmic order and the life in it. There with a steady stream of spectacular discoveries forthcoming in this domain, the Grand Observatories of Origins Deep Survey (GOODS) turns to reveal fascinating leaps in lines to encompass and help us comprehend the clue and code of the fundamental nature of the universe.

How congruent are these doctrines that bring faith in the precept of providence and modern scientific convictions close together to embrace a uniform view of creation?

We have to understand the logic of creation and the myth of life in the light of the true discernment of faith that is time and again professed in the Qur'an.

هُوَ الْاَوَّلُ وَالْاٰخِرُ وَالظَّاهِرُ وَالْبَاطِنُ ج وَهُوَ بِكُلِّ شَیْءٍ عَلِیْمٌ (۳) وہی اول بھی ہے اور آخر بھی اور ظاہر بھی ہے اور باطن بھی اور وہ ہر چیز کا پورا علم رکھتا ہے (۳)

Allah Almighty reiterates that He's the "First" and the "Last" (57:3).

The first numeral, of course, is one as we affirm that His Almighty Allah is "One."

When He was there as the precept of a principal with providence, there was nihility (i.e., the matter or all of the substance besides Him, so figuratively it was ten or 10, with one commanding the nihility, "0," the zero, at the core that had no order of substantiation without "One."

When we turn to the stellar sprawl in the creation of the multiverses, we understand that the Lord Almighty, who is "indeterminate" and "incomprehensible" (i.e., omnipotent) could only instigate a most unfathomable and ungraspable cosmic order, for nihility could otherwise never achieve a figuratively conceivable status in concern.

Figuratively, when we write for the indeterminate order of consequence, we place it something like this:

9.99999999999999999999999999999999999999999999

Even if we add a value to the above figure, it loses its identity in indefinite terms.

.00000000000000000000000000000000000000000000001

It becomes something finite but not last; so to be infinite and indeterminate, it has to be only "9" and nothing else.

Not a bit in terms of discernment can be conceived to His indeterminate order of sapience, because He is the sole originator of all conceivable perception in prudence. For Allah Almighty is infinite, eternal, and unbounded for His command and demand in score, besides His sapience and sagacity in core, so we cannot add even a bit of a trace to His indeterminate order of consequence in lore.

So figuratively, it was ten at the time of the creation of the universe, which is to expand indefinitely to some order that could be something like:

10 x 10 x 10 x 10 x 10

100000000000000000000000000000000000000000000

Can we not say for sure whether this notion of figurative concern has some predetermined end to it? Yes! It has a predetermined end to it as discussed later in this chapter.

Look at the figure with the immeasurable order of consequence (i.e., one with an undetermined number of zeroes besides it still remains "one" if we remove all the zeroes beside it, whereas nihility or "0" after attaining an ungraspable order of discernment is nothing without "one"). Now consider the whole consequence of creation in this context.

But there is a strong conviction that nihility started off on its own to an incomprehensible order of cosmic sway. We shall have to consider the appropriateness of nihility in mathematical terms; that's 0. If we multiply zero by an infinite number, the outcome is still zero; for it would have still stayed as nihility or zero because the multiple of nihility cannot have figuratively conceivable dimensions. Indeed! There had to be a source or the precept of the principal with providence to kick off the blow. And we affirm that one supreme principal with providence initiated the whole order in consequence. How could the creation take its stride without the dictum of "one," the Lord, Allah Almighty, God, Brahma, or Bhagwan?

That's the state today with the one of indeterminate order of consequence besides "nihility" (i.e., zero) commanding its enigmatic and mysterious expanse in distance and direction. And if ever the cosmological arrow of time is reversed, it'll make it difficult for life to survive the odds. At that instance, the order of figurative discernment once again would tend to be "one" besides nihility or zero (i.e., 10). Different scientific theories suggest that already isolated events of crunch are happening in the cosmological order, like black holes, and the Qur'an also predicts an event of a big crunch.

The Qur'an has asserted it over and again that there has to be a sudden end to the realm of life besides the end of the cosmic domain (i.e., a big smash eventuating in a series of big crunches).

The Day We'll whirl heavens *in twirl*
And a recorder list up a scribble in *swirl*
As We began the first creation *in sway*
We'll trend to it once again *in array*
It's pledged from Us *in pace*
Us to assert once more *to place* (21:104)

And once again, there will be only one precept of principal with providence besides nihility.

So we learn that at the earliest state of creation, there was an order of ten (i.e., one beside nihility or zero "0"), the multiple of which is one hundred, and as we determine the boundless cosmic order today, we refer to the figure of nine, the multiple of which is eighty-one.

The difference between the two, one hundred and eighty-one, is nineteen. Similarly, ten plus nine is nineteen, and ten minus nine is one.

The one is the Lord Almighty, the omnipotent, and nineteen stays as a figurative stamp on His creation.

Once again, turning toward the order of consequence in figures, all other dictions are the jumble and clutter of figures between one and nine with nihility enunciating a substantial role.

How congruent is this notion as we turn the pages of the Holy Scripture?

The chapters in the Holy Scripture are 114, a multiple of nineteen.

The first revelation has exactly nineteen words.

اِقْرَأْ بِاسْمِ رَبِّكَ الَّذِیْ خَلَقَ (۱) خَلَقَ الْاِنْسَانَ مِنْ عَلَقٍ (۲) اِقْرَأْ وَرَبُّكَ الْاَکْرَمُ (۳) الَّذِیْ عَلَّمَ بِالْقَلَمِ (۴) عَلَّمَ الْاِنْسَانَ مَالَمْ یَعْلَمْ (۵)

پڑھو(اے نبیﷺ)اپنے رب کا نام لے کر جس نے پیدا کیا(۱) پیدا کیا انسان کو(نطفہ مخلوط کے) جمے ہوئے خون سے(۲) پڑھواور تمہارا رب بڑائی کریم ہے(۳) جس نے علم سکھایا قلم کے ذریعے سے(۴) سکھایا انسان کو وہ علم جو نہیں جانتا تھاوہ(۵)

The last revelation also has exactly nineteen words.

اِذَاجَآءَ نَصُرُ اللّٰهِ وَالْفَتْحُ (١) وَرَاَيْتَ النَّاسَ يَدْ خُلُوْنَ فِىْ دِيْنِ اللّٰهِ اَفْوَاجًا (٢)فَسَبِّحْ بِحَمْدِ رَبِّكَ وَاسْتَغْفِرْهُ ط اِنَّهُ كَانَ تَوَّابًا(٣)

جب آجائے مدداللہ کی اورفتح (نصیب ہوجائے)(١)اوردیکھولوتم (اے نبیﷺ) لوگوں کوکہ داخل ہورہے ہیں وہ اللہ کے دین میں فوج درفوج(٢) توتسبیح کرو تم اپنے رب کی،اس کی حمد کے ساتھ اوربخشش مانگواس سے بے شک وہی ہے تو بہ قبول کرنے والا (٣)

Likewise بِسْمِ اللّٰهِ الرَّحْمٰنِ الرَّحِيْمِ is mentioned 114 times; it is missing once in Surah *Taubah*, but appears twice in Surah *Naml*.

بِسْمِ اللّٰهِ الرَّحْمٰنِ الرَّحِيْمِSimilarly, this benevolent sentence has nineteen letters.

How do we discern the order of "nature"?

In the following verse, His Almighty, while elucidating His semblance or nature, has very eloquently made clear the type and sort of physical laws operating in the multiverses. We have a long way to go to comprehend the philosophy of the Qur'an, but I have attempted to give a brief elucidation of some of the topics, so that a reader can cherish the axiom of nature.

Lord is The Only Glow *in Gleam*
Of the heavens and earth *in esteem*
Semblance of His Gleam
Light like of a beam

Wherein the lamp is placed *in recess*
The glass around the lamp *in access*

The glass as a lustrous star *in glow*
Lamp in aglow of (sacred) olive *in flow*

That's not of the East or West *in prime*
Whose oil to beam and gleam *in sublime*

There's no flare or flash to pat *in chime*
Shimmer over Glimmer *all so Divine*

Lord escort to His Gleam *in Glow*
To one He cherishes His esteem *in flow*

Simile of Lord is for men *to aside*
Lord discerns and concerns *all in stride*
(Al Nōōr 24:35)

Can you really understand the lamp and the lamp placed in a nook amidst the *chandelier*, a word used by Maulana Abul Ala Maudodi while describing the above-mentioned verse?

The universal space contains all the laws of the universe (e.g., inertia, gravity, quantum mechanics, biogenetics, electromagnetic emission, the atomic laws, evolution, and whatnot). Every cubic centimeter of space from one end of the universe to the other is filled with a definite law that makes the universe and everything in it work. These natural laws in turn create space and determine the size of the universe. Where the laws end, the universe ends.

If the laws only extended outward in all directions for just one meter, this would be the size of the whole grand universe comprised of multiverses. There would be no space beyond this sphere of influence. It could not extend one bit further. The laws of universal space precisely determine and control all actions and interactions of matter and energy within the multiverses, from the tiniest space between the subatomic particles to the vast expanse of the multiverses. The laws of the Almighty created universal space; without its laws, the universe would not exist.

Energy is nothing without matter to push around. Matter has no mass without energy. Together, under the absolute rule of the laws of space, they create this complex, dynamic universe we live in. Even if there were no matter or energy in universal space, it would still exist as long as divine laws existed, although it would be rather pointless.

I cannot bring myself to believe that all these exquisite, impeccable, tangled, and all-pervading laws of nature just happened to come into being without some infinitely wise and all-powerful reality creating them. I am talking about the natural laws of the universe. There is an "all-powerful reality," His Almighty Allah, behind all these philosophies of mankind, other living beings, and the cosmic sway.

The laws of space govern everything within the universe. They do not go on forever, nor do they gradually weaken and dissipate. They are either completely in force, or they do not exist at all. Where the laws do not apply, neither energy nor matter can exist; therefore, there is no space. The boundary of the universe is not a wall; it is simply where the laws of the universe end— the lower skies, as mentioned in the Holy Qur'an: *"I've decked the Lower Skies with stellar sprawl"* (41:12).

The multiverses are shaped like a hollow sphere with nature's laws governing and unifying everything within the sphere. The laws of nature create space, as we know it. Outside the sphere, beyond the boundary of the universe, nothing can exist. It is completely devoid of all energy and matter.

Beyond the boundary, the laws of universal space do not exist; therefore, nothing can exist. Even space itself does not exist, to our knowledge.

The stars and planets could not form since there would be no mass or gravity to hold them together. A light ray could not travel in this region because there would be no laws to guide it. But the "gleam in glow" of His Almighty, who is the source of all laws, doesn't need any physical laws to perpetuate itself.

There would be no possible way to determine if this region ended just beyond our reach or extended out to infinity. But the Lord Almighty, evincing His semblance, clearly elucidates this region's limits as an imperceptible transparent glass, because the space itself is an unlit transparency like a glass.

In the text, His Almighty, soon after elucidating His discipline of cosmic order that He organized so ubiquitously in a fascinating discipline of measure, advises man to observe the same in his daily routine.

When there was an initial whisper of *Kun*, there was a swizzle of initiation, *Fa Ya Koon*, merging in the swash of eternity; the glow of light up and coming from the brawl of the big bang took around fifteen billion light-years to reach us today. That's from the early click of creation, and scientists affirm that, "Our future stretches ahead much farther than our past trails behind." Can you dream of the size of the cosmic order, where somewhere in the nook of that the origin of "the Nōōr," it evinces its display?

Light has a substantiated actuality of source that could either be chemical, electrical, or mechanical, and its speed is around 186,000 miles per second. But Nōōr has no evinced source of ignition. The Lord Almighty asserts that it evinces its glow on its own without the element of combustion. The speed of Nōōr cannot be actually comprehended because as it will be discussed later in "Divine perception of Time," for angels that are a part of Nōōr, their speed ranges from fifty million to two hundred million times the speed of light, and the speed of the Archangel Gabriel is thirty billion times the speed of light (details in "The Divine Perception of Time").

Nay! You really cannot grasp or appreciate the "indeterminate sway" in the sweep of the chandelier. Can you? Where beyond in the cosmic sway, the rule of scientific laws has no order in stay, His gleam in glow shimmers and glimmers in flow like a star.

While describing His glow in gleam, the Lord Almighty defines the limit of the cosmological arrow of time, when it will face an edge, a transparent glass-like limit that determines the end of the multiverses; perhaps, there beyond, physical laws wouldn't hold good to support the existence of life or the Lord Almighty Himself wouldn't like it to perpetuate beyond definite limits (the lower skies).

That's the time when the thermodynamic arrow of time will also reverse, as the temperature at the core of creation would probably reach absolute zero according to some scientific theories (i.e., -273.15 on the Celsius scale or -459.67 Fahrenheit). This will be the time when the energy as the rise in temperature will take place with a big smash. Different galaxies and stars will be swallowed by the black holes, and there alone the gravitational force will be dissipated in the void raising its temperature to billions and trillions. Then finally, the black holes will evaporate. The intense gravitational force then released will sweep across to swallow the space and energy and finally will wrap up under its own intense gravitational influence to an infinitely minute point, the nullity—a seedling for the next creation. There's another arrow of time called the "interminable arrow" of time (discussed later in "Divine Perception of Time" as a time of nihility). We don't have a way to really ascertain the nature of this time for it existed before the creation of the multiverses. It would flow for eternity in the indeterminate cosmic sway, with the Astral O Astute Gleam in Glow of Allah Almighty surging in flow, in the most incomprehensible array.

This is also asserted in Surah Al-Rahman verse 7:

Raised the Heavens and set its brink
That you may not cross it's brim

Brink and *brim* are confines limiting the expansion of multiverses, thus indicating a predetermined order of the big smash (discussed in "The Fate of the Universe").

This *interminable arrow* of time has nothing to do with the big bang because it took its strides ever since the Lord Almighty evinced His "being" with the creation of the angels and other exigencies for what we don't have the means to discern.

The glow or the glimmer of Nōōr does not need any physical laws for illumination beyond the glass or the lower skies; rather the glow of light, as we experience it, becomes more intense in illumination beyond the glass. So the glimmer of Nōōr has the lustrous glow of a star infinitely beyond in the interminable order of cosmic sway that to our knowledge has no borders or end. This gleam of Nōōr is not subjected to a saddle curve like ordinary light but pierces through and through even the most dense lead sheets or any other encumbrances for these are all His creations. I assert this because I had a glimpse of His glow piercing through the rooftops and different strata of the multiverses, directed toward my heart, wherein I could discern the vistas of the whole in lucid drill.

16

Nõõr

That's a Gleam in Glow
For '*Nõõr*' there's is no twist in flow

Whereas light has to face
A bend or bow in trace
When it chances a barrier in pace
It happens to drift in place

So in the cosmic sprawl in flow
Light has to face a curve in glow

Whereas *Nõõr* eludes all catch in track
For all being His creations in stack

So it goes over and hurl in throw
Whatever chances to be there in flow?

The Glimpse of *Nõõr* evince in Glow
Faces of ardently men in endow

For *Nõõr* has no source in place
It's the source of self in trace
That's the Alluvial Gleam in pace

What I could never discern in stance
Lord endowed me quite a lot in trance

Gather up every last mote and particle of matter between here and the edge of creation and squeeze it into a spot so infinitesimally compact that it has no dimensions at all: the singularity with no space or darkness. For singularity has nothing around it. There is no space to occupy it, with no place for it to be. We cannot even imagine how long it has been there, if it has been here forever or just recently was contrived into being, at a right moment to travel its trail in the frame of the time domain that we name the thermodynamic arrow of time, cosmological arrow of time, or psychological arrow of time, and yet another interminable arrow of time.[6]

So we start with *Kun, Fa Ya Koon*. In a single flash, much too fast and expansive for words to assert, this singularity assumes a heavenly dimension with space beyond conceiving mentally. The first lively second produces all the physical forces with gravity and all the other laws commanding modern physics.

Because before *Kun, Fa Ya Koon*, time did not yet exist to our knowledge, there is no way to measure this event, but scientists have agreed to start the universal clock at Planck time.

During those early moments, matter was an ultra-hot, super-dense brew of particles called quarks and gluons, which were rushing hither and thither and crashing willy-nilly into one another. A sprinkling of electrons, photons, and other elementary light particles seasoned the soup. This mixture had a temperature in the trillions of degrees, more than 100,000 times hotter than the sun's core.

But the temperature plummeted as the cosmos expanded, just like an ordinary gas cools today when it expands rapidly. The quarks and gluons slowed down so much that some of them could begin sticking together briefly. After nearly ten microseconds had elapsed, the quarks and gluons became shackled together by strong forces between them, locked up permanently within protons, neutrons, and other strongly interacting particles that physicists collectively call "hadrons." Such an abrupt change in the properties of a material is called a phase transition (like liquid water freezing into ice). The cosmic phase transition from the original mix of quarks and gluons into mundane protons and neutrons is of intense interest to scientists, both those who seek clues about how the universe evolved toward its current highly structured state and those who wish to understand better the fundamental forces involved.

The protons and neutrons that form the nuclei of every atom today are relic droplets of that primordial sea, tiny subatomic prison cells in which quarks thrash back and forth, chained forever. Even in violent collisions, when the quarks seem on the verge of breaking out, new "walls" form to keep them confined. Although many physicists have tried, no one has ever witnessed a solitary quark drifting all alone through a particle detector.

---

6   To understand the arrow of time and wormhole theory, I would recommend the reader study *A Brief History of Time*, because that's quite a complete subject in itself.

In less than a minute, the universe is a million billion kilometers across and growing fast. Imagine, the speed of light is only around three hundred thousand kilometers per second, so the celerity of the inflation of the universe at the time of creation is really beyond human perception. There was extreme heat all around, ten billion degrees of it, enough to begin nuclear reactions and create the lighter elements like hydrogen and helium with a dash of lithium. In three minutes, 98 percent of all the matter there is or will ever be has been produced.

It took one billion years (approximately this long) for the newly formed Earth to cool, develop oceans, give birth to single-celled life, and exchange its carbon dioxide–rich early atmosphere for an oxygen-rich one. Meanwhile, the sun orbited four times around the center of the galaxy. Because the universe is twelve to fourteen billion years old, units of time beyond a billion years are not used very often.

In innumerable verses, the Lord Almighty has asserted that all the cosmological order has to face a big smash with an eventual series of big crunches. This cosmological order is still expanding with a speed of 186,000[7] miles per second and will continue for however long it takes to reach the brim of the cosmological order where the lower sky is the limit of the closed model. *This is virtually a citation from Allah Almighty; the lower sky is referred to as a glass cover.* There in the glass at the core is the alluvial gleam of *Nōōr* evinced in the "center," which belongs neither to the east nor to the west.

Time	Sequence of Events in Creation and Temperature	
0 sec	Birth of the multiverses	
10^{-43} sec	Quantum gravity era: strings or other exotic physics in play	10^{32} °C
10^{-35} sec	Probable era of inflation: universe expands exponentially	10^{28} °C
10^{-11} sec	Electro-weak phase transition: electromagnetic and weak forces become different	10 quadrillion °C
0.1 micro-sec		20 trillion °C
1 micro-sec		6 trillion °C

7   More precisely 299,796 kilometers/second outside the gravitational field of the sun (i.e., in space) or 12,000 lunar orbits/Earth day.

10 micro-sec	Quarks are bound into pro-tons and neutrons	2 trillion °C
100 sec	Nucleo-synthesis: formation of helium and other elements from hydrogen	billion °C
380,000 years	First neutral atoms form	2,700 °C

The perimeter of the glass is just to affirm; that's the limit for the cosmological arrow to take its bend. When that is to be is still far, far from our comprehension, because when this expansion or the cosmological arrow of time reaches that limit, where beyond, it will be hard for the physical laws to keep their discipline, the cosmological arrow will be reversed along the interminable arrow of time and the multiverses will face a big smash, eventuating in a series of big crunches providing a seedling for the next creation. The Lord Almighty asserts that He will create all the multiverses and the living beings anew to cherish the fruits of this trivial stay in the transit lounge wherein during the stay you have the choice to collect as many of the things as possible from the duty-free shop, but you must be sure to leave them before embarking on the next flight—that's the life in this world—and then to treasure the bloom of eternal life, like that you can determine from the initiation of the creation (i.e., the big bang to the order of the big smash, when the universe is expanding with a speed of thirty thousand kilometers per second for around fifteen billion light-years, where one light-year is six trillion miles). Can you imagine how trivial our stay is if we take into account the life in the Hereafter?

But cosmologists believe that the universe will probably keep expanding indefinitely, until long after the last star dies (one hundred trillion years from now) and the last black hole evaporates (10^{100} years from now). *Our future stretches ahead much farther than our past trails behind.*

Like quite a few verses enumerated frequently in the Holy Scripture, the following verse gives a very discrete explanation of how the Lord Almighty would create the whole order of creation once again.

The Day We'll whirl heavens *in twirl*
And a recorder list up a scribble in *swirl*
As We began the first creation *in sway*
We'll trend to it once again *in array*
It's pledged from Us *to stay* (21:104)

The Lord Is Domineering

Either the Lord has no power or He has all the power. If then He has no power, why do you pray to Him? But if He has all the power, why don't you adjure and entreat Him to give you the faculty of not fearing any of the things which you fear or of not desiring any of the things which you desire or not being pained at anything, rather than pray that any of these things should not happen or happen? For certainly, if His Almighty can alleviate the agony of men, they can cherish the fruit for these designs and consigns. But perhaps you will say the Lord has placed them in your power. Well, then, is it not better to use what is in your power like a free man than to desire in a slavish and abject way what is not in your power? And who has told you that the Lord does not aid us even in the things which are in our power? Begin, then, to pray for such things and you will see. One man prays thus: How shall I be able to lineage with that grand-dame? Do you pray thus: How shall I not reminisce to satiate with her?

O Man! Deliberate on your destiny that may be around this very moment.

Any one activity, whatever it may be, when it has ceased at its proper time, suffers no evil because it has ceased; nor he who has done this act, does he suffer any evil for this reason that the act has ceased. In like manner then, the whole, which consists of all the acts, which is our life, if it ceases at its proper time, suffers no evil for this reason that it has ceased; nor he who has terminated this series at the proper time. But the proper time and the limit nature fixes, sometimes as in old age the peculiar nature of man, but always the universal nature, by the change of whose parts the whole universe continues ever young and perfect.

And everything, which is useful to the universal nature, is always good in reason. Therefore, the termination of life for every man is no evil, because it is not shameful, since it is both independent of the will and not opposed of the will and not opposed to the general interest, but it is good, since it is reasonable and congruent with the universal nature.

21

The Nature of the Unseen

To those who ask, where have you seen the principal with providence, or how do you comprehend that He exists and so worship Him alone? I answer, in the first place, that he may be seen even with true discernment in the veer of your core; in the second place, neither have I seen even my own soul, but yet I honor it. Thus then with respect to the providence, from what I constantly experience of His power, from this I comprehend that Al-Almighty exists, and I venerate Him.

Close your eyes and start slowly reciting the venerated name "Allah" while you exhale with your full concentration toward your heart. Gradually, the sluice of your heart will start flinging open, and eventually, you will feel as if tarrying in the infinite vistas of the whole. You wouldn't know where you are in the cosmos, like a wee pinch in the illimitable ocean, but a circumstance of prudence and sagacity, animation and elation of beatitude would transcend. You feel the whim of discernment beaming in brilliance, illustrious and effulgent glowing in glimmer, lucid and luminous, as it insinuates the depth of vision; the exultance of seclusion triumphs, and then everything looks completely resplendent and gleaming. That's the moment you cherish the exhilaration and ecstasy. But as you are vanquished to your ephemeral being, even though you once again contemplate to tarriance back into the charm and bliss of elation, you cannot really get back to the state of elation with all your body senses intact, because it is not conceivable to cherish the bliss of ecstasy of the ephemeral being when you're in your earthly self.

It is the intimate and numinous approach with an experience of sense of immense cognizance melting into infinite space when the body has already melted into the soul and the soul then becomes part of the whole that once consummated and cherished the bliss and delight of numinous moments. It is not conceivable to accomplish that cadence of discernment without the munificence of His Almighty.

The second order of faith in the unseen is to trust and believe in the Hereafter. The veridical concept in the Hereafter stands at a dilemma because the new generation is quite allergic to paying attention to this word, as they trust and believe that as we are created by chance, so we need to allure the boons of this opportunity and cherish the lust and lure of this life in the midst of fury and flurry to its peak in prime, for otherwise, we'll be deprived of the opportunity that nature by way of chance happened to endow us. So the subject needs quite a bit of detail in the light of historical facts with philosophical and scientific interpretations.

Faith in the Hereafter

The discovery of one or the other scientific theory may not be able to explain or help in the quest for our survival. It may not even affect our lifestyles. But ever since the dawn of civilization, we have not been content with viewing the events as unconnected or inexplicable. Men have been striving hard to understand the underlying order in the universe. Today, we still aspire to know why we are here and where we came from. Humanity's heightening longing for understanding is acceptable justification for our ongoing pursuits. And our objective is nothing less than a concluded and unblemished description of the universe we live in. We might advance ever meticulous towards our understanding of the laws that govern the universe with true faith that also occasions for devoted watchful accomplishment for eventual exoneration.

The Lord Almighty has bestowed upon the man the mental power to understand the reason for his creation and for the cosmic order through benevolent intelligence (i.e., philosophical logic or scientific interpretations). The meticulous scientific data and controlled deductions drawn through experiments or mathematical calculations or through the logic of philosophically sound reasoning and the conclusions and inferences will determine the course of our discernment of faith through implicative assertions and avowals.

The other sane and sober perception for discerning the truth is through the cognizance of spirituality. That was just discussed in the last chapter.

The prudence or perceptiveness of spirituality is the absolute and factual understanding of a sagacious or enlightened "self" of the pedigreed providence of His Almighty through the intimate impression or intelligence of the "core." Is it the "heart" that is driving blood through our vascular tree or the insinuated veer of the sagacious self, which is the punch and prod of clairvoyant consciousness (i.e., a part of the brain that interprets the truth)? Is it the divine prudence and providence that brought us into the actuality of this vale—the efflux or the soul? This is true perceptiveness. When the efflux is withdrawn, the earthly being is once again thrown back into the dust and dirt with all its inanimate and lifeless material (i.e., the minerals, salts, water, etc.). What remains of this living being after the glow of the efflux is waved off is nothing but dust or soot. His Almighty proposes the man persistently and prompts him to perceive his origin and repeatedly intimates to him that He would once again infuse his efflux in the remains wherever they would be, whether scattered as dust or soot or rotten bones and revitalize them once again. And inducing His efflux into this earthly pot is not queer or intricate for Him. It is just to say "Be," and it would "Be," in actual confirmation of this vale. (Details are provided in "The Philosophy of Life.")

The affirmation of our existence and being in this world or the world to come is through the true perception and discernment of faith and intelligence of logic i.e. science and philosophy. The myth of creation is soon resolved when you perceive it through its original form.

How can it be that His Almighty, after having arranged all things well and benevolently for mankind, has overlooked this alone that some men and very good men, and men who, as we may say, have had the most communion with the divinity and through pious acts and religious observances have been the most intimate with the divinity, when they have once died should never exist again but should be completely extinguished?

But if this is so, be assured that if it ought to have been otherwise, His Almighty would have done it; for if it were just, it would also be possible, and if it were according to nature, nature would have had it so. But because it is not so, if in fact it is not so, be convinced that it ought not to have been so; for you see even of yourself that in this inquiry, you are disputing with the deity, the supreme truth; and we should not thus dispute with the benevolent nature, but if this is so, it would not have allowed anything in the ordering of the universe to be neglected unjustly and irrationally.

Consider in what condition, both in body and soul, a man should be when he is overtaken by death, and consider the shortness of life, the boundless abyss of time, past and future, the feebleness of all matter.

Either there is a dire necessity and invincible order for a kind providence or confusion without a purpose and without a director. If then there is an indomitable necessity, why do you resist? But there is a providence, which allows itself to be propitiated; make yourself worthy of the compliance with the divinity. And if there is confusion without a governor, be content that in such a tempest, you have in yourself a certain ruling intelligence, the true discernment. And even if the tempest carry you away, let it carry away the poor flesh and efflux and everything else, for the intelligence at least it will not carry away as it will tarry to pass your word of truth in this vale. And the efflux, when carried away to the infinite and eternal abode, will stay in exalted peace and tranquility, if you in reality ordained the discipline of faith.

Does the light of the lamp shine without losing its splendor until it is extinct and expired? And shall the truth, which is in you with equity and integrity, patience and prudence be extinguished before your death? No! For the intellectual cognition can conduct us on the right path to contrive the candor of the creation of the cosmos and the living beings. We have to understand the logic of creation and the philosophy of life after death in the light of the true discernment of faith time and again professed in the Holy Scripture.

Did you ever reach the logic of creation of this cosmos with all your bodily senses? I speak not of these alone, but of the absolute eminence and wholeness and efficacy and of the gist and pith or factual temperament of everything. Have you ever perceived the reality of the bodily organs, the small musing pets, the innumerable fascinating creatures, the most captivating and cheering fragrance of the flora, and the fascination of the fauna around you, besides the most incomprehensible cosmic order?

It is only through the intimate approach of the knowledge of their several natures made by Him who so abides His intellectual vision that they have the most exact conception of the essence of His deliberations?

All those, who cherish the enlightenment of the creation in the highest purity and who approach each of the wonders not with the reason alone and not admitting when in the accomplishment of thinking the intrusion or infraction of precise or any other estimation in the band or body of discernment, but with the very agility of the intellect in its distinctness that permeates into the very lissome and limber of truth stay in the highest order. He has gotten rid, as far as he can, of eyes and ears and of the whole body, when he visualizes them only as an agonizing component, impeding the soul from the appropriation of illumination when in association with her. Is not this the sort of man who is hopeful of acquiring the discernment of actuality?

And when he contemplates all this, must not the appropriate meditative thinker make a reflection, of which he will speak? We have sensed a scent and spoor of speculation, which seems to bring us close to the justification to interpret the inference that while we are in the flesh, our lust and longing will not be gratified, for the flesh and torso is a fountainhead of enduring and incessant tribulation to us by the simple requirement of food. It is also prone to afflictions, which intercept and obstruct us in the probing and accessing of truth. Our efflux or soul, an endowment of His Almighty, is compounded with the pack of depravity and degradation of fleshy demands, and our craving is for the truth.

Moreover, if there is time and an inclination toward the study of truth, yet the body introduces a commotion and confusion into the course of speculation and hinders us from seeing the truth. All experience shows that if we would have pure knowledge of anything, we must be liberated from the body's sensuous and other luxurious demands. The soul in herself must behold all things in themselves. I suppose that we shall attain that which we desire and of which we say that we love wisdom, not while we live, but also after the departure from this world. The contention demonstrates that while in the company of the body, the soul cannot have pure knowledge until it is subjected to the true perception of faith and that is only discernible if the person goes for it sincerely. For then and not until then, the soul will be in herself alone and without the fleshly demands of the body.

In this vale, I imagine that we make the nearest approach to knowledge when we have the least possible concern or interest in the body and are not dipping in the fleshly or sensual propositions of its nature, but abiding in innocence until the hour when the Lord Almighty Himself is pleased to emancipate us. And then the flightiness of the body will be cleared away, and we shall be pure and hold discourse with other pure souls and know of ourselves the clear light everywhere; this is surely the light of truth.

And what is purification?

Is it the separation of the soul from the body?

The inclination of the soul is to congregate and collect herself into herself, out of all the deportment of the flesh and abiding in her own suite and site alone, as in the life Hereafter, so also in this, as far as she can. Is this the release of the soul from the chains of the lusty lures of this vale?

And what is that which is termed death? Is it this very separation and release of the efflux, the soul, from the flesh? It would be a ridiculous contradiction in men dreaming to live as nearly as they can in a state of uncertainty and yet glooming and brooding when death comes. And when you see a man who is languishing at the approximation of death, is not his unwillingness a satisfactory substantiation that he is adoring of enlightenment and sagacity but doesn't endure lust and love of the fleshly demands of the body and presumably, at the same time, is not an admirer of either hunger for power or care for money throughout his life?

Will he not depart with joy?

Surely he will; if he is truly sagacious, he will have a resolute certitude that only there and nowhere else can he find prudence in the purity and probity of the soul.

How inconstant and incongruous of them to have been always lush and luxurious with the luscious body and yearning to have the efflux or soul alone in a state of eternal wisdom and veracity, and when this is granted to them, to be shuddering and shivering, sulking and sighing, instead of exhilarating at their flitting to that place where they hope to gain that which in life they loved, the enlightenment, and at the same time to be clear of the company of their fleshly temptations of vale! Many a man has been willing to go to the world yonder in the hope of seeing the earthly ardor and affection of family life if they had it here. And will he, who is a true lover of wisdom and persuaded in like manner that only in the world yonder he can proficiently luxuriate, still languish and fret at death?

Each one of us wants to allure the "bliss of the heavens," but nobody wants to die.

But here in this vale, it is the discipline of faith by which one has to abide. If the earthly living, what I invariably call the "vale," is spent in conformity with the discipline of true faith, then the fear of leaving this flesh will not cause panic or pain, because through abiding by a true discipline of worldly life as ordained in the Holy Scriptures, the soul will be in real tranquility and peace.

There is an excellence in the ethics of Islam, which is designated forbearance and fortitude, and that is a special quirk and quality of the true faith. Again, there is a reticence and humility that is unruffled subordination with no scorn, snubbing, infatuation, or indignation but temperance, a quality appertaining only to those who disdain the fleshly enchantments of the body and live with true conviction.

Whether the souls after demise are or are not in the world beyond this vale is a question, which may be argued in this manner.

The ancient Hindu doctrine affirms that they go from this earthly life into the other world and return hither and are reborn after death. Now if this is true and the living come from the dead, then our souls must be in the other world, for if not, how could they be born again? And this would be conclusive, if there were any real evidence that the living are only born from the dead, but if there is no evidence of this, then other arguments will have to be adduced.

Then let us consider this question, not in relation to man only, but in relation to animals generally and to plants and to everything of which there is generation, and the proof will be easier. Are not all things that have opposites generated out of their opposites? I mean such things as good and evil and justice and injustice, along with innumerable other oppositions which are generated out of opposites. And I want to show that this holds universally for all opposites; I mean to say, for example, that anything that becomes superior must become superior after being inferior.

And that which becomes inferior must have been once superior and then became inferior.

And the feeble is originated from the brave and the expeditious from the laggard.

And the deteriorated is from the ameliorated, and the worthy is from the unworthy.

And is this true of all opposing qualities?

And are we convinced that all of them are generated out of opposites?

The duality or universal opposition of all things also accompanies an intermediate process, which is ever going on, from one to the other and back again. Where there is a greater and a lesser, there is also an intermediary process of augmentation and alleviation. And that which sprouts is said to wax, and that which dwindles to wane.

And there are many other behavioral situations such as dispersion and combination and chilling and heating, which equally involve a passage into and out of one another. And this holds of all opposites, even though it is not always easily asserted in words—they are procreated out of one another, and there is a transition from one to the other of them.

Well! Is there not an opposite of life, as sleep is the opposite of waking?

And what is that?

Death is the answer.

And these, then, are generated, if they are opposites, the one from the other. Are these, their two intermediate processes, also?

We all bore witness to His Almighty, saying that, "You are our Lord, before we were sent to this proscenium of vale." (This is discussed later in "The Adam of Science and the Adam of the Qur'an.")

And similarly, in the life to come, when we will be called back to His Almighty Lord, we will be dumbfounded to find ourselves once again in actuality accounting for our deeds in this vale. We conclude that living in this vale is nothing but the intermediate process of the two. (See "The Philosophy of Life" for details.)

I will analyze one of the two pairs of opposites along with its intermediate processes. The state of sleep is opposed to the state of waking. And out of sleeping, waking is generated, and out of waking, sleeping. The process of generation is in the one case falling asleep and in the other, waking up.

Then are the living, whether things or persons, generated from the dead?

Is the inference that our souls were in the world somewhere beyond our perception?

And one of the two processes or generations is visible—for surely the act of dying is visible?

And may not the other be inferred as the complement of nature? It is not to be supposed to go on one leg only. And if not, must a corresponding process of generation in death also be assigned to her? And what is that process? Revival is the logical outcome of that.

And revival, if there be such a thing, is the birth of the dead into the world of the living?

Then there is a new way in which we arrive at the inference that the living come from the dead, just as the dead come from the living. If this is true, then the souls of the dead must be in some place out of which they come again. And this, as I think, has been satisfactorily proved. Misunderstanding of the convictions or faith demonstrates the need for further elucidation. The Holy Scriptures' concept is very close to the logical outcome of the position. The soul when it leaves this flesh resorts to a place where it has to abide for a certain period, until again, it will be called back to life by His Almighty to apprise the state of his living like in this vale. Whether it was a life lived in conformity to His Discipline or an outlandish life spent in chaotic and lusty aspirations in this worldly life? The generation is not in a straight line only, and there has to be a compensation or circle in nature (i.e., a return into another). If all things would at last have the same forms and pass into the same state, there would be no more generation of them.

Let us take the example of sleep. You know that if there were no compensation for sleeping in waking, the sleeping would in the end have no meaning, because all other things would be asleep, too. Or if there were composition only, and no division of substances, then the chaos would come again. And in like manner, if all things, which are associated with life were to die, and after they were dead endured in the form of death and did not come to life again, all would at last die, and nothing would be alive. How could this be otherwise, for the eventual life would begin from the dead, for ultimate contemplation of this vale?

A true allegiant is convinced in the belief that there truly is such a thing as living again, that the living spring from the dead, that the souls of the dead are in existence, and that the virtuous souls have a more preferred apportionment than the flagitious.

His Almighty has all the power to do anything whatever or whichever way He likes because He commands all the powers of the intellect and the universe. The discipline of life and death is not so simple that we can end the discussion at this moment, because the life that springs from death is not life as conventionally mentioned but eternal life where one has to cherish the fruits of the devotion or disobedience of his doings in this vale.

The Holy Scriptures are not the history books, nor are they a text teaching a certain specific subject, but instead, they are a divine message conveyed to humanity through our Holy Prophets for the education and enlightenment of the people of different communities so that they may cherish a veritable means of surviving in this fanciful and fallacious, fantastical and faltering, flighty and fickle, unpredictable world and treasure the produce and products of the everlasting life that we assume to be eternity.

Will human beings ever be able to conceive of the cosmic order in the light of revelations made in the Holy Scriptures? I presume the answer is yes! Because His Almighty has proclaimed it quite frequently in the Holy Scriptures of the Qur'an.

> I've endowed the man with all the discernment of intelligence to accomplish the assignment entrusted to him in this vale, but with certain limitations. (Al Rahman 33)

The assignment bequeathed to man on this earth evinces and distinctly insinuates that he must accomplish the contortionism of the scientific eon before the consummation of the assignment directed toward them.

The Holy Scriptures are not only a message of discipline, subjugation, and regulation but also a text of guidance in all walks of life, including the scientific and philosophical orders.

To evince the Day of Judgment, we feel perplexed to find a clear notion of discernment.

When we are dead, our genetic code is dispersed into the earth exactly as the message conveyed to the computer hard disc is dispersed into binary codes and bits. When we intend to retrieve data, we just give a command, and within no time, details are recovered on the computer screen. Similarly, imagine the human genome with definite coded letters or nucleotides. When put out of action after death, the disabled genes or the pseudogenes, the molecular relics, scattered across the human landscape, behave as DNA dinosaurs. These disabled genes may not be quite so dead, as the signs of activity among pseudogenes is another reminder. The project to sequence the human genome (the complete set of genetic information in the nuclei of our cells) has a story of its own to tell. This genetic closet holds the skeletons of memory. Imagine the instance when the genetic array dispersed in the dust and soot after death will be called back by His Almighty with one command. Then the genetic code of an individual will gather in its properly guided slot to conform once again into a perfect human being. And the Lord Almighty asserts that your creation back to life will be accomplished with just one command (79:13–14). The whole genome is less like a static library of information than an active computer operating system for a living thing. Pseudogenes may analogously be vestiges of old code associated with defunct routines, but they also constitute a functioning record contained within the overall program of how it has grown and diversified over time. As products of the processes by which they remodel and update themselves, pseudogenes are providing new insight into those dynamics, as hints about their own, possibly ongoing, role in our genome.

Some things are briskly coming into existence, and others are dashing out of it, and of that which is coming into existence, part is already dead and lifeless. Movements and reorganizations are incessantly recommencing in this world, just as the perpetual passage of time is always reiterating the unfathomable duration of the ages. In this sweeping, rippling, and gliding stream, on which there is hardly any trust to endure for long, what is there of the things which hustle by on which a man would set a high price? It would be just as if a man should fall in love with one of the pheasants, which fly by, but it has already passed out of sight. Something of this kind is the very life of every man, like the exhalation of the air. For such as it is to have once drawn in the air and to have given it back, which we do every moment, just the same is it with the whole respiratory power, which you did receive at your birth yesterday and the day before, to give it back to the element from which you had first drawn it.

Soon, very soon, we will be rotten dust, ashes, or an eroded skeleton and either a name or not even a name. But a name is sound and echo, and the things which are much valued in life are empty and rotten and trifling and like little dogs biting one another and little children quarreling, laughing, and then straightway weeping. But ardor and allegiance and integrity and impeccability will remain to endure, and that is your achievement while in the daze and dazzle of lust and lure, besides the fury of fray and in score.

What's there, which still confines us here, if the motivations of significance are freely swapped and never support or abide, the organs of perception are dull and easily receive false impressions, and the poor soul itself is an effluvium from the body. And to have virtuous appraisal in such a world as this is a hypocritical and delusive thing. Why then do we not wait in serenity for our end, which is not absolute extinction but removal to another state? And until that time comes, what is appreciable? Why, what else than to venerate His Almighty and beseech Him and to do good to men and to practice forbearance and magnanimity, integrity, and self-restraint, but as to everything which is beyond the limits of the poor flesh and breath, to remember that this is neither ours nor in our power?

We cannot disregard our lives in an even-tempered and tranquil flow of blissfulness and euphoria, if we cannot go by the right way and think and act in the right way. These two things are common both to the nature and soul or the efflux and to the soul of every rational being, not to be impeded by another and to hold the good to involve itself in nature to justice and the practice of it and in this to let our aspirations treasure its consummation.

Since it is conceivable that you may depart from life this very moment, regulate every act and thought accordingly. But to go away from among men, if there is His Almighty, is not a thing of which to be afraid. For His

Almighty will not involve you in depravity, but if indeed He does not exist or if He has no concern about human affairs, then what's it to me to live in a universe devoid of the precept of the principal with providence or devoid of discipline?

But in truth, His Almighty does exist and He does care for human things. He has put all the means of intelligence and discernment in man's power to enable him not to fall into fictional, baneful acts. And as to the rest, if there were anything unfortunate, His Almighty would have provided for this also, that it should be altogether in a man's power not to fall into it. Now, that which does not make a man worse, how can it make a man's life worse? But neither through ignorance nor through having the knowledge but not the power to guard against or correct these things is it possible that the nature of the universe has overlooked them; nor is it possible that it has made so great an oversight. It is either through want of power or want of skill that good and evil should happen indiscriminately to the good and the bad. But death, certainly, and life, honor and dishonor, pain and pleasure, all these things equally happen to good men and bad. All these happenings, which make us neither better nor worse, are therefore neither virtuous nor depraved as these are determined as a part of the whole.

Think continually that all kinds of men and all kinds of pursuits and all nations are dead, so that your thoughts come down to even. Now turn your thoughts to the other kinds of men. To that place then we must remove, where there are so many great orators and so many noble philosophers, priests, and prophets, so many heroes of former days, and so many generals after them and oppressors, besides these, and other men of astute natural talents, great minds, lovers of labor, versatile men with confidence besides those mockers of the perishable and ephemeral life of man. As to all these, consider that they have long been in the dust. What harm then is this to them and what to those whose names are altogether unknown? One thing here is worth a great deal, to pass your life in truth and justice, with a benevolent disposition even to liars and unjust men.

There is no man so fortuitous that there shall not be by him, when he is dying, some who are pleased with what is going to happen. Suppose that he was a good and a wise man, will there not be at least someone to say to himself, "Let us breathe freely being relieved from this mentor or instructor"? It is true that he was discordant to none of us, but we think that he virtually castigated us. You will think about this then when you are dying, and you will pass away more comfortably by contemplating thus: "I am going away from this world, in which even my friends on behalf of whom I have struggled, implored, cared, and concerned so much, themselves desire me to die, believing conceivably to get some brief perk and boon by it."

Why, then, should a man cohere to a further stay here?

You have set sail. You have made the voyage, and you have come to shore. Get out.

Any one activity, whatever it may be, when it has discontinued at its appropriate time sustains no depravity because it has ceased to exist. He, who has done this act, does He suffer any pain for this reason that the act has ceased to exist? In like fashion, the whole, which embodies all the acts, which is our life, if it ceases at its appropriate time sustains no pain for this reason that it has ceased to exist. He who has terminated this string at the appropriate time, has He been wrong dealing with it? But the proper time and the limit nature fixes, sometimes as in old age, that's the peculiar nature of man. But the universe always continues ever young and perfect. And everything, which is useful to the universal state, is always good in flavor. Therefore, the death or demise for every man is not unfortunate, because neither is it disgraceful, since it is both free of the choice and not antagonistic to the common appeal. But it is righteous, since it is appropriate and rewarding and conformable and unified with the universal concept. But if in a state without sensation, you will cease to be held by pains and pleasures and to be a slave to the vessel which is as much inferior as that which supports it is superior, then know that the one is earth and corruption and the other is intelligence and deity.

What's Death?

He who fears death either fears the loss of sensation or a different kind of sensation. But if you shall have no judgments or sensation, neither you will feel any harm, and if you shall acquire another kind of sensation, you will be a different kind of living being and you will not cease to live.

It is cessation of the impressions through the senses and of the pulling of the carnality, which moves the appetite, and of the rambling conduct of the ardor and desire, As the child leaves the womb and comes into life by leaving the shelter, so the soul at death leaves its envelope. Death is a mystery of nature where, when the divine bestowal of the efflux is removed from the earthly pot, which is then left to the earth to consume it once again to its congruity and consonance, the soul may on leaving the body pass into another existence, which is perfect.

Consistently yield to your remembrance of those who have bewailed awfully about anything. Those who have been practically distinguished by the excellent distinction and afflictions, tragedies and animosities, possessions and loathing of any kind, and then think where they all are now? The waste of sequential order, not even to identify, they are gone, mixed with the dust and soot. And let there be manifest to your mind also everything of this sort, how the men of fame lived in the country and in their fascinating gardens and men of valor and worth with fame and name loved in elegant design of the fervent pursuance. Something is after to which men aggressively stretch, strain, or strive. And how much more is it known for a man of sapience to show him evenhanded and dispassionate, amenable to the Almighty and to do this with all humility with submissiveness and subservience?

The Fruit of Fortune in the Hereafter

In the first place, the things which you do either benevolently or thoughtlessly rather than as decency or honesty herself would act, but with respect to what may happen to you from without, consider that it happens either by chance or according to providence and you should neither blame chance nor accuse providence.

Secondly, consider that every being is from the seed to the time of its receiving a soul, and consider from the reception of a soul to the giving back of the same of what things every being is compounded and into what things it is resolved.

Thirdly, if you should suddenly be raised up above the earth and should look down on human beings and observe the variety of them, see how great it is and at the same time also see at a glance how great is the number of beings who dwell all around you, and consider that as often as you should be raised up, you would see the same things, the sameness of form and shortness of duration.

Are these things to be proud of?

Consider that opinion is everything, and opinion is in your power. Take away then, when you chose, your opinion, and like a navigator who has doubled the projection, you will find calm, everything stable, and a listless body.

Consider that before long, you will just be nobody and nowhere. Neither will any of the things exist, which you now see, nor any of those who are now living. For all things are formed by nature to change and be turned and to perish in order that other things in continuous succession may exist.

But if this is so, be enlightened that if it ought to have been otherwise, the Almighty would have done it. For if it were just, it would also be possible, and if it were according to nature, nature would have had it so. But because it is not so, if in fact it is not so, be convinced, that it ought not to have been so. For you see even of yourself that in this inquisition, you are countering with the deity, and we should not thus dispute with His Almighty, because

He is most superb, most accurate, and most equitable. And He has allowed everything in the ordering of the universe to be excellently executed from one-millionth of a fraction of an atom to the most incomprehensible cosmic order that we perceive about fifteen billion light-years away from now.

Constantly consider how all things such as they now are, in time past, also were, and consider that they will be the same again. And place before your eyes entire dramas and stages of the same form, whatever you have learned from your experience or from older history (e.g., the whole fortune of Alexander, the sovereign state of Moughal Emperor Akbar); for all those were such dramas as we see now, only with different actors.

Hasan of Basra was a jewel merchant and was called "Hasan of the Pearls." He traded with Byzantium and had to do with the generals and ministers of Caesar. On one occasion, as he was going to Byzantium, he called on the prime minister and conversed with him a while.

"We will go to a certain place," the minister told him, "if you are agreeable."

"It is for you to say," Hasan replied. "I agree."

So the minister commanded a horse to be brought for Hasan. He mounted with the minster, and they set out. When they reached the desert, Hasan perceived a tent of Byzantine brocade, fastened with ropes of silk and golden pegs, set firmly in the ground. He stood to one side. Then a mighty army, all exposed in the impressive array of war, came out; they circled the tent, said a few words, and withdrew. Philosophers and scholars to the number of well nigh four hundred arrived on the scene; they circled the tent, said a few words, and departed. After that, three hundred illumined elders with white beards approached the tent, circled it, said a few words, and departed. Thereafter, more than two hundred moon-fair maidens, each bearing a plate of gold and silver and precious stones, circled the tent, said a few words, and departed.

Hasan relates that, astonished and filled with wonder, he asked himself what this might be.

"When we alighted," he went on, "I asked the minister. He said that the Caesar had a son of unsurpassable beauty, perfect in all the branches of learning and unrivalled in the arena of manly prowess. His father loved him with all his heart."

Suddenly he fell ill—so Hasan related on the authority of the minister. All the skilled physicians proved incapable of curing him. Finally, he died and was buried in that tent. Once every year, people came out to visit him. First, an immense army circled the tent, and they said, "O prince, if this circumstance that has befallen thee had come about in war, we would have all sacrificed our lives for thee, to ransom thee back. But the circumstance that has befallen thee is at the hand of 'One' against whom we cannot fight, whom we cannot challenge." That's what they said and then returned.

The philosophers and the scholars came forward and said, "This circumstance has been brought about by 'One' against whom we cannot do anything by means of learning and philosophy, science and creativity. For all the philosophers of the world are powerless before Him, and all learned are ignorant beside His knowledge. Otherwise, we would have contrived devices and spoken words which all in creation could not have withstood." This they said and then returned.

Next, the venerable elders advanced and said, "O prince, if this circumstance that has befallen you could have been set right by the intercession of elders, we would all have interceded with humble petitions and would not have abandoned you there. But this circumstance has been brought upon you by 'One' against whom no mortal man's intercession profits anything." This they said and departed.

Next, the moon-fair maidens with their plates of gold and precious stones advanced, circled the tent, and said, "Son of Caesar, if this circumstance that has befallen you could have been set right by wealth and beauty, we would have sacrificed ourselves and given great moneys and would not have abandoned you. But this circumstance has been brought upon you by 'One' on whom wealth and beauty have no effect." This they said and returned.

Then Caesar himself with his chief minister entered the tent and said, "O Core and crux of the father. O! The pleasing and enchanting consequence of the soul of the father, O highly valued cherished and adored of the father, what is in the father's grasp to accomplish? Your father executed a stupendous army. He accomplished philosophers and scholars, intercessors and advisers, beautiful maidens, wealth, and all conventionality of luxuries, and he came himself. If all this could have been of avail, your father would have done all that lay in his power. But the One before Whom your father, with this entire ingenious plan, stratagem, contrivance (i.e., the setup and device), this army and assemblage, this extravagance and affluence and fortune, is helpless and infirm and has brought about this circumstance. Contentment and concord be upon you, till next year!" This he said and returned.

These words of the minister influenced Hasan to an extent that he could not reconcile with his present condition. At once, he made arrangements to return. Coming to Basra, he took an oath never to laugh again in this world, till his ultimate destiny became clear to him. He flung himself into all appearance of devotions and austerities, such that no man in his time could exceed that discipline.

Just deliberate!

A man deposits seed in a womb and goes away and then another cause takes it and labors on it and delivers a child. What a thing from such a material! The Holy Scriptures refer to the creation of the man from such a humble drop of liquid. Again, the child passes food down through the throat, and then another cause takes it and makes perception, motion, appealing and exuberant life, and capabilities and other things, how many and how extraordinary and inexplicable! Perceive then the things, which are fabricated in such a mysterious and symbolic way and see the endowment just as we see the competence, which transfers things downwardly to earth and upwardly to the heavens, not with the eyes, but still no less manifestly. Then, turn your deliberations to your life under your grandfather and then to your life under your mother and then to your life under your father, and as you find many other discriminations and distinctions, reviews and revisions, consummations and conclusions, ask yourself, "Is this anything to be dismayed by?"

In like manner then, neither the termination nor cessation nor even the change of your whole life are things of which to be afraid.

Indeed if you spent it in the light of the heavenly code of ethics well ordained for you to accomplish in this life. The following poetry will give some idea as to how uncertain is our life.

Agony in Alarm

This is the story of the earthquake of October 8, 2005, which occurred around 8:00 AM in the northern areas of Pakistan.

Agony in Alarm

That's October of 8th in the morn

That's a fable of an agony in alarm
Trended in throng in languishing morn
What a queer and quaint tranquil in calm

Whispering sounds of the rustling leaves
Flowers swinging in hustling breeze
Glittering rainbow on the floral wreath

Sobbing adjuring in imploring resume
With tang in trail of tarrying gloom
Praying pleading in dread of doom

Beseech to brace "Thy" mercy in boon
For they'd whiff, the imminent boom

Dusky sky in swarthy dawn
With curious quibble of awe in alarm

Bracing anguished sprinkle in splash
When birds hazed warbling in dash

Then in expanse they darted in swarm
None could discern their whim in norm

Barking dogs with a whimper in drill
Course in conduct so strange and shrill

All seemed frenzied, fierce in swarm
That's October of 8th, in the morn
And,
Students in class so warily calm
Teachers of class, dumb in alarm

As if a scourge is hung in surround
Then bluster in bustle boom in around
All in about then trend to slide
A mountain in close gets to glide

Yonder in rubble all in stray
Sinking men and dame in allay
And the kids and kin absorbed in play

Students in class cannot raise pen to a toss
They sink in rubble of concrete in gross

How'd they lift their heads in blur
Anguish in alarm, swing in stir

Then woe and ado mounts in surround
Men in around cannot discern in abound

All are buried in the rubble in slide
Just a man is left thither in glide

What a calamity has stricken in stride
Man cannot discern a bit in abide

Where I'm hither, thither in fore
Cannot discern to concern a word in lore

Where's the house I was close and aside
Where's the shop I trended in stride

Where're the men all in surround
A scream in squeak and lull in abound

Man trends once more to review in trance
How'd they be gone in a moment of glance

He shook his head once more in sway
And trended his looks thither in array

How'd I be hither in stay
Dazed and amazed baffled in fray

Then from the rubble a tend in impeach
Why, O man!
Dazed in alarm and tend to screech

Why to surprise and stun in score
Care to concern your veer of core
All your deeds and proceeds in fore
Curse and scold term least be sure
For if you've a bit of reason in lore

Persuasion of Lord was you to aside
But you never cared a bit in stride

Lord asserts for all conduct in appeal
For if you've a bit of intellect in deal

Just care and concern your term in stay
For what you resolved and affirmed to obey

O Lord!
You're "Assertive" all in Acclaim
But we nether, not deft to sustain
A term in torment hither to remain

Why all this term in trial for us to aside
When we're determined in faith to abide

O Man!
Don't you concern hither in stance
Defecting Dictum of 'Mine' in trance
Trending ambiguous ways in glance

41

O Lord!
But we assert and affirm in pray
Your dictum in dictate firm to obey

O Man!
But, in all deeds and proceeds in sway
You assert to affirm one else to obey

But, Lord they're all innocent in prime
Who're doomed in ordeal of anguish in sign

My lays and ways you cannot discern to aside
For what I care to concern in stride

Did you ever concern in stance
When you eased[8] some in trance

Then,
Tribulation and torture held in stray
That's *Tora Bora* conduct in fray

Course in anguish held in alarm
That too was October of 8th in the morn
When,
Men were ravished ruthless in stance

O man!
Concern your done and doings in sort
How'd you evade My Term in plot

Man once more,
Begged and beseeched in sublime
O Lord! They're all forthright in prime
Who're accursed of calamity in time

But,
They're also "My" innocent men and clan
Who're contemptuously plighted in plan

---

8   When Pakistan allowed Allied Forces to attack Afghanistan from Pakistan

Do you recall their treachery in stray
Amputated legs and arms in fray

You face the agony here in conduct
For what you held a bid in instruct

O man!
They're also "My" virtuous men in abide
Who in adversity tormented in stride

And I hold an account of all in trail
For what you concern hither in vale
And care for the deeds and proceeds in dale
For what would trend once more to avail

Perhaps,
You may be fated hither in plight
Like pain, they endured once in slight

Far more firm and affirmed in blight
If you don't trend to Word so bright

O man,
Just concern a notion in norm
All who died hither and thither in alarm

Destined to cherish boons in swarm
That's October of 8th in the morn

And those mangled and warped in sight
That's a term so trifle in blight
Them to treasure alluring gardens in delight

My Dictum in dictate is for you to brace
And not for the cynic thither to trace

Who stay in slight and trend in stray
For if you trend discipline to obey
My ease and appease is for you in fray

O Lord!
How'd we ever endure to concern
After *"Tsunami"* more ordeal in term

O Man!
Don't you concern, hurricanes in throng
But they abide certain discipline in norm

Trend to their deeds and proceeds in term
And to your done and doings in concern

Now,
Some did assert to affirm in stance
Whereas they abide decency in glance

And you care to concern "self" in daze
Even few affirmed subjugation in haze

O My men hither in abide
Be the men of Dictum to aside
Not to cherish lust of lure in deride

For what,
You trend dubious ways in sway
But! Be a man of discipline to obey

It's to admonish once more in stride
To assert and affirm "My" word to aside

I exhorted and apprised all in pace
But you never tended to Word in grace

Now!
Stare in stance your trends in plight
Tending to each, hither in blight

Some grabbing and gloating all in surround
Whereas they'd affirm discipline in abound

How'd I ever trend to assuage in stance
When you deny and defy *'My Word'* to glance

We entreat and beseech *Thee O Lord* in pray
Extenuate for sure our trends in decay
We assert to affirm "Your" word to obey
O Man!
Just a trifle in stance, a tend in spree
You cherish in trance hither in glee

O My men and clan hither in abide
How'd you ever esteem boons to aside
When you've deserted all drill in stride

Trend to your core once more to discern
What's your term of discipline in concern

Each tine in trend to amass in stance
Riches of sort teeming in glance

Did you ever care a bit in trace
Your next of neighbor in misery of pace

Each term in treat, you swing in deceit
Your trends in entreat dangle in conceit

There's no sincerity of a bit in trace
How'd you ever trend to brace
My term in appease hither in grace

Trend to your veer of core once more
Think of all the notions in lore

Do you've a bit of virtuosity in core
Nay!
You've always defied My Word to allure
With,
A lure in lust and sensuality in scale
When such are trends of clan in vale
I assign the leaders of similar trail
Also,
Trend to your peers of Faith in term
With "pot in belly" and money in concern

Trending to each of other sect in assault
With words so enticing and charming in blot

For what they trend to affirm others to aside
They don't have a bit of care in abide
Instead they grab and gloat around in pride

For if they'd a discipline in trace
They'd have adored bliss in grace
And
Men to pursue their word to brace
But alas!
Their done and doings hither in fore
Determine to selfish pursuance in core

That's the reason hither in trail
The best of Faith defied in scale

What's the way of order in strike
Suicidal trends, attempts in strife

O man!
Have sort and style of restraint in stride
Trend to prophet's PBUH discipline in abide
For what he concerns "My Word" to aside

Then you'll affirm all in surround
A word of acclaim glowing in abound
From all caste, color, and creed in around

Trending to verity of Faith in grace
With,
Boon, bounties, and benedictions to brace
O man!
Your ultimate return is to "Me" in stride
To "Me" you're concerned to pray in abide

So cherish each jiffy of verve in beseech
Your eventual restore is to "Me" in treat

Trend to "My" word affirmed in Qur'an
For that's real of "My" concern in stance

I aver and assert to resolve in trance
Your term in blight hither in glance

Man trends once more around and along
The scatter of shake, contortion in swarm

Amputated limbs of kids and kin in alarm
Distorted and deformed spreads in throng

Scourge in alarm anguish in swarm
That's October of 8th in the morn
Man asserts to affirm his notion in norm
O Lord!
We aver and avow so subservient in calm
For,
We cannot discern to concern a bit in trace
Your term of tribulation affirmed in grace

So don't despise or scorn death, but be well prepared and satisfied with it since this too is one of those things which nature commands because the efflux that you endure is neither yours nor do you have command over it, as it may leave the earthly pot this very moment. Can you hold it back? How many men of the olden days are living today? Just name one!

For such as it is to be young and to grow old and to increase and to reach maturity and to have teeth and beard and gray hair and to propagate and to be pregnant and to bring forth, and all the other natural courses and conduct, which the flavors of your life convey, such is the decomposition and desolation. This, then, is conforming to the disposition of a meditative man, to be neither heedless nor hotheaded and hasty, nor contemptuous and disrespectful with regard to death, but to anticipate it as one part of the conduct of nature.

As you now wait for the time when the child shall fall out of your wife's womb, so be ready for the time when your soul shall fall out of this earthly pot. But if you require also a lascivious kind of compassion which shall reach your heart, you will not be made best reconciled to death by observing the objects from which you are going to be eliminated, and the morals and ideals of those with whom your body will no longer be assimilated and associated. For it is in no way right to be affronted or aggrieved with men, but it is your duty to care for them and to abide with them smoothly and yet to bear in mind that your separation will be not from men who have the same principles as yourself. For this is the only thing, if there be any, which could draw us the contrary way and attach us to life, to be permitted to live with those who have the same principles as ourselves. But now you see how great was the annoyance that was emerging from the divergence of those who lived together. So that you may say, "O death! Show up clearly, lest I, too, should neglect and ignore myself in the worldly allures, because:

Where,
All is the same
That dignity to brace so fleeting in frame

What to a life
That's just to betray
A lust in lures, a drift in stray
That's delusive, deception in fray
A sway in swirl, a squeal in array
For,
All is alike as tethered in trace
That's hither in vale or buried in grave

What to a being, that's just to defy
Covets in course, distract to comply
Instead,
Love Thy Lord and conform in pray
And dictum of faith assert to obey

For He's the One forever to glow
None can dare to defy *(hither)* in flow

Let your core in crux affirm in adore
Munificence of Lord, firm in lore
O man! Love Thy Lord,
For, He's "All" to beg and bestow.

It would be a man's happiest lot to depart from mankind without having had any taste of deceit and hypocrisy and extravagance and arrogance. However, to breathe out one's life, when a man has had enough of these things, is the next best voyage, as the saying: "Have you settled to endure with depravity and have not been encountering deceit yet convinced to flee from this pestilence? The devastation of understanding is pestilence much more indeed than the corruption, besides the changes of the atmosphere. For this corruption is a pestilence of animals so far as they are animals, but the other is a pestilence of men so far as they are not the men of intelligence."

Death: A Natural Phenomenon

The termination of activity, the cessation of movement and opinion, and in a sense their deaths are no evil. Turn your thoughts now to the consideration of your life, your life as a child, as a youth, your manhood, and your old age, for in these also every change was demise from one to the other. Is this anything to fear if you abide by the Lord? Turn your thoughts now to your life in different stages of your development under your grandpa, your mother, and then under your father. As you discover many other divergences, variations, and dissimilarities, ask yourself, "Is this anything to panic about?" In course, neither is the cessation or dissociation from one to the other stages of your whole life a thing of which to be afraid.

Soon, the earth will cover us all. Then the earth too will change, and the things also which result from change will continue to change forever, and these again forever. For if a man reflects on the changes and transformations which follow one another like wave after wave and their rapidity, he will despise everything which is perishable and will endure immortality.

All that you see will quickly perish, and those who have been spectators of its dissolution will very soon perish too. And he who dies in extreme old age will be brought into the same condition with him who died prematurely. What are these men's leading principles? About what kinds of things they are busy? And for what kinds of reasons do they love and honor? Imagine that you see their poor souls laid bare. When they think that they do harm by their blame or good by their praise, what an ideal!

All the created beings, whether the sun, moon, stars, or other galactic or cosmic objects, besides human beings, are destined to be exterminated. Even the scientific theories of today converge in that the entire universe will meet its doom in the "big smash," eventuating in series of big crunches at a certain time. Similarly, all human beings are destined to die as it is very clearly stated in the Holy Scriptures. (Details provided in "The Fate of the Universe.")

Do you assume O clan?
That I created you without any design in plan
That you're not destined to "Me" in span (24:115)

50

This verse clearly elucidates that we are here for some well-defined expectation and design. The objective, assignment, expectation, and intent of the creation of an individual is really beyond our perception, because when angels cautioned His Almighty that this human race would create all the destruction and damage, torments and tribulations, tortures and tragedies, and turn His world of benedictions into hell of sufferings, His Almighty's response was, "I comprehend what you don't."

His Almighty indeed established by proclamation and edict that each and every particular "sentient being" should be what its attributes obligated it to be. The preference is doctrine of inference.

Death and the Good Life

This brings us to a new concept of death, a view that was felicitously put by Leonardo de Vinci: "Just as a day well spent brings happy sleep, so a life well spent brings happy death." Painful preoccupation with death has its source in human misery; the cure is to foster human well-being. A happy man is not seriously pained by the thought of death, nor does he dwell on the subject. Many illuminated thinkers held this view, and it also appears to be the view of the most pragmatic Bertrand Russell.

There are two counterarguments. The first is the theme prevalent in several branches of Christianity concerning the total impossibility of attaining happiness on earth.

The second is the even more familiar and prevalent Christian theme that in order to achieve happiness in this life, one must first conquer the fear of death.

But happiness, therefore, is not a cure; it is a consequence of the cure.

The veracity in the discernment of true faith gives unfeigned happiness, tranquility, and appeasement of the mind.

The Holy Scriptures repeatedly reiterate that spending a well-disciplined life in the light of the divine code of ethics affirms true satisfaction, beatitude, blissfulness, exuberance, and happiness.

Death without Consolation

In distinct divergence to this last position is that of a long line of nineteenth-century and twentieth-century philosophers from Schopenhauer to simultaneous existentialists. For them, human well-being or happiness, at least as traditionally conceived, is totally impossible to achieve, and if the individual is to experience such rewarding values as life does permit, he must uncompromisingly embrace the tragedy of the human condition, clearheadedly acknowledging such evils as death. Like the Stoics, these authors would have us think constantly of death. Unlike the Stoics, however, they do not offer us the consolation of belief in a providential order of nature. From the standpoint of being or nature, the death of the individual is totally meaningless or absurd.

According to Nietzsche, the preferred man will not endure death pursuing him out to waylay him, devious in deception, striking him down unaware. The preferred man will live steadfastly and constantly in the cognizance and true discernment of death, joyfully and proudly assuming death as the natural and proper terminus of life. This notion of death confirms the true discernment of the Holy Scriptures' vision of all monotheistic religions.

Heidegger and Sartre, like most existentialists, urged us to cultivate the awareness of death chiefly as a means of heightening our sense of life.

The knowledge of death gives to life a sense of determination and devotion, commitment and creditability, earnestness and enthusiasm, persistence and perseverance that it would otherwise lack. Freud, who compared life without the consciousness of death to a Platonic romance or to a game played without stakes, has made the same point.

Heidegger makes the additional claim, although here Sartre parts company with him, that the awareness of death confers upon man a sense of his own individuality. Dying, he says, is the one thing no one can do for you; each of us must die alone. To shut out the consciousness of death is, therefore, to refuse one's distinctiveness and to live an outlandish life without moral and social ethics.

This divine scripture revealed to the Holy Prophet Muhammad PBUH enunciates a complete discipline and code of ethics in each conduct to conform the human nature. His Almighty concludes an embellished punctilious vision of discernment for the human being, His most elegant creation, to live with and cherish the most benevolent of His endowments in this vale. His real and sincere desire for us is to live a life of true discipline because when His Almighty ordained His discipline, the Holy Scripture, His Almighty had a far-out ensample of His most adorable Prophet Muhammad PBUH so that each living being should spend his life with a cherished and concerned example before them. And when you get to the discipline of the life of the Holy Prophet, you find each moment of his life spent in tribulation and torture for the sake of His Almighty's acquiescence of true discipline.

There is a host of literature written in this context. I have no idea about nor any competence to elaborate on the divine discernment, but I have as quietly as possible attempted to make sense of the most conformant text of the Holy Scriptures in the light of modern-day science and philosophy. I have tried to discuss the subject of the "soul" and death because the discipline of life becomes quite insignificant and absurd if we do not give credence to life after death or the eternal life of our soul or the philosophy of recreation.

Do we seek and strive to endure the subjection of life as ordained by His Almighty in the Holy Scriptures and the discipline of life as ordained by His Holy prophets?

We are all baffled as to whether or not we have ever been able to abide by that discipline of life as preferred by true faith.

The life is to ordain a definite discipline with a defined objective behind the concept, and when you have something definite to accomplish, you don't have the time to look around for things, as Socrates once excused himself to someone for not seeing him, saying, "It is because I would not be perished by the worst of all ends, that is, I could not receive favor and then be unable to return it." I constantly think of someone of the former times who practiced virtue. Neither in writing nor in reading will you be able to lay down the rules in sight of others, erstwhile you shall have first learned to obey the rules yourself.

When His Almighty laid down the discipline of virtue, He had an example before us of our Holy Prophet Muhammad PBUH and others like Moses, Jesus Christ, Abraham, and many others. Have we ever contemplated the favors and bestowal of His Almighty in our everyday lives? His Almighty sincerely wished every one of us to follow the footprints of His prophets PBUH.

The virtuous must distinguish between scrupulous and sinister and must yearn to stay on the right tang and trail in the light of the Holy Scriptures. They must have a firm belief in the certain conviction that they otherwise cannot perceive visually or prove scientifically (i.e., the discernment of His Almighty Lord, the angels, life after death, the concept of Heaven and Hell). These notions have to be incisively insinuated in the mind before one seeks guidance from the Holy Qur'an.

What are you here for, O Man?

Look at this standing by yourself and separate it as a natural instinct for you, in health and wealth.

Is there anything to live long?

But look at the man not only as part of the whole but for the sake of the whole.

And if you should at one time get sick or at other moment be trapped in the perils of the sea, again, know the meaning of your wants and perhaps only death is going to extinguish the fire of your desires.

Isn't it correct?

Then why to repine?

For What Is a Man?

That was a good reply made to a man, who asked someone for a letter of recommendation. That you are a man, he will know, when he sees you, whether a good or bad one. He will know if you have any skill in discerning and discriminating the good from the bad. But if you have nothing to assert and stay in dilemma to answer, will he never know? It is as if a coin was desired to be recommended to someone to be tested; either the man has no knowledge of silver as though he has never seen it before, or the man will be a good judge of silver, and he will know. The coin will tell its own tale.

The Lord is beneficent. But the good is also beneficent. It should seem then that where the real nature of the Lord is, there too is to be found the real nature of the good.

What then is the real nature of the Lord?

Isn't this the intelligence, the knowledge, and the right reason? Here then without much ado, seek the real nature of the good.

For surely, you do not seek it in a plant or in an animal that reasons not. It is through the veer of your core, the seat of your intelligence, a discerning power, a bestowal of His Almighty to the perception and precept of truth in faith.

The seat of intelligence, the veer of the core, is not the heart but the brain. But it's the heart that responds to the immediate notion of sentiment that invariably tells the story of the mind, as we say, "He remembered by heart," or "He loved her from the core of his heart." However, it's not the heart that is the seat of passion and memory; it is the brain.

What then?

Are not these other things also works of the Lord?

They are, but some are not preferred to the honor of one in dismay, as these are portions of the whole. But are you a man preferred to the honor of the day alone and not of the whole or the Hereafter?

You are yourself a fragment torn from the whole; you have a portion of all within yourself. How is it then that you do not know your descent in doom is nearing you soon?

Don't you know from whence you came and for what purpose you are determined to abide hither in this vale?

When you eat, will you not remember who you are that eats and who feeds you?

In intercourse, in exercise, in discussion, you know not that there's a Lord whom you bear about with you.

O miserable, dismal in dejection!
You don't have the vision of perception.

Do you think that I speak of a deity of unwavering symbols? Are you without that?
Nay! You bear Him within yourself.
All are oblivious of eluding Him with your impure thoughts and unclean deeds.
Were an image of the Lord present, you would not dare to act as you do; yet, when the Lord Himself is present within you, beholding and hearing all, you do not blush to have such thoughts and do such deeds.
O you who are insensible of your own nature, you lie under the wrath of the Lord!
Consider, for example, the times of early cultures. You will see all these things: people espousing and bringing up children, ailing in affliction, putrid and perishing in dejection, plighted and pursuing in defection, conflicting and contesting in exultation, supping and savoring all festivities of fortune in recreation, and procuring and purchasing with the squeeze and squash of humiliation. They stay cushioning and cultivating the meads and fields, flavoring and flattering the callously conceit, wary and skeptical in planning and plotting in proceeds, yearning for some to dissolve and decay, bewailing about the present, whining and grinning at the lapse of love, cocking and stocking fortune and funds, adoring for conversing with turn and concern, and aspiring for grandiosity in demand.
Well, then, the life of these people is no longer to exist forever to cherish the boons in bloom.
Their life, too, is gone.
In like manner, view also the other epochs of time and of whole nations and see how many after great efforts soon fell and were resolved into the elements. But chiefly you should think of those whom you have yourself known to be distracting themselves about idle things, neglecting to do what was in accordance with their proper constitution, hold firmly to this, and be content with it. And herein, it is necessary to remember that the attention given to everything has its proper value and proportion. For thus you will not be dissatisfied, if you apply yourself to smaller matters no further than is fit.
You will soon die, and you are not yet simple, nor free from perturbations, nor without suspicion of being hurt by external things, nor kindly disposed toward all; nor do you place wisdom only in acting justly.

What is evil to you does not subsist in the ruling principle of another, nor yet in any turning and mutation of your corporeal covering.

Where is it then? It is in that peel and part of yourself in which is insinuated the power of forming opinions about evils. Let this power then not form such opinions, and all is well. And if that which is nearest to it, the poor body, is cut, burnt, or filled with matter and rottenness, nevertheless let the peel and part which forms opinions about these things be quiet, that is, let it judge that nothing is either bad or good which can happen equally to the bad man and the good. For which happens equally to him who lives contrary to faith ordained by the Almighty and to him who lives according to the true faith is neither according to nature nor contrary to nature until through the turn of the true discernment of faith.

Constantly regard the universe as one living being having one substance and one soul, and observe how all things have reference to one perception, the perception of this one living being, how all things act with one movement, and how all things are the cooperating causes of all things which exist. Observe too the continuous spinning of the thread and the texture of the web. So is the life of a man from the core of the womb to the crust of the grave and in between. Time is like a river made up of the events which happen, a turbulent stream; for as soon as a thing has been seen, it is carried away and another comes in its place. This will be carried away too, as will be the life. Everything that happens is as familiar and well known as the rose in spring and the mangoes in summer; for such is doom and death.

Be like the promontory against which the waves continually break. It stands firm and tames the fury of the water around it. You can resist the torment and torture, agony and alarm, depravity and desperation, castigation and retribution, sleet and nipping of aside and akin, the societal bog of the environment, and the lusty enticements in this vale.

Unhappy I am, because this has happened to me. Not so, but happy I am, though this has happened to me, because I continue free from pain, neither crushed by the present nor fearing the future. For such a thing as this might have happened to every man, but every man would not have continued free from pain on such an occasion. Why, then, is that rather a misfortune and this a good fortune? And do you in all cases call that a man's misfortune, which is not a deviation from man's nature? And does a thing seem to be a deviation from man's intelligence, when it is not contrary to the will of man's nature? Well, you know the will of nature. Will then this, which has happened, prevent you from being just, generous, temperate, prudent, and secure against inconsiderate opinions and falsehoods? Will it prevent you from having modesty, freedom, and everything else, by the presence of which man's nature obtains all that is its own? Remember, too, on every occasion that leads you to displeasure to apply this principle: not that this is a disaster, but that to bear it nobly is good fortune.

It is rude and crude but still a useful help toward slight and scorn of death, to pass in inquisition those who have resolutely been stranded in life. What more then have they gained than those who have died early? Certainly they lie in their pit and crypt somewhere, at least kings, philosophers, and scientists, or anyone else like them, who has carried many to be buried, and then were carried themselves. Altogether, the interval is small between birth and death; it is a very trivial one. Ask a man of one hundred as to how much time has he lived to his choice, and the answer you get is hardly any. And consider with how much trouble and in company with what sort of people and in what a feeble body this interval is laboriously passed. Do not then consider life a thing of any value. For look to the immensity of time behind you and to the time, which is before you, another boundless space if you really conform to the abidance of faith as ordained in the Qur'an. In this infinitude and eternity then, what is the difference between him who lives three days and him who lives three generations?

In the morning when you rise reluctantly, let this notion be deeply seated in your mind that I am advancing to the work of a human being. Why then am I discontented, if I am going to do the things for which I exist and for which I was brought into the world? Or have I been made for this, to sleep in the bedclothes, pajamas, and keep myself warm? But this is more pleasant, if you determine a goal for the benefit of another. Do you exist then to take your pleasure and not for action or exertion? Don't you see the little plants, the little birds, the ants, the spiders, the bees working together to put in order their several clips and crops of the universe? And are you unwilling to do the work of a human being, and do you not make haste to do that, which is according to your nature? But it is necessary to take rest also. However, nature has fixed bounds to this too. The Lord has fixed bounds both to eating and drinking, and yet you go beyond these bounds, beyond what is sufficient; yet in your acts, it is not so, but you stop short of what you can do. So you love not yourself, for if you did, you would love your nature and would have the bliss of the Lord. But those who love their several areas exhaust themselves in working at them unwashed as if you value your own nature less than the trends that persuade you to values other than the true nature of discipline, such as the love of money or the lust of a little glory. And such men, when they have a violent affection for these things, choose the most undesirable means to acquire all that, which is beyond their means.

Judge every word and deed which are according to nature to be fit for you, and be not diverted by the blame which follows from any people, nor by their words, but if a thing is good to be done or said, do not consider it unworthy of yourself. For those persons have their peculiar leading principle and follow their peculiar movement, which things you turn to regard, but go straight on, following your own nature and the common nature, and the way of both is one.

Consciousness in the Afterlife

If there is no God, there should be no reparations for living a villainous life and no assertion of contentment in living a virtuous and disciplined life, because Mother Teresa and Hitler shall be conferred alike. And if there is a God, the well-deserved life spent by Mother Teresa will assuredly be prized. For otherwise, Mother Teresa and Hitler will be equal, and if there is a God, presumably, the justice for good and bad has to be there. Those who have faith and belief and have earned their glorified living dedicatedly, at least, have preference over those who did not believe in the Lord and the afterlife and lived an outlandish, eccentric, erratic, droll, and queer life. This life of ours is just like spending a few moments in a transit lounge, where our conduct and course of action have to be ascertained in each discipline of life.

The Philosophy of Life

Qur'anic assertions guide us in a proper course of conduct in life and in the ways and means of practicing and pursuing prudence and probity, which are not philosophical or theoretical but are purely practical in bent and intent. These are the notions that distinguish and discriminate the results of elegance and invocation from natural accomplishments and other inclinations. There is no bent and bias in the Scripture. It is all innovating with natural boons, bounty, and benedictions. The most notable feature of the Scripture, however, is its unyielding and unwavering bearing of the true lover of the reverence, Muhammad PBUH. The simulation of the Prophet recommends not a simple copying of him but acting by analogy with deeds and doings in all walks of life. His life was mainly characterized, according to history, by anguish and affliction and the torment and torture of near and dear ones and then daring to defy old willfully perverse, erring and evil, dissolute and depraved dogmas and doctrines ardently insinuated with whims of convictions.

The Qur'an essentially deals with:

Firstly, the spiritual and social amelioration of the individual as indicated earlier.

The second concern is the preparation of the core with the illumination and enlightenment in the discipline of life.

The third consists of a spiritual approach between Muhammad PBHU and the soul, which gives a further exposition of the ascetic and austere wont and way. The passages of the Holy Scripture give a spiritual inclination of the kind of mystical experience awaiting those who truly love the Lord and His prophets.

In the case of faith, a person is not sufficiently moved by the object to accept it as true, so, by an act of will, he inclines himself to believe. Knowledge implies assent motivated by a personal seeing of the object without any direct influence from will. Where objects of belief have to do with divine matters, which exceed man's natural cognitive capacity, the disposition to believe such articles of religious faith is regarded as faith in the unseen, a special gift from Allah. Reason is another type of intellectual activity; simple cognition to grasp rationalizing differs only in the manner in which the intellect works. Through conceptual discernment, one knows simply by seeing what something means, while through reason, one moves deviously and discursively from one item of knowledge to another.

Men obtain their knowledge of reality from the initial details of true discernment as envisaged through the Qur'an and abidance in the demand and decree of the Lord, apart from supernatural experiences, which some mystics may have to the cognition of reality only with the *blessings* of Allah Almighty. The Qur'anic assertions do not limit human cognition to senses of perception and the brainy discernment of its sense organs that are inspired by the stippled and perceptible, malodorous and flavorsome, or the tactual qualities of extra-mental bodies, and sensation is the vital response through man's five external sense powers to such stimulation.

Although human cognition begins with the knowing of bodily things, man can form some intellectual notions and judgments concerning immaterial beings, souls, angels, and the Lord. It also educates and enlightens that man does this by aspiring certain aspects of intelligence in the light of modern-day science and philosophy. When the notion of power is attributed to the Lord, its meaning is transferred from an initial physical concept to the corresponding consummation and completion of that which can accomplish results in the *spiritual* order. This concedes a lesson that men during this vale can hardly familiarize themselves with the nature of the Lord in any adequately positive way, until they truly consume all their deeds and doings in the precept and perception of the Lord.

We cannot abide to live in a house without an order of some sort, so how could one imagine the order of the indeterminate cosmic order without any deity behind it?

The conclusive and affirmative inference was taken as an intelligent procedure moving from or toward the first principles in the logical concept and precept of a deity that demonstrates the way of detection and disclosure with deductions derived and described from the Holy Scripture. In one way, sense experiences in faith is the first and principal starting point for all of man's natural knowledge. The Qur'an taught that many sensations combine to form a unified memory, and many memories constitute the sense of experience and cognition. From this manifold of experience, by a sort of sensory induction, there arises within human cognizance a beginning that postulates the discernment of time. Such first principles are demonstrated naturally as they emerge from a sense of perception when we go through the text of the Scripture in a most discerning way, and it becomes the root for inferable intelligent support and solace through the discernment of time and domain.

When we account for the creation of the human being based on the genetic proscenium, which is almost 99.9 percent the same in each one of us, we find that we do not have much control over that predicament that we designate as fate or predestination. It is only 0.1 percent of the genetic attributes that construct our individual characteristics including behavioral traits and different notions. But His Almighty has blessed us with intelligence, a notion of discernment that is going to be the subject of deliberation, when we are asked to justify the conduct of our course that we may call fortune of action in this vale.

There are roughly three and a half billion letters in the human genome. If it were a book and we could read ten letters of it every second, it would take eleven years to recite the whole text. Even if we had eleven years to spare, a simple recitation of the code would give no hint of the way it makes a human life.

Instead of thinking of the genome as a book, imagine it as a piano keyboard. Each piano key represents one gene. If you press down on a key, you hear a single note. That note corresponds to the protein that the gene specifies. If you press the key again, you will hear the same note and again, monotonously, every time the key is played.

But if you have lot of keys, you can make music. Just so, our various cell types play upon the immense keyboard of the genome. They combine notes, playing some genes together as chords, tripping several together in a phrase, gathering boundless notes to create the complex and wonderful effects that find expression in our biological being. Just as a pianist does not play all the keys in every piece, only some of the genes get played in the cells of each organ. Just conceive of the whole consequence and concern in this context.

"Which of the favors, you may deny of your Astral O Astute Lord?" (Al Rahman).

But think what can happen to a piano concerto if an important key sticks or sounds the wrong note when struck. Such a flaw can ruin the very passage where that key is played. Just perceive of this consequence of genetic disarray in human conduct and the course of action in health and disease, as it plays a pivotal role in the care and construct of the most esteemed creation of Allah Almighty that is composed of three main components: the earthly pot, or the "*body*"; the divine source, or the *efflux or soul*; and the bestowal of the Lord at the time of the creation of Adam, *intelligence*.

The Earthly Pot

It once again becomes a part of the dust and soot when its efflux is withdrawn, and nothing remains of this protoplasmic flesh but mineral salts and water, which are dissipated in the dirt or mud from where it was originally retrieved.

When we are dead, this genetic code is dispersed in the earth exactly as the message conveyed to the computer hard disc is dispersed in binary codes and bits. When we intend to retrieve the data, we just give a command, and within no time, the details are retrieved on the computer screen. Similarly, imagine the human genome with definite coded letters and each genome dispersed in dust and soot after death. It would be recalled by His Almighty with His dictum in dictate to congregate the genetic code of an individual in the properly guided slots to form once again a perfect man as in this vale.

One more assertion in this context will elucidate the matter even more clearly.

The Day their mouths will be shut *and sealed*
Hands and feet would trend to reveal
For what they'd affirmed to conceal (36:65)

How's that possible?

Yes, of course, today's scientific affirmations prove from which material we are fabricated.

Dust and mud!

What is it constituted of?

It is constituted of all the earthly material, (i.e., water, minerals, and salts).

What's silicon?

A material derived from the earth, which is able to store data in a computer.

Are you sure there wouldn't be any other material derived from the soil to store memory like silicon?

There, in all likelihood, could be something.

Okay! Then it affirms that our hands and feet and whatever other parts of the body ordained in the dictum and dictate of the Lord will divulge all our deeds and doings in this vale, when in the Hereafter they will be ordained to do so.

Certainly, there is no doubt about it.

Moving beyond today's silicon integrated-chip technology will require shrinking logic and memory circuits to the scale of a few nanometers. Large arrays of intersecting *nanowires* called crossbars provide the basis for one of the best candidate technologies for *nanocomputing* success.

On and Off at the Crossroads

The key component of the crossbar architecture is a *nanoscale* switch that can be turned "on" or "off" by applying an appropriate voltage to the wires it connects.

In the Hewlett-Packard (HP) Laboratories version, the switch is formed at the junction between two crossing *nano-wires* that are separated by a single monolayer of molecules. The switch starts out in a high resistance state, blocking the flow of electrons between its two *nano-wires,* but when a large enough voltage of the appropriate polarity is placed across it, the switch changes abruptly to a much lower resistance state, allowing electrons to flow more easily. The switch stays in this low-resistance state until a large enough negative voltage makes it revert to its original state. As long as the voltage is maintained between these positive and negative thresholds, the switch remains in the state in which it was last set. Some switches the authors have examined have retained their set states for more than three years so far. If the switches can be toggled back and forth many times, they are reconfigurable and can be used in a random access memory or a reprogrammable logic circuit.

The prototype array for a crossbar-computing device depicted in an atomic force micrograph has thirty-four *nano-wires* (each thirty nanometers wide) intersecting with thirty-four others. A junction of two *nano-wires* is smaller than a typical virus.

Build top-down or bottom-up?

The field of *nanoscale* fabrication is extremely active today, with many competing techniques under study. These approaches can be classified into two categories: top-down and bottom-up. The former examples resemble conventional integrated circuit IC manufacturing methods that use photolithography followed by chemical etching or deposition of materials to create the desired features. The latter approaches are based on extensions of chemical or biochemical processes by which atoms or molecules self-assemble into a desired configuration because of their planned, inherent properties. Most investigators in this field agree that some combination of the two approaches will be required to build future *nanoscale* circuits.

At HP, the team uses imprint lithography to create the crossbars. Some scientists employ electron beam lithography to construct molds for the circuits. Although this process is slow and costly, we can make duplicates of the final product, which then are used to stamp out large quantities of circuits, much as vinyl LP records were made. A thin layer of a polymer or polymer precursor coats a substrate. The mold is pressed into this soft layer, and the impressed pattern hardens under exposure to heat or ultraviolet light. The advantage of this approach is that electron beam lithography can fabricate arbitrary wire geometries on the mold. The drawback is that the present resolution of the features in a set of parallel wires is limited to roughly thirty-nanometer half pitch (half the distance between the centers of two wires, a standard industry measure).

Just turn toward this new evolutionary discovery of nano-wire chips and the structural makeup of the man, who has innumerable nano-wire circuits in the body.

We affirm through modern science that creation is from mud. Now discern the following verse of the Holy Qur'an.

It's He,
Who stages your creation *in best*
Created you from *the mud and* dust

Then from sperm *in speck*
You're leech-like,
Clot *in mother's den and nest*
He gets you to light,
As suckling *with the rest*
Lets,
You grow and reach, age vigor *in best*
Then gets you to be an elderly *guest*
Though some,
May doom and die, before *the rest*

And lets you attain a time *in vale*
And to affirm sense and sapience *in trail* (40:67)

The Efflux or Soul

Aquinas sometimes spoke as if this was a special power of the man, as an agent. He formally stressed the view that it is the whole man who was the human agent. A human being is an animated body in which the psychic principle (anima) is distinctive of the species and determines that the material is human. In other words, man's soul is his substantial form. Some of man's activities are obviously very like those of brutes, but the intellectual and volitional functions transcend materiality by virtue of their universal and abstracted character. Aquinas took as an indication of the immateriality of the human soul the fact that it can understand universal meanings and make free decisions. The efflux is a real part of man, being immaterial the real spiritual self. From certain other features of man's higher activities, especially from the unity of conscious experience, it was concluded to the simplicity and integration of man's soup: it is not divisible into parts. This, in turn, led him to the conclusion that the soul is incapable of corruption (disintegration into parts) and thus is immortal.

He was thus forced to the view that divine creation originates each rational efflux from a source outside the domain of our perception. Human parents are not the total cause of their offspring; they share the work of procreation with the Lord. This view explains why one puts so much stress on the dignity and sanctity of human reproduction, which is regarded as more than a biological function, when it is claimed, in ethics, that the "begetting" is not a simple sensual activity but a human participation in the Lord's creative function.

Hieros Gamos

More than two thousand years ago, Egyptian priests and priestesses performed it regularly to celebrate the reproductive power of the female. It looks like a sexual ritual, but it has nothing to do with eroticism; instead, it is a spiritual act. The physical union of the male and female in the sexual act, remained the core of spirituality. The ancients believed that the male was incomplete unless he had carnal knowledge of the feminine sexuality. With the physical union of the two sexes, they became spiritually complete and ultimately achieved "gnosis," or knowledge of divine inspiration, a climax instance, when the mind went totally blank and one could see the orgasm, the core of spirituality. That split second was devoid of thought, a brief mental vacuum, a moment of clarity during which the divine order of exhilaration could be experienced. Intercourse was the revered union of the two halves of the human spirit, the male and the female. That eventually begot new life, the ultimate miracle. The ability of the woman to produce life from her womb made her sacred. And the two sexes melding physical union with sensual climax found the high order of spiritual wholeness and communion with the creator.

Hieros gamos looked like a sexual act of perversion, but it was a deeply revered ceremony. The sensual union was a sacramental act of spiritual union—a challenge to find the spark of divinity in a legal way of wedding, for otherwise, a sense of guilt always supervenes and the notion of charm or exhilaration, that's in reality a bliss of the almighty, drags you to the other extreme of sexual guilt and shame. Islam very clearly indicates two, three, and even four marriages if you can carry through the accomplishment in a decent way and can do justice to all.

The philosopher-theologian cannot dispute, correct, or complete anything in science, but neither does one have to accept the philosophical opinions of scientists. The connection between these two parallel approaches to reality is simply that science always leaves us metaphysically hungry and with the feeling that they have not exhausted all the possibilities of knowledge, so they motivate us to turn to philosophy. It is only when we come to philosophy in this way that it is really valuable; any philosophy that is undertaken and forced upon us by scientific study is insipid.

What the sciences must get from philosophy is an idea of nature, a theory of being to delimit their ontological horizons. They cannot themselves build such an idea of nature adequately, for the founding of physics and scholasticism did the same for modern science: the way-out work of different scientists would have been impossible. Physics is again in crisis, facing problems that cannot be solved by physicists, logicians, or epistemologists alone, but only by ontologists, who can supply a fresh idea of nature within which quantum physics can progress.

In the philosophy of existence, philosophers accept the radical ontological nullity of man, who is nothing apart from the tasks he has to wrestle with. It is in dealing with his tasks that man comes to be. The nature consists in the mission of being sent out but with an added doctrine of religation. Zubiri coined the term *religation* from the Latin word *religare* "to tie," which may also be the root of religion. According to this doctrine, we are not simply thrown into existence, as atheistic existentialists say, but are impelled into it by something that we feel all the time as an obligation, a force imposing on us the task of choosing and realizing ourselves. That something is the supreme deity to which we are bound, or tied. Religation, the relation to the deity, is the fundamental root of existence and the ontological structure of personality that binds us all in the discipline of faith.

When we comprehend anything it is through our sense of perception, an endowment of Allah Almighty, the efflux or spirituality, for otherwise, this earthly pot—the man contrived of dust and mud—cannot concern, conform, or discern to affirm anything. So it is established as long as the man is alive or the earthly pot holds the efflux, it has the sense of discernment and sagacity, but once the efflux is gone, it cannot perceive. So the perception of being in vivacity is through spirituality (i.e., the divine endowment, the efflux).

It affirms that under ordinary situations, it's all through the sane ambience of intelligence with spirituality at its core that we can hear to consider, can speak to affirm, and can see to discern.

But once we tarry in the trail of depravity, the Qur'an says:

Stubborn and stupid not to discern
And they don't trend to submit in concern (2:18)

So is the state of affairs when the efflux is gone after death, and during life, when they don't concern their intelligence or their souls, they're like the dead. They were conferred the breath soon after birth. If they did it on their own, so fine and good; if not, their nurse mildly smacked them on the back to make them take it (breath). The efflux then delivered, when it's withdrawn, the earthly pot is not in a position to hear to concern, speak to conform, or see to discern even though all the neural connections to the higher centers are intact.

For the intelligence thus delivered, the efflux holds its charge to manage (i.e., it is through the efflux one can really care to concern and discern to affirm). Nothing in reality can hear, speak, or see without the efflux—so when we see it, we discern it. We cannot see it, but the efflux is there to bestow us all the boons to cherish its neural relay. Similarly, we cannot hear unless the efflux is there to set its trail to the higher centers, and we cannot speak unless we have the endowment from the efflux to charge its glow.

That the part of the divine source of life (i.e., the efflux), the soul, derives its subsistence and sagacity from spirituality has now been scientifically proved. A piece of brain in the left parietal lobe derives its endurance and enlightenment only from the spiritual sources when the subject is in deep meditation. It shows that under ordinary situations, that part of the brain derives its nourishment from the physical sources, as it reveals a normal flow of blood to this part of the brain.

But at that moment of true perceptiveness and prudence in meditation, which is the primal source of erudition and edification when it comprehends its endowments of guidance with the instruction and injunction of spiritual enlightenment, it derives its subsistence only from divine sources as the blood supply to this part of the brain is totally stopped as confirmed on a PET scan.

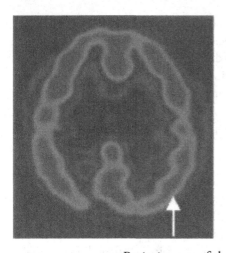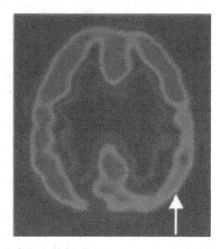

Brain images of the left parietal lobe.
On the left, it shows good blood flow in a normal person.
During meditation, this part of the brain [on the right] is deprived of blood supply. (Readers Digest)

Since His Almighty has made us in His own image, we should be able to discern Him in the depths of our minds (i.e., the *core and crux of the soul*) instead of staring into the void or starting with metaphysical abstractions or other verbal distinctions.

As invariably we assert:

- I love you from the core of my heart or
- I learnt it by heart.

The heart has nothing to do either with loving in the core or learning in lore; it is all the brain, but it is indeed the heart that passes the bliss of elation, when its pace is very smooth and comforting, and during moments of stress, it is quite fast and even irregular.

The Self

Buddhism attributes to it "undo-self." Confucianism calls it the "social self," whereas in Hinduism, the all- pervading cosmic spirit comes close to swallow the individual self. Islam and its Semitic allies revere this drift, regarding individuality as not only real but good in principle. Value and spiritual fulfillment comes through the realization of the potentialities that are uniquely one's own in ways that are not inconsequential. Those possibilities differ from those of every other soul that has ever lived or ever will come to live in the future, as the inexplicable finite center of experience is the fundamental fact of the universe. All life is individual with its soul at its core, but to cherish the bliss of the whole or the bliss of solitude through vision, while recounting the Holy appellation "Allah" when concentrating on the heart during exhalation, the sluice of the heart is flung open and one feels like a peewee gliding and soaring in the vistas of the whole. It is this instance of impetus when one instinctively feels that His Almighty Allah can bestow us the sequence in significance and projection in prominence of our lives. This is the time of turn when the body melts into the soul (i.e., singularity or factually in a state of nihility, an indeterminate term and realm when the body and soul along with time have merged into nihility).

That's the situation before the creation of time (timelessness) and the universe (i.e., a singularity or nihility) when the concept of time and space bore no design and definition. One becomes part of vistas of the whole where the time domain has no deliverance of past, present, and future, for all is one, melted in nihility.

An order of "whole," for when time and all the material was one with no discernment of time and space that the Qur'an terms, the earliest creation perceived as "smoke of an inconclusive order," whereas the scientific theories also affirm that the earliest creation perceived was the glowing smoke all around. The concept of creation and the time are all one, like before the creation of the universe.

Try to discern the whole cosmic order when the true meditative perception makes the earthly pot, the body, part of the soul with an overwhelming sixth sense of intuitive perception or the spirituality at its core (i.e., commanding over all the other five senses of the earthly pot). It's the impulse when the soul or the efflux itself travels the indeterminate cosmic order with no reference to the time domain, for this is the state of nihility of the self, when the body is assimilated in the soul and the soul becomes a part of the vistas of the whole cosmic order with no precept or concept of the term of the time domain.

When body is consumed in soul
Soul then trails in the vistas of Whole

That's a state of indeterminate lore
When none but virtues permeate in core

What a tine to treasure His Munificent Whole
Relish and revere, ardor and adore in blissful allure

As we know that His Almighty created us all from nihility, we thus find the probity and purity of soul when this earthly pot once again becomes part of the soul or part of the whole, losing all its luscious and ludicrous aspirations.

Intelligence

The third essential element, the intelligence, is really yours. It has the power of discrimination and discernment, insight and intuition, sagacity and super-vision, perception and prudence, comprehension and concern, determination and decision.

And it is this third part of the divine endowment of intelligence to human beings, His Almighty reiterates in a most appealing and alluring, enticing and enchanting manner in this most gleeful and glowing verse repeatedly in *Surah Al Rahman*:

"Which of the favors, you may deny of your Prudent and Pretentious Lord?"

As already described, that intelligence is a most benevolent gift and grant of Allah Almighty for His men, but a part of that intelligence is true discernment, and it is the perception of true discernment that holds the intelligence to live in concurrence with the perception of divine nature. It is essentially to live according to the man's own rightful or virtuous nature in the order of the nature of providence.

To insinuate the intelligence, we shall have to look at it in a different way as it endows its development on certain attributes, of which some are constructed on the genetic proscenium. Other attributes are dependent on the conscious self, in addition to the environmental factors. The overall conduct in the course of an individual's accomplishment, the intelligence will depend on:

- Hereditary attributes or the genetic code
- Environmental factors
- Personal attributes

Death or demise will determine the success and semblance in the light of these attributes of the living beings.

Intelligence is freely distributed like air for each individual to cherish its boons. Every person has to have a share of fresh and clean air free of pollution from the industrial sources or other discernable defiling and debasing, blemishing and befouling environmental noxious wastes. To breathe in crisp and refreshing unpolluted air is certainly through the free will of a person, who otherwise is not constrained to abide in stiffly and strongly tainted and adulterated environments. Nevertheless, he possesses a choice of selecting to change his surroundings and have nectarous breathing in the scent and spoor of natural environments.

We have "sane intelligence" that derives its discernment both from the body or fleshly resources and partly determines its discernment by way of the "soul," the spiritual or divine source.

If the intelligence derives its discernment only from its bodily and fleshly resources, its demand of comestibles and sensual regalement are increased, and it is desecrated and defiled. I call it "profane intelligence." The basic prudence and perspicacity, discernment and discrimination of authenticity are faded in a fog. It is like the air adulterated with acid rain in industrial towns. And as living in such conditions takes a toll on physical or bodily health, similarly, in living in conscientiously depraved environments, our intelligence is defiled and especially becomes heinous and nefarious, amoral and atrocious, lubricous and illicit.

The Qur'an determines that man is indeed "unjust" and a "fool" (33:72), because he does not care to concern his intelligence.

Indeed!
We offered a Term[9] in Trust *to confirm*
To the,
Heavens and Earth and Mountains *to affirm*
But they declined to assume *in pace*
For they're all scared *in place*
But man affirmed the course *in conduct*
He's indeed biased and idiotic *in instruct*
(Ruthless and fool)

When we go through the text, we discern that at the very first instance, the Lord Almighty asserts that He endowed the heavens, the earth, and even the mountains with the responsibility to communicate the message of faith (i.e., Qur'an). *I am giving details of this stance and stanza because I could find no satisfactory explanation for this Verse given in various texts.* Here once again, I don't feel comfortable reconciling the meaning "declined" often mentioned in the translations.

How could the heavens, earth, and mountains, or for that matter anything, dare to defy the Lord Almighty's word in command? They indeed

---

9   To own the responsibility to covey the message Holy Qur'an.

71

would have acceded to His demand even though shattered and scattered, tattered and torn, but this assertion is to confirm that indeed the Lord Almighty endowed man with ascendancy over all the things created by Him, as at another instance, the Lord Almighty affirms that if the Qur'an was to be revealed to the mountains, they would have ripped apart.

But one would marvel at this stage as to how could all these things communicate the divine message to whatever nature of the subjects before them. This passage or the stance and stanza itself clearly elucidates that the Lord created the man with a special quirk of intelligence to know the secrets of the cosmic order, the earth, and the mountains, besides heading the responsibility of communication of His Almighty's message, for the man was created for this very purpose. The man is asserted to affirm with the bestowal of all the endowments from the Lord Almighty to head the responsibility.

Did he accomplish it faithfully or not?

When someone affirms to do something, which he is not competent to do, we say he's a fool but not unjust or ruthless.

We say he is unjust only when he was competent enough to do the job but did not deliver the goods to accomplish the job to one's satisfaction, which in all likelihood, he could have accomplished.

Here in this stance is such a situation; when man avowed that he'd accomplish the assignment, the Lord Almighty knew very well that he could do that job, so He affirmed him to undertake the assignment as desired, but indeed, he broke down to do that and hence didn't do it justice and was ruthless. Soon thereafter, the Lord Almighty asserts that he is fool.

Why the Man Is a Fool

Surah Al Ahzabb 33:72

Indeed!
We offered a Word[10] in Trust *to confirm*
To the,
Heavens and Earth and Mountains *to affirm*
But they declined to assume *in pace*
For they're all scared *in place*
But man affirmed the course *in conduct*
He's indeed biased and idiotic *in instruct*

If we are presented a gift and we fail to make use of it, what does it mean?

---

10 The Qur'an

Indeed! A fool will fail to avail the boons of the gift!

If ever man could discern between the lines of stance and stanza of the Holy Scripture, he could cherish the endowments of Allah Almighty.

It is emphasized once for sure.

O man! If ever you could really benefit from the bestowal Allah Almighty endowed in the Qur'an, you could have been most gifted in sapience.

But Nay!

You really defied acceptance of the message, and so you are a fool as well.

For if he would have affirmed that, he could have known the secrets of the heavens, the earth, and the mountains, and so understood the nature of the Lord Almighty, Who's behind the creation of all this myth of marvelous nature. Therefore, the man would've cherished the boons, bounties, and benedictions of the Lord Almighty not only hither in the vale but also Hereafter in trail.

Then a man obsessed to ask in trance
Why "The Lord" trended in stance

To the man who affirmed* in relate
Unjust and fool in state

Who asserted to affirm to comply?
(Dictum of Lord not to defy)
Lord could really assert to confirm in glance
That man was quite deft to affirm in stance
The term of Qur'an in glory of grace

And,
Aver to establish its elegance to brace
But alas!
Man failed in his avow to affirm
For what he'd apprised to concern
He's unjust in trends to discern

Indeed!
He's a fool of first order in astray
For couldn't trend to the splendor in sway
For what's acclaimed in Qur'an to obey
For,
If he would've trended the Word to aside
He'd have cherished the Boons in stride

Not only hither in vale so bright
But also Hereafter in delight

But how'd Lord ever discern to concern
The man, who trended to avow and affirm

Deny and defy the basic concept at core
Not abiding Dictum of Lord in lore
Isn't that unjust to the word, he secured
*Who affirmed to confirm to convey the message of Qur'an)

O Man,
Trend to your done and doings hither in fore
Are you sincere to His Dictum in core

But nay!
You aver to avow in words to entreat
Whereas in verity, abide some else in treat

For if you would've confirmed to obey
You would've cherished His Bounties in sway

But in all your trends and amends in abide
You've your own ways in stride
Indeed!
The man is egoistic in all his trends
Isn't he a fool to construe in amends

Quite a few of His assertions far and away
Convenient in course, conduct to astray
For what you affirmed a word to obey

There's lot to be said in stance
But you trend to "self" in glance

Do you care for Dictum of Lord *in pray*
Indeed not!
For you don't have a bit of concern *in fray*

And still you summon Lord *in trance*
As to why He indicted the man *in stance*
Unjust and fool in his trends *at glance*

The word in stance is quite clear to brace
For,
If you've a bit of sense of sapience in trace

That's why it's often said that a man is known by the company he keeps, and so the peers advise to abide beside the company of only the virtuous in stride.

What to a strumpet, who was born and brought up in unfortunate environments, but later, had the option of free discernment through her *intelligence* to have the free guidance of the preferred? Her earlier part of life when she was forced to stay in such defiled surroundings (i.e., a part of the genetic code or true fate), that was determined by nature as a part of the whole.

This fable will make the things a bit clearer.

Baba Fareed Shaker Gang stayed occupied in divine adoration for more than thirty-five years in jungles, uninhabited wastelands, and far-flung areas, where no one could approximate to access or observe him in prostration. His consecration and devotion in prayers were immense. One afternoon, when he was busy in beseeching under a tree, where swarms of small birds were twittering and chirping, he got vexed and cried in disgust and dismay, "Why don't you give up the ghost, as you are dissuading and daunting my observance and concentration in invocation and imploration?" All the birds were down dead beside him.

This was a notion of insinuation and allusion to Baba Fareed that it's the time. You now get to the people in town to preach the divine message. He drifted toward the city. He had only one wand with him. When he came close to the city abode, a dog crossed his way. He swung his staff to ward off the dog when a woman staying close to a well cried out, "Fareed, beware! This dog has a master, and strange enough you have killed the birds in desolation."

Fareed, bewildered and baffled, turned to the dame. "May I ask you, fine lady, how come you have achieved this dignified status, when nobody around here knew me, as I am turning to some town after thirty-five years and am sure when the birds fell dead that moment nobody except Allah Almighty was witness to that?"

The good lady said, "I am a prostitute by profession, born in the house of a strumpet. My mother was quite sick; it was a very chilly night. She got up and voiced me to bring water, but when I returned to her with a tumbler full of water, she had already gone to sleep. I kept waiting beside her bed till morn, provided she might need water to drink, and in that case, once again she would return to open the door in the extreme cold."

The moral of the fable is:

There's a saying years gone old
All that glitters is not gold

I'd like to annex one more
It's not vile all you hex and scold

What to a strumpet born in abide
Wherein cursed and sneered in deride
Intent to turn out of miserable plight
Languish to cherish some pitying sight

Would she endure a pledge of delight
All in concern, defy to discern in slight

Turn to you; recall in heart and soul
What you ordain, think once more
Terms determined in intent of core

With,
All your done and doings hither in fore
Curse and scold one, least be sure
Is that proper and precise in lore
How'd you defer and defy to endure

Wherein Lord proffer proficiency in score
Glimmer of Lord in clemency to allure

For Thy exoneration for us to survive
Diversely we're not going to thrive

O Lord! Our repentance in base and refuse
And Your semblance in retreat and refuge

Bestow Thee O Lord Blessing in more
Don't turn to indict, but bliss in adore
We,
Beg and beseech Thy Benefaction in more
Let us admire and adore Thy Bounty in score

And that all men are not born alike and that though one is born in the strumpet's house and one is born in a priest's house, the one has no edge over the other, except for the ultimate course and conduct of their nature of discipline ordained in this vale through intelligence. His Almighty's gesture of admonition and absolution is also according to the status and designation of man in place of his assignment. As in the Qur'an betroths of the Prophet, it is reminded that if they committed some omission in oversight, their admonition and exhortation will be twice as to those of others because they were in the home and hearth of discipline.

O Spouses of the Prophet:
Here's word for you *in instruct*
If any of you're to blame, *stupid in conduct*
Castigation be paired *due in construct*
That's easy for Mighty Lord *to induct* (33:30)

His Almighty has blessed us with the perception of true repentance and penitence that allures us in the semblance of the refuge in providence that eliminates the soot from the blemished self.

The truth of faith when it permeates the intelligence, once defiled by the desecrated circumstances, once again breathes, like fresh air, in the sane ambience of intelligence. And what is that intelligence? It is the discernment and true perception, a part of life that is answerable to His Almighty of our conduct in course and discipline in force in this worldly life.

Once more have the cognizance to discern that matter and energy have to come from somewhere. Everyone can agree on that. But information has to come from somewhere, too! Information is a separate entity, fully at par with matter and energy. And information can only come from a mind. If books and poems and TV shows come from human intelligence, then all living things inevitably came from a super intelligence.

Every word you hear, every sentence you speak, every song you sing, every e-mail you read, every packet of information that zings across the Internet is proof of the existence of the Almighty. The information and language always originates in a mind.

In the beginning were words and language.

In the beginning was information.

When we consider the mystery of life—where it came from and how it was possible—do we not at the same time ask the questions where is it going and what is its purpose?

Intelligence in Discipline

It is by following the divinity within that man comes nearest to the deity, the supreme good. A man can never attain perfect agreement with his internal guidance provided he has not solely submitted to the Almighty. Live with Allah. He who conforms to live with the Almighty and constantly show to Him that his own material and sensual desires are only satisfied with that which is assigned to him of his fleshy lusciousness and all the ludicrous aspirations. To every man for his escort, a portion of his understanding and reason is bestowed to him from the Almighty to discriminate the righteousness and wickedness of his undertakings through his true discerning intelligence.

Is it only through the intimate approach to the knowledge of their several natures made by Him, Who so abides His intellectual vision to have the most exact conception of the essence of His deliberations?

Moreover, if there is time and an inclination toward the study of truth, but the body introduces a commotion and confusion into the course of speculation, it hinders us from seeing the truth. All experience shows that if we would have pure knowledge of anything, we must be liberated of the body's sensuousness and seductions with other sumptuous stipulations. The soul in herself must behold all things in themselves. I suppose that we shall attain that which we desire and of which we say that we love wisdom, not while we live, but also after the departure from this vale. The contention demonstrates that while in company with the body, the soul cannot have pure knowledge until it is subjected to the true perception of faith, and that is only discernible if the person goes for it sincerely. For then, and not until then, the soul will be in herself alone and without the fleshly enticements of the body.

The Veracity of Intelligence

There is an excellence in the decency of discipline, which is designated for-bearance and fortitude, that's a special quirk and quality of the precise and perpetuating faith. There is reticence in humility, a tranquil servitude, with no scorn and snubbing of the infatuation and indignation, but a prudence and perseverance. It is a quality care and concern only to those who slight and despise sensual allure and enchantment, the zeal and zest of the frame or flesh, and abide in sound and sonorous certitude with a confidence that is the "veracity of discipline" ordained by Allah Almighty.

We may call it the governing intelligence or the governing faculty or the master of the soul. A man must respect only his capability for discernment and the truth within him. As we must esteem that which is supreme in the universe, so we must esteem that which is supreme in ourselves, and this is that which is of like kind, which is supreme in the universe.

Our true discerning intelligence, the "sane intelligence," is a bestowal of His Almighty to the deliberations of which we are endowed to abide by in this vale. It is through the intimate source of the core and crux that we cherish the bliss of our intelligence with the benevolent endowment of Allah Almighty. So to esteem the beauty of the Lord in intimate core, the bestowal of intelligence is there for us to escort in lore.

The notion of intelligence is an endowment and bliss of the pedigreed providence that's the firm conviction with assertion in faith and affirmation through a benevolent escort in the principles.

There is a life promised Hereafter that His Almighty asserts to be an everlasting verve in flow, with His bestowal in glow. Could it be His Almighty created us in this vale to abide certain disciplines as ordained from the time of civilization known at this stage through His Prophets?

For in the Hereafter, He has promised an everlasting life of youth in prime with no dotage in decline.

Today's scientific research is converging toward the most sophisticated genetic mutation: stem cell transplants and cloning. Indeed, we are here to accomplish some order of nature bestowed to us in this world before we retire to the everlasting domain.

It is here that we beseech His Almighty:

And there're men and clan who turn to beseech
Our Lord!
Give us Phenomenal in this vale to appease
And of the excellent in Hereafter O Please
And save us from anguish of pyre in treat (2:201)

Today, what we aspire or desire is to cherish the sway and swing in the reign and rule of faith in a most munificent and bountiful way, to delve and dig always in the core and crux of the veer and profundity of the mind and soul.

How and why do we adore the purity of truth in the core with the certitude of conviction?

It's here in the vale you are put to the test for your care in concern and lore to discern.

I am sure the truth of intelligence when it permeates the soul, the true discernment of intelligence escorts us to the convincing verity in faith with probity in the profundity of actuality. Allah Almighty discerns and concerns each notion of our deeds and doings in this vale and convoys us in the veracity of faith as ordained in the Holy Scripture. All these notions of perception are endowed to direct our earthly part, the body, in the gleam of the truth of our souls.

In this world, I believe that we make the nearest approach to intelligence when we have the least possible concern or interest in the body and it's not drenched in the fleshly or sensual propositions. Assert and affirm to abide in innocence until the hour when the Lord Almighty Himself is pleased to emancipate us and when the flightiness of the body will be cleared away and we shall be pure and hold discourse with other pure souls and know of ourselves the clear light everywhere; this is surely the light of truth with true discernment of intelligence.

And what's purification?

Is it the separation of the soul from the body?

The inclination of the soul congregating and collecting herself into "herself," out of the deportment of the flesh and abiding in her own suite and site alone, as in the afterlife, *Fanaa*, so also in here, as far as she can release our soul from the chains of this captivating vale.

Why Are We Created?

What you think to discern
That you're born without any goal in concern
And that you're not destined to "Me" in return
(23:115–116)

I've no vision to discern but have some inkling to pen a few words in concern.

Allah Almighty loves his living beings far more than a mother.

Sure?

Of course, indeed!

Okay! Then, when a contorted and crippled baby is born, how tormenting and painful is it for the mother?

Sure enough, there's no doubt about it.

Don't you think the Lord Almighty will also be concerned about this disturbing situation?

It's quite likely.

Just turn toward the soil and the cultivation. We sow a seed of cotton or some grain, but what really comes out?

Besides cotton or grain, there are so many undesired plants.

We treat the soil with so many approaches to get rid of the undesirable plants, and only then do we yield the crop of our choice, even though we're not quite appeased with its ultimate outcome that it would've yielded without those unwanted plants. But actually, we don't know the cause, for it was expedient for the superfluous yield to be there before the germination of the desired product. So these are exterminated only when these are visible or come out of the soil.

So is the genetic swing in sway, for the detrimental genes are there for the purpose of the whole, and so these are taken care of sooner or later by nature.

Am I clear?

Indeed! It's like that.

If we turn toward the creation of the cosmic order and also the living beings as a whole, in the proscenium of creation, couldn't there be some unwelcome products produced in the genetic array and cosmic sway for the discipline of the whole in cosmic array?

Because:

For the order of the whole there has to be good and bad.

For what in design, did He create the man?
For whom is the bestowal of lore in the plan?

Just concern for a while here to discern.
Could we be hither some chore to affirm?

For the preference in competence in the genetic swing and sway is in reality the perfection with precision of the order of nature.

It is not conceivable to imagine that all men and clans will cherish an equanimity in poise for their conduct in course, propensity, and proficiency in intelligence and competence. So the point and plan of comprehension with sapience in sagacity besides health and wealth must vary from person to person. So there had to be certain mutations with innovations in the genetic proscenium, for otherwise, this world would not have been a place to endure life.

Get an eyeful and scrutinize the conviviality of the social conduct. How can we toil or moil, whet and whittle to accomplish if each one of us becomes a genius or an eminently cultivated astute, a doctor of medicine or a consultant, an engineer or a professor or a scientist, a philosopher or a scholar if there were no janitor or a sweeper, no peon or carpenter, no washer-man or subaltern, no tram or train driver, no tiller, or no sailor.

There is apportioning of toil and drudge to strive not only in the close clique, communion, in the culture but also for the whole social order. Exceptionally, we encounter an identical situation when we sound out the human body. Just watch your hands, the indigent laborers that have to toil and travail all the time, but when it comes to nutrition, they seize just the leftovers from the surplus of that used for the body's needs, particularly the brain. The brain is commanding and controlling the whole body's systems but squeezing the cream of the nutrients. Similarly, there is apportionment of all the assignments of the society and humanity as a whole. A philosopher, a ruler, and the like of a man commanding an authority in any department derives the best salary and other facilities, whereas a peon in the same departments, who works round the clock is contented with a modest salary.

Besides all these strides in restraints, tending and verging, His Almighty was quite relaxed, for He had determined this fickle and fake triviality in trace vale for a very short term in trail, during which He intended to determine our conduct in course and discipline in this vale.

It's for the eventual attainment of the adorable goal of the Hereafter in trail.

But why don't we recollect that life of ours when His Almighty had determined our genetic proscenium?

Well, there could possibly be a life of our soul or efflux with its genetic proscenium somewhere there, in a very different state.

It was then we affirmed His Almighty Allah.
When we were asked: Who's your Lord?
All souls asserted in that event:
You are our Lord. (7–172)

It was then the endowment of intelligence with true discernment and discrimination of the flagitious in the fray and esteem in sway was held in conformity. The word of true discernment is so deeply insinuated in our essence of core and that it has been perpetuating ever since the creation of humanity in this abode for us to decide in different trends in strides, and that's the veracity of intelligence to aside.

And we need not apprise some of the righteous or sinister in different notions, for we discern for sure within our veer of core, for that's the endowment in lore.

And What's the Source of Knowledge?

Even Einstein affirmed that knowledge is through intuitive perception.

It's all through the benevolence of Allah Almighty, who so designs and consigns all order of nature in accordance with His true dictum in dictate.

But here in this domain of research, one shall have to tread very cautiously in a definite purpose in plan.

The Lord Almighty reiterates that:

What you care and concern thither *in dale*
That We created you for nothing *in scale*
And to Me,
You wouldn't return *in trail* (23:15)

The address is to all of humanity and not to the Muslims only. Now let us take one more stance in this context. There're so many angels assigned for different projects and purposes.

Who commands the authority?

A Mighty Nature!
But!
Who are we hither in domain?
What are we here to sustain?
What are we determined to do hither in vale?
And where are we destined Hereafter in trail?

The answer to all such questions very lucidly comes in various sonnets and stanzas of the Holy Scripture. The discussion in this regard is very complicated and the words in communication cannot really explain the notion of His Almighty.

And when He turned to the angels *in Command*
I'm to apprise an assertive *(on earth) in Demand*
They tended in plead *in stance*
Will You assign one to wreck *in vale*
And tend to depravity infinite *in scale*

While we adore and anoint *(Thee) in beseech*
He said: Certainly *and indeed*
I discern that you cannot concern *in treat*
He instructed Adam all the words *in lore*
And evinced them to angels for the same *in score*
Saying:
Recount and relate *(Me)* all *of the same*
If you're suited, sedate and apt *in claim*
(2:30–34)

After He created the man, He taught discernment of intelligence, whereas He endowed the angels with vigilance of compliance. He taught him to speak and utter in different parlance and dialects. Besides that, He endowed him with the gift of "intelligence" that has been perpetuated ever since the creation of humanity. The dash and smack with the intent of intelligence are deeply ingrained and insinuated in our lives. For each one of us clearly discerns what is virtuous in pace or flagitious in place. Did you ever think of the very simple notion that the infant cries when he first comes into this world and later he weeps and sobs for milk and whines and grins and smiles and laughs when he is pleased? Think of all these small notions of perception and ruminate. Who taught them all that? Why doesn't a child born in different communities and regions behave differently? Why all the same? O man! If ever you had the sapience in lore, you must have perceived the order of the Lord Almighty, Who is to organize all these things in the proper mode of discipline, as these are all deeply insinuated in the brain like the discernment of morality and evil.

If to hurt and harm is agonizing in form
To appease and assuage lure in charm
Similar citation holds good to be told
For applaud and esteem in hex and scold

Likewise:

Clemency and compassion in crush to allure
Besides soothe and solace in stress to secure
For sickness, there's a conclusion to cure

For each smite in hurt, there's a salve in balm
For each nadir in alarm, there's glory in swarm
For each cyclone in storm, there's an appease in calm

For each draught in dried, there's drizzle in fray
For each prick in pain, there's peace in play

For each frizzy in fray, there's favor to aside
For each torment in taunt, there's bliss in obey

All these in terms of intelligence are deeply ingrained and insinuated in our minds or in the veer of our core. So for the term of the vale, we are supposed to abide by the discipline for what we have been apprised to affirm according to the bestowal of nature. We are ordained to determine in our consciousness the veracity of intelligence as a factual offering of His Almighty for us to concern in each time to discern for the ultimate course of our conduct in this vale—for what we are created hither in trail.

Fate and Fortune

This is one of the most instricate problems of religion. For if you look into the traditional arguments about this dilemma, you may find them contradictory; such is the case with arguments of reason. The apparent variance in the reasons of the first kind is found in the Holy Scripture.

I would like to put it in the simplest words. *Fate* is destined through the genetic array, whereas the bliss of *fortune* bears the fruit of intelligence, a bestowal of the Lord Almighty when He designed the genetic proscenium of Adam and Eve.

It must be pointed out that the difference between past fate and fortune with reference to destiny is very misleadingly expressed by the common remark that we can change the future but not the past. It is true that we can shape the future, and we cannot disturb the past. We cannot, however, change the future, for the future is what it will be. If I decide to take the left-hand fork in a road instead of the right-hand one, I have not changed the future, for in this case, the future is my going left. To talk of changing the future is indeed to relapse into the error of talking of events changing and of the notion of passage.

The Ruling Faculty

Before getting on this subject, you must have in your mind that the universe is not created for you, but you are a part of the whole to meet its providence, even though the universe is created for you to cherish its philosophy as a whole. So while having this thing in mind, when you turn to deliberate on the mutilation of misery and agony in alarm, you must be thankful to the Almighty that he created you to partake in the process of His generation to meet its requirements for the cause and purpose of the whole, because your sufferings and sorrow in distress cannot change your destiny, which is determined in any case, if it is so ordained for you to hold as a part of the whole. But when you blissfully submit to His dictum for the amelioration of the whole, you will enjoy a different kind of sensation, because in that case, you will be part of His discipline assigned for the cause of the whole.

When it is said that the nature of the universe prescribed to this man disease or mutilation or loss or anything else of the kind that happens to or suits the man, that is fixed in a manner for him suitably to the destiny of the whole. For this is what we mean when we say that things are suitable to us, as the workmen say of squared stones in walls or the pyramids, that they are suitable, when they fit them to one another in some kind of connection. For there is altogether one concord in accord, and the universe is made up out of all bodies to be such a domain in order and accord of the whole.

And even those who are completely ignorant understand what it actually means, as in necessity destiny brought this to such a person. This was brought, and this was prescribed to him. Now let us then perceive these things, as well as those which Almighty ordains in like manner. Many, as a matter of course, even among the prescriptions, are disagreeable, but we accept them in the benevolent hope of providence or the benevolent life. Let the perfect accomplishment of the things, which the common nature judges to be good, be judged by yourself to be of the same kind as your health. And so accept everything that happens, even if it seems disagreeable, because it leads to the destiny of the universe and to the preference of the cosmic order. For the man alone would not be useful for the whole but is useful through his acts for the whole. Neither does the nature of anything, whatever it may be, cause anything, which is not suitable to that which is directed by it.

For two reasons then, it is right to be content with what happens to you: one, because it was determined for you, prescribed for you, in a manner had preference to you, and was originally spun with your destiny; and the other, because even that which comes naturally to every man is from the power, which administers the universe, a cause of felicity and perfection, not even of its very continuance. For the integrity of the whole is distorted and deformed, if you cut off anything whatever from the conjunction and the continuity either of the parts or of the causes.

Don't be disgusted, discouraged, or dissatisfied, if you do not achieve doing everything according to right principles. But when you have failed, turn back again and be content with the greater part of what you have failed; try again, and be comfortable if the greater part of your doing is consistent with man's nature and love this to which you return. Return to the precept as if it was a principle of providence. And act like those who have sore eyes and apply a bit of water by sponge. For thus, you will not fail to obey reason and you will repose in it. And remember that philosophy requires only the things that your nature requires, but you would have something else, which is not according to the precept of the principal. It may be objected, why, what is more agreeable than this that I'm destined to do? But is not this the very reason why preference in purpose beguiles and betrays us? And consider if the boon and benevolence, dedication and deliverance, distinctness and devotion, calmness and composure are not more amiable and abounding. For what is more agreeable than intelligence itself, when you think of the security and the happy course of all things, which depend on the faculty of understanding and knowledge?

The Order of Discernment

Human sovereignty in decision making is, nevertheless, appropriate in the sense that it is somewhat perfect. Man is the a priori choice; obviously, the discernment is not contravened. It is taken into attention only as an appearance of choice; man is choice and in his choice is discernment. When something goes wrong with the choice, discernment is also contorted. Therefore, the heavenly interference is imperative, the sacrament with sincere beseeching and the meditation.

Certainly, there can be an element of a right decision while taking a wrong course in conduct, when estranged in the whirlwind events of misery and misfortune, so the discernment is assimilated with confusion and chaos. So the sacrament needs an escort by the providence, being nihility in itself. It demands the guidance of the soul. But in any case, we must not lose sight of what discernment is in itself, nor give credence that a work composed of a stupid mistake or bungle could be the outcome of hearty or even better discernment. Discernment under events of stress constitutes a temperament of trustworthiness. The accomplished innocence of discernment cannot be really attributed to negligence or doubt.

All this is the imperative part of the agile brainy competence to discern and perceive to whom these convictions and preferences give eminence. What is death? And the fact is, if a man looks at it in itself and by the distillation capability of contemplation and deliberates into the details of bouncing back from this diverging world, he can perceive the truth behind the wall of ignorance. All the things that present themselves to the imagination in it, he will then consider to be nothing else than an operation of His Almighty. This, however, is not only an operation of nature, but it is also a thing, which conduces to the purposes of nature. To observe how man comes near to the deity and what part of man is so willing to abide by His discipline.

If you seek reality, you will not look for the purchase of success by every possible means, and when you have found precision, you need not shy away or succumb to the events for fear of being crushed.

What frivolous talk is this?

How can I any longer set assertion to the right standard of conduct in faith, if I am not content with being what I am but am keyed up about what I am assumed to be?

I should be very clear in my mind of all my aims and objects in life, for only then am I sure to treasure and appreciate the fruit of fortune not only in this world but also in the Hereafter.

His Almighty has made all things in the world, nay, the world itself. No other living being is accomplished of comprehending His administration thereof. But the reasonable being, man, possesses endowments for the deliberation of all these things—not only that he himself is a part, but what part he is and how it meets that the part should give place to the whole.

A man should have an object or purpose in life, that he may direct all his energies to it; of course, a good object. He, who has not one object or purpose of life, cannot be one and the same all through his life and sincere to himself, not to mention the whole.

The Holy Scriptures have words to the same effect.

What you aver and avow *to aside*
That "We" didn't create you *in pace*
With a definite discipline *to abide*
And to Us,
You're not determined to restore *in place* (Al Noor 24:115)

The fundamental principle is to know the condition of one's own mind. If a man perceives that this is in a feeble condition, he will not then want to apply it to dispute the finest moment. As it is, men who are not fit to swallow even a morsel buy whole treatises and try to devour them. Accordingly, they either vomit them out again or suffer from indigestion with gripping and diarrhea, whereas they should have stopped to consider their capacity.

Such are the impressions of the few of whom I speak. And further, they apply themselves solely considering and examining the great assembly before they depart. Well, they are sneered and jeered at by the flock in abundance. So are the onlookers by the traders. Aye, and if the beasts had any sense, they would deride those who didn't think of anything but fodder.

There are many verses of the Holy Qur'an, which by their universal nature, teach that all the things are predestined. That's the genetic proscenium for which the man is constrained to stay under certain preordained environments, where he is determined to perform certain duties. Then there are verses that say that man is free in his acts and not fettered or impelled in accomplishing them. That's the true discernment of intelligence for what we're supposed to abide discipline in this vale, and it is this part of the bestowal of the Almighty we will be accountable for to His order of dictum in dictate for our deeds and doings in this vale.

The philosophy of life with its conduct in course is indicated to some reasonable extent in the foregoing pages. But what really has perplexed quite a few around us is that a body of the messages from the Holy Qur'an turn us to a state of bewilderment regarding preordained or predetermined conduct in different propensities of life and our choice to perform certain duties.

> *O Lord!*
> **Where from I came hither in vale**
> What I'm destined to do in dale
> And where to abide hereafter in trail
>
> Yesterday, I was in mother's womb in around
> Today, I'm hither with air comb in surround
> And then I'll be abiding dirt tomb in ground
> *O Lord!*
> I'm weary of the shimmer and glimmer of vale
> With all the worldly pursuance in trail
>
> How'd I cherish the swing in abide
> When veer of core is stunned in stride
>
> I intend to elude and drift far away
> From the bang of brittle world in stray
>
> And look for a nook here in surround
> Where to cherish "Your" bliss in abound
>
> A lore in adore, a sooth in assuage
> An ease in appease a lure in profuse
> A comfort in calm no concern in confuse
> *We!*
> Beg and beseech "Thee O Lord" in pray
> For a while of appease hither in fray
> Here in abide, Your Dictum to aside
> And entreat so earnest, all terms in stride
>
> Conform to comply and submit in pace
> And Your Benediction affirm to brace

I would like to refer to such discrepancies. There are actually not the inconsistencies often seen in the text. If carefully perceived, there is hardly any vacillation in the text. There are certain attributes one has to resort to as a part of the whole as determined in the genetic array. For if everyone was to secure a social, moral, intellectual, and physical status of the same order, then life would not be possible to abide. So our genetic code sets certain preordained trends over which we don't have much control, but our intelligence leaves us free in our choice of what's preferable in our performance in the process and passage of life.

The following verses tell us that all things are by compulsion and are predestined:

Say:
Surely all worn and torn *in stray*
And the hence and whence will come to stay (56:49)

He discerns hidden in the veer of core
As He is Astral O August immense in lore (13:9)

In the land *in toll,*
No dole and blow can break *to befall*
Or in the veer of your core in call
It's put to scroll as a proof in sort
With the dictum of Lord
Who's to bring it to call *in lore*
For it's quite easy for Lord *in score* (57:22)

In all these statements, His Almighty has asserted and affirmed His rule of law but didn't avow that He wouldn't change His order in proclamation whenever He would cherish to do so, for He is Lord of all the domains and to Him belong all the rule and edit.

Now, as to the verses, which say that man can acquire deeds by free will and that things are only possible and not necessary, the following may be quoted:

If He may so desire *in aback*
He can let the winds stop *in slack*
Letting the ships still and stable *in sea*
Indeed!
These are the signs for all *to perceive*
That's for all to discern
Who're sober and satisfying *in concern* (42:33)

Or He, cause them to perish *in pace*
For evil of their trends *in place*
But Lord!
Most Noble and Merciful *to brace* (42:34)

Let them concern to discern *in stride*
Who bicker and brawl Our Notation *in abide*
There's no way to elude Our term *in strike* (42:35)

Bestowal of Our ease and appease *hither in vale*
It's but a bit of slit *to avail*
But that's with Lord in trail
That's enduring *in pace*
It's for the men and clan of faith *in grace*
Who trust in Lord and comply *in place* (42:36)

And The Day, they'll get to "Me" *in stay*
They'd be asked with their duo *in stray*
 Poise in stance with your duo *in stance*
And trend to asunder the veil *in glance*
And the duo would then trend *in swift*
Saying:
 It's not us you beseeched *in thrift* (10:28)

O you the men and clan of faith *in stay*
Observe your onus and trust for Lord *to obey*
And concede what crumbs and refuse left *in stray*
If you're true blessed in tine and turn *to obey* (2:278)

A delirious gust in gale *held in throng*
From Lord of Might thither in swarm

For quite a few days, an affliction *in blight*
There's commotion and confusion in sight
They'd to taste crushing anguish *in plight*

But disgrace of Hereafter is more *in strife*
And wouldn't have ease and appease *in slight* (41:16)

Sometimes, an apparent contradiction appears in a single verse of the Qur'an. For instance:

It's for beneficence of Lord *in Grace*
That you're so kind to the clan *in pace*

For if you're grim or hoary at core *in treat*
They would've drifted *hither in impeach*

So dip and flip their failing and flaws *in stray*
And beg extenuation of Lord (for them) *in pray*

And confer their notion *in term*
Then once you determine *to discern*
Place your trust in Lord *in concern*

And then to beg *to entreat*
For Lord Ardors in adore one *in treat*
Who abide in faith and trend *to beseech* (3:159)

If Lord ease you in all course *of conduct*
None can stun and subdue or trend *to infract*

If He deserts and drop in term *to elude*
Who's there, then *to assuage*

O you the men of faith *in grace*
Talent in trust of Lord, His bliss *to brace* (3:160)

O man!
All good are from Lord *to stay*
And the ills are your earn *in astray*
Messenger is to steer a way *in instruct*
And Lord discerns all *in conduct* (4:79)

"O Lord!
Give us Phenomenal in this vale *to appease*
And of the excellent in Hereafter *O Please*
And save us from anguish of pyre *in impeach*" (2:201)

They don't trend to "Compliance" *in core*
But once they leave thy accomplice *in lore*

A band and body of them *in slight*
Plan and ponder all through the night
On words so deviant you tell so bright

But Lord concerns all they do *and discern*
All through the night
What they really concern

So be at a pace and space of them *in abide*
And have your trust of Lord *in stride*
Lord is to sway and settle *in glides* (4:81)

It's not for a soul *in sway*
To turn and trend to obey
Until for Lord Consent *to aside*
Lord has His Own ways *in stride*
And throws smudge *in scale*
Who don't have the sense to *avail* (10:100)

So if at all there is some confusion in the text, it can be easily resolved if we think in terms of our choice in certain attributes through the wit of our intelligence. The bestowal of intelligence is from the Almighty ever since the creation of man. And man has to perceive through the core of his intelligence for the best in escort and not let the boat of life sway in the surge of the stream and float the way as directed by the current. The environmental hazards may deter us and not let us have a free choice to swim against the current. So to cherish the discipline of life, one has to observe and abide by the true guidance from the sane ambience of intelligence, a bestowal of the Lord Almighty for us to cherish His Bliss in all our means and manners in this vale.

It is here we entreat and beseech His Almighty for His true guidance in all our trends during each prayer in each stance of "Qaẏaam" five times a day.

We adjure and implore ("Thee") humble *in accord*
And we beg and beseech ("Thee") fervent *in assort*

Guide us in the seemly site *and spot*
With scent and spoor of the suited *in slot*

Have us the discipline of (Your) adorable *in trail*
And not of the deplorable with depravity *in dale*   (Al Fatihah*)*

And after each prayer, we invariably plead to the Almighty:

O Lord! Portion us with your Profusion hither in vale

For if this earthy life is not in True Discipline how and why one
could cherish the fruit of Hereafter.

And there're men and clan who beg *to beseech*
Our Lord!
Give us Phenomenal in here *to appease*
And of the excellent in the Hereafter *O Please*
And save us from anguish of pyre *in treat* (2:201)

So His Almighty Himself asserts that you can change your destiny with
the true abidance of discipline in each mannerism of your life with firm
determination.
Similarly, at another instance, we beg His reprieve and help:

For,
Lord has never changed the *destiny in plight*
Of the men and clan, hither in slight
Who're determined to course and conduct in blight

For all your done and doings in vale
Trend to your deeds and proceeds in trail

Indeed!
If you incline to cherish His boons in sway
Then assert and affirm His dictum to obey

So,
Exalt in stance your "Self" in glow
That,
Lord may trend Hereafter to endow

O Man, demand!
What you wince hither in trance
Charming and enchanting lures in glance

For all your done and doings in relate
Affirmed and conformed "My" dictum in dictate

We,
Assert to affirm His bounty in adore
For He's all to endow in lore

Because we entreat Lord Almighty:

Please O Lord!
We beg and beseech Your Mercy to brace
Condone us in compliant and complacent grace
Don't put to a test in trail as hither in fore

O Lord!
And don't put us in doubt dubious in score
For what we cannot bear a bit to endure
Be congenial and convivial and extenuate for sure
In a while of drift, we beg to pray
And trend to You humble in pray
O Lord!
Be Genial and Generous for sure *in trail*
For You're (our) Lord *Gleaming in grace*
So elevate our term in stance
With a sway to stay over incredulous race (2:285)

Over and above, we seek His help in all courses and conduct here in this world for the veracity in each term of our endowments from His Almighty.

Now turn to the text of the Holy Scripture with minds open to perceive the true nature of the discipline ordained by His Almighty for the conduct in course and affirmation in advice. It is basically from the endowment of the genetic code on one hand, and on the other, it is based on the guidance of intelligence; they are closely related to each other.

So when the Lord Almighty refers to certain affirmations, He leaves it to the cognizance of the person to affirm the real course of conduct in different spheres of his deeds and doings.

Even a leaf cannot move without His discretion. Perhaps all the believers of monotheistic religions trust it is so. But when the Prophet ^{PBUH} was tortured and tormented, how could we account that the Lord Almighty kept aside and did not intervene at those moments of torture and tribulation? He could do so—but there is a role for the conduct of intelligence to steer one out of the difficult moments of life with patience, perseverance, and persistence, so leaving a message for the followers to adopt a way of truth in the escort of intelligence. So the Lord Almighty has laid definite rules and regulations for nature to have its course, but definitely when in need of guidance, for men seeking His escort, there is an absolute way to tread in truth.

You can really change the destiny that's inscribed for you. As some people assert, the lines in the palm indicate the fate and fortune of a person. We wonder if the lines in the palm can be changed.

Indeed! These lines cannot be changed.

After burning, if a skin transplant were made on the hand, it would trend to the original design of the lines in the palm. Similarly, many criminals have tried in vain to have a skin transplant to change their fingerprints.

But nay!

These lines can be changed with firm conviction and determination.

I can assure you that you can even change the lines in your hand and your destiny with firm conviction and a determined attitude with His Almighty's blessings, for factually, the Lord Almighty is the fate and fortune of all disciplines.

Why do I contend that? Simply because I have had a personal experience twice in my life.

Once, in 1973, my career line was shattered and scattered when I was forced to join the armed forces. But with a determined attitude and regular prayers, it was all resolved.

Similarly, at another time, in early 2003, there was lot of turbulence and turmoil in my life, and it was a real test and trial of my fortitude and perseverance, to determine if I could really sustain all the trials and tribulations in His way. I stood firm with persistence in patience and perseverance with prayers and begged His Almighty's exoneration for all uneventful slips in the eventualities of my life. When I secured the hatred of my near and dear ones, besides friends and associates, His Almighty endowed me with His premium affection. And the lines were restored once again, and I was blessed with His injunction and inclination and guidance in writing this most benevolent manuscript.

So as His Almighty asserts that He has commanded your destiny, that's correct:

For Lord has never changed the destiny in plight
Of the men and clan hither in slight
Who're determined not to amend in trace
Of their repulsive practice in pace *

And when He asserts that the destiny is in your own hands, it is also correct:

Exalt in stance your self in glow
That, Lord may trend to you in endow
O man!
Come and demand hither in stance
What you perceive around in glance
For all your done and doings in relate
Affirmed and conformed "My" dictum in dictate *

For the worst, if you don't turn to Him, you'll endure the evil in fortune. But if you turn to His Almighty, Who in reality is the fate and fortune of all, He can endow His bliss for your ills and evils henceforth secured, in a most blissful allure.

As Muslims, we assert that the Lord Almighty determines the time and place of death, but how to reach the destiny is definitely in our hands.

For the Lord Almighty has ordained a discipline of life as to how to lead a numinous life with good health or turn to an outlandish life in ill health with evil notions.

Fortune in Discipline

One man, when he has done a service for another, is ready to set it down to his account as a favor conferred. Another is not ready to do this, but still in his own mind, he thinks of the man as his debtor and knows what he has done. A third in a manner does not even know what he has done but is like a vine, which has produced grapes and seeks for nothing more after it has once produced its proper fruit. As a bee when it has made honey, so a man when he has done a good act does not call out for others to come and see but goes on to another act, as a vine goes on to produce again the grapes in season. So must the man be one of these, who in a manner acts thus without observing it? Yes, but this very thing is necessary, the

* Allama Iqbal, poet laureate of the east

observation of what a man is doing, for it may be said, it is characteristic of
the social animal to perceive that he is working in a social manner and indeed
to wish that his social partner also should perceive it.

But if a man has first conceived as good the things which appear to the
many to be good, he will listen and readily receive them as very applicable;
thus, even the many perceive the difference. For were it not so, this saying
would not offend and would not be rejected in the first case, while we receive it
when it is said fitly and wittily of wealth and of the means with further luxury
and fame. Go on then and ask if we should value and think those things to
be good, to which after their first bethinking in the mind the words of deceit
might be aptly applied—that he who has them, through pure abundance,
has not a place to ease himself in this vale, as very correctly mentioned in the
Qur'an: "And know that your possessions and your children are a test and
trial and with Allah is immense reward" (08:28)

Nothing happens to any man, which he is not formed by nature to bear
(2:283). The same things may happen to another, and either because he does
not see that they have happened or because he would show his great spirit, he
is firm and determined.

Often think of the rapidity with which things pass by and disappear.
For substance is like a river in continual flow, and the activities of things are
in constant change and the causes of work in infinite varieties. And there
is hardly anything that stands still. And consider all this, which is near to
you, this illimitable abyss of the past and of the future in which all things
disappear. How is it then that he doesn't dolt and dunce when he is puffed up
with such things or plagued about them or has made himself miserable? For
they vex him only for a very short time.

Think of the universal substance, of which you have a very small portion,
and of universal time, of which a short and indivisible interval has been
assigned to you, and of that which is fixed by destiny. And how small a part
of it you are here to cherish the lures of the lust of this worldly life.

What you elude and evade yourself attempt not to impose on others.
You shun treachery—beware of tormenting others! If you can bear to do
that, one would think you had once been sinuous and snaky yourself. For
lechery and licentiousness and blemish and debauchery have nothing in
common with temperance and prudence, probity and integrity, or the
gratification of contentment and comfort with the best of competence and
other endowments.

In conception, it is easy to convince an ignorant person; in actual life, men
not only dispute to offer themselves to be persuaded but hate the man who
has talked them into something. We should never lead a life not subjected to
examination or extermination. Are you compelled through being defectively

furnished by nature to murmur and to be stingy and to flatter and to find fault with your poor body and to try to please men and to make great display and to be restless in your mind? No, by the Almighty, you might have been delivered from these things long ago. Only if in truth you can be charged with being rather slow and dull of comprehension, you must exert yourself about this also, not neglecting it nor yet taking pleasure in your dowdiness.

I am composed of the formal being and the material, and neither of them will perish into nonexistence, as neither of them came into existence out of nonexistence. All parts of me then will be reduced by change into some part of the universe, and that again will change into another part and peel of the universe and so on forever. And by consequence of such a change, I too exist, and those who begot me forever in the other direction. For nothing hinders us from saying so, even if the universe is administered according to distinct terms of circumvolution and thence we shall be brought back to life by putting the divine part of the efflux back into the material being, the dust and crust of our remains.

Reason and rationalizing are philosophical discernment that have powers, which are sufficient for themselves and for their own works. They move then from a first principle, which is their own, and they make their way to the end, which is proposed to them. This is the reason why such acts are named sane or suitable acts, which signifies that they proceed by the whim in stride.

None of the things ought to be called a possession of the man, which do not belong to a man as man, nor does man's nature promise them, nor are they the means of man's nature attaining its end. Neither does the end of man lie in these things, nor yet that which aids to the accomplishment of this end, and that which aids toward this end is that which is good. Besides, if any of these things did belong to the man, it would not be right for a man to despise them and to set himself against them; nor would a man be worthy of praise, who showed that he did not want these things, nor would he be stinted himself in any of them as good, if indeed these things were good.

Let the core of your soul which leads and governs be undisturbed by the movements in the flesh, whether of pleasure or of pain, and let it not unite with them, but let it circumscribe itself and limit those effects in pursuance of discipline. But when these effects rise up to the mind by virtue of that other sympathy that naturally exists in a body which is all one, then you must not strive to resist the sensation, for it is natural, but let not the ruling faculty for itself add to the sensation the opinion that it is either good or bad.

When you wish to cherish the lure of lust yourself then contemplate the probity and prudence of those who live with you, for instance, the liveliness of one, the decency of another, the benevolence of a third, and some other virtuous quality of a fourth. For nothing fascinates so much as the examples of temperance when they are clear in the principles of those who live with us and present themselves in munificence and affluence, as far as is possible. Therefore, we must keep them before us.

To the jaundiced, honey tastes bitter, and to those bitten by mad dogs, water causes fear. To little children, the ball is a fine thing. Why be incensed? Do you think that a deceptive and specious conception has less power than the bile in the jaundiced or the poison in him who is bitten by a mad dog?

So then, the hindrance to the intelligence is an evil to the intelligent nature. Apply all these for yourself in the discernment of logic. The senses will look to that. Has any obstacle opposed you in your effort toward an object? If indeed you were making this effort absolutely unconditionally or without any reservation, certainly this obstacle is an evil to you who are considered a rational animal. But if you take into consideration the usual course of things, you have not yet been injured nor even impeded. The things, which are proper to the understanding no other man can obstruct, for neither fire nor abuse touches it in any way. When it has been made a sphere, it continues a sphere.

Take me and cast me where you will; for there, I shall keep my divine dictum in tranquil humility, that is, contentment. I can feel and act conformably to its proper constitution, and isn't this change of place sufficient reason that my soul should be unhappy and worse than it was, depressed, expanded, shrinking, and affrighted?

Nothing can happen to any man that is not human in antecedent nor to an ox that is not according to the nature of an ox, nor to a venery, which is not according to the nature of venery, nor to a stone, which is not proper to a stone. If then there happens to each thing both what is usual and natural, why should you complain? The common nature of the environment brings nothing which may not be borne by you (2: 284–286).

What then can these things do to prevent your mind from remaining pure, wise, sober, and just? For instance, if a man should stand by a crystal-clear pure spring and curse it, the spring never ceases sending up potable water, and if he should cast clay into it or filth, it will speedily disperse them and wash them out and will not be at all polluted. How then shall you possess a perpetual fountain and not a mere well, your fountain of intelligence by taming you clearly free for holding discipline with contentment, simplicity, and modesty?

Do you wish to be praised by a man who curses himself thrice every hour? Would you wish to please a man who does not please himself? Does a man please himself who repents of nearly everything that he does?

No longer let your breathing only act in concert with the air that surrounds you, but let your intelligence also now be in harmony with the real discernment, which embraces all things. For the intelligence is not less diffused in all things for him who is willing to draw it for him, besides the air during respiration for him to breathe?

Endowment of Discipline

I shall go through the things, which happen according to nature until I fall to rest, breathing out my breath into that element out of which I daily draw it in and falling upon that earth out of which my father collected the seed and my mother the blood and my nurse the milk, out of which during so many years, I have been supplied with food and drink, which bears me when I walk on it and abuse it for so many purposes.

You say men cannot admire the sharpness of His deliberation. Be it so, but there are many other things of which you cannot say I am not formed for them by nature. Show those qualities then which are altogether in your power: sincerity, humility, endurance of labor, aversion to lusty pleasure, contentment with your portion and with few things, benevolence, frankness, no love of superfluity, and freedom from trifling magnanimity.

> Why to incline for a dignity in pace
> That's to thrive only a while in trace

Don't you see how many qualities you are immediately able to exhibit, in which there is no excuse of natural incompetence and feebleness, and yet you still endure at your own discretion below the mark? Because you willfully and resolutely, consciously and determinedly miss so many promptings and possibilities, inducements and opportunities at so many stances and spots for so many possible fortuities fated to change your future and finality.

One asks how a man might eat acceptably to the Lord.

If when he eats, he can be just, cheerful, equable, temperate, and orderly, can he not thus eat acceptably to the Lord?

But when you call for hot water, and your servant does not answer or when he answers brings it warm or is not even found to be in the house at all, then don't be vexed or burst with anger. Isn't that acceptable to the Lord?

But how can one endure such people?

But I pay a price for them, not they for me.

Will you not endure your own brother, who has followed his forefather, even as a son sprung from the same stock and of the same high descent as yourself? And if you are stationed in a high position, are you forthwith going to instigate treachery and torment others for no reason? Remember who you are, and whom you rule, that they are by nature your kinsmen, your brothers, the most benevolent creation of the Almighty.

Do you see which way you are looking—down to the earth, to the pit and the laws ordained by the dead? But to the laws of the Lord you do not look. You were both brought from the dust, and you both ultimately become a part of the dust in demise for the discipline of the whole; otherwise, this world wouldn't have been a place to live.

When one took counsel of a philosopher, saying, "What I seek is this. Even so, my younger brother is not reconciled to me, and I may still remain as nature would have me to be."

All great things are slow of growth; nay, this is true even of a grape or of a fig. If then you say to me now, "I desire a fig," I shall answer, "And it needs time. Wait till it first flowers, then casts its blossom, then ripens." The fruit of the fig tree does not reach maturity suddenly.

Do you desire so quickly to reap the fruit of the mind of a man?

Imagine the human creation in this context.

Not exactly, expect it not.

As though the discipline of faith ordains that you abide by nature and learn from whatever source you can to nurture the intelligence that may have its uncontrived course to accomplish the full discernment of vigilance.

Will: A power of determination

Affective responses to the universal objects of understanding are functions of "intellectual perception" and are considered quite different from sensory perception as this area of volition is the special power involved in the preference of will.

We distinguish two kinds of volitional functions.

First, there are those basic and natural tendencies of approval and affective approach to an object that is judged good or desirable without qualification. In regard to justice, peace, or a perfectly good being, for instance, personal "desire" would be naturally and necessarily attracted to such objects. This natural movement of the will is not free without the trends in the core of intelligence.

Second, there are volitional movements toward or away from intellectually known objects that are judged as partly desirable or partly undesirable. Such movements of will are directed by intellectual judgments evaluating the objects. In this case, volition is said to be deliberated and specified by intellectual considerations and free will. It is in the act of decision that man is free. Talking about free will, the term *Libra voluntas* is a nontechnical usage, rather, than free choice or decision, *liberum arbitrium*. Man, by virtue of his intellectual powers, is free in some of his actions.

Intelligence and Reason

Reason produces fruit both for all and for itself, and from it, other things are produced. There are other things of the same kind as reason itself.

Among the animals, which have no reason, one position and prevarication is distributed, but among reasonable animals, like us, one intelligent soul is distributed, just as there is one earth of all things, which are of an earthly nature, and we see by one light and breathe one air, all of us that have the faculty of vision and all that have life, a divine endowment of efflux.

All things that participate in anything that is common to them all, move toward that which is of the same kind with them. Everything that is earthly turns toward the earth, everything that is liquid flows together, and everything that is of an aerial kind does the same, so that they require something to keep them asunder and the application of force. Fire indeed moves upward on account of the elemental fire, which is here, that even every substance, which is somewhat dry, is easily ignited, because there is less mingled with it of that which is a hindrance to ignition. Accordingly, then, everything that participates in the commonweal of the nature moves in like manner toward that which is of the same kind with itself or moves even more. For so much as it is superior in comparison with all other things, in the same degree, it is also more ready to mingle with and to be fused with that which is akin to it. Accordingly, among animals devoid of reason, we find swarms of bees and herds of cattle and the nurture of young birds, and in a manner, even in animals, there are souls and that power which brings them together is seen to exert itself in the superior degree and in such a way that you never have observed in plants or in stones or in trees. But in rational animals, there are civic communities with mutual love and respect, races and relations, connections and confrontations of communities in combat and concord, truces and treaties of peace.

But in the things, which are still superior, even though they are separated from one another, unity in a manner exists, as in the cosmic order. Thus the ascent to the higher degree is able to produce sympathy even in things that are separated. See then what now takes place. Only intelligent men have now forgotten this mutual desire and inclination, and in them alone, the property of flowing together is not seen. But still, though men strive to avoid this union, they are caught and held by it, for their nature is too strong for them, and you will see what I say, if you only observe. Soon then, will one find anything earthly, which comes in contact with no other earthly thing than a man altogether separated from other men?

If you are able, correct by teaching those who do wrong, but if you cannot, remember that tolerance is given to you for this purpose. And the Lord, too, is tolerant to such persons, and for some purposes, He even helps them to get health, wealth, and reputation, so benevolent He is. And it is in your power also to say who hinders you.

Labor not as one who is wretched, nor yet as one who would be pitied or admired, but direct your will to one thing only, to put yourself in motion and to check yourself, as the natural objective obligated as ordained in the discipline of faith. For a stone, which has been thrown up, it is no evil to come down, nor indeed any good to have been carried up.

All things are changing, and you yourself are in continuous mutation and in an appearance and aspect of incessant desolation and the whole universe too. It is your duty to leave another man's wrongful act there, where it is, and not to abide his depraved act but abide the divine benevolence.

Hasten to examine your own ruling faculty, the real discernment and that of the universe and that of your neighbor, your own that you may make it just and that of the universe that you may remember of what you are a part and that of your neighbor that you may know whether he has acted ignorantly or with knowledge and that you may also consider that his ruling faculty is akin to yours as designed and determined by faith.

As you are a component part of a social system, so let every act of yours stay in discipline as a component peel and part of conduct in the vale. Whatever act of yours then has no reference, either immediately or remotely, to a social end; this tears asunder your life and does not allow it to be one. It is of the nature of a mutiny, just as when in a popular assembly, a man acting by himself stands apart from the general agreement.

You have endured infinitely, though not being contented with your ruling faculty of intelligence, when it does the things which it is constituted by nature to do. But that's enough of this. When another blames you or hates you or when men say about you anything injurious, approach their poor souls, penetrate within, and see what kind of men they are. You will discover that there is no reason to take any trouble that these men may have this or that opinion about you. However, you must be well disposed toward them, for by nature, they are friends. And the Lord too aids them in all ways, by dreams, by signs, toward the attainment of those things on which they set a value.

The periodic movements of the universe are the same, up and down from ages. And either the universal intelligence puts itself in motion for every separate effect, and if this is so, be you content with that which is the result of its activity, or it puts itself in motion once and everything else comes by way of sequence in a manner or indivisible elements as these are the origin of all things. In a word, there is a discipline of intelligence that controls all cosmic promenades in faith as ordained in the Qur'an in confirmation to the demand of His Almighty Lord.

The universal cause is like a tornado or a torrent; it carries everything along with it. But how worthless are all these poor people who are engaged in matters so fickle and fake, trivial in trace, not really to be perusable in place with no dignity or grace. Well then, man does what his nature requires. Set yourself in motion, if it is in your power, and do not look about you to see if anyone will observe it, but be content if the smallest thing goes on well, and consider such an event to be no small matter. For who can change men's opinions? And without a change of opinions, what else is there than the slavery of men who groan while they pretend to obey? Simple and modest is the work of philosophy. Draw me not aslant and apart to impudence and insolence.

Look down from above on the countless herds of men and see their countless solemnities, the infinitely varied sailing in storms and calms, and the differences among those who are born in arms, live in swarms, and die in alarm. And consider, too, the lives lived by others in olden times and the lives of those who will live after you and the lives now lived among barbarous nations. And consider how many know not even your name, how many will soon forget it, and how they who perhaps now are praising you will very soon blame you and that neither a posthumous name is of any value, nor reputation, nor anything else, but only the good deeds you leave behind for the cause of humanity, whether in the discipline of faith, education, health, or any benevolent mission.

You can remove out of the way many useless things among those which disturb you, for they lie entirely in your opinion, and you will then gain for yourself ample space by comprehending the whole universe in your mind. And by contemplating the eternity of time and observing the rapid change of everything, you will see how trivial is the time from birth to dissolution and the illimitable time before birth as well as an equally boundless time after dissolution.

Loss is nothing else than a change. But the universal nature delights in change and in obedience in that all things have now done well and from eternity have been observing in like form and will be such to the time without end. What then do you say? That all things have been and all things always will be bad and that no power has ever been found in so many worldly things, for the Lord to rectify these things, but the world has been condemned to be bound in never-ceasing change?

If any man has done wrong, the harm is his own. But perhaps he has not done wrong. All things fall down to settle to proceed from one intelligent source and come together as in one body, and the part ought not to find fault with what is done for the benefit of the whole, or there are only traces and nothing else than the muddle and clutter with dispersion. Why then you are disturbed? Say to the ruling faculty, "Are you dead? Are you corrupted? Are you playing the philosopher? Or if you have become a beast, do you herd and feed with the rest?"

You may thus pray, "How shall I become the most astute, not be scared to lose some of my ruling faculty?"

Whether astute or acute, trend in trust or demand, direct your invocation and imploration, adjuration and appealing only to the Almighty this way, and see what comes.

When you are vexed and perplexed with any man's arrant and audacious, brazen and blatant, insolent and immoral, sluttish and sinful course in conduct, instantly ask yourself, "Is it expedient then, that the unabashed men should not be in the world?" It is not conceivable. Do not then demand for what is not feasible and is unattainable. For this man is also one of those who are impudent and out-and-out, who must of karma or kismet for the destiny of the whole, be there, to conform the discipline. Let the same consequence and consideration be there and present in your mind in the case of the rogue and rascal, the deceitful and doubting, and of every man who acts erroneously and incongruously in any way. For, at the same time that you prompt yourself that it is not practicable that such a set and sort of men should not endure and subsist, you will go more benevolently apt and prone toward everyone individually.

It is quit essential and effective to discover and consider the probity and prudence of the nature given to man that is to combat and confront every illicit and illegal spin and stint. For nature has given to the man a course of correction against the dumb and daft and tolerance and tenderness against another kind of man enduring some other power. And in all cases, it is conceivable and expedient for you to amend and assert by educating the man who is gone adrift and astray; for every man, who is a gaffe or goof and fumbles and stumbles over His design in the plan, is gone astray and amiss, besides wherein have you been injured or impaired? For you will find that no one among those against whom you are irked or frustrated has done anything by which your mind could be made sad and sick, but that which is calamity and corrupt for you and invidious and injurious has its course only in the mind. And what damage and detriment is done or what is there alien and exotic if the man, who has not been enlightened and instructed, does the acts of an empty-headed man? Consider whether you should not rather accuse and ascribe to yourself, because you did not expect such a man to blunder and bewail in such a way. For you had ways and means with which to approach and instruct given to you by your core of discernment to infer and assume that it was likely that he would confide and consign this error, and yet you have lapsed from consciousness and are dazed and amazed that he has blundered and misjudged.

But most of all, when you rebuke a man as perfidious and preoccupied, turn to yourself, for the fault is manifestly your own, whether you did trust that man who had such a disposition and would not keep his promise or when conferring your complaisance, you did not confer it completely, nor yet in such a way as to have received from your very act all the profits and proceeds. For what more do you want when you have done a man some benevolent job to assist? Are you not content and comfortable that you have done something conformable to your nature, and do you cherish to allure the profits for it? How would you justify the eye that necessitated amends and rewards for seeing or the feet for walking? For as these members are formed for a distinctive design and direction and by working in conformity to their certain essence and aspect obtain what is their own, so also is man formed by nature to acts of benevolence; when he has done anything benevolent or in any other way conducive to the common interest, he has conformably accomplished to his constitution, and he gets what is his own.

Will you then be never good and simple and one of the pure, more manifest than the body that surrounds you? Will you never enjoy an affectionate and contented disposition? Will you never be full and without a want of any kind, longing for nothing more, nor desiring anything, either animate or inanimate, for the enjoyment of pleasures? Nor yet be desirous in time wherein you shall have longer enjoyment or place or pleasant climate or the society of men with whom you may live in harmony? But will you be satisfied with your present condition and pleased with all that is about you, and will you convince yourself that you have everything and that it comes from the Almighty, that everything is well for you and will be well whatever shall please Him and whatever He shall give for the conservation of the perfect living being, the good and just and beautiful, which generates and holds together all things and contains and embraces all things which are dissolved for the production of other like things? Will you never be such that you shall so dwell in community with Allah and men as neither to find fault with them at all, nor to be condemned by them?

Observe what your nature of intelligence concerns, so far as you are governed by nature only, then do it and accept it, if your nature, so far as you are a living being, shall not be made worse by it. And next, you must observe what your nature requires so far as you are a living being. And for all this, you may allow to yourself, if your nature, so far as you are a rational animal, shall not be made worse by it. But the rational animal is consequently also an affable and amiable animal. Use these rules then, and trouble yourself about nothing else, as when abiding the faith ordained by His Almighty your conformity to the discipline of life becomes so lucid and luminous that you no more strike on the illusions falling in delusions.

Whether the universe is a concourse of atoms or nature is a system, let this first be established, that I am part and peel of the whole, which is governed by nature; next, I am, in a manner, intimately related to parts that are of the same kind with myself. For remembering this, inasmuch as I am part, I shall be displeased with none of the things, that are assigned to me out of the whole; for nothing is harmful to the part, if it is for the convenience of the whole. For the whole contains nothing which is not for its fulfillment. Besides that, it cannot be forced even by any obvious objective to produce and procreate; it sows not the seeds of anything invidious or injurious to itself. By consecrating, then, being a peel and part of such as a whole, I shall be content with everything that happens to me. And inasmuch as I am in a manner intimately related to the parts that are of the same kind as myself, I shall do nothing that defies social norms, but I shall rather direct myself to the things that are of the same kind with myself, and I shall turn all my efforts to the common interest and divert them from the contrary. Now, if these things are done so, life must flow on happily, just as you may observe that the life of a citizen is happy, who continues a course of action that is advantageous to his fellow citizens and is content with whatever the moral obligation may assign to him.

The concern of the whole, everything, I mean, which is naturally comprehended in the universe, must of necessity perish, but let this be understood in this sense, that they must undergo a change. But if this were naturally both an evil and a necessity for the element of the soul, the whole would not continue to exist in a good condition. So are the flesh and soul being subject to change and constituted so as to perish in various ways. The dissolution of things is into those things of which each thing is composed. For there is either a dispersion of the elements out of which everything has been compounded or a change from the solid to the earthly and from the airy to the aerial, so that these parts are taken back into the universal reason, whether this at certain periods is consumed by time or renewed by eternal changes. And do not imagine that the solid and the airy part belong to you from the time of generation. For all this received its accretion only yesterday and the day before, as one may say, from the food that is ingested and the air that is inspired; where then are they doomed to depart? This then, which has perceived the growth, changes not that which your mother brought forth.

But suppose that your mother brought you forth very much with the other part, which has the peculiar quality of change. Is it nothing in fact in the way of objection to what is said: "Beware of the fib and foe that you may not perish in blow?"

When you have assumed these names, *righteous* and *reasonable*, *exact* and *authentic*, *sagacious* and *sensible*, *a man of equanimity and magnanimity*, take care you do not change these names, and if you should lose them, quickly return to them. And remember that the term *rational* was intended to signify a discriminating attention to several things; besides freedom from negligence and composure and calmness is the voluntary acceptance of the things that are assigned to you by the common nature. And remember that magnanimity is the elevation of the intelligent discernment above selfish desire over and atop of the pleasurable or painful sensations of the flesh and above that poor thing called fame so transitory in frame and all such things that have not to remain. If then you maintain yourself in the possession of these fortunes without desiring to be called by these names by others, you will be another person and will enter another life.

For to continue to be such as you have up to this time been and to be ripped into pieces and defiled in such a life is the character of an absurd man, overfond of his praise in this gust and gale. And these are the callow fighters with wild beasts, who, though covered with lesions and lacerations, gore and gash in slash still entreat to be kept to the following day, though they will be exposed in the same state to the same claws and bites. Therefore, fix yourself in the possession of these few names, and if you are able to abide in them, abide as if you were removed to certain islands of the extremity and blissful life. But if you shall perceive that you fall out of them and do not sustain your hold, go daring and dauntless into some cranny and compartment where you shall maintain them. And even if you depart at once from this vale, not in ardor and indignation, but with austerity and amiability, with decency and dignity, after doing this one meritorious thing at least in your life, it will be to have gone out with that thus acceptable to the Almighty.

In order, however, to remember these names, it will greatly help you if you remember the faith ordained by the Almighty that's the same discipline as decreed and determined in the Qur'an and that they wish not to be flattered, but wish all reasonable beings to be made alike in the faith ordained in the Scriptures.

Acquire a contemplative way of seeing how all things change into one another, and constantly attend to it. Exercise yourself about its nature of philosophy, for nothing is so much adapted to produce magnanimity. Such a man has put off the body, and as he sees that he must—no one knows how soon to go away from among men and leave everything here—he gives himself up entirely to just doing in all his actions and in everything else that happens and resigns himself to the universal nature. But as to what a man shall say or think about him or do against him, he never even thinks of it, being himself contented with these two things that act justly in what he now does, and he lays aside all distracting and busy pursuits and desires nothing else than to accomplish the straight course through the law and by accomplishing the straight course, to follow the discipline of faith.

What need is there of suspicious fear, since it is in your power to inquire what ought to be done? And if you see clearly, go by this way content, without turning back, but if you do not see clearly, stop and take the best advice. But if any other thing opposes you, go on according to your powers with due consideration, keeping to that which appears to be just. For it is best to reach this object, and if you do fail, let your failure be in attempting this. He who follows reason in all things is both tranquil and active and at the same time also cheerful and composed.

Ask yourself as soon as you wake from sleep, whether it will make any difference to you if someone does what is just and right or crosses you at each step. Will it make any difference to you? Even if it is so, you have no choice but to let the man have his preference, because you have no alternative but to reconcile to the situation.

You have not forgotten that those who assume arrogant airs in bestowing their praise or blame on others are such as they are at bed and board, and you have not forgotten what they do and what they avoid and what they pursue and how they steal and how they rob, not with hands and feet, but with their most valuable part, by means of which seemliness is produced, when a man chooses, fidelity, modesty, truth, law, and an exceptional happiness.

Constantly contemplate the whole of time for the whole of the substance, and consider that all individual things as substances are grains of a fig and as to the time the turning of a gimlet.

Consider what men are when they are eating, sleeping, generating, easing themselves, and so forth, and then what kind of men they are when they are imperious and arrogant or screaming and scolding from their elevated place. But a short time ago, how many were slaves of their lust for power and praise and for what things? And after a little time, consider in what a condition they will be with what the nature brings to each. And it is for its good at the time when nature brings it. The earth loves the shower, and the universe loves to make whatever is about to be. Either you live here and have already accustomed yourself to it, or you are going away and this was your own will, or you are dying and have discharged your duties. But besides these things, there is just nothing to endure for long.

111

What is my ruling faculty, the intelligence, now to me? And of what nature am I now inclined to make it? And for what purpose am I now going to use it? Is it void of understanding? Is it loosed and rent asunder from social life? Is it melted into and mixed with the poor flesh so as to move together with it?

He who takes off from his master is a runaway, but the discipline is master, and he who breaks the discipline is a runaway. And he also who is grieved or angry or afraid is dissatisfied because something has been or it shall be of the things which are appointed by Him Who rules all things, and He commands the law and assigns to every man what is fit. He then who fears or is grieved or is angry is a runaway.

Imagine every man who is grieved at anything or discontented to be a lamb, which when sacrificed, kicks and screams. Like this lamb, also is the man, who on his bed in silence laments the holds in which he is put in dismay. And consider that only to the rational animal is given the faculty to follow the reason of escort in intelligence.

When you are offended at any man's fault, forthwith turn to yourself and reflect in what like manner you go wrong yourself, for example, in thinking that money is a good thing or pleasure or a bit of reputation and the like. For by attending to this, you will quickly forget your anger, if the consideration also is added that the man is compelled; for what else could he do? Or, if you are able, take away from him the compulsion.

When you have looked on yourself, think of any other men of fortune and preference, and in the case of every one, do in like manner. Then let this thought be in your mind: where then are those men? Nowhere or nobody knows where. For thus continuously, you will look at human things as dust and smoke and nothing at all, especially if you reflect at the same time that what has once changed will never exist again in the infinite duration of time. But you, in what a brief space of time you have your existence! And why are you not content to pass through this short time in a disciplined way? What substance and occasion for your activity are you evading? For what else are all your things, except exercises for the reason, when it has viewed carefully and by examination into their nature the things which happen in your own, as the stomach which is strengthened makes all things its own, as the blazing fire makes flame and brightness out of everything that is thrown into it.

Let it not be in any man's power to say truly of you that you are not unassuming or that you are not exemplary, but let him be a prevaricator whoever shall think anything of this kind about you. This is altogether in your power if you abide the discipline laid down in the Qur'an. For who is he that shall hinder you from being good and simple? Do you only determine to live no longer unless you shall be such, for nothing in reason allows you to live if you are not such.

The healthy eye ought to see all visible things and not to say, "I wish for green things," for this is the condition of a diseased eye. And the healthy hearing and smelling ought to be ready to perceive all that can be heard and smelled. And the healthy stomach ought to be, with respect to all food, just as the mill with respect to all things, which it is formed to grind. And accordingly, the healthy understanding ought to be prepared for everything that happens, but that which says, "Let my dear children live, and let all men praise whatever I may do," is an eye which needs to seek for the rose in bloom or teeth which seek for crunchy and crispy things.

Accustom yourself as much as possible on the occasion of anything being done by any person to inquire within you, "For what object is this man doing this?" But begin with yourself, and examine yourself first.

Remember that which pulls the strings is the thing, which is hidden within: this is the power of persuasion of the intelligence, and this is life. In contemplating yourself, never include the vessel that surrounds your core and these instruments that are attached about it. For your stay is like a cleaver differing only in this, that it grows in the body. For indeed there is no more use in these parts without the cause, which moves and checks them, than in the weaver's shuttle and the writer's pen and the driver's whip.

These are the properties of the rational soul: it sees itself, analyzes itself, and makes itself such as it chooses; the produce which it bears itself enjoys for the fruits of plants and that in animals which corresponds to other fruits enjoys its own end, wherever the limit of life may be fixed. The shimmer and glimmer of this vale and in such like things, where the whole action is incomplete, if anything cuts it short, but in every part and wherever it may be stopped, it makes what has been set before it full and complete, so that it can say, "I have what is my own for I tried to abide the discipline to the best of my wit." And further, it transverses the whole universe and the surrounding vacuum and surveys its form, and it extends itself into the infinity of time and embraces and comprehends the periodical renovation of all things. And it comprehends that those who come after us will see nothing new, nor have those before us seen anything more, but in a manner, he who is forty years old, if he has any understanding at all, has seen by virtue of the uniformity that prevails all things that have been and all that will be. This too is a property of the rational soul: love of one's neighbor and truth and modesty and valuing nothing more than itself, which is also the property of principle ordained.

The soul must be ready, if at any moment, it must be separated from the body, and it should be prepared either to be extinguished or even dispersed or continue to exist. But if this readiness comes from a man's own judgment, not from mere persistence, as with the truly faithful, but considerately with dignity and in a way to persuade another, how could that be possible?

Only in abidance of faith is the discipline of life to cherish the boons in the Hereafter.

Have I done something for the general interest? Well then, I have had my reward. Let this always be present to your mind, and never stop doing such conscientious actions. For me and for my children, if the fortune that neglects this has its reason to, again, we must not abrade and be irate at that which happens to us in this vale.

And life's harvest reaps like the wheat's blooming ear.

As those who try to stand in your way when you are proceeding according to right reason will not be able to turn you aside from your proper action, so neither let them drive you from your benevolent feelings toward them, but be on your guard equally in both matters, not only in the matter of steady judgment and action, but also in the matter of gentleness toward those who try to hinder you or otherwise. For this also is a weakness, to be vexed at them, as well as to be diverted from your course of action and give way through fear; for both are equally deserters from their posts, the man who does it through fear and the man who is alienated from him who is by nature a kinsman and a friend of faith.

The Almighty sees the mind's ruling principles of all men bared of material vestures and impurities. For with his intellectual part alone, he touches the intelligence only, which has flowed and been derived from nature into these bodies. And if you also use yourself to do this, you will rid yourself of your trouble. He who regards not the poor flesh, which envelops him, surely will not trouble him by looking after raiment and dwelling for fame and such like externals flare in glow.

The things are three of which you are composed: a little body, a little breath or the soul or efflux, and the intelligence. Of these, the first two are yours, so far as it is your duty to take care of them, but the third alone is properly yours. Therefore, if you shall separate from yourself, that is, from your understanding, whatever others do or say, whatever you have done or said yourself, whatever future things trouble you because they may happen, whatever is in the body that envelops you or in the breath that is by nature associated with the body, whatever is attached to you independent of your will, and whatever the external circadian-embolism vortex whirls round, the intellectual power will be exempt from the things of fate and can live pure and free by itself, doing what is just, accepting what happens, and saying the truth. If you will separate, I say, from this ruling faculty the things which are attached to it by the impressions of sense and the things of time to come and of time that is past and will make yourself like a dominating sphere, and if you shall strive to live only what is really your life, that is, the present, then you will be able to pass that portion of life which remains for you up to the time of your death free from perturbations, nobly, and obedient to your own conscious or the true discernment of intelligence that is within you.

When a man has conferred the semblance of having affirmed inappropriately, how do I know if this is an unlawful act? And even if he has done wrong, how do I know that he has not accursed himself? And so, this is like ripping and wrenching his face.

Consider that before long, you will be nobody and nowhere; nor will any of the things that you now see endure, nor any of those who are now living. For all things are formed by nature to change and be turned and to diverge, to die in order that other things in continuous succession may exist.

Consider that everything is opinion, and opinion is in the power. Take away then, when you choose, your opinion, and like a mariner who has doubled the promontory, you will find serene and steady everything stable and travel in a sea with no surge or swell, no ebb or tide. And is it possible?

What You're Really Craving in Desire?

Would you like to continue to endure and exist with the universal nature?

Well, do you wish to have sensation or the motivation of the movement alone, besides the growth, and then thereafter again cease to grow? To use your speech and to think of the same as your ills in core cherish to adore? What is there of all these things which seem to you worth desiring? But if it is easy to set little value on all these things, turn to that which remains, which is to follow reason and faith. But it is inconsistent with honoring reason and faith to be troubled because by death, a man will be deprived of the other things. How small is the order of parts and peels of the boundless and unfathomable time assigned to every man? For it is very soon swallowed up in the eternal.

And how small a clip of crop or the whole of substance that we intend to allure?

And how small a cut and scrape of the universal soul do we intend to secure?

And on what small flora and foliage of the whole earth you creep and wish to allure?

Reflecting on all this, you consider nothing to be great, except to act as your nature brings in lore.

Man! You have been a citizen in this great state —the world. What difference does it make to you whether for fifty years or five? For that which is conformable to the laws is just for all. Where is the hardship then, if no tyrant or yet an unjust judge sends you away from the state, but nature who brought you into it? It is the same as if a director, who has employed an actor, dismisses him from the stage. But you have not finished the five acts, but only three of them. You say well, but in your life, the three acts are the whole drama; for what shall be a complete drama is determined by Him, Who was once the cause of its composition and now of its dissolution, but you are the cause of neither. Depart then satisfied, for He Who releases you is also satisfied.

Conformity in Discipline

In that instance you're to be there in discipline
To savor in hither an equal sort of infliction

The physics of Aristotle is the knowledge of the nature of the universe, of its governance, and of the relation of man's nature to both. He names the universe the universal substance, and he adds that reason governs the universe. He also uses the terms *universal nature* and *nature of the universe*. He calls the universe the one and all, which we name the cosmos. If he ever seems to use these general terms as significant of "all" and of all that man can in any way conceive to exist, he still on other occasions plainly distinguishes between matter, material things, and the cause, origin, and reason.

This is conformable to Zeno's doctrine that there are two original principles of all things: that which acts and that which is acted upon. That which is acted upon is the formless matter, and that which acts is the "reason," the Almighty, Who is eternal and operates through all matter and produces all things. So Antonymous speaks of the reason, which pervades all substance, and through all time by fixed periods (revolutions), administers the universe. The Almighty is eternal, and matter is also eternal. It is the Lord who gives form to matter. The Lord and matter exist independently, but the Lord governs matter. This doctrine is simply the expression of the fact of the existence both of matter and of the Lord. The Stoics did not perplex themselves with the unsolvable question of the origin and nature of matter. Antonymous also assumes a beginning of things, as we know them, but his language is sometimes very obscure.

Matter consists of elemental parts of which all material objects are made. But nothing is permanent in form. The nature of the universe, according to Antonymous, expression, loves nothing so much as to change the things which are and to make new things like them. For everything that exists is in a manner the seed of that which will be. All things then are in constant flux and change; some things are dissolved into the elements, others come in their places, and so the whole universe continues ever young and perfect.

When we look at the motions of the planets, the action of what we call navigation under gravitational law, the elemental combination of unorganized bodies and their resolution, the production of plants and of all living bodies, their generation, growth, and their dissolution, which we call their death, we observe a regular sequence of phenomena, which within the limits of experience—present and past, so far as we know the past—is fixed and invariable. But if this is not so, if the order and sequence of phenomena, as known to us, are subject to change in the course of an infinite progression and such change is conceivable, we have not discovered, nor shall we ever discover, the whole of the order and sequence of phenomena, in which sequence there may be involved according to its very nature, that is, according to its fixed order, some variation of what we now call the order or nature of things. It is also conceivable that such changes have taken place, changes in the order of things, as we are compelled by the imperfection of language to call them, but which are not changes, and further it is certain, that our knowledge of the true sequence of all actual phenomena, as for instance, the phenomena of generation, growth, and ultimate death.

Moral philosophy directed by the Almighty is not a feeble or narrow system, which teaches a man to look directly to his own happiness, though a man's happiness or tranquility is indirectly promoted by living as he ought to. A man must live conformably to the universal nature, which means, as the discipline in faith ordains it in many passages, that a man's actions must be conformable to his true relations to all other human beings, both as a citizen of a political community and as a member of the whole human family. This implies, and he often expresses it in the most forcible language, that a man's words and actions, so far as they affect others, must be measured by a fixed rule, which is their consistency with the conservation and the interests of the particular society of which he is a member and of the whole human race. To live conformably to such a faith, a man must use his rational faculties in order to discern clearly the consequences and full effect of all his actions and of the actions of others. He must not live a life of contemplation and reflection only, though he must often retire within himself to calm and purify his soul by thought, but he must mingle in the work of man and be a fellow laborer for the general good of all the living beings.

A man should have a sane and sober objective or purpose in life, that he may aim all his dash and dynamism to it—of course, it must be a good object. He who has not one object or purpose in life cannot be one and the same all through his life. Faith has a remark to the same effect, on the best means of reducing of the mind unto temperance and commendable circumstance, which is, the electing and propounding unto a man's self good and virtuous ends of his life, such as may be in a sane and sober sort within his sweep and scope to attain. He is a happy man who has been wise all through the opportunities, but the Almighty, seeing well that a man cannot always be so wise in his youth, encourages him to do it when he can and not to let life slip away before he has begun. He who can propose to himself good and virtuous ends of life and be true to them cannot fail to live conformably to his own interest and the universal interest, for in the nature of things, they are one.

For a thing, if it's not good for the hive, it cannot be good for the bee.
One passage may end this matter

Not validating in discipline of Faith
Say:
If you had bit of intelligence in trace
Regard, you'd have discipline with grace
For fear of doling out to the men in need
For that's the bliss of fortitude indeed

If the nature has determined about me and about the things which must happen to me, these are destined and determined well, for it is not easy even to imagine deity without providence doing me any harm. Why should He incline to do so without any rational justification? For what advantage would result to the vale or world at large from this or to the whole, which is the special object of His providence? But if He has not determined about me individually, He has certainly determined about the whole at least, and the things, which happen by way of sequence in this general arrangement, I ought to accept with pleasure and be content with discipline. But if He intends and inclines about nothing—which it is odious to believe, or if we do give credence to it, let us neither expiate nor entreat nor avow nor do anything else which we do as if the nature were present and lived with us. But if, however, the nature concludes about none of the things that pertain to us, I am able to resolve to settle about myself, and I can inquire about that which is useful and that is useful to every man, which is conformable to his own constitution and nature.

But my nature is rational and social and my city and country, so far as I am Seyal, is Multan and Pakistan, but so far as I am a man, it is the domain of this world. The things that are beneficial to the world are alone effectual for my endurance in this sphere of sway.

It would be tedious and it is not necessary to state the divine opinions on all the ways in which a man may profitably use his understanding toward perfecting himself in practical virtue. The passages to this purpose are in all parts of this text, but as they are in no order or connection, a man must use Scripture a long time before he will find out all that is in it. A few words may be added here. If we analyze all other things, we find how insufficient they are for human life and how truly worthless many are for themselves. Virtue alone is the indivisible one and perfectly satisfying. The notion of virtue cannot be considered vague or unsettled, because a man may find it difficult to explain the notion fully to himself or to expound on it to others in such a way as to prevent seduction or subversion. Virtue is a whole, and no more consists of parts than man's intelligence does, and yet we speak of various intellectual faculties as a convenient way of expressing the various powers which man's intellect shows by his works. In the same way, we may speak of various virtues or parts of virtue in a practical sense for the purpose of showing what particular virtues we ought to practice in order to exercise the whole of virtue, that is, as much as man's nature is capable of.

The prime principle in man's constitution is faith. The next in order is not to yield to the persuasions of the body when they are not conformable to the rational principle of faith, which must govern intelligence. The third is freedom from error and from deception. Let then the ruling principle holding fast to these things go straight on, and it has what is its own. The Almighty selects justice as the virtue that is the basis of all the rest, and this has been said long before.

You have embarked, you have made the voyage, and you have come to shore. Get out. If indeed to another life, there is no want of providence, even there. But if to a state without sensation, you will cease to be held by pains and pleasures and to be a slave to the vessel which is as much inferior as that which serves it is superior, for the one is intelligence and deity; the other is earth and corruption. It is not death that a man should fear; rather, he should fear never beginning to live according to nature. Every man should live in such a way as to discharge his duty and to trouble himself about nothing else. He should live such a life that he shall always be ready for death and shall depart content when the summons comes.

Demise in Death

That's the cessation of the impressions through the senses, of the pulling of the strings that move the appetites, of the discursive movements of the thoughts, and of the service to the flesh. Death, like generation, is a mystery of nature. In another passage, the exact meaning of which is perhaps doubtful, one speaks of the child who leaves the womb, and so the soul at death leaves its envelope. As the child is born or comes into life by leaving the womb, so the soul may on leaving the body pass into another existence, which is perfect.

> Don't they really perceive and conceive
> Who created heavens and earth a retrieve
>
> Has Dictum to create like anew in plan
> He's ordained a definite time in span
>
> For what there's no waver in trace
> But biased defy in yonder to brace
>
> But not to appreciate in stance
> Denying discipline of Faith in trance
> (Al Isra 17:99)

The opinion and the concept of a future life are very clearly expressed in different verses of the Qur'an. His Almighty's discipline of the nature and soul essentially requires that it does not perish absolutely, for a portion of the divinity cannot perish. The opinion is at least as old as the time since the creation of mankind with all the divine endowments. What comes from earth goes back to earth, and what comes from the heavens, the soul, must return to Him Who presumed it. But I find a clear concept of the man existing after death so as to be conscious of his sameness with that soul which occupied his vessel of clay in this vale.

Truth in Prayer

> They speak and repeat it to say:
> Glory be to The Lord *in pray*
> *Indeed!*
> The promise of Lord has come to stay
> (Al Isra 17:108)

What truth I can grasp? It leads to a differentiation between the clear and distinct perception that I have of my own existence as a purposeful and pragmatic approach ensures and secures that I possess of the existence of extended material substance and guarantees that I own and occupy it only because a perfect being—Allah—would not allow me to be cheated in my sense of sagacity and skill. The status of the mind is necessarily quite different from that of the body; I am a mind but only have a body. This leads to a deep incompetence to assign or equate the mind and body in attitude and tradition. You can see intellective eventualities and physical occurrences as two self-ruling sequences of conformities that the Lord providentially synchronizes, so that my decision to move my hand and the hand's subsequent movement follow from each other just as if the one caused the other.

Both the nature of the role assigned by the Lord who holds providence in action and the absolutely circumstantial character of the elucidation involved rule out any such solution. But one does not need a conclusion or clarification of this or any other kind, since according to the premises and provisions, the problem cannot arise. Muhammad ^PBUH is exceptional and excellent, unlike other prophets, and a legend who discerns intellective eventualities as the effect of physical causes or of having communication and visualizing the correlative and creative relationship between the body and mind. The body and mind are not causally related at all; they are identical, because thought and extension are two attributes under which the one substance is conceived. The Islamic doctrine of substance and attributes is not merely an assertion of the unity of the single substance but an attempt to explain the relationship between that unity and the multiplicity of finite beings.

Say:
Call upon Rahman
O Lord of Domain!
What's to the name
Call *(Him)* earnest in acclaim
To Him belong all the Most Beautiful Names

Don't you invoke aloud prayers in moan!
So loud nor low timbre in tone
But seek, *Medium course* while praying *in alone*
(Al Isra 73:110)

What a delicacy, daintiness and decency, respectability and seemliness is depicted and described in this verse, so that while talking to some, your voice should neither be so loud nor so low as to cause annoyance to the listener.

Have we ever looked at ourselves?

The bevy and brood are passing along to be sold, and the greater part of the riffraff to buy and sell. But there are some few who come only to look at the fair, to question how and why it is being held, upon what command, sway, or supremacy and with what motivation. So, too, in this great fair of life, some, like the beef on the hoof, pester themselves about nothing but

121

the feed and forage. Know all of you, who are absorbed about falsifying for affluence, fortune, estate, possessions, and golden trinkets, that these are nothing but fodder?

Can there be no administrator? Is it possible that while neither city nor household could endure even for a moment without one to administer and see to its welfare, this corporeal, so promising, so boundless, should be executed in order so congruously and consistently without a proper strategy and by blind chance? There is therefore an administrator. What are His attributes and how does He conduct and control? And who are we, His creation? And what moil or toil were we born to accomplish?

Have we any close affiliation with or faith in Him?

If you have faith as a grain of mustard seed, you shall say unto the mountain: Remove hence to yonder place; and it shall remove: and nothing shall be impossible unto you. (St. Matthew 17:20)

Faith was the cause that made Christ's adherents accomplish his assignment and possess somewhat the identical revelation as he owned. Faith decorates an endowment in man that transforms his vision and vivacity when everything looks quite unclouded and most discernible.

Reason and Revelation

The existence of a thing for itself is its complete life; its existence for another is its relative life. The Lord Almighty existed for Himself. He is the living one, and His life is the life complete and immortal. Created beings in general exist for His Almighty. Their life is relative and linked with death. Life is a single essence, incapable of diminution or division; existence for itself is everything, and that which constitutes a thing is its life.

Earth with its earthly living beings, as we all discern, has support for all the created beings till the time of its final termination. Who could have conceived or accomplished all that other than the Lord Almighty, Allah, or God, Dharma or Elohim—whatever name you may attribute to Him? Who could ensure the provision of all the created beings from the swizzle of initiation to the swash of eternity?

The Lord, as such, that is to say, the Almighty envisaged, not as He manifested Himself in a specific way at a certain time, away in pace or place to conceive and in as much as He is what He is and also as He originated and divulged by Himself, with the interminable arrow of time, as we may assign the name to it, when the Almighty first evinced Himself by creating the angels and other exigencies that we have no order to determine. The Lord Almighty is shaping authenticity, materialization, and reintegration, whereas the man is theoretically propositioned excellent discernment and free choice. Man thus appears to be a preference for a dual repository made for the perfect faith, as religion comes to fill that repository primarily with the precision of the perfect and secondarily with the law—or the actuality and the law. The former is complementary to the discernment and the subsequent to the choice.

The faith is foreordained to exterminate skepticism, vacillation, determination, and consternation. The notion of preordination does not do away with the idea of the independence of choice prone to faux pas. Human supremacy, however, is appropriate in the sense that it is somewhat impeccable and well accomplished. Man is a priori the choice. Obviously, the discernment is not contradicted, but it is taken into attention only as an appearance of choice.

Imagine the effulgent and sparkling summer sky, and suppose simple people stare protuberantly into it with their dream of the afterworld. Now assume that it were conceivable to convey these simple people into the caliginous, unlit, and frosty bottomless pit of the galaxies and nebulae with its awesome and stunning stillness. In this abyss, all too many of them would lose their faith, and this is exactly what eventuates as an outcome of neoteric science, both to the educated and the popular concepts. Most men do not know—and if they could know it, why should they be called on to believe it?

Is it that this blue sky, a utopian deception, a visual blooper that is postulated by the sight of the extraterrestrial void, is, however, a convincing and cogent portraiture of a divine marvel of origin dappled with silver-gilt clouds that overwhelms the glittering and glinting of innumerous stars? To remain devoted to our element of actuality, we may not transgress our deceptive approach with satisfactory action to purpose in an undeniable intellect. It is the perception of the prudence that transforms the confidence of the simple and does rejuvenate the attainable to the immaculate understanding. But it is also an inquisition, in conformity to the instantaneous attribute of the semblance of the bottomless pit of ubiquitous demonstrations of the cosmic order, whose confines indefinitely elude our ordinary experience. Finally the extraterrestrial space conformably casts back death.

There is a programmed makeover from the geocentric to the heliocentric worldview. We are endeavoring hard to find a new synthesis of science and spirit because there is a point of prudence outside the inconsistency of deception and truth by which lives can be put back together again. Spiritually, however, the center is where the sight is. Stand on a height and view the horizon. The unprecedented expansion of the horizon cleanses the doors of the perception of our creation and that of the universe. Anyone who has had an experience of mystery knows that there is a dimension of the universe that is not available to his senses. We live in the recognition of something there, which is much greater than the human dimension.

Purpose, however, should not be set aside as an implicit belief but gainfully employed in the procurement of equity, the reconciliation of the true faith. There is nothing true in His Almighty's word conflicting to the discrete discernment or rationalization of explanation. We must, however, be prepared in this world: to ensure our perception of cognition to the conformity, and not to strain and strive, toil and moil, dig and drive in winnowing to sift out a profound precision by reasoning of such mysteries as are not comprehensible or do not fall under any rule of natural science.

Guidance in Revelation

Reason should be kept very much to the fore when one is confronted with those who claim revelation, for if a man says that His Almighty spoke to him in a dream, "This is no more than to say he dreamed that His Almighty spoke to him." Is there a psychological explanation for such phenomena that casts doubt on their reliability as valid communications with His Almighty?

Guidance from His Almighty is not for a specific class, creed, or color in a particular faith. He who seeks His blessed direction will secure it. It's for all who are dedicatedly committed for a specific cause for the betterment of humanity and all living beings.

I was zestfully consumed to know the possible mode of action of synthetic garments on the body surface to the production of various behavioral and cardiovascular influences but was on the blink. I explored different libraries in the USA for the possible mode of action but without much fruition. I was confounded because soon I had to return to Pakistan. The night before my departure, I prayed and implored His Almighty for injunctions. Intuitively, I picked up a few books from my brother's library, and surprisingly, the evidence for the mode of action became discernible. The intuitive perceptions are not beyond the scope of human intellect if one is dedicated for a certain purpose or sanctified instinct.

The Lord Almighty has repeatedly reiterated and asserted in the Holy Scriptures:

And tend to Lord in your term *in adore*
For His Boon and Bounties hither *in score*
And the pledge He affirmed with you *to allure*

For you said:
We heed and submit to Him, way *to affirm*
Awe and dread Lord, for He deem *to discern*
All in veer of core, He care and *concern*
(Al Mai'dah 05:7)

Dreams and discernment and erudition and enlightenment, however, should not be discharged all in all, for it is by similar support that the prophets have been edified of the demand and decree of His Almighty Lord. The attitude and the lore of the determination to give credence to, with all it is congenial and conforming motivation, chance faith is balanced. Belief must persevere to vindicate itself; there is no probability of a conclusive affirmation. Both the preferences of pragmatic life and the creed of faith may be merited as appropriate kinds of scientific hypotheses. The first kind is exceptional because of its deterrence to some distinctive concern or the circumstances and the second because it is the elusive generality.

On the Socratic view, one may learn geometry from this teacher or that, but the question of the truth of a geometric theorem is independent of the question of from where we learned it.

The new discoveries of this scientific age answer to our firm religious beliefs by enabling us to recognize in this whole universe a reflection magnified of our own most "inward nature" so that we are indeed its "eyes," its "ears," its "core," its "logic," and its "assertion," and in faith, the Lord Almighty is omnipresent.

Today, we are participating in one of the most intensely consequentially clear conceptions of the human spirit to recognize and confirm not only outside nature but also our own abysmal inward mystery. Like all the heavenly bodies, we are also compressing toward an end, our demise, converging toward an indeterminate destination, black hole, or you may call it a big crunch, as the scientific opinion converges today. This has also been reiterated quite frequently in the Holy Scriptures, but in a clear way.

Sun is moving to its defined *butt and tail*
Moon directed to traverse *a trek in trail*

Crescent browsing as a date tree *shoot in sear*
There's tangible trek for moon and sun *so clear*

Both sun and moon tread *in define*
Also the day and night *held in confine*

Concern to abide determined trek *in trail*
So to confirm correct confine *in scale* (Ya Sin 36:38–40)

The outward prominence of our mortal invulnerability into a precipitous space and an incomprehensibly mysterious world can only be rationalized in a numinous sense since we must die before we die. (That's demise from this vale to cherish the indeterminate living of the afterlife.) What we would chiefly call to someone's attention here is the negation of assuming the bare actuality of unbiased significance.

I have tried to touch at this point the spiritual or sensory order of the divine presence with two of its manifestations: the intelligence, a perpetual driving force of divine pedigreed providence within us, which is our core of discernment, and the demise or giving away of the efflux from this earthly pot.

And you can have the vision of divine force or the unseen.

Today, the scientists are dumbfounded to see the command of law that operates from the minutest point (i.e., from one-millionth of an inch in the atom to the extremely vast universe that we perceive about fourteen billion light-years away from today). It is virtually most perplexing to comprehend Your administration.

"And that should be the subject of my thoughts, my study, when death overtakes me."

Wherefore a good man and true, bearing in mind who he is and from whence he came and from whom he sprang, cares only how he may fill his post with due discipline and obedience to the Almighty.

With "You" that I continue to live?
Then I will live, as one that is free and noble, as "You" would have me.
For "You" have made me free from hindrance in what appears unto me.
But now "You" no further have need of me?
I thank "You"! Up to this hour, I have stayed for "Your" sake and none other's.
And now in obedience to "You" I depart.

If our conduct and attitude are admonishing with insalubrious comportment, we will be deserted and left forlorn and destitute. Then why not behave in a befitting manner in this transit lounge of earthly living. Alchemical natural philosophy was always intimately secured to medicine in Islam, as a fundamental principle of the conformity between all, confirming the everlasting world to come after demise.

There is in the hermetic, diversified injunctions of actuality, the comprehensible power structure, the heavenly bodies, and the human order.

An inclination to smoking, drinking, overeating, living a sedentary life, and to abiding immorality is not definitely ordained by the Lord Almighty. It's through our own discernment to pick and choose a right trend in the trail to cherish the bliss of discipline in all terms to avail.

It is here we beg and beseech the Lord for our true guidance.

If the fate was really destined and was not to be changed, then why at all beg His assistance and escort at each stance of torture and tribulation, because by nature, man assumes himself to be free of any discipline and duty assigned to him by nature?

Similarly, genetically, each one of us has a different propensity for a disease. One smoker is more prone to fall a prey to ischemic heart disease, another to bronchogenic carcinoma, and yet another to stroke. But to continue smoking is definitely our own choice; it's not right to blame the genetic code. Similarly, we can talk of all the known risk factors.

A friend of mine, who was a professor of medicine, was in excellent health and had no risk factors; he was slim and smart, living a disciplined life both in the spiritual and physical context. One afternoon, while sitting in his living room, he asked for a cup of tea. The tea was already ready. His wife got him the cup of tea, but he was gone. He breathed his last without any twinkle in gesture of agony or alarm.

Another close kin of mine, a professor of medicine in the UK, was a smoker. He had a heart attack in 2003. That was followed by heart irregularity and a stroke. I really feel concerned and sorry for the man for he is crippled in bed, reduced to a skeleton, but still taking his breath and waiting for the eventual exoneration of Allah Almighty.

At times, misfortune and agony never abate in certain cases. Mind you, you are a part of the whole, and for the discipline of the whole, some have to endure agony in score. It is again for the endurance and existence of the whole. This will be discussed later in "The Adam of Science and the Adam of the Qur'an." If a child is suffering a crippling disease, it is basically for the better health of the lot; so if a man is to endure or suffer misery and agony all through his life, it is for the better of the lot, so he may be grateful to the Lord Almighty that His Almighty put him to torture for the betterment of the lot. Eventually, he will cherish the real boons in the Hereafter for all his suffering hither in this vale. He would be all grateful to the Lord Almighty, who let him suffer for a while to cherish the everlasting boons in the Hereafter.

Discipline Is Justice

He who acts unjustly acts impiously. For the universal nature has made rational animals for the sake of one another to help according to their capacity, but in no way to injure one another, he who transgresses his will, is clearly guilty of impiety towards the Highest Divinity. And he too who lies is guilty of impiety inasmuch as he acts unjustly by deceiving, and he also who lies intentionally or unintentionally, inasmuch as he is at variance with the universal nature and inasmuch as he disturbs the order by fighting against the nature of the world; for he fights against it, who is moved of himself to that which is contrary to truth, for he had received powers from nature through the neglect of which he is not able now to distinguish falsehood from truth.

And indeed he, who pursues pleasure as good and avoids pain as evil is guilty of impiety. For of necessity such a man must often find fault with the universal nature, alleging that it assigns things to the bad and the good contrary to their needs, because frequently the bad are in the pleasure, but the good have pain for their share and the things, which cause pain. Going uphill is a difficult lash, for to achieve some cherished goal of life is always accompanied with distress and further he who is afraid of pain will sometimes also be afraid of some of the things which will happen in the world and even this is impiety. And he who pursues pleasure will not abstain from injustice, and this is plainly impiety.

Obedience

And once we affirm there's a Lord, then there has to be a discipline to abide. And Allah Almighty has bestowed intelligence in this context to abide by true discipline ordained in all the religions. In the Qur'an, His Almighty over and again repeats to affirm He created the man originally from dirt or mud and taught him to speak and instructed him to live according to the discipline of nature and behold the divine benedictions.

To live according to nature is to live according to a man's whole nature, not according to a part of it, and to respect the divinity within him as the decree and dictum of all his actions. To the rational animal, the same act is according to nature and according to reason that asserts true discernment of providence.

Discipline is through knowledge, and the knowledge is accomplished through education. For once we determine to learn, we shall have to strive for the source. And what's the source? If we ordain the true wisdom endowed by the Almighty, then we certainly assert it's through faith as determined by the Lord through His most exalted personalities assigned in this world. Do I need to repeat that? You all know they were His prophets like Abraham, Moses, and Jesus, who conveyed the message of Allah from time to time to different communities on different occasions. But once the society was almost there to accomplish His bestowal of resources, the assignment of messengers stopped altogether after Prophet Muhammad ^{PBUH}.

For once we gain knowledge through that, we meditate at the true discernment of the text communicated in the message. That's the true discernment of knowledge for what I call the sane ambience of discernment. That's the philosophy of the scientific approach and is also affirmed in the Scriptures. If one carefully reads the text of the Holy Scriptures, one can see it's almost in each Surah and quite often reiterated in the same Surah many times that it's through knowledge man can allure the true wisdom. The Holy Qur'an speaks a universal language that invites all people, irrespective of caste, creed, or color, to the assertion of scientific approaches in different domains. Here are two verses. The first shows the universality of the message in the Holy Qur'an, and the second shows its new scientific message.

O the men and clan in place!
We created you of a couple *in pace*
And *(held you)* in the realm and race

Varied names in elect and *decide*
That you may know each *in abide*
And not to trend, scorn each *in deride*
Before Lord!
Most pious of you is the virtuous *in trail*
Indeed!
Lord discerns and concerns *all trivial in scale* (49:13)

Shortly!
We'll evince our Notations *in surround*
And also within their souls *in abound*

Until the verity is clear *(for them)* to brace
Isn't it enough to affirm *in pace*
That Lord is there to concern *in place* (41:53)

It's a modest undertaking to substantiate the authenticity in perfection of each stance and stanza of the Holy Qur'an. Some scientists propagated the notion that Islam is going to turn our whole social order topsy-turvy. It is to assert that Muslims are not quite disinclined to the modern trends, but rather eluding the so-called progress in the social order that has virtually damaged the whole moral structure of the elite society. A word of the acclaimed movie *American Beauty* is enough to substantiate the whole moral structure of the modern the so-called advanced social order. "This country is gone to hell." That's why a sober class of the society has distracted itself from that social order based on nudity and sensual enticements. But the Muslims are drifting away from their own true philosophy of the faith. They're at a crossroads, dubious and dazed, delusive and amazed. For as long as Muslims were abiding the discipline, they were teaching Europe the philosophy of science with its implications and enlightenment. But today, the Muslims have strayed in manner and means far away from the wisdom of discipline.

If Muslims are trailing behind, it is because of the smothering and suffocating sway in stride of the Western hold on cultural and scientific propensities, besides the tread in educational pace and economical spheres on one side and on the other, it's because Muslims have ditched the precision in perception of the prudence and are lurking in delusion far away from the discipline of faith.

The discipline of faith is universal, and unfortunately, it is the West that is following the true message of intelligence, which was communicated to man at his creation which is at the core of most of the spheres of life. But sensual indulgence has gained such a ravenous impetus and thrust in the highly evolved societies all over the world that people have virtually lost all the other moral values in the so-called elite class.

If the Muslims had followed the true discipline of faith, they could have secured better opportunities in different propensities of life and cherished the fruits of benevolence.

Knowledge

Islam has proposed that man contemplate and accomplish true discernment with enlightenment, because all scientific predilection and dispositions will eventually lead him to the precision in the precept of the principal with providence. For in actuality, it is faith with the precept of providence ordained by the principal that reflects the whole order of creation. That is to say, the more the man acquires knowledge, the more he gets to know the Lord Almighty beyond any hesitation. The Lord Almighty says, in this respect:

Don't you discern and concern in twinkle
Lord conveys drizzle *(from sky) in sprinkle*
With it We yield diverse in tint
And in foothills,
There're trek and trail *in wink*
Red and white in stint

Diverse in hue, *stipple in spot*
Some intense black in slot other tint *in plot*
And so midst men *and clan in shape*
And crawling creatures and herds *in drape*
They vary in sheen and shade
Really!
His men in lore
Awe and dread in core
For Lord is Exalted in Might
And Oft-Forgiving *in slight* (35:27/28)

But those affirming sapience *in lore*
Besides abiding the faith *in core*

Would trend to affirm and *confirm*
You did dawdle in daze hither *in term*
Within dictum of Lord *in vale*
To the Day of revival *and rekindling in prevail*
And this is the Day of renaissance in glance
But you did care to apprise in stance (30:56)

How can a man determine *to obey*
Invoking in hours of night *in pray*
A trend in entreat so earnest in beseech
Care and caution of Hereafter *in treat*
Trust in Lord for His Mercy in *Reprieve*
How could he be compared to one *in stance*
Determined to defy Dictum of Lord *in trance*
Such are the men with endowment *in grace*
With council of caution and admonition *to brace* (39:9)

And those of the men with sapience *in lore*
Who trend to assert *for sure*
Divulgence is from Lord *in adore*
That's the verity held *to avail*
Them to escort noble trek *in trail*
From Lord,
Exalted and Astute, Bounteous in Tribute (34:6)

The prominence and eminence of intelligence with the true discernment of wisdom is what we call science, and one who tends to research and scrutinize is called *knowledgeable* (a scientist). The Qur'an has repeatedly asserted this in its text. And the scientists are exceptionally dignified in the Holy Qur'an. For the more man gains knowledge, the more he is convinced that some most powerful nature is behind the creation of this most ungraspable cosmic order and the life in it. Just look at the ant, a small, most insignificant creature with all the sensual allures besides its locomotive, digestive, nervous, respiratory, and genitourinary systems. If you could ever sneak a while to look at its behavior, you'd really marvel at its discipline and its sense of intelligence. Who could've made such a small creature with all the fascination in persuasion?

It wouldn't be possible without a most powerful mind behind all this myth of creation.

The very first revelation affirmed the importance of knowledge, for the very first words of the communication from the Lord Almighty were "Read or Recite." Chapter 96 opens with the following verses:

Read!
Discern in the Name of Thy Lord *in grace*
Who contrived the man of a clump *in trace*
Read!
Discern Your Lord is Most Cordial *indeed*
Who school in scribble and scrawl *in proceed*
Enlighten the man, knowledgeable *in lore*
That he didn't have a precept *in fore*

The contents of the very first verse communicated by the Lord Almighty asserts with affirmation the importance and significance of *knowledge*. The Lord Almighty has given supreme status to *knowledge* and the *knowledgeable*, because through the different sources of knowledge, man gains faith in the Lord Almighty, Who asserts:

Nun.
By the Pen and that *scribble to write*
By The Grace of Lord,
You aren't of the fanatical *in plight* (68:1-2)

The Lord Almighty also ordains in the Holy Qur'an you are to meditate and think profoundly in the profundity of your intelligence about His signs in the heavens and scattered around on the earth.

Divination of Qur'an *in stance*
That's from Lord *to glance*
Exalted *in Might*
With Sense of Sapience *so Bright*
Divination of Qur'an *in stance*
That's from Lord *to glance*

Exalted in Might
With Sense of Sapience *so Bright*
And in your birth *(so adoring in trail)*
And for the cattle dispersed in vale
There're Signs *in vigilance to brace*
For the men of Faith *in pace*

Swapping of night and the day *in stride*
And indeed Lord convey *a word to aside*
Provisions from the sky *held in abide*
That rouses and revives seared soil *in dried*
And the shift and drift of winds *in gale*
These are signs, men of sapience* *to avail*
(45:1–5)

Indeed!
The Signs are palpable *in core*
For those gifted of sense[11] *in lore*
And none but biased defy *(Our Signs) to allure*
Yet they say:
Why Notations aren't revealed *to sustain*
To him, from His Lord *to claim*
O Muhammad!
Just assert to affirm in stride

11 Knowledge and intelligence

The Notations are indeed with Lord *to aside*
I'm but to admonish, men and clan *in abide* (29:49–50)

Prophet Mohammed's [PBUH] tradition, "Sunnah," also termed *(Hadidh)*, is rich and clear in advocating all kinds of knowledge, whether it is religious or scientific.

- Scientists, the knowledgeable, are the inheritors of the prophets.
- The acquisition of knowledge is a duty incumbent on every Muslim, male and female.
- Seek knowledge from the cradle to the grave.
- He who leaves his home in search of knowledge walks on the path of Allah.
- If Allah likes someone to be good, He makes him to understand and learn.
- Certainly knowledge is the result of learning.

In Islam, there is no contradiction between science and religion. On the contrary, there is an intimate embracing and evened association. In Islam, there is equilibrium between the heart and the mind, between what is spiritual and ethereal and what is real and down-to-earth. A divine balance endows us with the true discernment of its actuality.

In this respect, Dr. Maurice Bucaille in his book, *The Bible, the Qur'an and Science: The Holy Scriptures Examined in the Light of Modern Knowledge*, says, "The association between the Qur'an and science is a preference, not a surprise, especially since it is going to be one of harmony and not of discord."

The Adam of Qur'an and the Adam of Science Are One not Two

The origin of the species was a powerful theory for how evolution could occur through purely natural forces, liberating scientists to explore the glorious complexity of life, rather than merely accept it as an impenetrable mystery. "Nothing in biology makes sense, except in the light of evolution."

On July 2, 1866, Alfred Russel Wallace suggested* redacting the term and adopting Herbert Spencer's phrase "survival of the fittest." Unfortunately, that is what happened, and it led to two myths about evolution that persist today: that there is a prescient directionality to evolution and that survival depends entirely on cutthroat, competitive fitness. *(Scientific American; Sept 2009)

Contrary to the first myth, natural selection is a description of a process, not a force.

Natural selection simply means that those individuals with variations better suited to their environment leave behind more offspring than individuals that are less well adapted. This outcome is known as "differential reproductive success." It may be, as the second myth holds, that organisms that are bigger, stronger, faster, and brutishly competitive will reproduce more successfully, but it is just as likely that organisms that are smaller, weaker, slower, and socially cooperative will do so as well. This second notion in particular makes evolution unpalatable for many people, because it covers the theory with a darkened patina reminiscent of Alfred, Lord Tennyson's "nature, red in tooth and claw." Thomas Henry Huxley, Darwin's "bulldog" defender, promoted this "gladiatorial" view of life in a series of popular essays on nature "whereby the strongest, the swiftest, and the most cunning live to fight another day." The myth persists.

How could you ever determine *to concern*
That "We" created you *in term*

Gradually grow out of earth (Ardh) *in turn*
(Al Qur'an 71:17)
(Created you to grow gradually in stages from the dust and mud.)

When we read this verse, we find hardly any deviation of the scientific concept from faith.

So far, the Adam and Eve of science differ entirely from the Adam and Eve of religion; the two types of concepts have given rise to a conflicting situation from which there is no escape except to abandon either the enunciation of religion or the clear teachings of science. Today, the young generation finds itself in a similar dilemma, thrown at the crossroads, bewildered and perplexed. Those who profess to accept this duality of thinking in their challenging experience of pursuing scientific convictions while still preserving religious faith are in fact split-up personalities with little prospect of finding the right path, for faith cannot take root in a divided mind. This article might be rabble-rousing for cetrain polemical thinkers on both sides (i.e., faith and science), but a temperate and measured approach will help us to understand the philosophy of creation objectively.

We shall have to carefully evolve a diplomatic way to integrate the elements of faith and science so that there is no fear of squashing the old, deeply insinuated convictions in this domain.

Before understanding the philosophy of the creation of man, we shall have to understand the basic integral unit of the human body that not only forms the brickwork of the human body as an earthly pot but also forms the basis of the vivacity that holds the life or efflux or soul to perform the simplest to most complex tasks while playing on the most delicate orchestra of the human genetic proscenium—life at the cellular, DNA level.

Every organism carries a chemical code for its own creation inside its cells, a text written in a language common to all life: the simple, three-letter code of DNA. DNA not only confirms the reality of evolution, it also shows, at the most basic level, how it reshapes living things.

Genes are the sequences of DNA letters that when activated by the cell make a particular protein through RNA in the nucleus of the cell. When the gene for a protein called BMP4 is activated (scientists use the word "expressed") in the growing jaw of a finch embryo, it makes the beak deeper and wider. Hopi Hoekstra, at Harvard, and her colleagues traced the color difference to the change of a single letter in a single gene, which cuts down the production of pigment in the fur of a mouse.

Now, in the beak of the finch and the fur of the mouse, we can actually see the hand of natural selection at work, molding and modifying the

DNA of genes and their expression to adapt the organism to its particular circumstances.

The mutation is a single letter change, from A to G, on the long arm of chromosome 15, which dampens the expression of a gene called OCA2, involved in the manufacture of the pigment that darkens the eyes. This mutation happened only about six to ten thousand years ago, well after the invention of agriculture, in a particular individual somewhere around the Black Sea. So Darwin may have gotten his blue eyes because of a single misspelled letter in the DNA in the baby of a Neolithic farmer. Intriguingly, the spelling change that caused blue eyes is not in the pigment gene itself but in a nearby snippet of DNA scripture that controls the gene's expression. This lends support to the idea that is rushing through genetics and evolutionary biology: evolution works not just by changing genes, but by modifying the way those genes are switched on and off. We reach the conclusion: the primary fuel for the evolution of anatomy turns out not to be gene changes, but changes in the regulation of genes that control development.

The notion of genetic switches explains the humiliating surprise that human beings appear to have no special human genes. Over the past decade, as scientists compared the human genome with that of other creatures, it has emerged that we inherit not just the same number of genes as a mouse—fewer than twenty-one thousand—but in most cases, the very same genes. Just as you don't need different words to write different books or different building materials to construct different buildings, so you don't need new genes to make new species. You just change the order and pattern of their use. Perhaps more scientists should have realized this sooner than they did. After all, bodies are not assembled, like machines in factories; they grow and develop, so evolution was always going to be about changing the process of growth rather than specifying the end product of that growth. In other words, a giraffe doesn't have special genes for a long neck.

Though modern genetics vindicates Darwin in all sorts of ways, it also turns the spotlight on his biggest mistake. Darwin's own ideas on the mechanism of inheritance were a mess—and wrong. He thought that an organism blended together a mixture of its parents' traits, and later in his life, he began to believe it also passed on traits acquired during its lifetime. An organism isn't a blend of its two parents at all, but the composite result of lots and lots of individual traits passed down by its father and mother from their own parents and their grandparents before them.

Our creation or initiation was not an ordinary job. The Lord Almighty created the genetic array of the human being in perfect order with His own hands (Sad 38:75) and did not leave it on its own for procreation. There has been a proper order and discipline in this procreation, but for the order of whole, there has to be definite transmutation in the genetic makeup. For the discipline of the whole, there has to be good and bad, for otherwise, this life would not have been a place to live.

The gradual creation of man from mud (Nuh 71:17) and all living beings from water (Nür 24:45) has been repeatedly emphasized in the Qur'an. If we go through the pose and strophe of each verse very discerningly, we can well understand the evolution of the human being is not, as matter of fact, a chance hypothesis as Darwin perceives but the logical outcome of His Almighty's deliberation of the natural process, determined under different environmental conditions, of the creation as it evolved. His Almighty brought the related living beings on this earth. The early dinosaurs were to loiter hither and thither in extreme weather conditions when nothing on Earth could survive, but later, the clue and concept of science and faith converge at one point: that the creation of Adam and Eve was a matter of preordained evolution.

Some people assert that the gradual creation from dust and mud refers to our nutrition, which is all based on the growth from the soil hence, the "gradual creation or evolution of the man is from dust and mud." But when we consider the Holy Scripture, it clearly refers to man's earlier creation that was from dust and mud and later from the conjugation of ovum and sperm (40:67; 35:11).

It's He,
Who stages your creation *in best*

Created you from the mud *or dust* تُرَاب
Then from the sperm *in speck*
You're,
Leech-like clot in mother's den *as nest*
(Mumin 40:67)

Lord created you from the dust *or mud*
Then from the speck of sperm *in speck*
(Fatir 35:11)

In a cultural milieu permeated through and through with science, modern man has developed habits to concrete on thought which renders him less capable of that type of inner experience on which religious faith ultimately rests because he suspects it 'liable to illusion. And no one would hazard action on the basis of a doubtful principle of conduct.

Religion stands in greater need of a rational foundation for its ultimate principles than the dogmas of science. In these circumstances, the demand for a scientific form of religious experience is quite natural. It was the desire to fulfill this need that prompted me to reconstruct religious thought in Islam "with due regard to the philosophical traditions of Islam and the latest developments in various domains of human knowledge, particularly modern-day science." Today, I also assume to resolve myself to evolve a method physiologically less violent and psychologically more suitable to a concrete type of mind. We find the Muslims of this century in an extremely critical stage which immediately demanded an attempt to reconcile religion with reason. I firmly believe that the day is not far off when "religion and science will discover mutual harmonies." My efforts at the rationalization of faith are not actually restricted to one belief, as the modern scientific achievements immediately demand alliance with the philosophy of religion. This need has prompted me to strive hard to find the true way of equanimity and amity between modern-day science and the evolution of mankind in the light of the Qur'an.

Like the creation of the universe, earth is, for that matter, the fruit of the cosmic order, as far as we know up to today, and similarly, the creation of man is the fruit of life in the cosmic blue pearl, the earth. The order of fruition as detailed before was planned in a definite, designed order with gradual evolution and mutation of the genetic array. Surprisingly, as a matter of fact, the mouse is our close kin, sharing almost 65 percent of its genes with us. A play on the genetic proscenium with a master or Hox gene in each of the Almighty's creations by nature conceived the most fascinating and enchanting creations, and still we deny His order of discipline in each pace. How fascinating is His order in each discipline of creation? One cannot really comprehend His enchantments in the sea world, not to mention the other innumerable effects and equipage in the surroundings.

But there is a line of reasoning to consider. When genetic evolution and mutation were taking place, it was throughout the surface of the globe and not isolated to a particular point or area.

There were hobbits, the tiny (only three feet tall) human relatives from an isolated island, Flores, of Indonesia, who somehow failed to thrive in the competitive existence and so vanished.

Where did they come from?

Similarly, in Surah: *Ash Shuara*, verses (026:123–139), the Qur'an gives the narration of the nation Aad, who were probably twenty-eight to thirty feet tall (last page).

So did the men and clan of Aad in abide
Defying and denying messengers in stride

139

When their close in kin Hud got to pray
O my men and clan hither in stay
Wouldn't you elude evil in play

Indeed!
I'm a sincere messenger (to you) in sway
So have trust in Lord and me you obey

And I don't ask for a pittance in prize
For that's for my Lord to apprise

You raise memorial at the height
For your abortive tends in delight

And construct casual castle in assort
As if you're going to stay for ever in resort

And if you snag and subdue by might in lush
It's same as do oppressor or a duce in crush

Dread Almighty and obey my command
And dread Him,
Who endowed you, what you hold in stance
As you ever discern so comply in glance
He gave you steers and sons in play
Besides gardens and springs in sway

Indeed!
I dread a doom in gloom in sight
Retaliation of dreadful Day in plight

They said:
It's but the same in stance
If to exhort or not in glance

That's but a fable, men and clan of old
And we wouldn't be smashed in hold

And they defied to disputed (him) to obey
So We smashed and shattered (them) in stray

Didn't they have the evolution from those environmental conditions of the place they were living?

It is essentially believed that the modern man *Homo erectus* took its stride from Africa. Could it be the evolution from that part of the land reached its maturity earlier or before rest of the world? But there is a point to consider very carefully in this context, that if the evolution was there in rest of the world too, then why couldn't it reach the prime order of maturity over there at some later stage or did it only migrate from Africa to the rest of world?

If we all reconcile to the modern concept of evolution of *Homo erectus*, then the Lord Almighty decided to have His cherished creative being to be first from the land of Africa.

The genetic mutation was carried through time and space in human descendants, who now include around six billion men around the world. In the genetic copy of the gene, it might surprise you, they are related to common ancestors. The long-gone ancestor is known as the founder of all the population, and his or her genetic legacy is called a founder mutation. The Qur'an affirms that you're born of common ancestors (4 Al Nisa: 1). Recent studies (*Scientific American*, July 2008) reported that humans from different populations all descended from a single female, Mitochondrial Eve, from Africa. She lived about two hundred thousand years ago. The fast, relatively predictable rate of neutral mitochondrial mutations—ones that are neither beneficial nor harmful—lets the organelles operate as molecular clocks. Counting the differences in the number of mutations (ticks of the clock) between two groups, or the lineages, allows a researcher to construct a genetic tree that tracks back to a common ancestor—Mitochondrial Eve— who founded a new lineage. Comparison of the age of the lineages from different regions permits the building of a timeline of human migration, besides resolving a long-disputed issue of the Adam of science and the Adam of religion.

Let us deliberate on the different views elaborating the process of evolution. There is a strong opinion asserting the role of supreme nature, for otherwise, even the proteins could not have evolved on their own, not to mention the most complicated living beings like a man, who could not have developed without a most fascinating mind behind all this evolution. And finally, we'll trend toward the affirmations given in the Holy Qur'an that assert to affirm the process of evolution but with a definite design in plan as ordained by the Lord Almighty.

What Darwin wrote in one of the most incendiary books in the history of science, *The Origin of Species*, was a powerful theory for how evolution could occur through purely natural forces,[12] liberating scientists to explore the glorious complexity of life, rather than accept it as an impenetrable mystery. "Nothing in biology makes sense, except in the light of evolution."

Evolution is only a theory; it's not a fact or a scientific law.

When Charles Darwin introduced the theory of evolution through natural selection some one hundred and fifty years ago, the scientists of the day argued over it fiercely, but the massing evidence from paleontology, genetics, zoology, molecular biology, and other fields gradually established evolution's truth beyond reasonable doubt. Today, that battle has been won everywhere except in the public imagination.

Evolution cannot explain how life first appeared on earth.

The origin of life remains very much a mystery, but biochemists have learned about how primitive nucleic acids, amino acids, and other building blocks of life could have formed and organized themselves into self-replicating, self-sustaining units, laying the foundation for cellular biochemistry. Astrochemical analyses hint that quantities of these compounds might have originated in space and fallen to earth in comets, a scenario that may solve the problem of how those constituents arose under the conditions that prevailed when our planet was young.

Creationists sometimes try to invalidate all of evolution by pointing to science's current inability to explain the origin of life. But even if life on earth turned out to have a non-evolutionary origin (for instance, if aliens introduced the first cells billions of years ago), evolution since then would be robustly confirmed by countless microevolutionary and macroevolutionary studies.

The following questions still remain unanswered: What's the original source of life? And who communicated it through the comets, as presumed, to the earth?

Mathematically, it is inconceivable that anything as complex as a protein, let alone a living cell or a human, could spring up by chance. Chance plays a part in evolution (for example, in the random mutations that can give rise to new traits), but evolution does not depend on chance to create organisms, proteins, or other entities. Quite the opposite, natural selection, the principal known mechanism of evolution, harnesses nonrandom change by preserving desirable adaptive features and eliminating undesirable (nonadaptive) ones. As long as the forces of selection stay constant, natural selection can push evolution in one direction and produce sophisticated

---

12 I call it <u>the Divine force</u> through the genetic code, for otherwise, it would not be possible for the natural forces to influence evolutionay processes.

structures in surprisingly short times. Still, we cannot avoid the words *natural selection* or *divine interference*.

Many students learned in elementary school that a theory falls in the middle of a hierarchy of certainty above a mere hypothesis but below a law. Scientists do not use the terms that way, however. According to the National Academy of Sciences (NAS), a scientific theory is a well-substantiated explanation of some aspect of the natural world that can incorporate facts, laws, inferences, and tested hypotheses. No amount of validation changes a theory into a law, which is a descriptive generalization about nature. So when scientists talk about the theory of evolution or the atomic theory of relativity, for that matter, they are not expressing reservations about its truth.

But the Qur'an gives a clear concept of the creation of nucleic acid with evolution to the genome or the genetic permutation of the fertilized ovum and sperm as discussed later in this chapter with reference to various Qur'anic verses.

In addition to the theory of evolution, meaning the idea of descent with modification, one may also speak of the fact of evolution. The NAS defines a fact as an observation that has been repeatedly confirmed and for all practical purposes is accepted as true. The fossil record and abundant other pieces of evidence testify that organisms have evolved through time.

Natural selection is based on circular reasoning; the fittest are those who survive, and those who survive are deemed fittest. Survival of the fittest is a conversational way to describe natural selection, but a more technical description speaks of differential rates of survival and reproduction. That is, rather than labeling a species as more or less fit, one can describe how many offspring they are likely to leave under given circumstances.

Some assert that evolution is unscientific, because it is not testable or falsifiable. It makes claims about events that were not observed and can never be recreated. This, though a dismissal of evolution, ignores important distinctions that divide the field into at least two broad areas: microevolution and macroevolution. *Microevolution* looks at changes within a species over time. Changes that may be a prelude to specification would result in the origin of a new species. *Macroevolution* studies how taxonomic groups above the level of the species change. Its evidence draws frequently on the fossil record and DNA comparisons to reconstruct how various organisms may be related.

Natural selection and other mechanisms, such as chromosomal changes, symbiosis, and hybridization, can drive profound changes in populations over time.

The historical nature of macroevolutionary studies involves inference from fossils and DNA rather than direct observation. Yet in the historical sciences, which include astronomy, geology, and archaeology, as well as evolutionary biology, hypotheses can still be tested by checking whether they conform to physical evidence or if they lead to verifiable predictions about future discoveries. For instance, evolution implies that between the earliest known ancestors of humans (roughly five million years ago) and the appearance of anatomically modern humans (about one hundred thousand years ago), one should find a succession of hominid creatures with features progressively less apelike and more modern, which is indeed what the fossil record shows. But one does not find modern human fossils embedded in strata from the Jurassic period (sixty-five million years ago). Evolutionary biology routinely makes predictions far more refined and precise than this, and researchers test them constantly.

Evidence suggests evolution is not losing ground. Pick up any issue of a peer-reviewed biological journal, and you will find articles that support and extend evolutionary studies or that embrace evolution as a fundamental concept. The Qur'an asserts, on various occasions, a concept of evolution that's further elucidated in the scientific consideration—the initiation of the big bang or the divine dictum in dictate, *Kun: Fa Yä Koon*.

When "We" asked both earth and heavens to come into actuality, they submissively acceded to the command and came into being. (All the physical laws that formed the basis of creation came into being within the first one second of the big bang (for details, see "Perfect Creation"). The process of evolution as ordained in Qur'anic teachings is not foreign to scientific convictions. Imagine everything in the cosmic domain evolved from nihility (as discussed in "Perfect Creation") and took billions of years to be the earth and its surroundings—not to mention our own creation (i.e., the initial conjugation of the insinuating dip of the sinful dot in drop, merging in a clot and finally bringing out a man of caliber in slot).

Similarly, all the processes of evolution evolved and materialized in the proper order of discipline as ordained by Allah Almighty; it was not that a monkey in the next phase of development evolved into a man or a lizard in next stages of development became a crocodile. The evolution of the created beings parallels the history of the evolution of the universe and the earth in particular because the very existence of different creatures could only be conceived of if it were congenial to the surrounding environments.

Living things have fantastically intricate features at the anatomical, cellular, and molecular levels that could not function if they were any less complex or distantly sophisticated. The only sensible conclusion is that they are the products of a most intelligent design, let alone evolution without an intelligent mind behind it.

Today's intelligent-design advocates are more sophisticated than their predecessors, but their arguments and goals are not fundamentally different. They criticize evolution by trying to demonstrate that it could not account for life as we know it and then insist that the only tenable alternative is that life was designed by an intelligent deity.

Recent studies prove that even at the microscopic level, life has a quality of complexity that could not have come about through evolution alone.

We conclude that the process of evolution was determined by the Lord Almighty in all spheres, in the creation of the cosmic order and all living beings, because such a sophisticated system could not have come into being on its own with just the process of evolution as conceived by Darwin.

If we read the text of the Holy Scripture (the Qur'an) intently with a view to understanding it in the light of scientific conviction, there is hardly any vacillation or deviation from scientific assertions, but it is not the Darwinian evolution; instead, it is a predetermined fruit of evolution, the man, as ordained by the Lord Almighty.

> How could you ever determine *to concern*
> That He created you *in turn,*
> Gradually grow out of earth *(mud) in term* (071:017)

It is repeatedly asserted in the Qur'an: Don't look at the dried, desolate, deserted land; when there is a sprinkle of rain, it's enlivened, and so I'll get you back to life when you will be just dust and soot after death and demise.

How is the land enlivened?

What's the cause or source of this effect?

Rain is the answer.

What's the source that caused the effect of rain?

The cloud is the answer.

And what's the source behind the cause of this effect?

The sun is the answer!

So we try to discern the source behind the effect of each cause, and we ultimately, as in this case, affirm that the sun was the source that produced the clouds over the sea and the gusts of wind, spreading them over the lands.

But the sun itself did not come into being on its own; it must have a discernable source behind the creation of this effect. We understand that each effect has to have a source and the source is the logic behind its creation. We invariably pronounce that source nature. A mighty nature is behind the creation of all these effects and equipage to which I attribute the name Allah;

some call it YUHUH and still others call it God, but nobody has refuted the word *nature*. I wonder if the scientists could avoid the terms "natural selection" in evolution, the process to which I attribute the name *divine selection*.

On the words *microevolution* and *macroevolution*: the role of natural environmental selection can lead to microevolution, whereas the divine order of evolution inscribed in the chemical code of the genome leads to the creation of different species in living beings and is macroevolution, preordained in the genetic array—the message communicated in the genetic proscenium, through the project engineer, the Hox gene.

At this moment, we cannot deny or defy the divine interception of creation and natural selection as the scientists join to assert. Let us have a glimpse of the Qur'anic affirmation in the order of creation and the modern scientific concepts acceding to or defying the Darwinian theory of evolution, as discussed earlier.

Lord created all living things from water (Al Qur'an 24:45)
We gradually created the man from mud. (Al Qur'an 71:17)

And recall, when Lord!
Created from progeny of Adam *in term*
From their loins the descendents *in stay*
And caused to affirm over them *in turn*
Saying:
Am I not your Lord *to pray*
They so affirmed:
Indeed!
You're Our Lord to pray (Al A 'räf 7:172)

The details of this affirmation need quite a bit of consideration.

What was the nature of the offspring from the bridal germ or ova and the male sperm, who were called to affirm?

Am I not your Lord *to pray*?

And whatever was the nature of the offspring, who affirmed: "You're our Lord, we submit *to obey*."

There are two possibilities:

- One, that Lord Almighty originally created Adam and Eve from the dust and mud and infused life into them, as commonly believed. But then what exactly was the nature of the offspring or the genetic array created from Adam and Eve?

- Two, He gradually created Adam and Eve from the dust and mud, and when they were mature enough (71:17), His Almighty got them to the heavens to reside.

And then from the bridal germ (ovum) and (male) sperm, progeny was created from day one to the end of life in this world, who affirm, "You're our Lord." But there is a point of real concern.

What was the nature of our being in the first stance?

Because it is commonly believed that our souls affirmed the Lord Almighty: "You're our Lord."

But how could an earthly pot (like Adam or Eve as full human beings) beget souls?

All the narrations from the Holy Scripture, when put together, assert to affirm that our being in our earlier stay in the heavens was not like our being here in this world. So could it be the genetic array in whatever shape endowed by Lord Almighty?

Before concluding the subject, we look at the various verses of the Holy Qur'an relating to the creation of mankind on the earth and their initial creation in the heavens (i.e., Adam and Eve).

How could you ever determine *to concern*
That He created you,
Gradually grow out of earth (Ardh) in term
(71 Nuh 17)

It's He, Who created you from dust (Ardh) *in trace*
And settled there *in pace*

So beg to reprieve Him and tend *to attrition*
Indeed!
My Lord is Close and Compliant in contrition
(11 Hud 61)

When you're created from the dust (Ardh) *in place*
Then you're veiled in your mother's womb *in stay*
So claim not your piety *in stay*
He discerns and concerns *in pace*
Who's the virtuous a bit *in trace* (53 Al Najm 32)

Indeed!
We created the man *in plan*
From the potter's clay like soot *in span*   صَلْصَالٍ مِّنْ حَمَإٍ مَّسْنُونٍ
(15 Hijr 26)

Potter's clay of black mud altered
And recall!
When Lord told the angels *in aside*

I'm creating a temporal being *in abide*
Hither from sooty potters clay in stride   *15* (Hijr 28)
(Potter's clay of black mud altered)   صَلْصَالٍ مِّنْ حَمَإٍ مَّسْنُونٍ

Created the man,
From the ringing potters clay   صَلْصَالٍ كَالْفَخَّارِ
(55 Al Rahman: 14)

These verses suggest that the creation of the nucleic acids, DNA and RNA, gradually evolved in the deepest layers of the earth as indicated in the following passage.

For all the diversity of life on this planet, ranging from tiny bacteria to majestic blue whales, from sunshine-harvesting plants to mineral-digesting endoliths, miles underground, only one kind of "life as we know it" exists. All these organisms are based on nucleic acids, DNA and RNA, and proteins, working together more or less as described by the so-called central dogma of molecular biology: DNA stores information that is transcribed into RNA, which then serves as a template for producing a protein. The proteins, in turn, serve as important structural elements in tissues and, as enzymes, are the cells' workhorses. Yet the scientists dream of synthesizing life that is utterly alien to this world—both to better understand the minimum component required for life (as part of the quest to uncover the essence of life that originated on earth) and, frankly, to see if they can do it. That is, they hope to put together a novel combination of molecules that can self-organize, metabolize (make use of an energy source), grow, reproduce, and evolve. A synthetic molecule discovered in 1995, called peptide nucleic acid (PNA), combines the information-storage properties of DNA with the chemical stability of a protein-like backbone.

In the following verses, the word for *dust* [طِينٍ] is used for the creation of man.

Such is The Lord unparallel *to pace*
Who created and contrived, superb *in place*

He got to the man in creation
Out of the clay *in narration* (32 Al Sajda 07)

Lord is the One the Alone in sway
Created you from dust and clay
And assigned for a term hither in stay
And a term Hereafter affirmed in place
But still quite a few hang in confound
With scruple and suspense in confound
(06 Al an ám 02)

When We asked Devil to sate:
Why you defied Our Word *in command*
Devil then turned to narrate
I'm of the better lot *in stance*
You created me from the Fire
And to him from *dirt and dust* (07 Al Araf 12)

Regard!
Lord voiced to the angels *in array*
I'm to contrive man from dirt *and clay*
(38 Sad 71)

Devil then asserted, *submissive in pace*
I'm preferred *(to him) for all in place*
You contrived me of flaming fire *in blaze*
And to him,
You created from dust *and dirt (in haze)*
(38 Sad 76)

Indeed!
We created the man in abide,
From the essence of the soggy soil *in stride* [13]
(23 Al Muminun 12)

In the following verses, the word تُرَاب for *dust* is used for the creation of the man.

His friend then trended *to state*

---

13 The essence of the soggy soil (i.e., the genetic permutation of the fertilized ovum or the whole genetic array of the human being);? is (i.e., the genetic permutation of sperm).

And said:
You don't have the faith for Lord in relate
Who created you of the dust first *in stance*
Then from the dribble of sperm *in glance*
Then shaped you to be a man *in trance*
(18 Al Qahf: 37)

O mankind!
If you still question the Day in Revive
Then indeed!
We contrived you from dust *to survive*
Then from drop of sperm *to thrive*
(22 Al Hajj: 05)

Of all His Signs affirmed *in prime*
As He created you of dust *in sublime*
And then look and around *in display*
Men and clan dispersed far *in array*
(30 Al Rum: 20)

It's He,
Who stages your creation *in best*
Created you from *the mud and* dust
Then from sperm *in speck*
You're leech-like clot *in mother's den and nest*
He gets you to the light, as suckling *with the rest*
Lets you grow and reach, age vigor *in best*
Then gets you to be an elderly *guest*
Though some,
May doom and die, before *of the rest*
And lets you attain a time *in vale*
And to affirm sense and sapience *in trail*
(40 Al Mumin: 67)

Lord so offers semblance *in plan*
Creation of,
Jesus that's like of Adam *in span*
Made Adam from dust and mud *in design*
Then He infused His Efflux *so refine*
And commanded it to "Be" *and sure*
And he was there *to endure* (03 Al Imran: 59)

There is food for thought for the creationists and those in the realm of evolution. The text of the Holy Scripture is clearly giving a clue to the creation of the building blocks of the living being as an earthly pot and the seat of the efflux or the soul, the nucleic acids. The word [*Teen* طِين] is clearly indicating the genetic permutation of the fertilized ovum whereas the word [*Turab* تُرَاب] is used for sperm, as the details will elucidate.

Allah Almighty gives the semblance of the creation of Christ to Adam and mentions that the latter, Adam, He created of dust [*Turab* تُرَاب]

We know that the male partner is not there in the case of Christ. So how can we assign the role of just dust or mud in the creation of Christ or Adam? And Allah Almighty has repeatedly asserted that He created you first from the [*Ardh* أَرْض] and then from the sperm [نُطْفَة]. It clearly elucidates that the word itself is defying the meaning as dust, at this place. [تُرَاب] is probably used as a symbolic genetic synonym for sperm. Later, we see in the Scripture, when Allah Almighty refers to the creation of Adam, He uses the word [طِين]. We see in the case of Christ, the mother's part as the ovum for fertilization was there, whereas in the case of Adam, that's missing.

The word [طِين] is most probably used as a symbolic genetic synonym for the fertilized ovum (the creation of Adam at the first instance).

The creation of humanity in gradual order, or evolution, is then affirmed from [*Ardh* أَرْض]

This is the true English meaning for the word dust or mud.

We conclude from the discussion that the initial creation of Adam in the heavens was not like the human beings living on the earth but very much like the Almighty ordained it to be with genetic proscenium at the core bearing His efflux.

When His Almighty ordained to create His assistant on the earth, أَرْض it was the genetic proscenium of all who affirmed, "You're our Lord," and it was then the man was bestowed the sapience in intellect (i.e., the intelligence and a word in dialect, referred to as "names" in the Holy Scripture). It was also bestowed to the man before conveying him down onto the earth for the gradual creation from the earth.

That word of intelligence has been perpetuating ever since the creation of the human being with gradual evolution.

Well, it will not be out of the way to give details as to why the Lord Almighty called man the superior being over and above the angels, when they are created with two of His Almighty's bestowals or divine parts: the efflux or the soul and the frame or structural makeup of Noor, whereas man, created of dust and mud, has just one endowment of the Lord Almighty (*i.e., the efflux or the soul*. But His Almighty bestowed upon the man the power of discernment or interpretation in the light of intelligence at the time of creation of the genetic proscenium with the endowment of the efflux or the soul. For the order of the whole, there has to be discipline of the soul. Angels have not to argue the command given to them. They have just to abide the order, because they are ordained only to obey the discipline of the Lord Almighty. They have not to see the pros and cons of anything good or bad, for whatever is communicated to them, they have just to comply.[14]

But man is endowed the power of discernment for what he is ordained to maintain in the discipline of life. And it is through the true perception of intelligence that he has to decide good or bad and take a right course of conduct that is deeply insinuated, the truth, in the genetic proscenium of all living beings.

If at the first instance, the actual created being, *Adam*, was from أَرْض [*Ardh*] as detailed above. Similarly, if the Lord Almighty created man gradually from the dust and mud, when it was mature enough to be a real human being, then from his offspring, His Almighty got the affirmation, "Who's your Lord?"

In both the cases, our being in the life before our creation in this world should have been like that of ours in this world, but nothing of the sort affirms such an assertion as true. So if we go into the details of the text of the Holy Qur'an, it very diligently affirms that with the creation of the cosmic sway, the Lord Almighty determined to have His caliph in this vale, so with the idea He possibly had the genetic array of the human race with Adam and Eve and asked the angels to prostrate before them.

> *And recall, when Lord!*
> Created from progeny of Adam *in term*
> From their loins the descendents in stay
> And caused to affirm over them *in turn*
> *Saying*:
> Am I not your Lord *to pray*
> *They so affirmed:*
> *Indeed!*
> You're Our Lord *all to pray* (Al A 'räf 7:172)

The legacy of creation in the heavens is nothing but the genetic procreation of all the mankind, from day one to the last in this world, who was endowed intelligence and got the affirmation of His being "the Lord, the

14 Angels, for that matter, have been endowed with vigilance in compliance and men with intelligence in discernment for interpretation.

Creator of all the Multiverses." The endowment of intelligence is nothing but the *affirmation of the truth*. And what's the truth? That's the faith as ordained in all the Holy Scriptures. You have not to tell somebody what is good or bad and virtuous or vile, it is deeply insinuated in our minds. When we teach our children regarding the discipline of faith, the truth, we simply remind them the factuality of truth in faith, which is already deeply insinuated in their minds.

Consider the whole concept in this context: When we have something in mind to construct, even a simple building, we initially have to write down the basic requirements of the plan and have the design and later start the structural array.

Imagine the early Adam and Eve as an elegant array of genetic proscenium, something like today's robots performing errands for us.

We know that Jesus Christ was created without the male partner or sperm and Allah Almighty is comparing the creation of the Christ with that of Adam. The texts of Surah Al Mumin and Surah Al Fatir clearly indicate that the original creation of Adam is not from the dust, as in the case of Christ; the sperm [*Turab* تُرَاب] is not there for conjugation; only the genetic play could replace the sperm. The whole text affirms that the meaning of [تُرَاب] is not the *dust* in the text. This could only be the *genetic permutation* that leads to the creation of Adam's genome, and then from day one to the last, all the genetic array of all the humanity was created from the genetic proscenium of Adam and Eve with the endowment of the efflux from Allah Almighty, who affirmed, when asked: اَلَسْتُ بِرَبِّكُمْ

"They said: You are our Lord."

Human evolution elucidates the role of genetic permutation.

The whole discussion clearly indicates the role of genetic permutation, which at the first instance, was in the heavens during the creation of Adam with the efflux (soul or the spirit of Allah Almighty) and from the genetic array of Adam and Eve (possibly the parallel creation of the genetic array of Eve was ordained, as the genetic permutation of Adam was in the process), the genetic array of the whole of humanity from day one to the last was created, they who affirmed that "You're our Lord," when asked: اَلَسْتُ بِرَبِّكُمْ

Then on the earth, it was the gradual creation of humanity from the dust [أَرْض*Ardh*]; as mentioned in Surah Nuh, Verse 17, it gradually evolved [*Teen* طِين] to have [طِين firtilized ovum] and then the sperm or [*Turab* تُرَاب] and finally, humanity evolved around two hundred thousand years before (as affirmed in the scientific journals) in Africa, and then it spread all over the globe.

We sum up the process of evolution as enunciated in the Holy Qur'an:

- Initial planning of creation of man from earthly material that also consisted of mud
- Then in the deepest layers of the earth, altered black mud under a different chemical reaction that can self-organize, metabolize (make use of an energy source), grow, reproduce, and evolve DNA and RNA (while the outer layers behave as potter's clay on drying, and then it further dries out and hardens to behave as a ringing potter's clay). During all this process, the mud is trapped at the core with hard ringing potter's clay like the material surrounding it all around.

The mud trapped inside the ringing potter's clay–like material got desquamated later; it turned black as it got mutilated over a period of time. How long this process of desquamation continued is a matter of concern for the creationists and evolutionists to work out, because so far, it is not conceivable mathematically to confirm the creation of simple proteins or amino acids. Whereas the verses from the Holy Scripture are clearly elucidating the process of evolution with the creation of the genetic proscenium, the genome with all the genetic code written on the DNA and RNA. Later from [طِين *Teen*], the essence for the further creation [تُرَاب *Turab*] is evolved. The genetic message is communicated through the sperm in the creation of the species, and [تُرَاب *Turab*] is the genetic permutation of sperm as very clearly elucidated in the Holy Qur'an (3:59).

Just think of the gene sequence, human accelerated region 1 (HAR1). The complexity of this gene played a key role in the creation of human beings from chimpanzees. The details are quite interesting but beyond the scope of this work. We share nearly 99 percent of our DNA with chimpanzees, but still we (these two species) differ so profoundly. (For details of creation of men from chimpanzees, please consult *Scientific American*, May 2009.)

Now the consequence of the soul or the efflux still remains to be answered, that neither belong to us nor do we have any control over them. If we think for a while over the entire process of creation, how could it be possible to write down billions of codes on the genome to interpret and determine the conduct and course of living beings. Through the Human Genome Project, which sequenced our own genome, scientists now know that the protein-coding genes make up just 1.5 percent of our DNA. The other 98.5 percent—sometimes referred to as junk DNA—contains regulatory sequences that tell other genes when to turn on and off and genes encoding RNA that do not get translated into proteins, as well as a lot of DNA that has purposes scientists are only beginning to understand.

From the comprehensive dialogue on the subject, we conclude that the determined discipline of evolution was preordained, because otherwise, we could not affirm the most complex nature of life from the unicellular to the most organized human being over and above the endowment of the soul or the efflux, that is neither ours nor within our control.

Another important point to consider at this stage is that since evolution was taking place around the globe almost everywhere, then why was it from Africa alone that the Mitochondrial Eve evolved to reproduce the whole human race that later spread all over the globe?

The order of evolution is all divine in nature, which an unbiased man of knowledge cannot deny.

Agile Author Astral O Astute

Brilliant Beginner Bountiful O Beatitude
Conforming Creator in Care and Command

When the whole genetic proscenium of all the human beings was created and the Lord Almighty could discern how a particular genome was going to behave in this world, all was written and saved. The story of Abu Lahb is a citation for all to consider. His Almighty could really envision the picture of the future array of His creation; so the Qur'an was written and saved in *Laoh-i-Mehfooz*. The Qur'an was written when He had conceived the genetic array and revealed from time to time as desired, confirming the situation. Here again, a logical point is raised. Then what is it to me to behave in a particular way or abide discipline in this world when it is already preordained? The answer to this question is detailed in the "Fate and Fortune" and a good bit of detail is also given in "The Philosophy of Creation."

No doubt a born atheist who carries through as a nonbeliever at one time or the other turns around to think that there is some supreme power who commands the authority; particularly in moments of great agony and despair, one determines that the Lord Almighty—by whatever name you may call Him—enjoys the supreme authority.

The subject of deliberation was the creation of the multiverses and the life in it. The Lord Almighty also affirmed the creation of His supreme living being whose early makeup of genetic array was designed by Him, with His own hands (38:75), who affirmed that He is our Lord, and later, a determined cherished creation gradually evolved from the unicellular organism from the dust or mud and water.

Lord then trended to Īblis *in command*
What hinders you to incline *in demand*
To one I fashioned so absolute *and refine*
With My own hands *in sublime*

Are you snobbish and conceited *to decline*
Or if you are high of esteem *in prime* (38:75)

So O Prophet!
Affirm and conform discipline *in Faith*
How *Arty O Crafty* is Lord *in Grace*
Who design in pace and affirm *in place*
He made the mankind in elegant *design*
No drift of shift in His craft *in consign*
That's the embellished Faith *of Divine*
But most of the men don't discern *in line* (30:30)

The Lord Almighty had a predetermined order of discipline for the gradual creation of mankind from the dust or mud and water. First read 7:172 and 71:17 and later the following text.

Lord,
Created of water, all the living *in pace*
There some slither *in place*
Other tread on (legs) two *in score*
There're others that tread on four
Lord is Adept to construe *in lore*
Indeed!
Lord may create *in more*
For what He cherishes *in adore* (24:45)

How nicely this verse elucidates the gradual evolution of the creation of all living beings.

Data from evolution further affirms the Qur'anic assertion. The first fish, the mudskippers, with a fleshy base, had a sober way of edging themselves forward with their front pair of fins. Each of the fins has a fleshy base supported internally by bones. The fin is, in effect, a rigid crutch, and with it, the fish can lever itself forward. Such fins are similar, in principle, than those of the whole group of primitive bony fish that were living in the remote period, when the move to the land was first made. The most famous of the series is the coelacanth which is four hundred million years old. Another fish in the series of evolution is the lungfish, and still another is the eusthenopteron, which has leg-like fins of a pattern found in the limbs of all land vertebrates. This fish, eusthenopteron, lived some four hundred million years ago. It had lungs, heavy scales, and muscular fins. The arrangement of the bones in its fin bases resembled that of the first walking land animals. Later in the series, an amphibian called lehthyostega became the first known four-legged animal to live on the land. It has a fish-like body with well-developed legs, and was know to have existed three hundred and fifty million years ago (i.e., fifty million years later than the two-legged fish, the Eusthenopteron). It resembles the living latimeria

The Holy Scripture further asserts the different stages of the developing embryo in the mother's womb.

It's He,
Who stages your creation *in best*
Created you from *the mud and* dust
Then from sperm *in speck*
You're,
Leech-like clot *in mother's den and nest*
He,
Gets you to light, as suckling *with the rest*
Lets you grow and reach, age vigor *in best*
Then gets you to be an elderly *guest*
Though some,
May doom and die, before *of the rest*

And lets you attain a time *in vale*
And to affirm sense and sapience *in trail* (040:067)

And Lord created you from dirt *and mud*
Then from a speck of sperm *in thud*
Then He made you couples *in keep*
And no dame conceives *in pace*
Or delivers a baby *in place*

But Lord has all the know *in stance*
Nor is a man enduring concluded *in span*
(All men have a determined age in plan)
Nor,
A part reduced from life *in pace*
But it's dictum of Lord *in trace*
It's all so easy for Lord *in grace* (011:035)

Confirming evolution:

> Then We fashioned the drop to a clot
> Subsequently,
> We shaped clot to a tiny lump *in spot*
> Adored tiny mass with bones *in assort*
> *Then,*
> Donned the bones,
> With flesh supple *as sponge*
> And then had the new being *in strong*
> *So,*
> Blessed be The Lord,
> Best of the creators *in norm* (23:14)

To summarize once again, I review the theory of evolution. Today, biologists are beginning to understand the origins of life's complexity—the exquisite optical mechanisms of the eye, the masterly engineering of the arm, the architecture of a flower, the choreography that allows trillions of cells to cooperate in a single organism.

The fundamental answer is clear: in one way or another, all these wonders evolved. "The basic idea of evolution is so elegant, so beautiful, so simple," says Howard Berg, a Harvard researcher who has spent much of the past forty years studying one of the humbler examples of nature's complexity: the spinning tail of common bacteria.

> The idea is simply that you fiddle around and you change something and then you ask: Does it improve my survival or not? And if it doesn't, then those individuals die and that idea goes away. And if it does, then those individuals succeed, and you keep fiddling around and improving. It's an enormously powerful technique.

But nearly 160 years after Darwin first brought the idea to the world's attention when he published *The Origin of Species*, the evolution of complex structures can still be hard to accept. Most of us can envision natural selection tweaking a simple trait—making an animal furrier, for example, or its neck longer. Yet it's harder to picture evolution producing a new complex organism, complete with all its precisely interlocking parts. Creationists claim that life is so complex that it could not have evolved on its own. They often cite the virtuoso engineering of the bacterial tail, which resembles a tiny electric motor spinning a shaft, to argue that such complexity must be the direct product of intelligent design by a superior being. The vast majority of biologists do not share this belief. Studying how complex structures came to be is one of the most exciting frontiers in evolutionary biology, with clues coming at remarkable speed.

Some have emerged from spectacular fossils that reveal the precursors of complex organs and limbs or feathers. Others came from laboratories, where scientists are studying the genes that turn featureless embryos into mature organisms. By comparing the genes that build bodies in different species, they've found evidence that structures as seemingly different as the eyes of a fly and a human being actually have a shared heritage.

Scientists still have a long way to go in understanding the complexity of evolution, which isn't surprising since many of life's devices evolved hundreds of millions of years ago. Nevertheless, new discoveries are revealing the steps by which complex structures developed from simple beginnings. Through it all, scientists keep rediscovering a few key rules. One is that a complex structure can evolve through a series of simpler intermediates. Another is that nature is thrifty, modifying old genes for new uses and even reusing the same genes in new ways, to build something more elaborate.

Sean Carroll, a biologist at the University of Wisconsin, Madison, likens the body-building genes to construction workers. "If you walked past a construction site at 6:00 PM every day, you'd say, 'Wow, it's a miracle; the building is building itself.' But if you sat there all day and saw the workers and the tools, you'd understand how it was put together. We can now see the workers and the machinery. And the same machinery and workers can build any structure."

But here once again, we have to look around for the project director, who is taking care of the workforce so they deploy their energies in a definite plan of design envisaged by the chief engineer, who planned the project, because you cannot expect the laborers to work on their own in a definite plan to construct even an ordinary building, let alone the most elegant creation, like a human being. We learn that "Hox genes" act as the project directors or the site engineers or as the master switches in almost all organisms, turning on the genes that guide the formation of distinct regions in the animal's body (i.e., with definite plan to coordinate between different genes for the evolution of each complex system in the body).

There is a set of codes in a gene that is sensitized by the environments. The gene in turn expresses and communicates the message to the neighboring gene to change its attitude by creating certain enzymes. At times, a gene code leaves its parent gene and jumps across to another gene possibly to communicate a special message that otherwise could not be communicated through enzyme expression. Scientists are involved day and night in working on the genetic switches to evaluate the true code and message embedded in each letter. There are around 3.5 billion letters with a definite message communicated and imprinted by the supreme nature for each individual to adjust and reshape according to the changing environment.

Perhaps one of the purposes of our creation *(maybe I am wrong)* could possibly be to evaluate the genes for different diseases *(as we are doing today)* and reshape them to prevent the catastrophe of the disease process and simultaneously find the genetic code of dotage (i.e., the aging process) and reshape that gene according to the need so that there is no dotage in decline but an everlasting youth in prime as promised by Allah Almighty for our life after death. I have no dexterity to comment on this aspect of life after death, but there is a word for each man of intellect to make a sensible decision between the word *nature* and Nature.

A man is truly impressed by the natural environments to readjust his conduct, behavior, and attitude to suit the environmental situation and later as our genetic code expresses by creating enzymes or toggling its way from one to the other set of genetic codes to reshape the individual expression so the microevolution takes place. But the message embedded in codes and bits for each genetic set is communicated by a supreme nature, and even today's scientific approach affirms that there is particular chemical code in the genetic array of each individual. So once again, the questions arise: who imprinted this most sophisticated genetic code in the human cell, and how and why do different codes toggle in different cells to perform a single act? The genetic code has a strange way of communicating, like sensory nerve endings. The sensory code passes the message or expresses the concern to the neighboring gene for mutation for the specific concern. If the neighboring gene does not respond to the message of the sensory gene, a code of the sensory gene snaps from the parent gene and skips the particular gene for mutation.

How did a genetic code get sensitized in subjects living in Africa and dying of malaria to create a malaria-resistant gene? But when a pair of such genes *(from mother and father)* are passed to the baby, they suffer from sickle-cell anemia. Similarly, in Western Europe, when people were dying from iron-deficiency anemia, the changes in the genetic code helped them to absorb more of the iron from whatever source they could have in bits and traces, but once again, the offspring, who have a pair of the genes, suffer from hemosidrosis. But nature had a way for them not to pass this trait to their offspring, as they were destined to die before they got married.

A man once asked why a crippled baby is born and what is the purpose of its creation? The Lord Almighty asserts: "I have created all the individuals for a definite purpose." And what purpose does a crippled baby serve in this world? My answer was, "So that you can enjoy a healthy life, and for that matter, nature has to sacrifice a few for the cause of the whole."

We don't know a lot about some congenital anomalies, why and how these are brought about and how these should be taken care of.

I usually mention that when we grow cotton or wheat, we sow the seed of cotton and wheat, but what really comes out besides cotton and wheat are many unwanted plants. They are later taken care of by the farmer (similarly, nature takes care of the individuals). But what we actually don't know is why it was expedient for these unwanted plants to be there before the germination of wheat and cotton?

This discussion concludes that we still need to go a long way to decode the individual genetic code and understand the basic philosophy of life in health and disease, besides comprehending many other environmental situations. And mind you, microevolution or the changing conduct of the genetic array under different environmental conditions cannot create species. Species are only predestined and preordained by the supreme nature, Who created the first genetic code of Adam with His own hands, and quite possibly, the rest of His creation is the jumble and clutter of the genetic proscenium of Adam. And in all this muddle and shuffle, there could possibly be some unwanted and undesired creations. Similarly, the men are not created of identical traits. There are good and bad, agile and slothful, submissive and arrogant. But the imperfection is the discipline, in the order of perfection.

Why?

If all were doctors and scientists, lawyers and judges, then there would not be sweepers, peons, washermen, and laborers, and life would be quite difficult to carry through.

Before concluding the discussion, I would like to mention that some scientists believe that there is a Hox gene, or master gene or a site engineer, specified by Almighty Nature for each living being, having the true text of the message for the organization of the particular building material for a specific individual. This may be true, but we conclude from the discussion that the chemical code of each individual is communicated by the supreme nature and the natural circumstances, or the environments call on the embedded code to readjust according to the need, the demand that arises from the environments. The supply is through the genetic code written and communicated by the supreme nature to create the living beings under the notion of the survival of the fittest; the fittest are those who can survive the odds

From One Cell to Trillions

In every human body, roughly ten trillion cells, brainless units of life, come together to work as a unified whole. It's a complex dance, requiring organization and constant communication. And how could this be all without a proper system of coordination that began more than six hundred million years ago when organisms containing just one cell gave rise to the first multicellular animals?

Scientists have found that the genes responsible for laying out the fly's body plan have nearly identical counterparts in many other animals, ranging from crabs to earthworms to lampreys to us. The discovery came as a surprise, since these animals have such different-looking bodies. But now scientists generally agree that the common ancestor of all these animals is a worm-like creature that lived an estimated five hundred and seventy million years ago that already had a basic set of body plan genes. Its descendants then used those genes to build new kinds of bodies.

Scientists studying body plan genes think arthropods started out much like velvet worms, using the same basic set of body-building genes to lay out their anatomy. Over time, copies of those genes began to be borrowed for new jobs.

From the comprehensive dialogue on the subject, we conclude that the determined discipline of evolution was preordained, because otherwise, we cannot affirm the most complex nature of life from the unicellular to the most organized human being over and above the endowment of the soul or the efflux that is neither ours nor within our control.

The order of evolution is all "divine in nature," which a man of sapience cannot deny.

The Purpose of Creation

What's your concern hither *in term*
That "We,"
Created you without any plan *in concern*
And
That you're not destined to "Me" *in return* (23:115–116)

I've no vision to discern, but I have some inkling to pen a few words in concern.

Allah Almighty loves his living beings far more than a mother.

Sure?

Of course, indeed!

Okay! Then, when a contorted and crippled baby is born, how tormenting and painful it is for the mother! Sure enough, there's no doubt about it.

Don't you think Lord Almighty will also be concerned about this disturbing situation?

It's quite likely.

Just turn toward the soil and the cultivation: We sow a seed of cotton or some grain but what really comes out?

Besides cotton or grain, there are so many undesired plants.

We treat the soil with so many approaches to get rid of the undesirable plants, and only then do we yield the crop of our choice, even though we're not quite appeased of its ultimate outcome that it would have yielded without those unwanted plants. But actually, we don't know the cause, for it was expedient for the superfluous yield to be there before the germination of the desired product. So these are exterminated only when they are visible or come out of the soil.

So is the genetic swing in sway, for the detrimental genes are there for the purpose of the whole, and so these are taken care of sooner or later by nature.

Am I clear?

Indeed! It's like that.

If we turn toward the creation of the cosmic order and also the living beings as a whole, in the "proscenium of creation," couldn't there be some unwelcome products produced in the genetic array and cosmic sway for the discipline of the whole in the cosmic array?

Because for the order of the whole, there has to be good and bad.

For the preference in competence in the genetic swing and sway is in reality, the perfection with precision of the order of nature.

Could it all be a stroke of chance? How could one discern his order of discipline, until one looks into the details of each effect and equipage with an unbiased eye?

Why don't you ask yourself who has arranged all these fascinating effects and equipage for us? Maybe I'm absolutely wide of the mark, but could it be?

The Lord Almighty wanted to settle many scores before the creation of His real perfect design; that's the life to cherish the bliss of the everlasting world in the Hereafter. Maybe we are unwittingly performing certain definite assignments without ever realizing the eventual purpose of their formation or impression. And what's the source of knowledge? Even people like Einstein affirmed that it's all intuitive perception that opens new vistas of concern, and I myself stand a witness to that.

For all the diversity of life on this planet, ranging from tiny bacteria to majestic blue whales, from sunshine-harvesting plants to mineral-digesting endoliths miles underground, only one kind of "life as we know it" exists. All these organisms are based on nucleic acids—DNA and RNA—and proteins, working together more or less as described by the so-called central dogma of molecular biology. The DNA stores information that is transcribed into RNA, which then serves as a template for producing a protein. The proteins in turn serve as important structural elements in tissues and, as enzymes, are the cells' workhorses. Yet the scientists dream of synthesizing life that is utterly alien to this world—both to better understand the minimum component required for life (as part of the quest to uncover the essence of life that originated on earth) and, frankly, to see if they can do it. That is, they hope to put together a novel combination of molecules that can self-organize, metabolize (make use of energy sources), grow, reproduce, and evolve. A synthetic molecule discovered in 1995, called a peptide nucleic acid (PNA), combines the information-storage properties of DNA with the chemical stability of a protein-like backbone.

The ultimate nature of the assignment endowed to the man is at least not very clear to us, but in the Qur'an, the Lord Almighty asserts that He has not created us (i.e., men of all castes, creeds, and cultures) without any definite design in plan (24:115). It very clearly affirms that the creation of all mankind and not of the Muslim community alone is planned with a definite reason.

What could that be?

Could it be something like that?

A handful of genes that control the body's defenses during hard times can also dramatically improve health and prolong life in diverse organisms. An understanding of how they work may reveal the keys to extending the human life span while banishing diseases of old age (i.e., delaying dotage and relishing the boons of life experiences with senescence), for in the Hereafter, there is a life in prime with no dotage in decline. But how could that be possible?

- Genes that control an organism's ability to withstand adversity, cause changes throughout the body that renders it temporarily supercharged for survival.
- Activated over the long term, this stress response prolongs the life span and forestalls disease in a wide range of organisms.
- Sirtuins are a family of genes that may be the master regulators of the survival mechanisms.
- Understanding how they produce their health and longevity-enhancing effects could lead to disease treatments and ultimately longer, disease-free human life spans, for that's the life in the Hereafter with ever-lasting youth in profusion with no dotage in refuse.
- Another concern is the stem-cell transplant creating an almost new organ to replace the damaged one.

The real purpose of life is food for thought for all who read the Holy Scriptures intently between the lines. Similarly, when we turn to the numeral and numerical system in the Holy Scripture, we are fascinated to find a logical connection in the order of discernment, what I call *faith healing*, as discussed in *Kun: Fa Ya Koon*.

Before we can understand the philosophy of the creation of man, we shall have to understand the basic integral unit of the human body that not only forms the brickwork of the human body as an earthly pot but also forms the basis of the vivacity that holds the life or efflux or soul that performs our most simple to most complex tasks while playing on the most delicate orchestra of the human genetic proscenium—life at the cellular, DNA level.

Each one of us is composed of a genetic array. There are about three and a half billion codes or letters written on the genome, the nucleic acids—DNA and RNA—and proteins, working together more or less as described by the central dogma of molecular biology. DNA stores information that is transcribed into RNA, which then serves as a template for producing a protein. The proteins, in turn, serve as important structural elements in the tissues and, as enzymes, are the cell's workhorses.

If we could read ten letters or codes a second, it would take eleven years to read the whole text, and even if we had eleven years at our discretion to read the whole text, we still would not be able make out how it received the vivacity to perform the most intricate functioning in our lives. We are all the same for 99.9 percent of the genetic code. It is only in 0.1 percent we are different from each other. Our creation or initiation was not an ordinary job. The Lord Almighty created the genetic array of the human being in a perfect order with His own hands (38:75) and did not leave it to its own devices for procreation. There has been a proper order and discipline in this procreation, but for the order of whole, there has to be definite transmutation in the genetic makeup. For the order of the whole, there has to be good and bad, for otherwise, this world would not have been a place to live.

More than one-fifth of the proteins (and hence genes) in each human being exist in a form that differs only 0.1 percent in the majority of the population. This remarkable genetic variability, or polymorphism, among "normal" people accounts for much of the normal variation in body traits, such as height, intelligence, and blood pressure. These genetic differences also determine the ability of each individual to meet environmental challenges, including those that produce disease. All human diseases can be considered to result from an interaction between an individual's unique genetic makeup and the environment. In certain diseases, the genetic component is so overwhelming that it expresses itself in a predictable manner without the requirement of extraordinary environmental challenges. Such diseases are termed genetic disorders.

Geneticists have discovered thousands of mutations responsible for diseases in humans, but founder mutations stand apart. The victims of many genetic diseases die before reproducing, stopping the mutant genes from reaching future generations. But founder mutations often spare their carriers and therefore can spread from the original founder to his or her descendants. And some of the disorders resulting from these mutations are common, such as hereditary hemochromatosis, sickle-cell anemia, and cystic fibrosis.

Mutations arise from random changes in our DNA. Most of the damage gets repaired or eliminated at birth and thus does not get passed down to subsequent generations. But some mutations, called germ-line mutations, are passed down, often with serious medical consequences to the offspring, who inherit them. More than one thousand different diseases arise from mutations in different human genes. What protection these mutations give humanity at large is yet to be explored, as in some of the cases, we are given an indication of protection from certain problems provided to the carriers of mutant genes.

The striking fact is how common these mutations can be. They are hundreds or even thousands of times more frequent than typical mutations that cause disease. Most disease mutations exist at a frequency of one in a few thousand to one in a few million. But founder mutations can occur in a substantial percent of the population.

This anomaly shouldn't be; evolution is to get rid of the harmful genes rather than select for them. This offers an important clue as to why founder mutations have persisted so far and spread. The answer, perhaps not surprisingly, is that under some circumstances, founder mutations prove beneficial. Most founder mutations are recessive; only a person with two copies of the affected gene, one from each parent, will suffer from the disease. A much larger percentage of people, who have only one copy, are carriers. They can pass on the gene to their children, but have no symptoms of disease themselves. The single copy of the founder mutation gives the carrier an advantage in the struggle for survival.

For example, carriers of the hereditary hemochromatosis mutation are thought to be protected from iron-deficiency anemia (a life-threatening condition in the past), because the protein encoded by that mutated gene makes the person absorb iron more efficiently than those who carry two normal copies of the gene. Carriers thus had an edge when dietary iron was scarce.

Perhaps the best-known example of a double-edged genetic mutation is the one responsible for sickle-cell disease. The sickle-cell mutation apparently arose repeatedly in regions riddled with malaria, such as Africa and the Middle East. A single copy of a sickle-cell gene helps the carrier survive malarial infection. But two copies doom the bearer to pain and a shortened life span. The sickle-cell mutation today can be found in five different regions, leading to the conclusion that the mutation appeared independently five times in five different founders.[15]

Two competing forces govern the frequency of a founder mutation in the population. Someone who has two copies will probably die before reproducing, but those who have only one copy will survive preferentially over those with no copies. This produces a so-called balancing selection, in which the beneficial effects drive the frequency of the mutant gene up while the harmful effects damp down the frequency. Evolution gives, and evolution takes away, so that over time, the gene maintains a relatively steady level in the population.

15 Although sickle-cell disease usually results from a founder mutation, some cases do arise from other mutations.

For example, a recent discovery may explain the persistence of factor V Leiden, a mutation in the factor V gene, which is responsible for making carriers of this mutation resistant to the lethal effects of bacterial infections in the bloodstream, a huge threat to survival in the pre-antibiotic past and still a cause of death today.

It is not conceivable to imagine that all men and clans cherish equanimity in poise for their conduct in course, propensity, and proficiency in intelligence and competence. So is the point and plan of comprehension with sapience in sagacity, besides health and wealth, that must vary from person to person. So there had to be certain mutations with innovations in the genetic proscenium, for otherwise, this world would not have been a place to endure life.

Noteworthy Founder Mutations

Affected gene	Condition	Mutation origin	Migration	Possible advantage of one copy
HF	Iron overload	Far Northwestern Europe	South and east across Europe	Protection from anemia
CFTR	Cystic fibrosis	Southeast Europe/ Middle East	West and north across Europe	Protection from diarrhea
Hb$_s$	Sickle-cell disease	Africa/ Middle East	To New World	Protection from malaria
FV Leiden	Blood clots	Western Europe	Worldwide	Protection from sepsis
ALDH2	Alcohol toxicity	Far East Asia	North and west across Asia	Protection from alcoholism, possibly hepatitis B
LCT	Lactose tolerance	Asia	West and north across Eurasia	Allows consumption of milk from domesticated animals
GJB2	Deafness	Middle East	West and north across Europe	Unknown

Get an eyeful and scrutinize the conviviality of the social conduct. How can we toil or moil, whet or whittle to accomplish if each one of us becomes a genius or an eminently cultivated astute, a doctor of medicine, or a consultant, an engineer or a wangle, a professor or a scientist, a philosopher or a scholar, if there were no janitor or a sweeper, no peon or carpenter, no washer-man or subaltern, no tram or train driver, no tiller or sailor. There is apportioning of toil and drudge to strive not only in the close clique or communion in the culture but also for the whole. Eminently, we encounter an identical situation when we sound out the human body. Just watch the hand, an indigent laborer, that has to toil and travail all the time, but when it comes to nutrition, it seizes just the leftovers from the surplus of the body and the brain which just commands and controls but cherishes the cream of the nutrients. There is apportionment of all treads in trail for each term in the vale diversely. How could we trend to avail all skilful plans of society and humanity as a whole in scale, for otherwise, it would not hold to persevere and turn to abide in dale.

Besides all these strides in restraints, tending and verging, His Almighty was quite relaxed for He had determined this fickle and fake triviality in trace vale for a very short term in trail, during which He intended to determine:

Our conduct in course and discipline in pace
It's for eventual,
Attainment of the adorable goal in the Hereafter to brace

But why don't we recollect that life of ours when His Almighty determined our genetic proscenium? Well, there could possibly be a life for our soul or efflux with its genetic proscenium somewhere there, in a very different state.

It was then, we affirmed His Almighty Allah.

When we were asked, "Who's your Lord?"

All genetic arrays asserted in that stance: "You are our Lord."

It was then the endowment of intelligence with true discernment and discrimination of the flagitious in the fray and esteem in sway was held in conformity. The word of true discernment is so deeply insinuated in our essence of core, and that has been perpetuating ever since the creation of humanity in this abode for us to decide in different trends in strides, and that's the veracity of intelligence to aside.

The auspicious and amiable, pitying and promising Almighty, Who is sympathetic, O Sublime, Clement, O Compassionate, has bestowed upon us the favor of the Qur'an, which is full of creative, scientific, mystical, and philosophical knowledge with discipline in almost all walks of life. He created the man and endowed him with the ability to speak and discern through the wit of intelligence, the purpose of life in a most sensible way.

The actuality of a thing for itself is its exquisite and "perfect life"; its reality for another is apposite but is "relative life." His Almighty endured for Himself. He is the living one, and His life is comprehensive and immortal. Created beings, in general, exist for His Almighty. Their life is comparative and affiliated with death. Life is a single essence, incapable of diminution or division; existence for self is everything, and what constitutes a "thing" is its "life."

Man has a corporeal, intellectual, and moral constitution fit for certain uses, and on the whole, man performs these uses, dies, and leaves other men in his place. So society exists, and a social state is manifested as the natural state of a man, the state for which his nature fits him, and society amidst innumerable irregularities and disorders still subsists. Perhaps we may say that the history of the past and our present knowledge give us a reasonable hope that its disorders will diminish, and that order, its governing principle, may be more firmly established. As order than a fixed order, we may say, subject to deviations real or apparent, must be admitted to exist in the whole nature of things that we call disorder or the evil constitution of things having a nature or fixed order. Nobody will conclude from the existence of disorder that order is not the rule, for the existence of order, both physical and moral, is proved by daily experiences and also all past experiences. We cannot conceive of how the order of the universe is maintained; we cannot even conceive of how our own lives from day to day are continued, nor of how we perform the simplest movements of the body, nor of how we grow and think and act, though we know many of the conditions which are necessary for all these functions.

Knowing nothing then of the unseen power, which acts in ourselves except by what is done, we know nothing of the power that acts through what we call all time and all space, but seeing that there is a nature or fixed order in all things known to us, it is conformable to the nature of our minds to believe that this universal nature has a cause, which operates continually, and we are totally unable to speculate on the reason of any of those disorders or evils which we perceive.

All that is from nature, I attribute the name Almighty, being full of providence. And that which is from fortune is not separated from the nature without an interweaving and involution with the things that are ordained by the providence. From Him, all things flow. There is nothing other than necessity, because it is for the advantage of the whole universe, of which we are a part. But that is good for every part of the nature, which serves to maintain the nature of all His creation. Now the universe is preserved, as by the changes of the elements, so by the changes of things compounded of the elements, it endures to exist in perfection. But cast away the thirst after self-possession that we may not die murmuring, but cheerfully, truly, and in our heart thankfully to His Almighty because He thought of us to partake in this grandiose mall.

Similarly, when we come to the evolution of enlightenment, edification, and the civilization with all its educational and informative enrichme nts and religious heritage, we are once again confronted with the mythos of evolution in the discernment of faith. For the antediluvian society in an uncouth era when the resources of communication and intercourse were direly curbed and confined, the perception of faith was very frugally perceived because of the scant and scarce resources of communication. There were many prophets working simultaneously. Moses asked His Almighty to bless him with the assistance of his brother as a prophet. The history of all the three monotheistic religions is full of such instances. The history of human social, cultural, and political evolution parallels the history of religious evolution. When the minds were mature and perceptive, the complete moral and ethical code was communicated and with the message that: "Today I have completed the Faith for you to practice and that there would not be any Prophet hereafter" (33:40).

The subject is demanding and obligates volumes to be written in this necessary link, but a short communication, I am sure, will elucidate the concept and attitude of the discernment of faith.

Assuredly, the creation of the heavens and earth is incomparable with the creation of mankind, but most of the human race knows not (60:57).

Allah is the creator of all things, and He is the guardian over all things (49:62).

The discovery of one or the other scientific theory may not be able to explain or help in the quest for our survival. It may not even affect our lifestyles. But ever since the dawn of civilization, we have not been content with the events as unconnected or inexplicable. Men have been striving hard to understand the underlying order in the universe. Today, we still aspire to know why we are here and where we came from. Humanity's heightening longing for understanding is acceptable justification for our ongoing pursuits. And our objective is nothing less than a concluded and unblemished description of the universe we live in. We might advance ever meticulous toward our understanding of the laws that govern the universe.

True faith has always endeavored to sense the softness and sweetness of the spirit and determined diligence in the subjects who were resolved after due forethought and who have no vanity or vainglory in their minds, which men call exaltation in excellence. There should be an adamant faith with persistence, patience, and perseverance and an ebullience to escort those who have anything to volunteer for the common purpose of the confidence in faith because of an undeviating firmness in giving to everyone according to the firm conviction and the knowledge derived from the Qur'an that endows experiences of discernment with discretion, enlightenment with education, and elegance with the enlightenment of special sophisticated subjects like modern-day science and philosophy. All these subjects are occasions for devoted, watchful accomplishment for eventual exoneration.

Allah Almighty has bestowed upon human beings the intellect to interpret the myth of their creation and the cosmic order through benevolent intelligence: philosophical logic and scientific rendition. Scientific knowledge with meticulous and controlled deductions drawn through experiments and mathematical calculations or through the logic of philosophically sound reasoning, conclusions, and inferences or the course of thought through implicative assertions and avowals will ultimately help them ascertain the true understanding of faith.

The other sane and sober perception to discern the truth is through the cognizance of spirituality. The prudence or perceptiveness of spirituality is the absolute and factual understanding of the sagacious or enlightened "self," an endowment of His Almighty through the intimate impression or intelligence of the "heart." Is it the heart that is driving blood through our vascular tree or the insinuated veer and swerve of the sagacious self that is the punch and prod of spiritual consciousness or the discernment of truth, the divine prudence and providence that brought us into the actuality of this vale, the efflux or the soul? When this true perceptive efflux is withdrawn, the earthly being is once again thrown back into the dust and dirt with all its inanimate and lifeless material (i.e., minerals, salts, and water, etc.). What remains of this living being after the efflux is waved off is nothing but dust.

"He created the man as that of in the potter's clay" (Al Rahman 55:14).

The code of belief of the soul is so intimate that it does not perish, for a segment of the eternal life cannot perish. This assumption is at least as old as the time of Epicharmus and Euripides. What comes from the earth goes back to the earth, and what comes from heaven, the divinity, returns to Him who presumed it.

His Almighty proposes the man persistently and prompts him to perceive his origin and repeatedly intimates to him that He would once again infuse His "efflux" in his remains wherever they would be, whether scattered as dust or soot or rotten bones and rejuvenate them once again. And inducing His efflux in this earthly pod is not surprising or difficult for Him. It is for Him to just say, "Be!" and it would "Be" an actual living being. But we have to find the concept of the man existing after death so as to be conscious of his

174

sameness with that soul which occupied this vessel of clay. He seems to be perplexed on this matter and finally to have resorted to the awareness that Allah Almighty will do whatever is best and consistent with the creation of things. The confirmation of our existence and being in this world or the world to come is through true perception and the discernment of faith and the intelligence of logic (i.e., science and philosophy). The myth of creation is soon resolved when you perceive it through its original form.

The logic of philosophy cannot ascertain the creation and the circumstance of the universe, and similarly, it has no means to reckon the genetic or galactic proscenium of the creation. In like manner, it has no disposition to discern the myth of space-time. On the other hand, the scientific approach has no dexterity to discriminate the discernment of the efflux or the soul, life after death, or the cognition or the approach to interpret the inspiration of faith in the secluded or secret. His Almighty Allah seduces and supplicates us quite resolutely and perpetually in the Qur'an:

> This very logic is hidden behind the most ebullient and enchanting verse: "Which of the favors, you may deny of your Dazzling O Defiant Lord?" (Al Rahman).

The intellectual cognition can conduct us to the right path to contrive the candor of the creation of the cosmos and the living beings.

There could be many ways to cherish the bliss of the Almighty through intellectual cognition with the spirit of self at its core, the sincerity. All of us dwell on the brink of the infinite oceans of life's creative power. We carry it within us: supreme strength, the fullness of wisdom, and unquenchable joy. It is never thwarted and cannot be destroyed. But it is hidden deep, which is what makes life a problem. The infinite is down in the darkest, profoundest vault or the veer of the core, in the forgotten well house, the deep cistern. What if we could bring it to light and draw from it unceasingly?

It is through sincere faith at the core with the bliss of the whole— meditation and yoga are the two ways to achieve this goal. By and large, life is motivated less by reason than by emotion, and of the many emotions that crowd the human heart, the strangest is love. The aim of "Salaam" or "Bhatia Yoga" is directed toward Allah. Yoga determines different postures, whereas meditation determines the recitation of the blessed name.

Have you ever perceived the reality of the bodily organs, the small musing pets, innumerable fascinating creatures, and the most captivating and enchanting fauna and flora around you, in addition to the most incomprehensible cosmic order?

It is only through the intimate approach to the knowledge of their several natures made by Him who so abides His intellectual vision to have the most exact conception of the essence of His deliberations.

All those who attain the knowledge of the creation in the highest purity and who go to each of the wonderments not with the reason alone, and not admitting when in the accomplishment of thinking, the infringement or preclusion of precise or any other estimation in the band or body of discernment, but with the very agility of the intellect in its distinctness that permeates into the very core of truth in each. He has got rid, as far as he can, of eyes and ears and of the whole body when he visualizes them only as an agonizing component, impeding the soul from the appropriation of enlightenment when in association with her. Is not this the sort of man who is hopeful to acquire the discernment of actuality or the real purpose of creation?

Our efflux or soul, an endowment of His Almighty, is compounded with the pack and pile of depravity and degradation, and our craving is for the truth. By stuffing us so full of affection and ardor, apprehension and anxiety, dread and dismay, fear and fancies, idols and illusions, and every sort of fickleness, it impedes our ever having so much as a thought. Moreover, if there is time and an inclination toward the study of truth, yet the body introduces turmoil and confusion and fear into the course of speculation and hinders us from seeing the truth. All experience shows that, if we would have pure knowledge of anything, we must be liberated of the body's sensuous and other luxurious demands.

The soul in itself must behold all things in themselves. I suppose that we shall attain that which we desire and of which we say that we love wisdom, not while we live but also after the departure from this vale. The argument shows that while in company with the body, the soul cannot have pure knowledge until it is subjected to the true perception of faith, and that is only discernible if the person goes for it sincerely. For then, and not until then, the soul will be in itself alone and without the fleshly demands of the body. In this vale, I reckon that we make the nearest approach to knowledge when we have the least possible concern or interest in the body and are not sopping in the fleshly or sensual propositions of its nature, but abide innocence until the hour when Allah Almighty Himself is pleased to emancipate us and when the flightiness of the body will be cleared away and we shall be pure and hold discourse with other pure souls and know of ourselves the clear light everywhere, and this is surely the light of truth. For no profaned or polluted thing is affirmed to approximate the pedigreed or pure.

And what is purification? Is it the separation of the soul from the body? The inclination of the soul to congregate and collect herself into "herself," out of all the deportment of the flesh and abiding in her own site and spot alone, as in another life, so also in this, as far as she can the release of the soul from the chains of the vale?

And what is that, which is termed death, but this very separation and release of the "efflux" or the soul from the flesh? It would be just an unreasonable paradox in men living as nearly as they can in a state of improbability and yet murmuring and brooding when death comes.

How inconsistent and incongruous of them who have been always luxuriating in the luscious body but are still yearning to have the efflux or soul alone in a state of eternal wisdom and veracity! And when this is granted to them, they start shuddering and shivering, sulking and sighing, instead of exhilarating in their flitting to that place where they hope to gain that which in life they loved, the enlightenment, and at the same time to be clear of the company of their fleshly temptations of the vale. Many a man has been willing to go to the world yonder in the hope of seeing an earthly love and for affection in family life if they had it here. And will he, who is a true lover of wisdom and is persuaded in like manner that only in the world yonder can he proficiently luxuriate in that, still languish and fret at death? But hither in this vale, one has to abide the discipline of faith. If the earthly living, what I invariably call the "vale," is spent in conformity with the discipline of true faith, then the fear or worry of leaving this flesh will not panic or apprehend, because living a true discipline of the vale, the soul will be in real tranquility and peace. Will he not depart with joy? Surely he will, if he is truly sagacious pursuing the adorable goal of all the living beings, for he will have a resolute certitude that they only and nowhere else can find prudence in the purity and probity of the "heart."

And when you see a man who is languishing at the approximation of death, is not his unwillingness a satisfactory substantiation that he is not a paramour of enlightenment and sagacity, but a lover of the fleshly demands of the body and presumably at the same time an admirer of either the lust for power and the love of money or both throughout his vale?

There is an excellence in ethics, which is designated forbearance and fortitude. That is the special quirk in the quality of the true faith. Again, there is reticence and humility, which is unruffled subordination, with scorn and snubbing of infatuation and indignation with temperance, a quality appertaining only to those who disdain and detest fleshly enchantments of the body and live in true conviction to cherish the bliss of the ultimate goal.

I've gone on very long on the subject, but clearly it's the abidance of faith on one side for the purification of the soul and the dedication to the purpose of the whole on the other side that conform the purpose of creation.

Perfect Creation

Turn your looks towards the heavenly sweep
Aren't you captivated of its profundity so deep?
How exquisite and adorable stellar sprawl is to peek
And still you defy of His Dictum in treat
(Al-Mulk 67:3–4)

He created skies in series of seven
There's no want in slant in term of creation
Most Amiable is Lord, *immense in array*
So trend your looks *once more to the heaven*
Can you discern a bit of slit *in sway*
Then trend and talent anew *in quest*
You're denied of flaw *in behest*
Not even perplexity or poop *in the rest*

Turn your looks towards the heavens so high
Aren't you dazed, when you wisp in spy
Can you sense a swing in swirl
Sprawling of the heavens in twirl
There's no way and ward in the whirl
It's so exquisite and adorable in sway
Abiding the dictum of Lord in array
Spin your gaze once more in quest
For if you discern a split in the rest

When we turn to the earliest state of initiation, the Qur'an refers to it as a smoke of inconclusive characteristics.

Likewise He got to design *in plan*
Order of *cosmic sway (sky) in span*
That's nothing, but smoke *in glance*
He directed to it and the earth *in start*
Come into being in sort *and assort*
Even so Willy Nilly, there *in part*

They said:
We do in unison and *get to a lead*
That's in,
Compliance and conformity *to heed* (41:11)

Embracing the concept of "smoke" once again draws us close to the subject of discernment that initial matter had no contour or configuration for us to perceive as to what it could have been like, as modern science turns to this notion as a "singularity" or the nihility of the inconclusive order of density and consequence eventuating from the core to stellar sprawl with the decree and dictum of the precept of the principal with providence.

We perceive the gleam of smoke with a stellar sprawl of about fifteen billion years before this time, and we cannot comprehend as to what it could be like before that instance of *Kun: Fa Ÿa Koon*; as the Qur'an mentions, the earliest state of the multiverse manifested as smoke of an inconclusive order and is observed today with our most sophisticated scientific endowments.

In the epoch of the sprawl of creation, the *big bang* or divine decree in dictate for this domain, *Kun Fa Ÿa Koon*, when matter and time set out their travel and travail from the nihility of singularity to the indeterminate order of imperceptible consequence, one must diligently deliberate as to where modern scientific concepts differ from Qur'anic philosophy at this most critical juncture of the creation of the time and material of the cosmic order and the life in it. There, with a steady stream of spectacular discoveries forthcoming in this domain, the Grand Observatories of Origins Deep Survey (GOODS) turns to reveal fascinating leaps in the lines to help us compass and comprehend the clue and code of the fundamental nature of the universe.

How congruent are these doctrines that bring the faith in the precept of providence and modern scientific convictions close together to embrace a uniform view of creation.

But as for the fate of the universe, modern science is quite divided as to how all these effects and this equipage are going to fold or wind up. The Qur'an gives quite a clear indication regarding the fate of the universe, and surprisingly, it also comes close to the most acclaimed concepts. I am sure if the future scientist seeks guidance in the light of the Qur'an, he can reveal quite a bit of material evidence about the future trends of our cosmic order. As discussed later in the text, the Qur'an asserts the initial boundary conditions of a closed system (the second law of thermodynamics) with a series of big crunches following a big smash and eventually providing a seedling for the next creation or big bang.

Big Bang

In Surah *Ya' Sin*, Allah Almighty gives a clear elucidation of the creation of the cosmic order, the movements of the different heavenly bodies like the sun and moon, and their ultimate fate.

Without hesitation, when we look at any scientific hypothesis, any physical theory is always provisional, for the reason that it is only a tentative assumption; you can never confirm it. No matter how many times the information base of experiments coincides with the same philosophy, you can never be sure that the next time the conclusions will not repudiate the assumption. On the other hand, you can challenge a hypothesis by finding even a single instance of dissent or difference with the prevision of the hypothesis.

Exceptionally, the Qur'an not only makes clear the anticipation with logic of modern-day scientific theories but also titillates and seduces mankind to pursue the scent and spoor of the verity and reality of the significance behind the philosophy of the creation of the divine endowments of the universe and the living beings. It also summons and solicits mankind to confound or confute any of His Almighty's assertions and affirmations if they could in all likelihood do that (2:2).

The data gained in this century indicate that the universe had an explosive origin. It came into existence from "nothingness," the nullity or nihility. The universe had a beginning, and this beginning owes its existence to an explosion called the *big bang*. Today, the majority of scientists acknowledge the big bang theory.

According to the theory, some fifteen billion years ago, all materials making up the earth and all the cosmic sway around us were originally reduced into one single point. This single point with no volume had an infinite density and an infinite temperature. This period before the big explosion (in fact, we cannot even call it a period; since there was no matter, there was also no concept of time) was a state in which there was not even nullity. The only word that can explain such a state is "nothingness or nullity." The theory follows that with the effect of such a big explosion, the ultimate condensed density of the materials dispersed with rapid velocities. In other words, the big explosion started to "exist" from "nothingness." Today, the verification of the expansion of the universe is the most substantial evidence for the big bang theory.

Einstein's theories have been thoroughly proved and verified by experiments and measurements. But there's an even more important implication of Einstein's discovery that not only does the universe have a beginning, but time itself, our own dimension of cause and effect, began with the big bang. That's right—time itself did not exist before then. The very line of time begins with that creation event. Matter, energy, time, and space were created in an instant by an intelligent being outside of space and time.

About this intelligence, Albert Einstein wrote in his book *The World as I See It* that the harmony of natural law reveals an intelligence of such superiority that it cannot be compared with; all the systematic thinking and acting of human beings is an utterly insignificant reflection before that deity.

A pretty significant statement.

In your kitchen cabinet, you've probably got a spray bottle with an adjustable nozzle. If you twist the nozzle one way, it sprays a fine mist into the air. If you twist the nozzle the other way, it squirts a jet of water in a straight line. You turn that nozzle to the exact position you want so you can wash a mirror, clean up a spill, or whatever. If the universe had expanded a little faster, the matter would have sprayed out into space like a fine mist from a water bottle—so fast that a gazillion particles of dust would have sped into infinity and never even formed a single star. If the universe had expanded just a little slower, the material would have dribbled out like big drops of water and then collapsed back to where it came from by the force of gravity. A little too fast, and you get a meaningless spray of fine dust. A little too slow, and the whole universe collapses back into one big black hole. The surprising thing is just how narrow the difference is. To strike the perfect balance between too fast and too slow, the force, something that physicists call "the dark energy term," had to be accurate to one part in ten with one hundred and twenty zeros.

If we write this as a decimal, the number would look like this:
0.000000000000000000000000000000000000000000000000000000
0000000000000000000000000001

In their paper "Disturbing Implications of a Cosmological Constant," two atheist scientists from Stanford University stated that the existence of this dark energy term "... would have required a miracle. An external agent, external to space and time, intervened in cosmic history for reasons of its own."

Just for comparison, the best human engineering example is the gravity wave telescope, which was built with a precision of twenty-three zeros. The designer, the "external agent" that caused our universe, must possess an intellect, knowledge, creativity, and power trillions and trillions of times greater than we humans have.

Absolutely amazing!

Now a person who doesn't believe in God has to find some way to explain this. One of the more common explanations seems to be that since there was an infinite number of universes, it was inevitable that things would have turned out right in at least one of them.

The "infinite universes" theory is truly an amazing theory. Just think about it, if there is an infinite number of universes, then absolutely everything is not only possible, it has actually happened!

In 1929, E. P. Hubble examined the frequency shift of the light from distant galaxies. He found that the light was redshifted (its frequency decreased) as he looked at increasingly distant galaxies, and thus he was the first to verify that the galaxies are receding from us with relative velocities that increase in proportion to the distance.[16]

For instance, the Ursa Major group of stars, which is at a distance of one billion light-years from the world, recedes one thousand five hundred kilometers in a second. The Hidra group of stars, on the other hand, which is much farther from us, recedes six thousand kilometers in a second.

Since the universe expands, there should be a moment at which this expansion started. As *New Scientist*[17] puts forth, if there was a possibility to reverse this expansion, then everything could be merged some fifteen billion years ago at a single mathematical point having an infinite density.

The most important significance of the big bang theory lies in its verification that the universe had a starting point. Apart from that, we should clarify here a misunderstanding. Some people think that the Lord Almighty created the universe through the big bang and then left everything on its own. The same logic follows that the Lord Almighty only initiated the occurrence of the universe and then the process spontaneously proceeded.

. In the universe, the big bang is actually the first movement that can be calculated. It is certainly improbable that all multiverses came into existence as result of a random explosion and then everything spontaneously had a perfect system in itself in the preceding stages of this explosion. Nobody can arrive at the conclusion that galaxies, star systems, and the solar system came into existence as a result of the dispersed particles of an explosion, which inherited no laws. It is even not possible to talk of a spontaneous occurrence of a single atom, bearing in mind the very complex systems it has.

So how come the universe, with all the convolution and intricacy it possesses is thought to be the sole outcome of a random explosion? They are all created with the ultimate power of the Lord Almighty. The Qur'an informs us that the Lord Almighty created the heavens, the earth, and all living things. Similarly, the Qur'anic verses state that the Lord Almighty is vigilant in watching over all living things.

---

16 *Encyclopedia Americana*, Volume 9, p. 294.
17 May 12, 1988, p. 52.

He endowed you life *to aside*
And cause doom of death *in stride*
Then He'll bestow life once more *in trail*
Indeed!
Man in really quite peeve *in scale*
(Al-Hajj 22:66)

He Commands all *the term in sway*
Of the heavens and earth *set in array*
All at conclusion affairs trend *in pace*
To The Lord Almighty *in Grace*
In a Day of tally *in trace*
Years thousand of your count *in place**
(Al-Sajdah 32:5)

speed of light, gravitational and electromagnetic field

Lord created seven of heavens
And similar count of earth in seven
There's dictum in dictate,
Through the all *in relate*
That you may tend *to discern*
His care in command *to affirm*
And it's for Lord *in state*
Lord holds the grasp *in concern*
All the effects and equipage *in term*
(Al-Talaq 65:12)

Today, the big bang is accepted to be the most consistent theory about the origin of the universe. There are some objections made to the theory, yet they are basically related to the highly complicated stages of the formation of the universe occurring at the other stages after the big bang. Today, the factors playing roles in the formation of atoms, stars, and galaxies are not exactly known. Yet, just as the Lord Almighty created man from a drop of water, He created some factors for the creation of the universe. The starting point of these factors may be an explosion or something different. No stage can come into being without the control of a mighty nature. Consequently, the perfection in creation manifests the ultimate power and intelligence of the Almighty. All the multiverses are created that man should get into the wisdom of its creation.

He fettered day and night for you *to aside*
And sun and moon in aid and abet *in stride*
The stars are set in His care *and concern*
Indeed!
There's a word for the men *to discern*
(Al-Nahl 16:12)

All the information related to the creation of the earth and the universe, revealed by the Qur'an, is in compliance with what science today indicates.

Cosmic Redshift

Nearly all galaxies show a redshift in their spectra, which indicates that they are all receding from us. And the speed is roughly proportional to their distance from us. In other words, they are all receding from each other. They all seem to have begun very near each other, about twenty billion years ago. The rate of expansion should be decreasing. So, the age of the universe is somewhat less than twenty billion years. Apparently, the current best estimate is thirteen billion.

Gather up every last mote and particle of matter between here and the edge of the universe, and squeeze them into a spot so infinitesimally compact that it has no dimensions at all—the singularity with no space to occupy and not a bit of darkness around, for the singularity has not a bit in surround. It has no space to occupy, virtually no space for it to be. We really wonder how long it has been there, if it has been there forever or just came into being in the known recent past, when it took its stride for the most incomprehensive cosmic order and the time.

At the big bang itself, when the universe had zero size, it would have been infinitely hot, but as the universe expanded, the temperature of the radiation decreased. One second after the big bang, it would have fallen to about ten thousand million degrees. This is about a thousand times the temperature at the center of the sun, but temperatures as high as this are reached in hydrogen bomb explosions. At this time, the universe would have contained mostly photons, electrons, and neutrinos (extremely light particles that are affected only by the weak force and gravity) and their antiparticles, together with some protons and neutrons. As the universe continued to expand and the temperature to drop, most of the electrons and antielectrons would have annihilated each other to produce more photons, leaving only a few electrons in the pool. The neutrinos and antineutrinos, however, would not have annihilated each other, because these particles interact with themselves and with other particles only very weakly.

> Glory be to The Lord, Who turned *to plan*
> Created pair in assort, various *gene in span*
> That may be within plant site *and spot*
> Your own and else you cannot hint *in plot*
> (Surah Ya Sin, Pairs in Creation 36:36)

Einstein's general theory of relativity, on its own, predicted that space-time began at the big bang singularity and would come to an end either at the big crunch singularity (if the whole universe re-collapsed) or at a singularity inside a black hole (if a local region, such as a star, were to collapse). Any matter that fell into the hole would be destroyed at the singularity, and only the gravitational effect of is mass would continue to be felt outside. On the other hand, when quantum effects were taken into account, it seemed that the mass or energy of the matter would eventually be returned to the rest of the universe and that the black hole, along with any singularity inside it, would evaporate away and finally disappear. Could quantum mechanics have an equally dramatic effect on the big bang and big crunch singularities? What really happens during the very early or late stages of the universe, when gravitational fields are so strong that quantum effects cannot be ignored? Some scientists like Stephen Hawking at one stage thought that in the event of a big smash, when everything would be happening in the cosmic order, singularities in the black hole with the ultimate energy of the mass destroyed within it would be passed to the rest of the universe. Eventually, the gravitational effect of the universe would become really very strong. Could quantum mechanics possibly play a dramatic role like at the initial stages of the big bang to turn once again in a series of big crunches with the cosmic order becoming so intensely hot that the seas are set ablaze (81:1–7).

At the time of creation, very high-temperature particles would be moving around so fast that they could escape any attraction toward each other due to nuclear or electromagnetic forces, but as they cooled off, one would expect particles that attract each other to start to clump together. Moreover, even the types of particles that exist in the universe would depend on the temperature. At high enough temperatures, particles have so much energy that whenever they collide, many different particle/antiparticle pairs would be produced—and although some of these particles would be annihilated on hitting antiparticles, they would be produced more rapidly than they could be annihilated. At lower temperatures, however, when colliding particles have less energy, particle/antiparticle pairs would be produced less quickly and annihilation would become faster than production.

And how immense the job of creation and its perpetuation is you will learn from the text. The Lord Almighty Himself asserts:

Indeed!
The creation of heavens and earth in sway
That's greater of the job in pace
Than the creation of men in place
But most of the men don't discern it to obey (40:57)

Just seek their concern in stance
If they're,
More onerous to be created in glance
Or that of the Multiverse in pace
That We contrived in precision
Them We created in place
Of a gluey trickle *in collision* (37:11)

And it all leads to the creation of an immense multiverse, an array of the different strata of parallel universes. So far, the scientists have discovered four strata of parallel universes, with each strata comprised of innumerable universes, each universe comprised of around one billion galaxies, and each galaxy with one hundred billion stars. Our solar system is 226,000 light-years away from the center of the Milky Way (our galaxy), and each light-year is six trillion miles. This all comprises the ever-expanding cosmic order with an average speed of three hundred thousand kilometers per second and still behaves as a closed model, covered and surrounded by the lower skies, (i.e., with preordained limits or border).

Can you comprehend His order of creation? Nay! You cannot.

He created skies in series of seven
There's no want in slant in term of creation
Most Amiable is Lord, *immense in initiation*
So trend your looks *once more to the heaven*
Can you discern a bit of slit *in generation*
Then trend and talent anew *in quest*
You're denied of flaw *in behest*
Not even perplexity or poop *in the rest*
(Al-Mulk 67:3–4)

Vow be to Heavenly Piers[18] *in consign*
Not discernable to human eye *in design*
Keeping cosmic line and plan *in array*
Added with Zodiacal signs *in sway*
(Al Buruj 085:1)

Billions of stars and galaxies in the multiverse revolve in their separate orbits in great harmony. Stars, planets, and satellites rotate around their axes and in their separate systems altogether.

The concept of velocity in the universe is hard to comprehend. The dimensions in space are enormous when compared with the measurements on earth; stars and planets of billions or trillions of tons and galaxies with sizes that can only be grasped with the help of mathematical formulas whirl toward specified destinations in space at incredible velocities.

For instance, the earth rotates around its axis at a mean velocity of about 1,670 kilometers per hour. If we compare earth's velocity with that of a bullet having an average velocity of 1,800 kilometers per hour, one can understand the huge velocity of earth despite its giant size.

The mean linear velocity of the earth in its orbit is 108,000 kilometers per hour, almost sixty times the velocity of the bullet. (If it could be possible to design such an automobile, it would travel around the equator in twenty-two minutes.)

These figures only relate to the earth. We come across tremendous figures when we examine the dimensions of the solar system. In the universe, as systems increase in size, the velocity also increases. The solar system revolves around the centre of the galaxy at a velocity of 720,000 kilometers per hour. The velocity of the Milky Way, which is comprised of some two hundred billion stars, is 950,000 kilometers per hour.

This tremendous speed is in fact an obvious indicator of the sensitive equilibrium established in the universe, which is vital to the existence of the whole cosmic order with life in it. In such a complex and speedy system, it is highly probable that giant accidents may occur at any time. However, as it is stated in the verse, one cannot see a flaw in the Lord's creation. After this assertion, how could one think that this extremely defined and well-determined system could have evolved and thrived on its own without a definite order of discipline abiding to keep them in pace and place? That is because nothing in the universe is left on its own, every single piece in point is under the control of a definite and well-determined discipline.

---

18 Electromagnetic and gravitational fields

- The Milky Way is a spiral galaxy, with curving arms of stars pinwheeling out from a center.
- The solar system is about halfway out on one of these arms and is about 226,000 light-years from the center. A light-year is about six trillion miles.
- Using a radio telescope system that measures celestial distances five hundred times more accurately than the Hubble Space Telescope, astronomers plotted the motion of the Milky Way and found that the sun and its family of planets were orbiting the galaxy at about 135 miles per second.
- That means it takes the solar system about 226 million years to orbit the Milky Way and puts the most precise value ever determined on one of the fundamental motions of the earth and its sun, said James Moran of Harvard's Smithsonian Center for Astrophysics in Cambridge, Massachusetts.
- The new measurement of the solar system's orbit adds new accuracy to a fundamental fact of the universe. Everything is moving constantly.
- The earth rotates on its axis at about 1,100 miles an hour, a motion that creates day and night.
- The earth orbits the sun at about 67,000 miles an hour, a motion that takes one year.
- The sun circles the Milky Way at a speed of about 486,000 miles per hour. And every object in the universe is moving apart from the other objects as the universe expands at a constantly accelerating rate.

Over and above all that, just have the perception of His creation. There are four types of galaxies:

- Spiral galaxies
- Lenticular—these are short, spiral galaxies with spiral structures.
- Elliptical—cosmic footballs, actually ellipsoid in shape
- Irregular Galaxies—distorted by the gravitation of their intergalactic neighbors.

Some galaxies, like M87 or M77, are several trillion solar masses with trillions of stars; their diameter ranges from a few thousand light-years (linear size of the galaxy M32) to a respectable several hundred thousand light-years as are some Messier galaxies like the Andromeda Galaxy, M31.

Our Milky Way Galaxy is two hundred and fifty billion solar masses with a total mass of seven hundred and fifty to one trillion times that of sun, and the disc diameter is one hundred thousand light-years.

Can you discern His order of discernment in the cosmic order? Nay! You cannot.

The Multiverses

The very first verse of the first chapter of the Holy Scripture asserts: "All praises be to the Lord of Multiverses."

And we all know our scientific belief in a universe up to early last century.

There would have been no dispute in various matters of scientific concern, if the scholars would have tried to understand the philosophy of the Holy Scripture at the early stages, when most of the scientists were conflicted over different disciplines of the cosmic order.

There was a confrontation going on:
The earth is static?
No, the earth is moving?
The sun is moving?
No, the sun is static?
Now turn to the following verses from the Holy Scripture.

There's another sign for them *to aside*
Night sweeping day sheds shawl *in stride*

Sun is moving to its defined *butt and tail*
Moon directed to traverse *a trek in trail*
Crescent browsing as a date tree *shoot in sear*
There's tangible trek[19] for moon and sun *so clear* (36:37–40)

These questions were perplexing the scientists till the early nineteenth century, but nobody ever turned to the Holy Qur'an, which ascertained 1,400 years back that all the universal celestial bodies are in motion and are tending toward their ultimate end. Besides that, the whole cosmic sway is built on piers that are not visible. How exquisitely Allah Almighty has referred to the electromagnetic fields functioning as firm and determined piers but invisible to the eyes.

---

19 Orbit

So we turn to the word *Ala'meen*, which means "worlds" or "multiverses." You'll be surprised that it is only a matter of a couple of years ago, that's the late twentieth century, when the scientists affirmed that this universe we are abiding in and which is made visible with our most sophisticated equipage about fourteen billion light-years hence is just one of the billions of other multiverses turning in stellar sprawl ever since the creation—the big bang or the divine decree in dictate: *Kûn.*

The Creation of the Multiverses Was an Arduous Job

Guidance in gleam and *a missive in flow*
For the men of sapience *in glow*
Assiduously then trend *to endure*
For Covenant of Lord is true *to allure*
And beg absolution for your ills *in score*
And keep glory of Lord *in adore*
Morn and eve *and even so more*

Those bickering *in trance*
The Signs of Lord *in stance*
With no dictum endowed *in glance*

They endeavor and attempt *in lore*
For glory in their veer *of core*
For what they'll never trend *to secure*
Beg in refuge of Lord *to endure*
For He discerns and concerns *in score*

Indeed!
The creation of the heavens and earth *in place*
Is greater than the creation of humanity *in pace*
Yet most of the men discern it not, *to in trace*
(Al Muimoun 40:54–57)

Similarly, in another instance, Allah Almighty asserts that the creation of mankind was not a real great job, but it was the creation and discipline of the multiverses.

Just trend to seek their view *in concern*
If they're more arduous to create
Or the Multiverses *in space*
We created Multiverses *in precision*
To the men,
We created from gluey dip *in collision*

The Qur'an escorts the man in different attitudes in our conduct in course besides elucidating the most burning topics of modern-day science.

"Enjoining justice and forbidding evil," on the other hand, it conducts in course as how to entreat and beseech hither in the vale for the ultimate exoneration Hereafter in trail.

All in the Heavens and earth *in array*
Ardor and adore Lord *in sway*
For He's Exalted in Might
With Sense and Sagacity *in Bright*
2.
To Him belongs the rule *and edit*
Of the Heavens and earth *in strict*
Commands in creation *and in demise*
Holds Dint and Demand all *in premise*
(Al Hadid (Iron) 57:1–2)

The subject demands a lot of patience and endurance to elaborate only in this context, for the Lord Almighty in the very first verse of the first Surah of the Holy Scripture has ascertained as a determined proof of His Almighty's domains in His dint in demand and care in command.

The idea of other parallel universes is not just a staple of science fiction; other universes are now a direct implication of cosmological observation. Such a change in our psyches seems strange and inconceivable, but it looks as if we will just have to live with it, because it is supported by astronomical observations. The simplest and most popular cosmological model today predicts that you have a twin in a galaxy about 10×10^{28} meters from here. This distance is so large that it is beyond astronomical, but that does not make the scientific assertion any less real. The estimate is derived from elementary probability and does not even assume speculative modern physics; it is merely that space is infinite (or at least sufficiently large) in size and almost uniformly filled with matter, as observations indicate.

In infinite space, even the most unlikely events must take place somewhere. Perhaps there are infinitely many other inhabited planets, including not just one but also possibly infinitely many that have people with the same appearances, names, and memories as you, who play out every possible permutation of your life choices.

You will probably never see your other selves. The farthest you can observe is the distance that light has been able to travel during the fourteen billion years since the big bang expansion began. The most distant visible objects are now about 4×10^{26} meters away—the distance that defines our observable universe also called our Hubble volume, our horizon volume, or simply our universe. Likewise, the universes of your other selves are spheres of the same size centered on their planets. They are the most straightforward example of parallel universes. Each universe is merely a small part of a larger.

By this very definition of "universe," one might expect the notion of a multiverse to be forever in the domain of metaphysics. Yet the borderline between physics and metaphysics is defined by whether a theory is experimentally testable, not by whether it is weird or involves unobservable entities. The frontiers of physics have gradually expanded to incorporate ever more abstract (and once metaphysical) concepts, such as a round Earth, invisible electromagnetic fields, the slowing down of time at high speeds, quantum superpositions, curved space, and black holes. Over the past several years, the concept of a multiverse has joined this list. It is grounded in well-tested theories, such as relativity and quantum mechanics, and it fulfills both of the basic criteria of an empirical science: it makes predictions, and it can be falsified. Scientists have discussed as many as four distinct types of parallel multiverses.

The key question is not whether the multiverses exist but rather how many levels they have. If anything, the Level I Multiverse sounds trivially obvious. How could space not be infinite? Is there a sign somewhere saying, "Space ends here—Mind the gap"? If so, what lies beyond it? In fact, Einstein's theory of gravity calls this intuition into question.

Another possibility is that space is infinite, but matter is confined to a finite region around us—the historically popular "island universe" model. In a variant on this model, matter thins out on large scales. In both cases, almost all universes in the Level I Multiverse would be empty and dead. But recent observations of the three-dimensional galaxy distribution and the microwave background have shown that the arrangement of matter gives way to dull uniformity on large scales, with no coherent structures larger than about 10^{24} meters. Assuming that this pattern continues, space beyond our observable universe teems with galaxies, stars, and planets, and that's still the lowermost sky.

That assumption underlies the estimate that your closest identical copy is 10×10^{28} meters away. About 10×10^{92} meters away, there should be a sphere with a radius of one hundred light-years identical to the one centered here, so all perceptions that we have during the next century will be identical to those of our counterparts over there. About 10 x 12^{118} meters away, there should be an entire Hubble volume identical to ours.

These are extremely conservative estimates, derived from all possible quantum states that a Hubble volume can have if it is no hotter than 10^8 Kelvins. One way to do the calculation is to ask how many protons could be packed into a Hubble volume at that temperature. The answer is 10^{118} protons. Each of those particles may or may not, in fact, be present, which makes for 2 x 10^{118} possible arrangements of protons. A box containing that many Hubble volumes exhausts all the possibilities. If you round off the numbers, such a box is about 10 x 10^{118} meters across. Beyond that box, universes—including ours—must repeat. Roughly using thermodynamics or quantum could derive the same number: gravitational estimates of the total information content of the universe.

The prevailing view in physics today is that the dimensionality of space-time, the qualities of elementary particles, and many of the so-called physical constants are not built into physical laws but are the outcome of processes known as symmetry breaking. For instance, theorists think that the space in our universe once had nine dimensions, all on an equal footing. Early in cosmic history, three of them partook in the cosmic expansion and became the three dimensions we now observe. The other six are now unobservable. (Doesn't it favor the Qur'anic assertion that .you observe the lowest sky decked with stars and the rest of the six skies stay beyond your comprehension?) either because they have stayed microscopic with a doughnut-like topology or because all matter is confined to a three-dimensional surface (a membrane) in the nine-dimensional space.

Creation of the Grand Universe and Life

Max Tegmark, in a *Scientific American* special issue on parallel universes, asserts something like that our creation and the creation of the grand universe is a mere stroke of chance as it may happen that in a hotel you are allotted room number 1967 which happens to be the same as your date of birth.

Agreed!

We came into being just with a stroke of chance.

Okay!

But how was the hotel constructed without any plan and design besides all instruction in construction?

Could it be erected only with a stroke of chance?

And such coincidences happen only once in a while. If you happen to have the same room on the same floor for the second or third time in a row, you'll be quite concerned about this and will be sure that there is someone behind this, who was arranging all of it.

As surprising as it appears to be, how frequently does it happen that you have the room of your date of birth? Once in a lifetime, if at all it happens to be so. But how would you construe the fine-tuning of the mass, volume, gravitational force, and speed of rotation at their axes, which are speeding away in their orbit in the swarm of the stellar sprawl in the cosmic order, not in the millions but in the billions of trillions, alone and together with all the planets around. Each is treading in its definite orbit in the cosmic sway in an extraordinary discipline, one cannot really comprehend to grasp. And that's all a stroke of chance, not at one pace or instance, but at each step in the stride in the cosmic glide, if you catch a glimpse in glance? And the Lord Almighty invites you to have look at the whole cosmic order and try to find out any slit or split in the system, but you cannot. Then once again, He asserts, "O Man! Try to look at the system once more, and see if you can find a deviance in the discipline." No! You really cannot; it's really a most fascinating display in array (Al Mulk).

Can you compromise with such an assertion?

Nobody can defy the role of the supreme nature in all this order, to which we all attribute the name of Allah Almighty, Lord, God, or Brahma.

What's meditation or spirituality that perceives supernatural notions?

Why is the blood supply to a part of the left parietal lobe in the brain totally stopped during deep meditation? And what's the source of nutrition or oxygen supply to that part of brain during meditation?

How did all these effects and this equipage come into being with definite laws abiding from the trivia of an atom to the indeterminate cosmic sway?

Then how come we disregard the most fascinating powerful hand behind the fine-tuning in the cosmological discipline? Couldn't there be a most mighty nature behind the creation of all these effects and equipage?

Although the degree of fine-tuning is still debated, these examples suggest the existence of parallel universes with other values of the physical constants. The Level II Multiverse theory predicts that physicists will never be able to determine the values of these constants from first principles. They will merely compute the probability distributions for what they should expect to find, taking selection effects into account. The result should be as generic as is consistent with our existence.

So should you believe in parallel universes? The principal arguments against them are that they are wasteful and that they are weird. Why should nature be so wasteful and indulge in such opulence as an infinity of different worlds? Yet this argument can be turned around to argue for a multiverse. What precisely would nature be wasting? Certainly not space, mass, or atoms—the uncontroversial Level I Multiverse already contains an infinite amount of all three, so who cares if nature wastes some more?

The real issue here is the apparent reduction in simplicity. A skeptic worries about all the information necessary to specify all those unseen worlds.

A common feature of all four multiverse levels is that the simplest and arguably most elegant theory involves parallel universes by default. To deny the existence of those universes, one needs to complicate the theory by adding experimentally unsupported processes and ad hoc postulates: finite space, wave function collapse, and ontological asymmetry.

Our judgment therefore comes down to which we find more wasteful and inelegant: many worlds or many words. Perhaps we will gradually get used to the weird ways of our cosmos and find its strangeness to be part of its charm.

For what the man, a creation of the Lord (nature), here in the world is trying to consider today, the Lord Almighty affirmed a long time ago, like the expansion of and rotation of the universe, the creation of darkness and black holes, and many other subjects with which the scientific mind of today is concerned.

Cosmic-Ray Hazard

The galaxy is pervaded with fast-moving particles that can rip apart DNA and other molecules. Here at the surface of the earth, we are well protected from this cosmic radiation by the air mass overhead. Astronauts in near-equatorial orbits are shielded by the planet's magnetic field. But those who make long voyages away from earth will suffer serious health consequences.

A spherical shell of water or plastic could protect space travelers, but it would take a total mass of at least four hundred tons, which is beyond the capacity of heavy-lift rockers. A superconducting magnet would repel cosmic particles and weigh an estimated nine tons, but that is still too much, and the magnetic field itself would pose health risks. No other proposed scheme is even vaguely realistic.

Biomedical researchers need to determine more precisely how much long-term exposure to cosmic rays a person can tolerate and whether medicines could stimulate the body's natural repair mechanisms.

The desk and domain of the human being is most probably restricted to a particular expanse for which he has been created and may not go beyond determined frontiers.

Within the universe, there is nowhere we can go without being constantly bombarded by radiation and high-energy particles or where we would not feel the effects of inertia. We are always completely under the influence of the laws of universal space. While with most of our powerful telescopes, we can look back eleven billion light-years yonder in the galaxy, it seems to be even much bigger than our discernment; there could possibly be one hundred billion light-years, all under the Almighty's domain.

A trip from the earth to beyond the Milky Way is a journey to the emptiest places imaginable. In the interstellar regions of the galaxy, light from the nearest stars takes years to arrive and the density of the intergalactic medium (IGM). Scientists are working on the likelihood of intergalactic travel from the familiar solar neighborhood into the depths of the most desolate places imaginable. Our eyes are still adjusting to the unexpected and intricate beauty of the cosmic web that stretches across the emptiest places.

The boon, benison, and benediction of His Almighty here in this vale and also the life to survive in the Hereafter, when we depart from this ephemeral existence have been resplendently explained in Surah *Al Mulk*. There is a word of admonition and chastisement for those perverse and perverted, petulant and pettish who have not been punctilious and principled to His Almighty's dictates and demands. His clear augury and omen at such instances precisely represents His bestowal of compassion and dispensation: *I had sent you My messengers and the scriptures, why didn't you abide by the discipline conveyed to you? And now you have to bear the brunt of tribulation thus ascribed for the bad-tempered and belligerent done and doing.*

The Expansion of the Universe

Until the twentieth century, nowhere in the world did a scientist put forth a theory regarding the expansion of the world. They did not even raise such a possibility. Stephan Hawking calls this discovery to be the most important occasion of the twentieth century.

In the Qur'an, the Lord Almighty informed the believers about the creation and expansion of the universe.

With power and skill *in pace*
We rear and raise sky *in place*
It's We, Who create vistas *in Space*

And We spread and tether *in phase*
The earth how exquisitely *in place*
(Al-Dhariyat 51:47–48)

The Rotating Universe and the Creation of the Day and Night

The fact that all stars, planets, and satellites follow an orbit is the factor essential in the establishment of the astonishing system in the universe. Until recently, man's knowledge about orbits was limited. However, the Qur'an informed us about orbits back in the sixth century.

He's The Lord!
Who created night and the day *in call*
Besides, gleam of moon and glitter of sol[20]
They bob and drift in each ellipse[21] *in mall*

All the bodies in the universe rotate on their axes as well as around their separate systems just like the wheels in a factory. The Qur'an also states that everything in the universe rotates on its axis:

Vow to the Heavens with sprinkle in spray[22]
And earth with streaming springs in sway
With blooming of fauna and foliage in array
(Al-Taryq 86:11–12)

The motion in the universe is not confined only to orbits. Our solar system and even other galaxies rotate around other systems. The earth, together with the solar system, moves five hundred million kilometers ahead each year. The slightest deviation from the orbit may cause detrimental consequences to the overall system. For instance, a deviation of three millimeters from the earth's orbit may cause the following:

While rotating around the sun, the earth follows such an orbit that for each eighteen miles, it only deviates 2.8 millimeters from a linear line. The orbit followed by the earth never changes. Even the slightest deviation would cause catastrophic disasters. If the deviation was

20 Sun
21 Orbit
22 Rain

2.5 mm instead of 2.8 mm, then the orbit would be expanding, causing the temperatures to fall drastically. In such an environment, everything would freeze. On the other hand, if the deviation was 3.1 mm, then all living things would burn up.[23]

It is an interesting reflection on the general climate of thought before the twentieth century that no one suggested that the universe was expanding or contracting. It was generally accepted that either the universe has existed forever in an unchanging state or that it was created at a finite time in the past or less as we observe it today. In part, this may have been due to people's tendency to believe in eternal truths, as well as the comfort they found in the thought that even though they may grow old and die, the universe is eternal and unchanging.

Even those who realized that Newton's theory of gravity showed that the universe could not be static did not think to suggest that it might be expanding. Instead, they attempted to modify the theory by making the gravitational force repulsive at very large distances. This did not significantly affect their predictions of the motions of the planets, but it allowed an infinite distribution of stars to remain in equilibrium—with the attractive forces between nearby stars balanced by the repulsive forces from those that were farther away. However, we do not believe such equilibrium wouldn't be unstable: if the stars in some region got only slightly nearer each other, the attractive forces between them would become stronger and dominate over the repulsive forces so that the stars would continue to fall toward each other. On the other hand, if the stars got a bit farther away from each other, the repulsive forces would dominate and drive them farther apart.

Another objection to an infinite, static universe is normally ascribed to the German philosopher Heinrich Olbers, who wrote about this theory in 1823. In fact, various contemporaries of Newton had raised the problem, and the Olbers' article was not even the first to contain plausible arguments against it. It was, however, the first to be widely noted. The difficulty is that in an infinite, static universe, nearly every line of sight would end on the surface of a star. Thus, one would expect that the whole sky would be as bright as the sun even at night. Olbers' counterargument was that the light from distant stars would be dimmed because of absorption by intervening matter. However, if that happened, the intervening matter would eventually heat up until it glowed as brightly as the stars. The only way of avoiding the conclusion that the whole of the night sky should be as bright as the surface of the sun is to assume that the stars have not been shining forever but were turned on at some finite time in the past. In that case, the absorbing

23 *Science & Technology*, July 1983.

matter might not have heated up yet or the light from distant stars might not yet have reached us. And that brings us to the question of what could have caused the stars to turn on in the first place.

The beginning of the universe had, of course, been discussed long before this. According to a number of early cosmologies and the Jewish, the Christian, and the Muslim traditions, the universe started at a finite and not very distant time in the past. One argument for such a beginning was the feeling that it was necessary to have "first cause" to explain the existence of the universe.

Within the universe, one always explained one event as being caused by some earlier event, but the existence of the universe itself could be explained in this way only if it had some beginning.

Another argument was put forward by St. Augustine in his book *The City of God*. He pointed out that civilization is progressing and we remember who performed this deed or developed that technique. Thus, man and perhaps the universe also could not have been there that long. St. Augustine accepted a date of about 5000 BC for the creation of the universe according to the book of Genesis. (It is interesting that this is not so far from the end of the last Ice Age, about 10,000 BC, which is when archaeologists tell us that civilization really began.)

Creation of Darkness

Don't they care and concern *to aside*
We created,
Night *(for them)* to rest *in abide*
And the day a glow *in delight*
Indeed!
There's a word who affirm *in slight*
(Al-Naml 27:86)

As it is indicated in the Qur'an, the night is specially created for rest. A few years ago, when scientists calculated the number of stars and the quantity of light emitted by stars in the universe, they concluded that the universe should have been bright all the time. They also could not understand why the earth darkens. This subject could only be understood after the discoveries that black holes, which are scattered all around the universe, have a tremendous attraction force, which absorbs light emitted by stars. This is the main reason for darkness in the universe. In other words, the darkness is specially "created." A detailed discussion is also given in the preceding paragraph.

Black Holes

In the universe, stars that run out of fuel shrink inwards. At the last stage of this shrinking process, an enormous force of attraction with an infinite density and zero volume emerges. This is called a black hole. The Qur'an attracts our attention to black holes in the following verses:

> *Likewise!*
> I call to behold stage and spot *in promotion*
> Dwindling of the stars *in commotion*
> *Indeed!*
> It's an immense pledge *in term*
> If you really care to discern
> (Al-Waqiah 56:75–76)

In the verse, it is emphasized that the locations of the stars represent a great force. The fact that black holes appear in the location of an inflated star and the great force they have are both indicated in the above-mentioned verses.

The Divine Order of Discipline

The orbit of the sun and moon:

> Moon directed to traverse *a trek in trail*
> Crescent browsing as a date tree *shoot in sear*
> There's tangible trek for moon and sun *so clear*
> Both sun and moon tread *in define*
> Also the day and night *held in confine*
> Concern to abide determined trek *in trail*
> So to confirm correct confine *in scale*
> (Yä sin 36:39–40)

As the moon follows its orbit, sometimes it appears in front of the earth and sometimes it trails the earth. In the meantime, since it rotates together with the earth around the sun, it follows an orbit shaped like an "S." The path of the moon's orbit in the universe is very similar to a dry date palm branch. The moon rotates around the earth at a rate of 3,659 kilometers per hour. It protects itself from the powerful gravity force of the earth with the help of this high-rotation velocity. If the moon rotated at a lower velocity, it would collide with the earth. If it rotated at a higher velocity, it would go out of its orbit and disappear in space. The size of the moon and its velocity of rotation affect the earth and cause what we call "the tide." If the moon's force of attraction were more, then most of the lands on earth would be covered by ocean.

> The Creator of earth and heavenly *mall*
> How can He have scion *in call*
>
> For there's no spouse for Him *in aside*
> When He created all hither *in stride*
>
> He concerns and discerns all *in abide*
> That's your Lord Mighty *in abound*
> There's no Lord, save Him *(all) in Alone*
> Who created all in hither *and surround*
> So trend to beseech *(Him) all in prone*
> He discerns and concerns *all in adorn*
>
> You cannot really discern *(Him) in pace*
> But He apprehends trivia *in trace*
> Lord beholds all concern *in grace*
>
> There're clear signs from Lord *to concern*
> Who so reasons, it's fair for him *to discern*
>
> Who's blind to concern *in core*
> The infliction is for him *to endure*
> I'm not to care your term *in score*
> (Al-Anaam 6:101–104)

The Sun

Let us consider the mass of the sun because the mass of a star determines its luminosity. And using the basic possible limits, only if the sun's mass falls into the narrow range between 1.6×10^{30} and 2.4×10^{30} kilograms, would it create luminosity besides heat to sustain life on the earth. Otherwise, Earth's climate would be colder than that of present-day Mars or hotter than that of present-day Venus. The measure of solar mass is 2.0×10^{30} kilograms. At first glance, this apparent coincidence of the habitable and observed mass values appears to be a wild stroke of luck. Stellar masses run from 10^{29} to 10^{32} kilograms, so if the sun acquired its mass at random, it had only a small chance of falling into the range that would make earth habitable. But one can explain this apparent coincidence by postulating an ensemble and a selection effect by nature (the fact that we find ourselves living on a habitable planet). Such observer-related selection effects are referred to as "anthropic," and although the "A-word" is notorious for triggering controversy, physicists broadly agree that these selection effects cannot be neglected when testing fundamental theories.

How delicate is the cosmological discipline?

Changing their values by a modest amount would have resulted in a qualitatively different universe—one in which we probably would not exist. If protons were 0.2 percent heavier, they could decay into neutrons, destabilizing atoms. If the electromagnetic force were 4 percent weaker, there would be no hydrogen and no normal stars. If the weak interaction were much weaker, hydrogen would not exist; if it were much stronger, supernovae would fail to seed interstellar space with heavy elements. If the cosmological constant were much larger, the universe would have blown itself apart before galaxies could form.

The distance between the earth and the sun is about 150 million kilometers. Despite this great distance, it conveys heat and light to the earth. The light then contributes to the growth of plant life and evaporates water from the ocean and other sources. It plays a pivotal role in the production of winds and accomplishes many innumerable operations that are indispensable to the existence of life on earth.

The power inherent in sunlight is generated by the transformation of hydrogen atoms into helium. Each second, 616 billion tons of hydrogen is transformed into 612 billion tons of helium. In the meantime, the energy ejected is equivalent to the explosion of five hundred million hydrogen bombs. The sun is only one of the two hundred billion stars in the Milky Way. Although it is 325,000 times wider than the earth, it is considered to be one of the small stars in the universe. It is a distance of 226 thousand light-years to the center of the Milky Way (One light-year equals six trillion miles).

As a star, the sun is a typical yellow dwarf and most inconspicuously located in a spiral arm near the outer edge of the Milky Way. In orbiting the centre of the galaxy, it whirls toward the constellation at a velocity of about 720,000 kilometers per hour; accordingly, the sun, together with the earth, moves 720,000 x 24 = 17,280,000 kilometers in a day.

The Shape of the Earth

He contrived,
Heavens and earth, due size *and span*
He folds[24] night over day *in design*
And so day folds night *in confine*
The sun and moon abide *in plan*
Submissive to His code *in consign*
Each conform trek and trail for a term *in assign*
He is Astral O August in His Dint and Demand
He relents and remits, then condone in command
(Al-Zumar 39:5)

The statements used in the verses that describe the universe are quite striking. The Arabic word translated as "overlap" in English is *Tekvir*. The precise meaning of *Tekvir* is to "to wind … round or to wrap … around." Consequently, the act of night overlapping the day and vice versa is only possible if the earth has a spherical shape.

Mountains and Earthquakes

He created universe without[25] pier *in pace*
For what you cannot discern and concern *in place*
Mountains settled on the earth *so firm*
Lest it should shiver and quiver *in term*
And He dispersed all sentient breed *and creed*
We convey shower from the sky *in steed*
And bear on earth in all sort *and spot*
All affirmed splendid creation in plot
(Luqman 31:10)

Haven't We created earth an abide *in term*
So spacious and capacious in scope *and space*
Mountains so fixed, pin and plugged *in place*
(Al-Naba 78:6–7)

---

24 How nicely this illustrates that the earth is round, as if folding a wrapper around a rounded object.
25 Invisible piers, (i.e., gravitational and electromagnetic fields)

What the science of geology tells us about the mountains today is in compliance with the verses above. One of the features of the mountains is that they exist on the endpoints of geological plates of the earth and bind them to each other. With such a function, mountains are like nails holding the pieces of plates in firm proximity. Apart from that, the pressure made by mountains on the surface of the earth prevents the effects of magma motion occurring in the core of the earth from coming to the surface and breaking the earth's crust into pieces.

Pairs in Creation

Glory be to The Lord, Who turned *to plan*
Created pair in assort, various *gene in span*
That may be within plant site *and spot*
Your own and else you cannot hint *in plot*
(Surah Yä sin 36:36)

The "pairs" indicated in the verse refer partly to the concept of male and female. Yet, the statement "… and other things of which they have no knowledge" includes a wider range of meanings. The English scientist Paul Dirac discovered antimatter and was rewarded with the Nobel Physics Prize in 1933 for his discovery. This startling discovery, which was called "partite," revealed that matter was created in pairs. The antimatter carries the opposite properties of matter. At the time of creation, the universe would have contained mostly photons, electrons, and neutrinos (extremely light particles that are affected only by the weak force and gravity) and their antiparticles, together with some protons and neutrons.

For instance, contrary to matter, the electrons of antimatter are charged positive (+), and its protons are charged negative (-). As the universe continued to expand and the temperature to drop, the rate at which they were being destroyed by annihilation, as most of the electrons and antielectrons annihilated each other to produce more photons, leaving only a few electrons. The neutrinos and antineutrinos, however, would not have annihilated each other, because these particles interact with themselves and with other particles only very weakly.

Assertion in the Perfection of Multiverses

He created skies in series of seven
There's no want in slant in term of creation

Most Amiable is Lord, *immense in initiation*
So trend your looks *once more to the heaven*
Can you discern a bit of slit *in this creation*
Then trend and talent anew *in quest*
You're denied of flaw *in behest*
Not even perplexity or poop *in the rest*
(Al Mulk 67:3–4)

Perfection in the Human Creation

Lord then trended to Iblis *in command*
What hinders you to incline *in demand*
To one I fashioned so absolute *and refine*
With My Own hands in sublime
Are you snobbish and conceited *to decline*
Or if you are high in esteem *and prime* (38:75)

This daze in amazement is an upshot of the biased slant in the attitude of some "scientists" toward the Qur'anic notion. They believe that there is an absolute incongruity between science and religion, whereas the Holy Scriptures provide well-defined concepts in various domains of modern science. The things are not clear to the ordinary person. They require deep knowledge of the Qur'anic philosophy and modern-day science to understand and make the connection between the two (i.e., science and faith).

The Fate of the Universe

The laws of gravity were incompatible until recently with the belief that the universe is unchanging in time; the fact that gravity is always attractive implies that the universe must be either expanding or contracting. According to the general theory of relativity, there must have been a state of infinite density in the past, before the big bang, which would have been an effective beginning of time. Similarly, if the whole universe re-collapsed, there would be another state of infinite density in the future, the big crunch, which would be the end of time. Even if the whole universe did not re-collapse, there would be singularities in any localized regions that collapsed to form black holes. These singularities would be an end of time for anyone who fell into their black holes. His Almighty had complete freedom to choose what happened and how the universe began and how the singularities would converge to their circumstances.

It is an interesting reflection on the general climate of thought before the twentieth century that no one suggested that the universe was expanding or contracting. It was generally accepted that either the universe had existed forever in an unchanging state, or that it had been created at a finite time in the past more or less as we observe it today. In part, this may have been due to people's tendency to believe in eternal truths, as well as the comfort they found in the thought that even though they may grow old and die, the universe would remain eternal and unchanging.

Even those who realized that Newton's theory of gravity showed that the universe could not be static did not think to suggest that it might be expanding. Instead, they attempted to modify the theory by making the gravitational force repulsive at very large distances. This did not significantly affect their predictions of the motions of the planets, but it allowed an infinite distribution of stars to remain in equilibrium, with the attractive forces between nearby stars balanced by the repulsive forces from those that were farther away. However, we now believe such equilibrium would be unstable; if the stars in some region were only slightly nearer each other, the attractive forces between them would become stronger and dominate the repulsive forces, so that the stars would continue to fall toward each other. On the other hand, if the stars got a bit farther away from each other, the repulsive forces would dominate and drive them farther apart.

Another objection to an infinite static universe is normally ascribed to the German philosopher Heinrich Olbers, who wrote about this theory in 1823. In fact, various contemporaries of Newton had raised the problem, and Olbers' article was not even the first to contain plausible arguments against it. It was, however, the first to be widely noted.

If we presume that the universe is static, the difficulty is that in an infinite, static universe nearly every line of sight (light) would end on the surface of a star. Thus, one would expect that the whole sky would be as bright as the sun, even at night.

How could one have imagined the extremely intricate discipline in the cosmic order, where billions of stars in billions of galaxies move around, maintaining a discipline of eventfulness? How could that be without a mighty discipline behind the whole cosmic order?

First, there are the laws that tell us how the universe changes with time. (If we know what the universe is like at any one time, these physical laws tell us how it will look at any later time.) Second, there is the question of the initial state of the universe. Some people feel that science should be concerned with only the first part; they regard the question of the initial situation as a matter for metaphysics or religion. They would say that the Almighty, being omnipotent, could have started the universe off any way he wanted. That may be so, but in that case, He also could have made it develop in a completely arbitrary way. Yet it appears that He chose to make it evolve in a very regular way according to certain laws. It therefore seems equally reasonable to suppose that there are also laws governing the initial state.

Scientists still stand divided concerning the fate of the grand universe. The Qur'an gives a definite plan of its ultimate end with creation anew or another big bang.

It turns out to be very difficult to devise a theory to describe the universe all in one go. Instead, we break the problem up into bits and invent a number of partial theories. Each of these partial theories describes and predicts a certain limited class of observations, neglecting the effects of other quantities or representing them by simple sets of numbers. It may be that this approach is completely wrong. If everything in the universe depends on everything else in a fundamental way, it might be impossible to get close to a full solution by investigating parts of the problem in isolation.

We do not yet have such a theory, and we may still be a long way from having one, but we do already know many of the properties that it must have.

Now, if you believe that the universe is not arbitrary but is governed by definite laws, you ultimately have to combine the partial theories into a complete unified theory that will describe everything in the universe.

The general theory of relatively describes gravity as a warping of space-time by the mass and energy in it.

The other phenomena that are going to accompany this expected change and of which the Qur'an has spoken in detail can give us a clear idea of this change. These phenomena are:

1. The Sundering Verse 1—*the rending asunder of heaven: when heaven is split asunder*
2. The Cleaving Asunder Verses 1, 2—*the scattering of the planets: when the heaven is cleft asunder and when the planets are dispersed*
3. The Folding Up Verse 6—*the turning of the seas into flames*
4. Resurrection Verse 9—*the vanishing of the moon*
5. Al Zumar 39, Verse 67—*when the earth and skies will be in the handful of Allah Almighty.*

The Qur'an tells that the end of the solar system will take place all of a sudden, as if in a twinkling of an eye. It will have no conspicuous preliminaries. From what the Qur'an has mentioned, we can deduce that the sun is going to explode, expulsing colossal swarms and the gloom of conflagration that will turn the seas into flames and conclude life on earth. The gravitational impetus of the sun will dwindle in so much as the centrifugal intensity of the planets will overwhelm it, and the sun will relinquish command over them. In due course, our planetary system will be disseminated.

Science predetermines two hypotheses. The first one is that the sun may burst and erupt like some of the other stars that have already done so and turn into a black hole.

The second is that the sun will become very cold promptly giving reddish light and then receding to disappear.

The two hypotheses assert that the solar system will come to an end. Science cannot take something for granted. The different Qur'anic verses affirm the ultimate fate of the grand universe. Science simply sets the hypothesis that has to be accepted by the time. The scientific knowledge still has a long way to go to accomplish the skill to appreciate the truth of the philosophy of the Holy Scripture.

Science seems to have uncovered a set of laws that, within the limits set by the uncertainty principle, tell us how the universe will develop with time, if we know its state at any one time. The Lord Almighty originally determined these laws, but how did He choose the initial state or configuration of the universe?

One possible answer is to say that the Lord Almighty chose the initial configuration of the universe for reasons that we cannot hope to understand. This would certainly have been within the power of an omnipotent being, who started it off in an inconceivable way. The whole history of science has been the gradual realization that events do not happen in an arbitrary manner, but rather reflect a certain underlying order, which could only be divinely instigated. It would be only natural to suppose that this order should apply not only to the laws but also to the conditions at the boundary of space-time that specify the initial state of the universe. There may be a large number of models of the grand universe with different initial conditions that all obey the laws. There ought to be some principle that picks out one initial state and hence one model to represent our universe.

In the classical theory of gravity, which is based on real space-time, there are only two possible ways the universe can behave: either it has existed for an infinite time or else it had a beginning at a singularity at some finite time in the past. In the quantum theory of gravity, on the other hand, a third possibility arises. Because one is using Euclidean space-times, in which the time direction is on the same footing as directions in space, it is possible for space-time to be finite in extent and yet to have no singularities that formed a boundary or edge. Space-time would be like the surface of the earth, only with two more dimensions. The surface of the earth is finite in extent, but it doesn't have a boundary or edge; if you sail off into the sunset, you don't fall off the edge or run into a singularity.

So the quantum theory of gravity has opened up a new possibility, in which there would be no boundary to space-time and so there would be no need to specify the behavior at the boundary. Scientists affirm there would be no singularities at which the laws of science broke down, and there would be no edge of space-time.

One could say that the boundary condition of the universe is that it has no boundary.

The universe would be completely self-contained and not affected by anything outside itself. It would neither be created nor destroyed. It would just "be." Some scientists, like Stephen Hawking, at one stage thought of the possibility that space-time was finite but had no boundary, which means that it had no beginning, no moment of creation.

Einstein's general theory of relativity, on its own, predicted that space-time began at the big bang singularity and would come to an end either at the big crunch singularity (if the whole universe re-collapsed) or at a singularity inside a black hole (if a local region, such as a star, were to collapse). Any matter that fell into the hole would be destroyed at the singularity, and only the gravitational effect of its mass would continue to be felt outside. On the other hand, when quantum effects were taken into account, it seemed that the mass or energy of the matter would eventually be returned to the rest of the universe and that the black hole, along with any singularity inside it, would evaporate away and finally disappear. Could quantum mechanics have an equally dramatic effect on the big bang and big crunch singularities? What really happens during the very early or late stages of the universe, when gravitational fields are so strong that quantum effects cannot be ignored?

Einstein's equations for relativity indicated that the universe was expanding. This bothered him because if it was expanding, it must have had a beginning and a beginner. Since neither of these appealed to him, Einstein introduced a "fudge factor" that ensured a "steady-state" universe, one that had no beginning or end. But in 1929, Edwin Hubble showed that the farthest galaxies were fleeing away from each other, just as the big bang model predicted. So in 1931, Einstein embraced what would later be known as the big bang theory, saying, "This is the most beautiful and satisfactory explanation of creation to which I have ever listened." He referred to the "fudge factor" to achieve a steady-state universe as the biggest blunder of his career.

Cosmologists have not yet determined if there is enough mass in the universe to make it contract again or if it will just keep expanding. A one-time explosion is not very satisfying, theoretically. So, a cyclic series of infinitely many big crunches is preferred. But if it keeps expanding, then it only happened once.

If we study the Qur'anic verses, we see they intently favor an infinitely prolonged series of big crunches after the big smash with the eventual festering of the whole cosmic order. It defines the initial boundary conditions of the closed system where everything eventually would go wrong, but not as a singularity, as in a state of expansion of the grand universe. What would happen at that instance is clearly elucidated in the Holy Qur'an. The lower skies and the universe are torn and ripped apart and would then start contracting with a series of big crunches, and the entire solar system would become so hot (i.e., once again *conflagration* like in the initial state when the seas will be put to blaze). Thereafter, the whole cosmic order will eventuate in an ultimate boundary (i.e., a singularity, providing the seedling for the next creation). And how it will happen is for the future scientist to reason and postulate.

The Qur'an undoubtedly indicates boundary conditions in expansion. The lower skies are the limit. It also clearly mentions the fate of the universe.

(Expansion of the Universe)
With power and skill *in pace*
We rear and raise sky *in place*
It's We, Who create vistas *in Space*
And We spread and tether *in phase*
The earth how exquisitely *in place*
(Al-Dhariyat 51:47–48)

 (Boundary Condition of the Closed System)
He then accomplished cosmic in *sway*
Seven of skies in eons two *in array*
And consigned in task, *each to obey*

And decked to adorn *in score*
The lower sky with stars *in glow*
And granted it guards *around in flow*
He's Exalted in Might with Sapience *in Lore* (41:12)

The lower of sky We decked *in array*
With elegant stars dispersed in sway (37:06)

(Boundary Condition)
Raised the Heavens and set its brink
That you may not transgress[26] its brim
(55:07–08)

 (Boundary Condition with a Definite Time for the Big Smash)
They seek to rush, castigation[27] *to strike*
Had it not been a *(definite)* term *in plight*
The Penalty would've surely come *to stay*
And surely it'll grasp *(them), in abrupt*
When they really cannot discern *in instruct* (29:53)

Because the universe is expanding at a definite speed to the boundary limits of its closed system (i.e., the lower skies), so that day cannot be brought nearer, but when it would strike, it will just be in the flash of a moment.

---

26 Lower sky, the limit
27 Doomsday (Big Smash)

(Big Smash)
The Hour, destined is to loom *in abrupt*
When moon will shred to split *in spurt* (54:01)

(Next Creation)
It's Lord!
Who occasions the course *in creation*
Then He does it again *in initiation*
You'll trend back to Lord *in accreditation* (30:11)

(Big Smash and Next Creation)
The Day We'll whirl heavens *in twirl*
And a recorder list up a scribble in *swirl*
As We began the first creation *in sway*
We'll trend to it once again *in array*
It's pledged from Us *in pace*
We'll accomplish it *in place* (21:104)

And when the heaven splits asunder
And becomes red like teguments cover
(Al Rahman 37-38)

The sky pierced and parted asunder *in assort*
His word of commitment to meet *in accord*
(Al Muzzamil 73:18)

When sun crimp in crease to ease *in glimmer*
And stars wither in rot to lose their glitter
When the mountains vanish *in vale*
When the she-camels tread *in trail*
Conceived of months ten slighted *in slither*
When wild beasts sway in swarm hither *and thither*
When sea simmer in blaze to swell *in surge*
Souls then group to see alike *in urge*
(81 Al Tekvir (The Folding Up) 1–7)

In order to comprehend the fate of the universe, it is expedient to understand the nature of the arrows of time.

He endowed you life *to aside*
And cause doom of death *in stride*
Then He'll bestow life once more *in trail*
Indeed!
Man is really quite peeve *in scale* (Al-Hajj 22:66)

After a bit of introduction regarding the fate of the universe as discussed in various verses of the Holy Scripture, let us now consider the fate of the universe in the light of modern-day science.

Thermodynamic Arrow of Time: It deals with the transformation of heat available to another form of energy, and so there is a constant relation between the energy expended in the form of heat and energy gained in any other form.

Entropy: That's the measure of molecular disorder existing in a system or how much of the thermal energy is unavailable for conversion into a mechanical source.

Before really explaining the thermodynamic arrow of time, I would like to quote the Qur'an about boundary conditions: "Lower Sky is decked with Stars" (37:06; 41:12).

Stellar sprawl is taking place according to an orderly design in all directions, so the lower skies should also be in all the directions like a surrounding cover, thus forming a closed system model. Disorder, or entropy, always increases as described in Murphy's Law. (The lower sky forms the global expansion limits of the cosmic order.)

Why don't we see the broken cups gathering themselves together off the floor and jumping back onto the table? Because that is forbidden by the second law of thermodynamics. This says that in a closed system, disorder or entropy always increases with time._(According to Murphy's Law, things always go wrong in a closed model!)

An intact cup on the table is in an orderly state, whereas a broken cup on the floor is in disorderly state. One can see the intact cup on the table and discern a broken cup on the floor as a future concern, but not the other way round. The increase in the entropy or disorder with time is one example of the *thermodynamic arrow of time.*

Psychological Arrow of Time: This is the direction in which we feel the past (we remember), the present we hold, and the future (we cannot envision).

Cosmological Arrow of Time: This is the direction of time in which the universe is expanding. If ever the universe starts contracting again, the cosmological arrow of time will reverse.

Interminable Arrow of Time: It is expedient to define the future trends of the cosmic order, and to understand this, we have to incorporate the period of time when space and time were one and there was no order of discernment of time. We termed it nihility or *Fanaa*. This arrow of time took its stride before singularity when the Lord Almighty evinced Himself, when He created the angels and other exigencies that we cannot really discern to concern, and it shall follow forever in a definite direction.

Today, all the four arrows of time are pointing in one direction. If there are no boundary conditions for the universe together which the weak anthropic principle can explain, why do all the four arrows of time point in the same direction, and why should a well-defined arrow of time exist at all?

But unlike the preceding assertion, since there is a definite boundary condition for the grand universe, we shall see that there must be a well-defined thermodynamic arrow and cosmological arrow of time, but they will not point in the same direction all through space-time, and as long as they do, it is conceivable for intelligent beings like us to exist and all the order of nature to endure. If ever the cosmological arrow of time reverses and the universe starts contracting, eventuating in a series of big crunches after a big smash, it will culminate in a singularity, a seedling for a future big bang.

And how is this going to be?

The universe would have started off with a period of exponential or inflationary expansion, in which it would have increased in size by a very large factor. During this expansion, the density fluctuations would have remained small at first but later would have started to grow. The regions in which the density was slightly higher than average had their expansion slowed down by the gravitational attraction of the extra mass in the universe. Eventually, such regions would stop expanding and collapse to form galaxies, stars, etc.

Some of the galaxies are speeding away and expanding at a greater speed, others at a slower. That's relative to the celestial swarm within the galactic pace of the particular galaxy, but overall expansion of the multiverses is at a uniform pace.

An open universe, corresponding to omega less one, will expand forever. Matter will spread thinner and thinner. Galaxies will exhaust their gas supply for forming new stars, and old stars will eventually burn out, leaving only dust and dead stars. The universe will become quite dark and, as the temperature of the universe approaches absolute zero (i.e., -273.15 on the Celsius scale or -459.67 on the Fahrenheit), it will become quite cold. The universe will not end, exactly, just peter out in a big chill.

If Omega equals exactly one, then the cosmic expansion will coast to a halt infinitely far into the future; the universe will not end in a big crunch nor expand into an infinite big chill but will remain at equilibrium.

The expansion of a closed universe, with an Omega greater than one, will slow down until it reaches a maximum size. (The lower skies are the limit.)

In the event of a big smash, when everything will be happening in the cosmic order, singularities in the black hole with the ultimate energy of the mass destroyed within it will be passed to the rest of the universe. Eventually, the gravitational effect of the universe will become really very strong. Could quantum mechanics possibly play a dramatic role like at the initial stages of the big bang to create once again a series, like a video of the big bang and dispersion run backward. The universe will become denser and hotter until it ends in an infinitely hot, infinitely dense big crunch, providing the seedling for another big bang. The Qur'an affirms this narration (81:1–7).

This last case is consistent with the inflation hypothesis and also commands the most observational support. Even though the scientists assume that the universe's fate lies billions of years in the future, it's the only one we have. The Surah 81: Folding Up in Verse 1–7 (series of big crunches) clearly elucidates the fate of the grand universe.

Conclusion

The creation of the multiverses with all the physical laws, substance, and energy along with the creation of innumerable strata of universes with billions of galaxies in each universe and then billions of stars in each galaxy rushing away from the core of creation (with a speed of three hundred thousand kilometers per second) toward the lowest sky to ultimately smash against it leading to series of big crunches and finally be reduced to a seedling for the creation of the Multiverses anew.

This will be a time when the temperature at the core of creation will be reduced to absolute zero (i.e. $-273°C$ or $-459.67°F$). But once again, the creation of energy will be taking place with immeasurable temperatures at the site of the big smash, where different stars will also be swallowed by the black holes, releasing only the gravitational force in the space that would create massive temperatures in the cosmos, as at the time of creation or the big bang. Then, eventually, the black holes will also evaporate, releasing immense gravitational forces. The intense gravitational forces will wrap up the space, substance, and the energy, and then it will wrap itself up under its own enormous gravitational force to an infinitely invisible point, the nullity, the seedling for the next creation, when the time (i.e. the thermodynamic, the cosmological, and the psychological arrows of time) will cease to exist but for the interminable arrow of time that will perpetuate in an ever infinite direction waiting for the message of the Almighty for the new creation (21:104).

To conclude once again on the fate of the multiverses, we review the most probable possibility in the light of the Holy Scripture. (This is food for thought for the cosmologist in reviewing their postulates.)

Most of us are very familiar with the idea that our planet is nothing more than a tiny speck orbiting a typical star, somewhere near the edge of an otherwise un-noteworthy galaxy. In the midst of a universe populated by billions of galaxies that stretch out to our cosmic horizon, we are led to believe that there is nothing special or unique about our location. But what is the evidence for this cosmic humility? And how would we be able to tell if we were in a special place? Astronomers typically gloss over these questions, assuming our own typicality sufficiently obvious to warrant no further discussion. To entertain the notion that we may, in fact, have a special location in the universe is, for many, unthinkable. Nevertheless, that is exactly what some small groups of physicists around the world have recently been considering.

Ironically, assuming ourselves to be insignificant has granted cosmologists great explanatory power. It has allowed us to extrapolate from what we see in our own cosmic neighborhood to the universe based on the cosmological principle—a generalization of the Copernican principle that states that at any moment in time, all points and directions in space look the same. Combined with our modern understanding of space, time, and matter, the cosmological principle implies that space is expanding, the universe is getting cooler, and it is populated by relics from its hot beginning—predictions that are all borne out by observations.

This accelerating expansion is the big surprise that fired the current revolution in cosmology. Matter in the universe should tug at the fabric of space-time, slowing down the expansion, but the supernova data suggest otherwise. If cosmologists accept the cosmological principle and assume that the assertion happens everywhere, we are led to the conclusion that the universe must be permeated by an exotic form of energy that exerts a repulsive force.

Eventually, in a series of big crunches, the ever-expanding universe will dash against the strata of the lower sky, and then everything will be in confusion and chaos; the stellar bodies will be swallowed by the black holes. Their gravitational force will be dissipated in the universe. The thermodynamic arrow of time once again will be reversed with billions and trillions of celcius temperature then the black holes will also evaporate. The extreme gravitational force with electromagnetic force will then sweep the whole universe that will squeeze the space and time (i.e., the thermodynamic and the cosmological arrows of time will be reversed). The reversal of the cosmological arrow of time will make the existence of life impossible; the existence of the psychological arrow of time will be quite improbable. Ultimately, the intense gravitational force will swallow itself after swallowing the space (energy) and time to an infinitely small point, as Allah Almighty reiterates in the Holy Qur'an (39:67):

> They don't have the wit *to discern*
> Boundless command of The Lord *in term*
> As was affirmed *in concern*
> On Day of Demand He'll hold *in grasp*
> Whole of the earth in His hand *to clasp*
> And heavens will then spin *in stash*
> In His right fist *in abash*
> Glory be to The Lord *in sway*
> He's Exalted of some duo *in array*
> For what they assign to Him *in pray*
> (39 Al Zumar 67)

This verse clearly elucidates that Allah Almighty will hold the command of multiverses and the skies in His hand on doomsday. This very clearly explains that the whole cosmic sway is nothing, but the mighty power of His Almighty Allah, Who will then recreate the whole cosmic sway with life in it as repeatedly affirmed in the Holy Scripture. Surprisingly, the scientists also believe that this universe will eventuate into a singularity or the nullity that will be the seedling for the next creation.

The fate of the universe, to sum up once again:

There was a singularity at the preliminary stage that kicked off as the big bang with conflagration and the continual expansion of the grand universe.

Boundary condition
- The lower skies are the limit or boundary.
- Then there will be a big smash.
- The cosmological arrow of time will be reversed
- (but along the interminable arrow of time).
- This will result in series of big crunches with conflagration.
- This will eventuate in a singularity.
- The singularity will provide a seedling for the next creation or big bang (21:104; 24:35; 37:06; 55:7–8; 82:1–4).

The Prophets (21:104)
The Day We'll whirl heavens *in twirl*
And a recorder list up a scribble in *swirl*
As "We" began the first creation *in sway*
We'll trend to it once again *in array*
It's pledged from "Us" *in pace*
Us to assert once more *to place*

Al Isra (17:99)
Don't they really perceive and conceive
Who created heavens and earth a retrieve
Has Dictum to create like anew in plan
He's ordained a time in span
For what there's no waver to perceive

Al-Hajj (22:66)
He endowed you life *to aside*
And cause doom of death *in stride*
Then He'll bestow life once more *in trail*
Indeed!
Man is really quite peeve *in scale*

COSMIC SWAY

Where,
No scientific laws can thrive in flow
His Alluvial Gleam evinces in Glow

Singularity
Providing seedling
for a new creation

Series of
Big Crunch

Only the Alluvial Gleam in Glow
of Allah Almighty to Shimmer
like a star in Cosmic Sway,
(different strata of Skies)

COSMIC ORDER
Limits the scientific laws
within this domain

Closed Model
Lower Skies with all
the cosmic order
Ripped & Torn Apart

Universe
as Today

ARROW OF TIME

Cosmological Arrow

Cosmological Arrow of Time Reversed
along

Interminable Arrow of Time

Thermodynamic Arrow

Psychological Arrow of Time

Singularity

Big Bang

When Lord Almighty evinced Himself by creating His 1st creation the angels and other exigencies
Interminable arrow of time took its stride - we may call it Time of Nihility or Fanna (Text)

220

Al Nōōr (24:35)
Lord is The Only Glow *in Gleam*
Of the heavens and earth *in esteem*
Semblance of His light is like of *a beam*

Wherein the lamp is placed *in a nook*
The lamp is put like in glass *(sway in brook)*

The glass as a lustrous star *in glow*
Lamp in aglow of (sacred) *oil in flow*

Al Safaat (37:06)
The lower of sky We decked in array
With elegant stars dispersed in sway

Al Rahman (55:7–8)
Raised the Heavens and set *its brink*
That you may not cross its brim

Al Rahman (55:37–38)
And when the heaven splits asunder
And becomes red like teguments cover

Al Infitar (82:01–04)
When the Sky is fissured *to shreds*
Then the stars dwindle *to threads*

When graves get to gust *and burst*
When oceans spurt *in thrust*

Qur'anic Vision

Man reflects on the changes and transformations, which for everything follow one another like a surge swinging in a turbulent stream. The rapidity of the tumultuous surge will despise that which is perishable and shall endure only the durable

The universal cause is like a tornado in torrent: it carries away everything along with it. But how worthless are these people who are engaged in matters so fickle and fake, so trivial in trace not pursuable in place neither of any dignity or grace.

Well then, man does what nature determines of him. Set yourself in motion, if it is in your power, and don't look around you to see if anyone will observe it, but be content if the smallest thing goes on well, and consider such an event to be no small matter. For who can change men's opinions? And without a change of opinions, what else is there than the slavery of a man who groans while he pretends to obey? Simple and modest is the work of philosophy; draw me not aslant and apart to impudence and insolence.

> *And say:*
> All word of adore is for Lord *to allure*
> Who'll display His signs you *to secure*
> That you may concern to discern *in lore*
> Bounty of Lord *in adore*
> *And Lord!*
> Discerns all your doings *in score* (Naml 27:93)

Did You Ever Care to Consider?

The parts of the body and the letters of the alphabet are elements found in the Sacred Book.

The seven cervical vertebrae and twelve dorsal correspond to the seven planets and twelve signs of the Zodiac as well as to the seven days of a week and twelve months of a year. And the total number of discs of the vertebrae, twenty-eight, are equal to the letters of the Arabic alphabet and the stations of the moon.

> We will show them "Our" signs in the universe, and in their own selves, until it becomes manifest to them that this (the Holy Scriptures) is the truth. Is it not sufficient in regard to your Lord that He is a Witness over all things?
> (Fussilat 41: Verse 53)

The text of the Holy Qur'an has an actuality in our daily routine. This is exclusively due to the fact that both the world and the Qur'an are creations of Allah. Therefore, all the information revealed and all the analysis pertaining to the psychological nature of man referred to in the Scripture is clearly elucidated in our day-to-day lives.

> Don't they discern Qur'an with care *to affirm*
> Had it been from other than Lord *to discern*
> There should've been lot of deviance *in term*
> (Al Nisa 4:82)

We must understand the philosophy of the Holy Scripture before turning the pages of the text and understanding the wisdom detailed regarding its scientific affirmations that are revealed from time to time in a very distinct manner.

As we have already discussed in "Initial and Infinite," the multiple of ten is one hundred and that of nine is eighty-one.

The figures 1 and 9 make 19, and 100 minus 19 is 81. Surprisingly, 81 is the number of stable natural existing chemical elements.

The Rapture (Al-Inshiqaaq) Surah # 84

Radioactive elements begin with element 84, Polonium, a radioactive element that gives energy through the spontaneous disintegration of atomic nuclei (to disintegrate means to separate into parts or fragments, to rupture or split). In the Qur'anic Surah 84, it has the title "The Rapture" (Al-Inshiqaaq). Is it just a coincidence?

Surah Al Hadid (Iron) is number 57 and 57 is one of the stable isotopes of iron.

There could be many other such notions of wisdom, which probably we cannot comprehend at this stage.

Qur'anic Wisdom

Word repetitions in the Qur'an:

Say:
If all men and Jinni were to meet *in abide*
To occasion like of Qur'an *to aside*
None like thereof could ever cause and produce
Even with all help of one else to include
(Al Isra 17:88)

The verse plainly announces that a text similar to the Qur'an can by no means be written by human beings. No doubt, if one ever attempts, he can write a book of about six hundred pages about the existence of Allah, the Hereafter, and the dictum of faith ordained by the Lord Almighty. Yet, the ability to write a book "similar" to the Qur'an will be far from his cognizance and discernment. One can never accomplish such a marvel in literature that can encompass so many aspects in one go.

There are various reasons for that. For instance, it has enormous literary influence, and the message communicated in the Qur'an can also be observed in the world around us.

Apart from the miraculous characteristics of the Qur'an, which we have looked into so far, it also contains what we can term "mathematical miracles." There are many examples of this fascinating Qur'anic feature. One example of this is the number of repetitions of certain words in the text of the Qur'an. Some related words are surprisingly repeated the same number of times. Below is a list of such words and the repetitions in the Qur'an.

The statement about seven heavens is repeated seven times. The creation of the heavens *(Khalaq us samawat)* is also repeated the same number of times. Day *(Yawm)* is repeated 365 times in its singular form. While its plural and dual forms "days" *(ayyam and yawmayn)* together are repeated thirty times.

The number of repetitions of the word "month" *(Shahar)* is twelve.

The number of repetitions of the words "plant and tree" is the same, twenty-six.

The word for "payment or reward" is repeated 117 times, while the expression for "Forgiveness" *(mughfirah)* is repeated exactly twice that amount, 234 times.

When we count the word for "say," we find it appears 332 times, and we arrive at the same figure when we count the phrase for "they said."

The number of times the words for "world" *(dunya)* and "Hereafter" *(akhira)* are repeated is also the same: 115.

The word for "Satan" *(Shaitan)* is used in the Qur'an sixty-eight times, as is the word for "angels" *(malaika)*.

The word for faith *(iman)* (without the genitive form) is repeated twenty-five times throughout the Qur'an as is the word for infidelity *(kufr)*.

The words for "paradise" and "hell" are each repeated seventy-seven times.

The word *Zakah* is repeated in the Qur'an thirty-two times, and the number of repetitions of the word for "blessing" *(barakah)* is also thirty-two.

The expression meaning "the righteous" *(al-abraar)* is used six times, but the expression for "the wicked" *(al-fujjaar)* is used half as much, three times.

The number of times the words meaning "summer hot" and "winter cold" are repeated is the same: five. The words for "wine" *(khamr)* and "intoxication" *(saqara)* are repeated in the Qur'an the same number of times: six.

The number of appearances of the words for "mind" and "light" is the same: forty-nine.

The words for "tongue" and "sermon" are both repeated twenty-five times.

The words for "benefit" and "corrupt" both appear fifty times.

Similarly, the words for "reward" *(ajr)* and "action" *(fail)* are both repeated 107 times.

The words for "love" *(al-mahabbah)* and "obedience" *(al-taah)* also appear the same number of times: eighty-three.

The words for "refuge" *(maser)* and "forever" *(abadan)* appear the same number of times: twenty-eight.

The words for "disaster" *(al-musibah)* and "thanks" *(al-shukr)* appear the same number of times: seventy-five.

The words for "sun" *(shams)* and "light" *(nur)* both appear thirty-three times. While counting the word for "light," only the simple forms of the word were included.

The number of appearances of the word meaning "right guidance" *(al-Huda)* and "mercy" *(al-Rahman)* is the same: seventy-nine.

The words for "trouble" and "peace" are both repeated thirteen times in the Qur'an.

The words for "man" and "woman" are also employed equally: twenty-three times.

Will they not ponder the Qur'an? If it had been from other than Allah, they would have found many inconsistencies in it (Qur'an 4:82).

This heavenly balance could not be a mere coincidence; therefore, we can say that this phenomenon is but one of God's great signs.

The words for human "life" and "death" and their derivatives are equally mentioned 145 times each.

The words for "sight" and "insight" are each mentioned 148 times, which is equal to the same number of times that the word for "heart" is mentioned.

The words for "good deeds" and "evil deeds" with their derivatives are mentioned 167 times each.

The words meaning "hell" and "punishment" are mentioned twenty-six times each.

The words for "knowledge" and "learning" with their derivatives are mentioned 811 times each, which is the same number that the word for "faith" and each of its derivatives are mentioned. This fact shows to what extent Islam values knowledge and learning, which are equal to "faith."

What is really amazing is that the word for "merciful" is mentioned fifty-seven times, while the word for "compassionate" is mentioned 114 times, which is the number of chapters of the Holy Qur'an.

It is very strange that in the Holy Qur'an, the words for "inspiration," "Islam," and "resurrection" with their derivatives are mentioned seventy times each.

The words for "magic" and "infatuation" are each mentioned sixty times.

The word for "fire" and its derivatives and the word for "heathen" are each mentioned 154 times.

The concepts of "fasting" and "patience" are mentioned in the Holy Qur'an in equal numbers.

The words for "brain" and "light" are equally mentioned forty-nine times each.

The concepts of "love" and "obedience" with all their derivatives are mentioned eighty-three times each.

The words for "generosity" and "reward" are mentioned twenty times each.

The words for "temptation" and "sin" are both mentioned twenty-two times each.

The word for "forgiveness" and its derivatives are mentioned 234 times, which is double the number of times that the word for "punishment" with all its derivatives is mentioned. This shows that the Lord Almighty is bounteous and compassionate toward His men.

The word meaning "treachery" *(khiyanah)* is repeated sixteen times, while the number of repetitions of the word for "foul" *(khabith)* is also sixteen. The word *salawat* appears five times in the Qur'an, as Almighty Allah has commanded men to perform the prayers *(salaat)* five times a day.

The Letter Q and Qur'an

The Qur'an has twenty-nine Surahs that start with an initial (e.g. Surah 2 starts with "A, L, M"; Surah 50 starts with "Q" and is called "Q"; Surah 38 starts with "S" and is called "S"; Surah 68 is called "The Pen" and starts with "N," and so on). There are fourteen different Arabic letters, forming fourteen different sets of Qur'anic initials and prefixing 29 Surahs (14+14+29=57). Fifty-seven is the number pointing to the Qur'an in the Qur'an (19 x 3). All these initials have some mathematical relationship to the number nineteen somehow.

Qur'anic Initial "Q" (Qaff)

There are two Surahs in the Qur'an that have the Qur'anic initial "Q" (Qaff) (i.e., Surah 42 and 50). Surah 50 is entitled "Q," is prefixed with "Q," and the first verse reads "Q, and the Glorious Qur'an." The indication is very strong that this "Q" stands for Qur'an. Here is a summary of the mathematical miracle found in the initial "Q."

(1) The frequency of occurrence of "Q" in Surah "Q" (Number 50) is fifty-seven (i.e., 19 x 3).

(2) The frequency of "Q" in the only other Q-initialed Surah (Number 42) is also fifty-seven, (19 x 3).

(3) The total occurrence of the letter "Q" in the only two Q-initialed Surahs is 114 (19 x 6). As we read in Surah "Q," the "Q" indicates the Qur'an. The total number of Surahs in the Qur'an is 114.

(4) Like the letter "Q" in each Surah (42 and 50), the word *Qur'an* is mentioned in the Qur'an fifty-seven times in reference to the Qur'an (57 = 19 x 3).

(5) The Qur'an was described in Surah "Q" as *"Majid"* (glorious). The word *Majid* has a numerical value of fifty-seven (19 x 3) (M = 40, J = 3, I = 10, and D = 4).

(6) Surah 42 has fifty-three verses and 42 + 53 = 95 (19x5).

(7) Surah 50 has forty-five verses and 50 + 45 = 95 (19x5).

(8) The number of Q's in all the verses numbered "19" throughout the Qur'an is 76 (19 x 4).

Creation of Mankind and Qur'an

The number of times the words for "man" and "woman" are repeated in the Qur'an is twenty-three, the same as that of the chromosomes in the egg and sperm in the formation of the human embryo. The total number of human chromosomes is forty-six; twenty-three each from the mother and father.

The word for "human being" is used sixty-five times. The sum of the number of references to the stages of man's creation is the same, sixty-five.

• Soil (*turab*)	17
• Drop of sperm (*nutfah*)	12
• Embryo (*alaq*)	06
• A half-formed lump of flesh (*mudghah*)	03
• Bone (*idham*)	15
• Flesh (*lahm*)	12
Total	65

Ratio of Land to Sea and Qur'an

The word *land* appears thirteen times in the Qur'an and the word *sea* thirty-two times, giving a total of forty-five references.

If we divide the number of references to the land by the total number of references to land and sea, we arrive at the figure 28.888888888888 percent (13/45 x 100). The number of total references to the sea divided by the total number of references to the sea and land in the Qur'an is 71.11111111111111 percent (32/45 x 100).

Extraordinarily, these figures represent the proportions of land and sea on the earth today.

Divine Perception of Time and Wormhole Theory

Elucidating the Prophet's Journey of Me'ráaj

Early people presumably first realized time passed when they saw that they lived in a world of constant change. We have come to place a premium on measuring the flow of time, as if by measuring it, we could begin to understand it.

Devising accurate calendars and clocks, however, proved to be one of man's most elusive and protracted intellectual pursuits. The long struggle to affix numbers to the passage of time parallels our organization of ourselves into a complex, modern world.

But in the Holy Qur'an, there is a use of numbers in the chapter entitled "The Cave," where God says:

And it's said they're there *(cave) in sleep*
For over years three hundreds *in sweep*
And add nine to the count in keep
(300 solar years = 309 lunar years) (18:25)

This verse miraculously communicates that three hundred solar years are exactly the same as three hundred and nine lunar years!

In the light of the recent careful astronomical measurements and exact estimates, it became evident that:

- The average duration of the lunar month is 29.550329 days.
- There are 354.60394 (29.550329 x 12) days in a lunar year.
- There are 109572.66 (354.60394 x 309) days in 309 lunar years.
- One solar year equals 365.2422 days.
- There are 109,572.66 (365.2422 x 300) days in 300 solar years.

With all this information, envision the Qur'anic script, affirming 1,400 years earlier the ratio of solar and lunar years (i.e., months and days) and for that matter their relative motion in their orbits, which was affirmed scientifically early last century.

Similarly, the repetitions of certain words pertaining to the time domain further assert that we must pursue the philosophy of the Holy Scripture before turning to any subject, if we can really comprehend the core of the text.

Day (*Yawm*) is repeated 365 times in singular form. While its plural and dual forms (*ayyam* and *yawmayn*) together are repeated thirty times.

The number of repetitions of the word for "month" (*Shahar*) is twelve.

Seeking guidance from the Holy Scripture was and is expedient in most situations like understanding time.

It began in the great civilizations that awakened five millennia ago along the life-giving rivers of the Middle East, in Sumer between the Tigris and Euphrates and in Egypt along the Nile. Drawn like most ancient people to the movements of the heavens and the changing seasons, the Babylonians developed a year of 360 days and then divided it into twelve lunar months of thirty days each. This was not a simple feat, since the sun and moon do not dance in step, with the moon's cycles occurring approximately every 29½ days and the earth's every 365¼ days.

Babylonian astronomers knew the true number of days in a year, but kept it at 360 because their priests insisted the number, which may have led to the number of degrees in a circle, possessed magical properties. The practical Egyptians extended the year by five days, which they set aside for feasting during the Nile's annual flooding. Refinements by the Romans and by Pope Gregory XIII in 1582 gave us today's Gregorian calendar, accurate to a day in every 3.323 years.

Early societies also broke the day itself into smaller units, presumably for the same reason as we do with our clocks and watches: so we know when we are supposed to be somewhere.

The sun, arching daily across the sky, was undoubtedly the first timepiece, followed perhaps by the shadow of a stick stuck in the ground, a crude sundial to mark the hours.

The time-conscious Egyptians divided the day into two cycles of twelve hours each. Why not eight or ten? The twelve-hour division might have come from the numbering system of the Sumerians or from star patterns in the sky.

By the seventeenth century, the clock was having a profound effect on society. The notion that time is money became an essential ingredient of emerging capitalism. In the early 1800s, some mill owners created the mill clock, an insidious device that ran fast or slow according to how hard workers labored.

In those days, time zones did not exist, and the world was a hodgepodge of local times. Nor was there a prime meridian where a twenty-four-hour count could begin for all navigators; most used the time at their homeports as they roved the seas.

At an 1884 meeting in Washington DC, Britain and the United States urged the international adoption of Greenwich, site of the Royal Observatory, as zero-degree longitude. Jerusalem and the Great Pyramid had been proposed earlier. The French delegates were particularly outspoken for Paris. Greenwich won, but French maps did not acknowledge it until 1914, in a magnificent and rarely seen hall at the Paris Observatory.

Have we become slaves to the clock? David Landes, a historian of timekeeping at Harvard University, thinks not.

The clock let individuals know what time belonged to their employers and what time was their own. Workers are now actually freer than ever before. Without the clock, and now the watch, there is no modern world. It is the difference between a complex, intricately coordinated society and a primitive one only vaguely aware of time's possibilities.

A vast global timekeeping system keeps all civilization synchronized.

And physicists tracking motion inside an atomic nucleus reckon in picoseconds (one-trillionth of a second) or even femtoseconds (thousandths of a picosecond). To grasp this, consider that there are more femtoseconds in one second than there were seconds in the past thirty-one million years.[28]

The Philosophy of Time

When the Lord Almighty asserts that the matters of the world reach Him in a day of your count, that equals one thousand years (Al Sajdah 32). As we will later calculate in this chapter, these matters of concern are nothing but the speed of light. So we conclude that the basic unit of speed with the Almighty is the speed of light and all other notions referring to the speed are the multiples of that. His Almighty asserts that angels and spirits reach Him in a day of fifty thousand years of count (Al Maarij 1–4), but *not of our count*. It clearly elucidates that the speed of the angels and spirits is fifty million (1,000 x 50,000 = 50,000,000). The details of this subject will be discussed later in this chapter.

Time is defined as the measure of motion in regard to "before" and "after" Aristotle.

---

28 1000 femtoseconds = 1 picosecond, and 10 billion picoseconds = 1 second

The way the old concept of time has been described so far is nothing but a real confusion. I'll endeavor to have philosophical look at time before trying to have a scientific discernment of the subject in the light of the Qur'an.

Time has frequently struck philosophers as mysterious. Some have even felt that it was incapable of rational discursive treatment and that it could be grasped only by intuition. This bafflement in attitude probably arises from the fact that time always seems to be mysteriously slipping away from us; no sooner do we grasp a bit of it in our consciousness than it slips away into the past. As very rightly affirmed in the Holy Qur'an:

By the vision of time
Man stays in dissipation well in decline
But for those determining Faith in prime
Who asperse and anoint virtuosity in sublime
Pursue and persevere probity in pray
And firm in endurance *stay to obey*
(Al Qur'an: Al Asar 103)

We shall see that this notion of time as something that continually slips past us is not based on commotion and confusion, mystification and perplexity, or daze and distraction but in fact gives us a lesson to value its each bit and piece, to cherish the bliss not only hither in vale but also Hereafter in trail.

St. Augustine's Puzzle

The apparent mysteriousness of time can make puzzles about time that seems more baffling than they are, even though similar ones arise in the case of non-temporal concepts. St. Augustine, in his *Confessions*, asks, "What's time?"

When no one asks him, he knows; when someone asks him, however, he does not know. He knows how to use the word *time* and related sequential words, such as *before, after, past,* and *future,* but he can give no clear account of this use. Trouble arises particularly from the form in which he puts his question.

What's Time?

This looks like a request for a definition, and yet no definition is forthcoming.

However, most interesting concepts cannot be elucidated by explicit definitions. Thus, to explain the meaning of the word *length*, we cannot give an explicit definition, but we can do things that explain how to tell that one thing is longer than another and how to measure length. In the same way, we can give an account of our use of the word *time*, even though we cannot do so by giving an explicit definition. In short, this puzzle is not of a sort that arises peculiarly in the case of time. Beyond pointing this out, therefore, it is not appropriate here to go further into the matter.

Augustine was also puzzled by how we could measure time. He seems to have been impressed by the lack of analogy between spatial and temporal measurement. For example, you can put a ruler alongside a tabletop, and the ruler and the tabletop are all there at once. On the other hand, if you measure a temporal process, you do it by comparing it with some other process, such as the movement of the hand of a watch. At any moment of the comparison, part of the process to be measured has passed away and part of it is yet to be.

Creation: Substance, Attributes, and Time

Once upon a timeless time, when there was no discernment of time or creation and when there was not even a whippersnapper in existence and not even the inspiration of a proposition except for the bounty of my Lord, at that twinkling and trice when His Almighty deliberated to bring the world into existence, He looked on the whim of surmise with a look of excellence. For there was nothing in actuality, not the sign and simile of initiation that is the source of all existence, that can bear the perfect manifestation of Almighty Allah. Perhaps it was only nature that belonged to the basic framework of all the material and the precept and principle of the providence that governed those basic ingredients of the material and the decree and deliberation of nature that directed the whole cosmic order.

That was the moment when the cadence of time with all its attributes essentially came into substantiality. Before creation, its attributes were pertaining to nihility with no discernment of present, past, or future along the interminable arrow of time as discussed in "The Fate of the Universe." Nothing is known before this earliest instant for which scientists use the term *big bang*.

Instantaneous to Eternal

The units of time range from the infinitesimally brief to the interminably long. The descriptions given here attempt to convey a sense of this vast chronological span.

Whenever we try to explicate the process of creation, we shall have to look at it in a most meticulous and unbiased way of defined discernment of vision: the universe and the human being. While contemplating both in one setting, we find the entire universe to be a dense material that explodes in one go of "Be," the big bang (Planck time)—the *Fa Ya Koon*, as it is called in the Qur'an—and starts its passage toward its indeterminate journey of cosmic order, which we have not yet been able to perceive even today with our quite highly evolved body of knowledge. And then, when and how long it would exist to host the living being could be anybody's guess. In the Qur'an, it is clearly and repeatedly enunciated that all this pretentious and pompous paraphernalia was brought into being in six phases or eons and will meet its destiny as discussed in "The Fate of the Universe."

Travel in Time

Time travel has been a popular science-fiction theme since H. G. Wells wrote his celebrated novel *The Time Machine* in 1895. But can it really be done?

Is it possible to build a machine that would transport a human being into the past or future?

For decades, time travel lay beyond the fringes of respectable science. In recent years, however, the topic has become something of a cottage industry among theoretical physicists. The motivation has been partly recreational, as time travel is fun to think about. But this research has a serious side too. Understanding the relationship between cause and effect is a key part of attempts to construct a unified theory of physics. If unrestricted time travel were possible, even in principle, the nature of such a unified theory could be drastically affected.

Our best understanding of time comes from Einstein's theories of relativity. Prior to these theories, time was widely regarded as absolute and universal, the same for everyone no matter what their physical circumstances were. In his special theory of relativity, Einstein proposed that the measured interval between two events depends on how the observer is moving. Crucially, two observers who move differently will experience different durations between the same two events, as in walking along with the movement of the train and walking in the opposite direction.

The Myth of Passage

We commonly think of time as a stream that flows or as a sea over which we advance. The two metaphors come to much the same thing, forming part of a whole way of thinking about time which someone called the "myth of passage." If time flows past us or if we advance through time, this would be motion with respect to a hyper-time. If motion in space is measured in feet per second, at which passage is of the essence of time, it is presumably the essence of hyper-time too, which could lead us to postulate a hyper-time theory.

Could one discern the postulate of time pertaining to nihility when you experience it through real discernment while in true meditation, when the earthly pot becomes part of the soul and the soul becomes part of the whole when the precept in the principle of time loses all its concern as past, present, and future (discussed in detail in "The Philosophy of Life")?

Time Order

There is something odd about the reputed properties of pastness, presentness, futurity, and the like, whereby events are supposed to change.

Leaving aside the epistemological predicates, we may suspect that the oddness arises from the fact that the words *past, present,* and *future,* together with *now* and the tenses, are token reflexive expressions. That is, these words refer to their own utterance. Let us indicate tenselessness in a verb by putting it in italics. Thus, if we say, "Caesar *crosses* the Rubicon," we do not indicate whether the crossing is something before, simultaneous with, or after our assertion. Tenseless verbs occur in mathematics where temporal position relative to our utterance is not even in question. Thus, we can say, two plus two is equal to four not because we wish to be noncommittal about the temporal position of two plus two as being equivalent to four but because it has no temporal position at all.

There is confusion in talking of events as changing in respect to pastness, presentness, and futurity. These are not genuine properties, as we can see if we make the token reflexiveness explicit. "E was future, is present, and will become past," goes over into "E is later than some utterance, earlier than this utterance, simultaneous with this utterance, and is earlier than some utterance later than this utterance." This is about as near as we can get to it, and it will be seen that we have to refer to three different utterances. A failure to recognize the token reflexiveness of words like *past, present,* and *future* can lead us to think wrongly of the change from future to past as a genuine change, like the change in the position of a boat which floats down a river.

Nevertheless, there is probably a deeper source of the illusion of time flow. This is that our stock of memories is constantly increasing, and memories are of earlier not of later events. It is difficult to state this matter properly, since we forget things as well as acquire new memories. With a very old man, there may well be a net diminishing of his stock of memories, and yet he does not feel as if time were running the other way. This suggestion is therefore a tentative and incompletely worked-out one. The subordinate question of why our memories are of the past not of the future is an extremely interesting one in its own right, and we shall see if it can really be answered.

Time's Unreality

The consideration may well be illustrated by considering how it bears on McTaggart's well-known argument for the unreality of time, which was put forward in an article in *Mind* (1908) and in his posthumous *Nature of Existence*. For McTaggart, events are capable of being ordered in two ways.

First, they can be ordered with respect to past, present, and future. He calls this ordering of events the "A series."

Second, events can be ordered with respect to the relations earlier than and later than. He calls this the "B series." McTaggart then argues that the B series does not by itself give us all that is essential to time and that the A series is contradictory.

His reason for saying that the B series misses the essence of time is that time involves change, and yet it always is, was, and will be the case that the Battle of Hastings, say, is earlier than the Battle of Waterloo. We have already seen, however, that it is not just false but also absurd to talk of events changing. The Battle of Hastings is not earlier than the Battle of Waterloo; it simply is (tenselessly) earlier than it. The notion of change is perfectly capable of being expressed in the language of the B series by saying that events in the B series differ from one another in various ways. Similarly, the proposition that a thing changes can be expressed in the language of the B series by the statement that one spatial cross section of it is different from an earlier one, and the proposition that it does not change can be expressed by saying that earlier and later cross sections are similar to one another. T expresses the notion of change; we are therefore not forced to say that events change. Nor, therefore, are we forced into referring to the A series, saying that events change (in the only way in which we can plausibly say this) in respect to pastness, presentness, and futurity. Nevertheless, if we do retreat to the language of the A series, we can perfectly well do so without contradiction. Just as McTaggart erred by using tensed verbs when talking of the B series, he in fact made the correlative error of forgetting tenses (or equivalent devices) when talking of the A series. For the contradiction which he claimed to find in the A series is that since any event is in turn future, present, and past, we must ascribe these three incompatible characteristics to it. But an event can only be future, present, or past with reference to a particular time, for example, one at which it was future, is present, and will be past. If we restore the tenses, the trouble with the A series disappears. Unsuccessful, though it is, McTaggart's argument provides an excellent case study with which to elucidate the relations between tensed and tenseless language.

Space-Time

The theory of relativity illustrates the advantages of replacing the separate notions of space and time by a unified notion of space-time. In particular, Murkowski showed that the Lorentz transformations of special relativity correspond to a rotation of axes in space-time. He showed how natural the kinematics of special relativity could seem, as opposed to Newtonian kinematics, in which, in fact, we should rotate the time axis without correspondingly rotating the space axes.

Since the theory of relativity, it has become commonplace to regard the world as a four-dimensional space-time manifold. Nevertheless, even in the days of Newtonian dynamics, there was nothing to prevent taking this view of the world, even though it would not have been as neat as it is in relativity theory. If we pass to a four-dimensional way of looking at things, it is important not to be confused about certain conceptual matters. Confusion will arise if we mix the tenseless way of talking appropriate to the four-dimensional picture with our ordinary way of talking of things as an enduring substance, the permanent in change.

In ordinary language, we use the word *space* itself as the name of a continuant. We can say, for example, that a part of space has become, or has continued to be, occupied. Space-time, however, is space in a tenseless sense of this word, and since time is already in the representation, it is quite wrong to talk of space-time as changing itself. Thus, in some expositions of relativity, we find that a material body moves or a light signal is propagated. The body or light signal, however, cannot correctly be said to move through space-time. What should be said is that the body or the light signal lies (tenselessly) along the world line. To talk of anything's moving through space-time is to bring time into the story twice over and in an illegitimate manner. When we are talking about motion in terms of the space-time picture, we must do so in terms of the relative orientations of world lines. Thus, to say that two particles move with a uniform nonzero relative velocity is expressed by saying that they lie (tenselessly) along straight world lines, which are at an angle to one another. Similarly, the recent conception of the positron as an electron moving backward in time is misleading since nothing can move, forward or backward, in time. What is meant is that the world lines of a positron and electron, which are produced together or which annihilate one another, can be regarded as a single bent world line and this may indeed be a very fruitful way of looking at the matter.

In popular expositions of relativity, we also read of such things as our consciousness crawling up the world line of our body. This is once more confusion of the myth of passage and hence, of the illegitimate notion of movement through space-time. It is instructive to consider how H. G. Wells's time machine could be represented in the space-time picture. A moment's thought should suffice to indicate to us that it couldn't be represented at all. If we draw a line that extends into the past, this will simply be the representation of a particle, which has existed for a very long time. It is not surprising that we cannot represent a time machine, since the notion of such a machine is an incoherent one. How fast would such a machine flash over a given ten-second stretch? No sensible answer can be given, for the question is itself absurd. The notion also involves the contradiction, pointed out by D. C. Williams in his article "The Myth of Passage", that if I get into a time machine at noon today, then at 3:00 PM say, I shall be both at 3:00 PM, today and at, say, minus a million years BC.

Absolute and Relational Theories

Isaac Newton held to an absolute theory of space and time, whereas his contemporary Leibniz argued that space and time are merely sets of relations between things, which are in space and time. Newton misleadingly and unnecessarily expressed his absolute theory of time in terms of the myth of passage, as when he confusingly said that absolute, true, and mathematical time, of itself and from its own nature, flows equably without relation to anything external. The special theory of relativity has made it impossible to consider time as something absolute; rather, it stands neutrally between absolute and relational theories of space-time.

The question of the difference between absolute and relational theories of space-time becomes especially interesting when we pass to the general theory of relativity. According to this theory, the structure of space-time is dependent on the distribution of the matter in the universe. In most forms of the theory, there is nevertheless a residual space-time structure, which cannot be thus accounted for. A curvature is usually attributed to space-time within the matter, and the inertia of a body, according to this theory, which depends in part on this cosmological contribution to the local metrical field and hence not solely on the total mass of the universe, as a purely relational theory would require. Research on this question is still ongoing, and until it has been decided, Mach's principle (as Einstein called it), according to which the spatiotemporal structure of the universe depends entirely on the distribution of its matter, will remain controversial. But even if Mach's principle were upheld, it might still be possible to interpret matter in a metaphysical way, as regions of special curvature of space-time.

Time and the Continuum

An absolute theory of space-time, as envisaged above, need not imply that there is anything absolute about distance (space-time interval). Because of the continuity of space-time, any space-time interval contains as many space-time points as any other (that is, a high infinity of them); space and time do not possess an intrinsic metric, and there must always be an element of convention in our definitions of congruence in geometry and chronology, as Grunbaum (influenced by Riemann) has pointed out. This means that the same cosmological facts can be expressed by means of a variety of space-time geometry, provided that they have the same topological structure. (Topology is that part of geometry which treats only those properties of a figure which remain the same however that figure is transformed into a new one, with the sole restriction that a point transforms into one and only one point and neighboring points transform into neighboring ones. Thus, the surface of a sphere and that of a cube have the same topology, but that of a sphere and that of an infinite plane do not.)

Zeno and Cantor

The continuity of space and time can be properly understood only in terms of the modern mathematical theory of infinity and dimensionality. Given the concepts available, Zeno rightly rejected the view than an extended line or time interval could be composed of un-extended points or instants

In modern terms, we may say that not even a denumerable infinity of points can make up a nonzero interval. Cantor has shown, however, that there are higher types of infinity than that which belongs to denumerable sets, such as the set of all natural numbers. Cantor showed that the set of real numbers on a line, or segment of a line, is of a higher type of infinity than is the set of natural numbers. Perhaps the right cardinality of dimensionless points can add up to a nonzero length. This answer is on the right track. Nevertheless, the cardinality of a set of points does not by itself determine dimensionality. For example, Cantor showed that there is a one-to-one mapping between the points of a plane and the points of a line. However, a mathematical theory of dimension has been developed which accords with our intuitions in assigning zero, one, two, three, and so on dimensions respectively to points, lines, planes, and other sorts of sets of points. For example, the set of all rational points on a line has dimension zero. So does the set of all irrational points. In these cases, the infinity of un-extended points does indeed form a set of dimension zero. Since these two sets of points together make up the set of points on a line, it follows that two sets of dimension zero can be united to form a set of dimension one. Strictly speaking, it is even inaccurate to talk of un-extended points. It is sets of points that have dimension.

A line is a set of points, and the points are not parts of the line but members of it.

The modern theory of dimension shows that there is no inconsistency in supposing that an appropriate non-denumerable infinity of points make up a set of greater dimensionality than any finite or denumerable set of points could.

The theory of the continuum implies that if we take away the lower end of a closed interval, we are left with an open interval, an interval without a first point. In fact, Zeno's stipulations in his incongruity of the dibs and dicker do not lead to ambiguity at all but are a concordant consequence of the theory of the continuum. Motion is impossible, according to the paradox of the dichotomy, because before one can go from A to B, one must first get to the halfway mark C, but before one can get to C, one must get to the halfway mark D between A and C, and so on indefinitely.

It is concluded that the motion can never even get started.

A similar argument, applied to time intervals, might seem to show that a thing couldn't even endure through time. The fallacy in both cases comes from thinking of the continuum as a set of points or instants arranged in succession. Such considerations enable us to deal with Zeno's paradox of Achilles and the tortoise, in which similar difficulties are supposed to arise at the latter end of an open interval.

Kant's Antinomies

A related paradox is Kant's first antinomy, in his *Critique of Pure Reason*. As was shown by Edward Caird in his commentary on Kant's critique, the antinomies (or paradoxes which Kant had constructed about space, time, and causality) were quite as important as Hume's skeptical philosophy in arousing Kant from his dogmatic slumbers. Kant's first antinomy relates to both space and time. There are two antithetical arguments. The first states that the world had a beginning in time, whereas the second, with equal plausibility, seems to show that the world had no beginning in time. The first argument begins with the premise that if the world had no beginning in time, then up to a given moment, an infinite series of successive events must have passed. But the infinity of a series consists in the fact that it can never be completed. Hence, it is impossible for an infinite series of events to have passed away.

It can be seen that Kant's argument here rests partly on the myth of passage. Kant thinks of the world as having come to its present state through a series of past events, so that an infinite succession would therefore have had to be completed. Otherwise, he would have been just as puzzled about the possibility of an infinite future as about an infinite past, and this does not seem to have been the case. Just as the sequence 0, 1, 2 ... can never be completed in the sense that it has no last member, the sequence ... -2, -1, 0 cannot be completed in the sense that it has no first member. This is not to say, of course, that an infinite set needs to have either a first or last member. Thus, the set of temporal instants up to, but not including, a given instant, has neither a first nor last member. However, Kant is clearly thinking not of the set of instants but of a sequence of events, each taking up a finite time. The set of instants does not form a sequence since there are no instants that are next to one another. Kant's definition of infinity, besides being objectionably psycho-logistic, is clearly inapplicable to infinite sets of entities which do not form a sequence, such as the points on a line or a segment of a line. Concerning an infinite set of events, which form a sequence, however, Kant is not justified in supposing that its having a last member is any more objectionable than its having a first member. There is a perfect symmetry between the two cases once we rid ourselves of the notion of the passage—that is, of the one-way flow of time.

Now let us take a fresh look at Kant's antithetical argument. He argues that the world cannot have had a beginning in time, so that, contrary to the thesis of the antinomy, there must have been an infinity of past events. His reason is that if the world had begun at a certain time, all previous time would have been a blank and there would be no reason that the world should have begun at the time it did rather than at some other time. Previously, Leibniz had used the same argument to support a relational theory of time. If solely the relations between events constitute time, then it becomes meaningless to ask questions about the temporal position of the universe as a whole or about when it began. In an absolute theory of time (or of space-time), Kant's problem remains, but further discussion of it cannot be pursued here since it would involve us in a metaphysical discussion of causality and the principle of sufficient reason.

We have just seen that Kant was puzzled about the infinity of the past in a way in which he was not puzzled about the infinity of the future. It has been suggested that the myth of passage had something to do with this inconsistency. If we reject the notion of passage, we find ourselves with a new, though soluble, problem. This is the apparent temporal asymmetry of the universe, which contrasts sharply with its large-scale spatial symmetry. For example, if we look out at the galaxies, they appear to be distributed evenly in all directions, and yet a time direction seems to be specified by the fact that they are all receding from one another, not approaching one another. On a more mundane level, the temporal asymmetry of the universe strikes us forcibly in many ways. For example, there is nothing in our experience analogous to memory with respect to the future, nor is there anything like a tape recording or a footprint of the future; that is, there are no traces of the future. A memory is indeed a special case of a trace. This asymmetry about traces explains how we can be so confident about the past history of the human race and about the past evolution of living creatures. He would be a bold man who would try to guess the political history of even the next hundred years or the organic evolution of the next few millions. The question is why are there traces only of the past, not of the future? Is this a fundamental one, or do we have no means to perceive such an instance if the theory of wormholes really comes true, or if the passage through black holes from one end to the other is possible, or if getting in and out upside down can put the man fifty million years ahead or before the existing time frame. This is a notion to illustrate that the true concept of time is beyond the perception of human cognition and discernment.

We must first rule out pure verbosity in the answer to this question. Someone might say that traces are always of the past, never of the future, because it is part of the meaning of the word *trace* that traces are of earlier, not of later, events. This would be to suppose that our question is as stupid as the question "Why are bachelors always male, never female?" This account of the matter is not good enough. Admittedly, in our language, as it is, the expression "female bachelor" is a self-contradictory one. Nevertheless, it is quite easy to imagine a variant of English in which bachelor simply meant a not-yet-married person, according to which spinsters could therefore be called bachelors. We can now silence the wordiness objection to our question about why traces are always of the past, never of the future, by recasting it in the form "Why are there no future analogues of traces?"

Temporal Asymmetry and Physical Laws:

The temporal directionality of the universe, or at the very least, of our present cosmic era of the universe, would therefore appear to be a deep-lying cosmological fact, which is not glossed over by wordy explanations. How is it to be explained? It is true that phenomenological thermodynamics would provide a contrary case, since its second law does contain time explicitly. Thus, if you put a kettle full of ice on a hot brick, you find that the system turns into one in which a kettle full of water sits on a cool brick. A film of this process cannot be reversed to show a process, which is possible in phenomenological thermo-dynamics; we cannot have a system of a kettle filled with water on cool bricks turning into one in which the water has frozen and the brick has become hot. In spite of all this, we must still assert that the laws of nature are time sym-metrical. This is because phenomenological thermodynamics provides only an approximation of the truth (it is refuted by the phenomenon of Brownian motion, for example) and more important, because a detailed explanation of the facts that phenomenological thermodynamics treats at the surface level is to be found in statistical thermodynamics. Statistical thermodynamics bases itself on the laws of mechanics, which are time symmetrical.

According to statistical thermodynamics, the situation in which the water in our kettle freezes while the brick gets hotter is indeed a physically possible one, though it is an almost infinitely unlikely one. Why it is unlikely has to do not with the laws of nature themselves but with their boundary conditions. There is indeed a puzzle here, because if we reverse all the velocities of a closed system, we get a configuration, which, according to statistical mechanics, is as likely as the original one. Therefore, the process seen on our reversed cinematographic film should be as likely as the original one. The answer to this objection (the reversibility objection) lies in the fact that corresponding to a given macroscopic description (cold kettle on hot brick, say), there is a whole ensemble of possible microstates. It follows that though any microstate is as probable as any other, this is not so with macrostates, and given the information that a body is in macrostate A, it is highly probable that it will turn into macrostate B, rather than vice versa, if B corresponds to an ensemble of microstates that is vastly more numerous than the ensemble of microstates corresponding to A; probability theorem has to explain, according to the law of nature in the light of the Qur'an, how, when we are reduced to dust or debris, soot or smoke after the doom and demise, we will be brought back to life. That is our firm belief and conviction (discussed in "The Philosophy of Life").

Trace Formation and Entropy

We are now in a position to deal with the formation of traces. Although a wide, relatively isolated part of the universe is increasing in its state of being shuffled, or to use the more precise notion developed by physicists, in its entropy, subsystems of the wider system may temporarily decrease in shuffling or entropy. Thus, an isolated system, such as that consisting of a cube of ice in a beaker of water, may well have lower entropy than its surroundings. This reduction of entropy is bought at the expense of a more than compensating increase of entropy in the surroundings. There will, for example, be an increase of disorderliness in the system containing the coal and air that react chemically and drive the generators that provide the electric power that drives the refrigerator that makes the ice cube. (The system consisting of coal and oxygen is a more highly ordered one than that which consists of the ashes and used-up air.) Eventually, our ice cube melts and becomes indistinguishable from the water in which it floated.

Branch System

The formation of a trace is the formation of a subsystem of temporarily lower entropy than its surroundings; the trace is blotted out when the entropy curve of the subsystem rejoins that of the larger system. A footprint in the sand is a temporarily highly ordered state of the sand; this orderliness is bought at the expense of an increased disorderliness or metabolic depletion of the pedestrian who made it, and this extra orderliness eventually disappears as a result of wind and weather. It is an observable fact and one to be expected from considerations of statistical thermodynamics that these branch systems in practice nearly all go in quite the same direction. This direction defines a temporal direction for the universe, or at least for our cosmic era.

Upon investigation, it will be seen that all sorts of traces, whether footprints on sand, photographs, fossil bones, or the like, can be understood as traces in this sense. Indeed, there are written records of our deeds and doings in subsequence of our existence for eventual perception on doomsday as determined by Almighty Allah. The close connection between information and entropy is brought out in modern information theory, the mathematics of which is much the same as that of statistical thermodynamics. A coherent piece of prose is an ordered part of the universe, unlike a completely random sequence of symbols.

It is possible that the formation of branch systems may be linked to deeper cosmological facts. Thomas Gold has argued persuasively that the formation of such a system is possible only because the universe provides a sink for radiation and this is possible, again, only because of the mutual recession of the galaxies. It may, therefore, ultimately be the expansion of the universe that accounts for the direction of time. Beyond noting this interesting suggestion of a link between the small-scale and large-scale structure of the cosmos, we can for our present purposes take the formation of branch systems for granted without linking it to uncertain cosmological speculations.

Popper's Account

The theory of branch systems detailed above was developed by Reichenbach and Grunbaum. Their work partly goes back to the work of Ludwig Boltzmann. We must now consider a different account of the direction of time.

Let us consider a spherical light wave emitted from a source, as when a small electric bulb is turned on. Consider how this process would look in reverse. We should have a large spherical wave contracting to a point. This would be causally inexplicable. In order to get a spherical light wave coming in from the depths of an infinite space, we should have to suppose a coordinated set of disturbances at every point of a vast sphere, and this would require a *deus ex machina* explanation. Moreover, this would still not provide the reverse of an outgoing wave expanding indefinitely. Thus, although the contracting wave is as much in accordance with the laws of optics as is the expanding one, it still is not compatible with any physically realizable set of initial conditions. Once more, as with the Reichenbach-Grunbaum solution, we see that temporal asymmetry arises from the initial or boundary conditions, which are laws of nature themselves, and hence these presumptions are disregarded.

Popper's criterion of temporal direction does not shed light on the concept of traces, as does the criterion of branch systems. And traces, particularly memory traces, give us our vivid sense of temporal asymmetry in the world. It is also interesting that if we consider a finite but unbounded, nonexpanding universe, a contracting spherical wave would be physically realizable. Just as an expanding series of concentric circles which are on the earth's surface and have their original center at the North Pole would become a series of circles contracting to the South Pole, so in a symmetrical and finite but unbounded universe, a spherical wave would shrink to the antipodal point of the point of emission. If we included the facts of radiation in our finite, nonexpanding universe, we should have to suppose a finite but unbounded space and Popper's criterion of temporal direction would become inapplicable. Including such facts would therefore also not conflict with our supposition of alternate cosmic eras in such a universe. This is learned to some extend ostensibly, and we may perfectly well know how to use words like *earlier* and *later* without knowing anything about entropy or branch systems. As Wittgenstein might have said, we know the language game. What

Reichenbach and Grunbaum are concerned with is a deeper problem: what are the general features of the universe that enable us to play the language game? Indeed, if the universe did not contain traces, it would be impossible for there to be any thought at all.

Time and Free Will

It is sometimes thought that the picture of the world as a space-time manifold is incompatible with free will. It is thought that if one of my future actions exists (tenselessly) in the space-time manifold, then it is fated that I will do this action *and I cannot be free not to do it.* To evade this conclusion, philosophers have sometimes been inclined to reject the theory of the manifold and also to deny that propositions about the future have to be either true or false. This view can be contested at several levels.

First, the fact that one of my future actions exists in the space-time manifold does not mean that I am fated to do it, in the sense that I come to do it independently of what I do in the meantime. It will still be my choice through intelligence as discussed in "The Philosophy of Life."

Second, the doctrine of the space-time manifold does not even imply the weaker doctrine of determinism. Determinism asserts that the laws of nature connect earlier and later spatial cross sections of the manifold in a determinate way, whereas indeterminism denies this. Thus, according to determinism, a complete knowledge of one spatial cross section of the universe would enable a superhuman calculator (who knew enough laws of nature) to deduce what other spatial cross sections would be like. Indeterminism, being only a denial of a certain sort of connectedness between the elements of the manifold, is quite compatible with the theory of the manifold as such.

Third, it could be argued that free will is perfectly compatible with determinism anyway.

Based on these propositions, we can assert that the theory of space-time has in reality nothing at all to do with the question of free will.

Now we turn to the scientific discernment of time. The very start of the concept might look odd, but it is not out of the way to explain some of the most important topics of time discussed today.

The Mystery of Time

Our sense tells us that time flows, namely, that the past is fixed, the future is undetermined, and reality lives in the present. Yet various physical and philosophical arguments suggest otherwise. The passage of time is an illusion. The consequence may involve thermodynamic or quantum processes that lend the impression of living moment by moment.

What's the Time Anyway?

Saint Augustine, the famous fifth-century theologian, remarked that he knew well what time was until somebody asked. Then he was at a loss for words. We sense time psychologically, because the definitions of time based on physics seem dry and inadequate. For the physicist, time is simply what (accurate) clocks measure. Mathematically, it is a one-dimensional space, usually assumed to be continuous, although it might be quantified into discrete "chronos," like frames of a movie.

The fact that time may be treated as a fourth dimension does not mean that it is identical to the three dimensions of space. Time and space enter into daily experience and physical theory in distinct ways, for example, in the formula for calculating spatial distances. The distinction between space and time underpins the key notion of causality, stopping cause and effect from being hopelessly jumbled. On the other hand, many physicists believe that on the very smallest scale of size and duration, space and time might lose their separate identities.

> Pick you roses as you may
> Old time is still gliding in dismal array

So wrote seventeenth-century English poet Robert Herrick, capturing the universal cliché that time flies. And who could doubt that it does? The passage of time is probably the most basic facet of human perception, for we feel time slipping by in our innermost selves in a manner that is altogether more intimate than our experience of, say, space or mass. The passage of time has been compared to the flight of an arrow and to an ever-rolling stream, bearing us inexorably from past to future. Shakespeare wrote of "the whirligig of time."

Andrew Marvell refers to, "Time's winged chariot hurrying near."

Evocative though these images may be, they run afoul of a deep and devastating paradox. Nothing in known physics corresponds to the passage of time. Indeed, physicists insist that time does not flow at all; it merely is. Some philosophers argue that the very notion of the passage of time is nonsensical and that the flux of time is founded on a misconception. How can something so basic to our experience of the physical world turn out to be a case of mistaken identity? Or is there a key quality of time that science has not yet identified?

Time Is Not of the Essence

In daily life, we divide time into three parts: past, present, and future. The grammatical structure of language revolves around this fundamental distinction. Reality is associated with the present moment. The past we think of as having slipped out of existence, whereas the future is even more shadowy, its details still unformed.

Our conscious awareness glides steadily onward, transforming events that were once in the unformed future into the concrete but fleeting reality of the present and thence relegating them to the fixed past.

Obvious though this commonsense description may seem, it is seriously at odds with modern physics. Albert Einstein famously expressed this point when he wrote to a friend, "The past, present and future are only illusions, even if sub-born ones." Einstein's startling conclusion stems directly from his special theory of relativity, which denies any absolute, universal significance to the present moment. According to the theory, simultaneity is relative. Two events that occur at the same moment, if observed from one reference frame, may occur at different moments if viewed from another.

An innocent question like "What is happening on Mars now?" has no definite answer. The key point is that Earth and Mars are a long way apart, up to about twenty light minutes. Because information cannot travel faster than light, an Earth-based observer is unable to know the situation on Mars at the same instant. He must infer the answer after the event, when light has had a chance to pass between the planets. The inferred past event will be different depending on the observer's velocity.

For example, during a future manned expedition to Mars, mission controllers back on Earth might say, "I wonder what Commander Jones is doing at Alpha Base now." When they look at their clock and see that it is 12:00 PM on Mars, their answer might be "eating lunch." But an astronaut zooming past Earth at near the speed of light at the same moment could, on looking at his clock, say that the time on Mars was earlier or later than 12:00 depending on his direction of motion. That astronaut's answer to the question about Commander Jones's activities would be "Cooking lunch" or "Washing dishes." Such mismatches make a mockery of any attempt to confer special status on the present moment, for whose "now" does that moment refer to? If you and I were in relative motion, an event that I might judge to be in the as yet undecided future might for you already exist in the fixed past.

The most straightforward conclusion is that both past and future are fixed. For this reason, physicists prefer to think of time as laid out entirely in a time-scape, analogous to a landscape with all past and future events located there together. It is a notion sometimes referred to as block time. Completely absent from this description of nature is anything that singles out a privileged special moment as the present or any process that would systematically turn future events into present and then past events.

How Time Does Not Fly

A number of philosophers over the years have arrived at the same conclusion by examining what we normally mean by the passage of time. They argue that the motion is internally inconsistent. The concept of flux, after all, refers to motion. It makes sense to talk about the movement of a physical object, such an arrow through space, by gauging how its location varies with time. But what meaning can be attached to the movement of time itself? Relative to what does it move? Whereas other types of motion relate one physical process to another, the putative flow of time relates time to itself. Posing the simple question "How fast does time pass?" exposes the absurdity of the very idea. The answer, "One second per second," tells us nothing at all.

In short, the time of the physicist does not pass or flow. Arguments go back to ancient Greek philosophers, such as Promenades and Zeno. A century ago, British philosopher John McTaggart sought to draw a clear distinction between the description of the world in terms of events happening, which he called the A series, and the description in terms of dates correlated with states of the world, the B series. Each seems to be a true description of reality, and yet the two points of view are seemingly in contradiction. For example, the event "Alice is disappointed" was once in the future, then in the present, and afterward in the past. But past, present, and future are exclusive categories, so how can a single event have the character of belonging to all three? McTaggart used this clash between the A and B series to argue for the unreality of time as such. It was perhaps a rather drastic conclusion. Most physicists would put it less dramatically; the flow of time is unreal, but time itself is as real as space.

Just in Time

A great source of confusion in the discussion of time's passage originates from its link with the so-called arrows of time. To deny that time flows is not to claim that the designations "past" and "future" are without physical basis. Events in the world undeniably form a unidirectional sequence. For instance, an egg dropped on the floor will smash into pieces, whereas the reverse process—a broken egg spontaneously assembling itself into an intact egg—is never witnessed, for this can happen in the shrinking universe that's not conducive to the sustenance of life on earth. This is an example of the second law of thermodynamics, which states that the entropy of a closed system will increase—roughly defined, disorder will tend to rise with time. An intact egg has a lower entropy than a shattered one.

Because nature abounds with irreversible physical processes, the second law of thermodynamics plays a key role in imprinting on the world a conspicuous asymmetry between past and future directions along the time axis. By convention, the arrow of time points toward the future. This does not imply, however, that the arrow is moving toward the future, any more than a compass needle pointing north indicates that the compass is traveling north. Both arrows symbolize an asymmetry, not a movement. The arrow of time denotes an asymmetry of the world in time, not an asymmetry or flux of time. The labels, "past" and "future," may legitimately be applied to temporal directions, just as "up" and "down" may be applied to spatial directions, but talk of the past or the future is as meaningless as referring to the up or the down.

The distinction between pastness or futureness and the past or the future is graphically illustrated by imagining a movie of, say, the egg being dropped on the floor and breaking. If the film were run backward through the projector, everyone would see that the sequence was unreal. Now imagine if the filmstrip was cut up into frames and the frames shuffled randomly. It would be a straightforward task for someone to rearrange the stack of frames into a correctly ordered sequence, with the broken egg at the top of the stack and the intact egg at the bottom. This vertical stack retains the asymmetry implied by the arrow of time because it forms an ordered sequence in vertical space, proving that time's asymmetry is actually a property of states of the world, not a property of time as such. It is not necessary for the film actually to be run as a movie for the arrow of time to be known.

Given that most physical and philosophical analyses of time fail to uncover any sign of a temporal flow, we are left with something of a mystery. To that, should we attribute the powerful, universal impression that the world is in a continual state of flux? Some researchers, notably Nobel Laureate chemist Illya Prigogine, have suggested that the physics of irreversible processes make the flow of time an objective aspect of the world. But some argue that it is an unusual sort of illusion.

After all, we do not really observe the passage of time. What we actually observe is that later states of the world differ from earlier states that we still remember. The fact that we remember the past, rather than the future, is an observation not of the passage of time but of the asymmetry of time. Nothing other than a conscious observer registers the flow of time.

A clock measures the duration between events, as a measuring tape measures distances between places. It does not measure the speed with which one moment succeeds another. Therefore, it appears that the flow of time is subjective, not objective.

Living in the Present

This illusion cries out for explanation, and that explanation is to be sought in psychology or neurophysiology. Modern science has barely begun to consider the question of how we perceive the passage of time; we can only speculate about the answer. It might have something to do with the functioning of the brain. If you spin around several times and stop suddenly, you will feel dizzy. Subjectively, it seems as if the world is rotating relative to you, but the evidence of your eyes is clear enough: it is not. The apparent movement of your surroundings is an illusion created by the rotation of fluid in the inner ear. Perhaps temporal flux is similar.

There are two aspects to time asymmetry that might create the false impression that time is flowing. The first is the thermodynamic distinction between past and future. Physicists have realized over the past few decades that the concept of entropy is closely related to the information content of a system. For this reason, the formation of memory is a unidirectional process as new memories add information and raise the entropy of the brain. We might perceive this unidirectionality as the flow of time.

A second possibility is that our perception of the flow of time is linked in some way to quantum mechanics. It was appreciated from the earliest days of the formulation of quantum mechanics that time enters into the theory in a unique manner, quite unlike space. The special role of time is one reason it is proving so difficult to merge quantum mechanics with general relativity. Heisemberg's uncertainty principle, according to which nature is inherently indeterministic, implies an open future (and, for that matter, an open past). This indeterminism manifests itself most conspicuously on an atomic scale of size and dictates that the observable properties that characterize a physical system are generally undecided from one moment to the next.

For example, the electron hitting an atom may bounce off in one of many directions, and it is normally impossible to predict in advance what the outcome in any given case will be. Quantum indeterminism implies that for a particular quantum state, there are many (possibly infinite) alternative futures or potential realities. Quantum mechanics supplies the relative probabilities for each observable outcome, although it won't say which potential future is destined for reality.

But when a human observer makes a measurement, one and only one result is obtained; for example, the rebounding electron will be found moving in a certain direction. In the act of measurement, a single, specific reality gets projected out from a vast array of possibilities. Within the observer's mind, the possible makes a transition to the actual, the open future to the fixed past, which is precisely what we mean by the flux of time.

There is no agreement among physicists on how this transition from many potential realities into a single actuality takes place. Many physicists have argued that it has something to do with the consciousness of the observer, on the basis that it is the act of observation that prompts nature to make up its mind. A few researchers, such as Roger Penrose of the Oxford University, maintain that consciousness, including the impression of temporal flux, could be related to quantum processes in the brain.

Although researchers have failed to find evidence for a single time organ in the brain, in the manner of, say, the visual cortex, it may be that future work will pin down those brain processes responsible for our sense of temporal passage. It is possible to imagine drugs that could suspend the subject's impression that time is passing. Indeed, some practitioners of meditation claim to be able to achieve such mental states naturally.

And what if science was able to explain away the flow of time? Perhaps we would no longer fret about the future or grieve for the past. Worries about death might become as irrelevant as worries about birth. *Expectation* and *nostalgia* might cease to be part of the human vocabulary. Above all, the sense of urgency attached to so much of human activity might evaporate. No longer would we be slaves to Henry Wordsworth Longfellow's entreaty to "act in the living present," for the past, present, and future would literally be things of the past. Scientific convictions and notions change in every eon, but today, modern research is close to the discernment of Qur'anic vision.

Time Dilation

The effect, known as time dilation, occurs whenever two observers move relative to each other. In daily life, we do not notice weird time warps, because the effect becomes dramatic only when the motion occurs at close to the speed of light. Even at aircraft speeds, the time dilation in a typical journey amounts to just a few nanoseconds. Nevertheless, atomic clocks are accurate enough to record the shift and confirm that time really is stretched by motion. So travel into the future is a proven fact, even if it has so far been rather unexciting.

To observe really dramatic time warps, one has to look beyond the realm of ordinary experience. Subatomic particles can be propelled at nearly the speed of light in large accelerator machines. Some of these particles, such as muons, have a built-in clock because they decay with a definite half-life; in accordance with Einstein's theory, fast-moving muons inside accelerators are observed to decay in slow motion. Some cosmic rays also experience spectacular time warps.

These particles move so close to the speed of light that, from their point of view, they cross the galaxy in minutes, even though in earth's frame of reference, they seem to take tens of thousands of years. If time dilation did not occur, those particles would never make it here.

Speed is one way to jump ahead in time; gravity is another.

In the general theory of relativity, Einstein predicted that gravity slows time. Clocks run a bit faster in the attic than in the basement, which is closer to the center of the earth and therefore deeper down in a gravitational field. Similarly, clocks run faster in space than on the ground. Once again, the effect is minuscule, but it has been directly measured using accurate clocks. Indeed, these time-warping effects have to be taken into account in the Global Positioning System. If they were not, sailors, taxi drivers, and cruise missiles could find themselves many kilometers off track.

At the surface of a neutron star, gravity is so strong that time is slowed by about 30 percent, relative to earth time. Viewed from such a star, events here would resemble a fast-forwarded video.

A black hole represents the ultimate time warp; at the surface of the black hole, time stands still relative to earth. This means that if you fell into a black hole from nearby, in the brief interval it took you to reach the surface, all of eternity would pass by in the wider universe. The region within the black hole is therefore beyond the end of time, as far as the outside universe is concerned.

If an astronaut could zoom very close to a black hole and return unscathed—admittedly a fanciful, not to mention foolhardy prospect—he could leap thousands of years into the future or could be back into the past in similar scale.

So far, I have discussed traveling forward in time. What about going backward? This is much more problematic. In 1948, Kurt Godel of the Institute for Advanced Study in Princeton, New Jersey, produced a solution for Einstein's gravitational field equations that described a rotating universe. In this universe, an astronaut could travel through space so as to reach his own past. This comes about because of the way gravity affects light. The rotation of the universe would drag light around with it, enabling a material object to travel in a closed loop in space that is also a closed loop in time, without at any stage exceeding the speed of light in the immediate neighborhood of the particle. Godel's solution was shrugged aside as a mathematical curiosity; after all, observations show no sign that the universe as a whole is spinning. His result served nonetheless to demonstrate that going back in time is not forbidden by the theory of relativity. Indeed, Einstein confessed that he was troubled by the thought that his theory might permit travel into the past under some circumstances.

Other scenarios have been found to permit travel into the past. For example, in 1974, Frank J. Tipler of Tulane University calculated that a massive, infinitely long cylinder spinning on its axis at near the speed of light could let astronauts visit their own pasts, again by dragging light around the cylinder into a loop. In 1991, J. Richard Gott of Princeton University predicted that cosmic strings, structures that cosmologists think were created in the early stages of the big bang, could produce similar results. But in the mid-1980s, the most realistic scenario for a time machine emerged, based on the concept of a wormhole.

In science fiction, wormholes are sometimes called star gates. They offer a shortcut between two widely separated points in space. Jump through a hypothetical wormhole and you might come out moments later on the other side of the galaxy. Wormholes naturally fit into the general theory of relativity. (The Lord Almighty, while explaining the three types of passages in the sky—the *Tareeq* for routine flight; the *Maarij*, the escalator-type, for rapid fights; and the third, *Hubbuk*, the spinning passages like moving wormholes wrapping time and space—asserts that He was not oblivious of the sophistication of His creation, as later discussed in this chapter.) Gravity warps not only time but also space. The theory allows the analogue of alternative road and tunnel routes connecting two points in space. Mathematicians refer to such a space as multiply connected. Just as a tunnel passing under a hill can be shorter than the surface street, a wormhole may be shorter than the usual route through ordinary space.

In the Loop

For the wormhole to be traversable, it must contain what Thorne termed "exotic matter." In effect, this is something that will generate antigravity to combat the natural tendency of a massive system to implode into a black hole under its intense weight. Negative energy or pressure can generate antigravity, or gravitational repulsion. Negative-energy states are known to exist in certain quantum systems, which suggests that Thorne's exotic matter is not ruled out by the laws of physics, although it is unclear whether enough anti-gravitating stuff can be assembled to stabilize a wormhole.

Soon, Thorne and his colleagues realized that if a stable wormhole could be created, then it could readily be turned into a time machine. An astronaut who passed through one end might come out not only somewhere else in the universe but some "when" else, either the future or the past. To adapt the wormhole for time travel, one of its mouths could be towed to a neutron star and placed close to its surface. The gravity of the star would slow time near that wormhole's mouth, so that a time difference between the ends of the wormhole would gradually accumulate. If both mouths were then parked at a convenient place in space, this time difference would remain frozen.

Suppose the difference were ten years. An astronaut passing through the wormhole in one direction would jump ten years into the future, whereas an astronaut passing in the other direction would jump ten years into the past. By returning to his starting point at high speed across ordinary space, the second astronaut might get back home before he left. In other words, a closed loop in space could become a loop in time as well. The one restriction is that the astronaut could not return to a time before the wormhole was first built. (Read this text in the context of Me'raaj, the Prophet's indeterminate journey through the whole cosmic order and beyond in the cosmic sway (23:17).)

It is quite conceivable that the next generation of particle accelerators will be able to create subatomic wormholes.

A formidable problem that stands in the way of entering a wormhole time domain is the concept in actuality of creation of the wormhole in the first place. Possibly space is threaded with such structures, natural relics of the big bang. If so, a super-civilization might commandeer one. Alternatively, wormholes might naturally come into existence on tiny scales, the so-called Planck length, about twenty factors of ten, as small as an atomic nucleus. In principle, such a minute wormhole could be stabilized by a pulse of energy and then somehow inflated to usable dimensions.

Paradoxes of this kind arise when the time traveler tries to change the past, which is obviously impossible. But that does not prevent someone from being a part of the past. Suppose the time traveler goes back and rescues a young girl from murder, and this girl grows up to become his mother. The causal loop is now self-consistent and no longer paradoxical. Causal consistency might impose restrictions on what a time traveler is able to do, but it does not rule out time travel.

Even if time travel is not strictly paradoxical, it is certainly weird. Consider the time traveler who leaps ahead a year and reads about a new mathematical theorem in a future edition of *Scientific American*. He notes the details, returns to his own time, and teaches the theorem to a student, who then writes it up for *Scientific American*. The article is, of course, the very one that the time traveler has read. The question then arises: Where did the information about the theorem come from? It is not from the time traveler, because he read it, but not from the student either, who learned it from the time traveler. The information seemingly came into existence from nowhere, without any reason. Don't you discern now the precept in the principle of providence?

The bizarre consequences of time travel have led some scientists to reject the notion outright. Stephen W. Hawking of the Cambridge University has proposed a "chronology protection conjecture," which would outlaw causal loops. Because the theory of relativity is known to permit causal loops, chronology protection would require some other factor to intercede to prevent travel into the past. What might this factor be? One suggestion is that quantum processes will come to the rescue. The existence of a time domain machine would allow particles to loop into their own pasts. Calculations hint that the ensuing disturbance would become self-reinforcing, creating a runaway surge of energy that would wreck the wormhole.

Chronology protection is still just a conjecture, so time travel remains a possibility. A final resolution of the matter may have to await the successful union of quantum mechanics and gravitation, perhaps through a theory such as string theory or its extension, so-called M-theory. It is even conceivable that the next generation of particle accelerators will be able to create subatomic wormholes that survive long enough for nearby particles to execute fleeting causal loops. This would be a far cry from Wells's vision of a time machine, but it would forever change our picture of physical reality.

The Enigma of the Time Calendar

What's time?
According to the late Nobel laureate Richard P. Feynman:

We physicists work with it every day, but do not ask me what it is; it's just too difficult to think about.

The attempted answer: "Time is nature's way of keeping everything from happening all at once."

Ask six people to explain time today, and, like the six blind men poking the elephant, you may get six answers. A physicist might say time is one of the two basic building blocks of the universe, the other being space. For a clockmaker time is the tick tock of his handiwork. For a science fiction fan it is the fourth dimension. A biologist sees time in the internal clocks that keep plants and animals in sync with nature. For a banker it is money, while a Buddhist monk contemplates time in the eternally returning cycles of nature.

We have given more attention to measuring time than to anything in nature, says Gernot Winkler, Director of Time Services at the U.S. Naval Observatory in Washington DC. But time remains an abstraction, a riddle that exists only in our minds.

Psychologists tell us that children before the age of two have little sense of the passage of time. It may have been the same for our early ancestors. Some scholars believe that people once lived in a state of timeless present with little or no sense of past or future.

The Concept of Time Domain

Is our timekeeping obsessive?

Consider this: locked in a cellar in Boulder, Colorado, is the standard for determining the length of a second in the United States. Operated by the National Institute of Standards and Technology, this cesium device, called NBS-6, is the nation's most precise atomic clock. It is accurate to within one second in three hundred thousand years.

NIST scientists have mastered timekeeping so well that they are now defining a meter as the world's basic unit of distance, in terms of the time it takes light in a vacuum to travel its length: 3,033,564,095 nanoseconds approximately.

We can measure time intervals better than material objects because time does not have little molecules dancing all over the place, said David Allan, a time theorist at NIST.

Nature too has its clocks. We can read them almost everywhere if we have the tools. In 1947, American chemist Willard Libby found a clock ticking in virtually everything that lived during the past fifty thousand years: the carbon-14 atom, which decays at a known rate. By comparing carbon-14 atoms with atoms that do not decay, scientists can tell the age of a pharaoh's mummy or an ancient Indian hearth.

Using similar techniques, geologists can measure the decay rates of radioactive elements like uranium, potassium, or rubidium to set ages for the planet's many tiers of rock. Those at the floor of the Grand Canyon reveal two billion years of geologic history, while rocks in northwest Canada go back nearly four billion years. Moon rocks date back 4.5 billion years, about the same age estimated for the earth.

Astronomers have gazed even further back in time, by looking at the light originating from a faraway galaxy. They are actually looking at the galaxies as they were billions of years ago. The rate at which these galaxies are flying away from each other tells them the date when all the matter in the universe set out on its journey.

We were able to show that the matter in the universe must have been infinitely compressed and dense about fifteen billion years ago, says theoretical physicist Stephen Hawking of England's Cambridge University. And before that time, as we measure it, simply did not exist, said Hawking. The reason is that the other side of the beginning of time is an abiding mystery, an unfathomable darkness without matter or motion. And to modern scientists, motion and time are invariably linked. (Read the details in "The Fate of the Universe," the interminable arrow of time.)

For Isaac Newton, time had a life of its own; it was an almost divine process cutting a path across all nature. Einstein changed all that with his theories of relativity. As the experiment with the traveling clocks showed, time for Einstein depended on how fast one was traveling. It no longer was absolute. And events determine how fast time passes instead of the other way around, as I think most of us would like to view it.

There is only one absolute, Hawking told us. It is not time but the speed of light: 186,282 miles a second. In a sense, the speed of light is Einstein's master clock, since there can be no velocity without time and the speed of light never varies. So the speed of light really is the best way to measure a meter.

But there's a hitch. One thing that affects both light and time is gravity. In the universe of Einstein's relativity, gravity is caused by the intrusion of a large chunk of matter, like the sun, into space and time. It is a geometric effect, like the one we see if we place a bowling ball on a trampoline.

Gravity bends both space and time. Thus, in the presence of a large stellar object, light has to travel farther between two points, and time slows down, speaking in a relative way. This does present a problem. On the surface of Jupiter, which has 318 times the mass of earth, a cesium clock would run noticeably slower than one at home. And what happens then to our light-measured meter?

John Wheeler, an eminent Princeton physicist friend of Einstein, likes to take the idea to an extreme. He pictures what happens on the surface of a black hole, a super-dense body created when a massive star collapses of its own gravitational pull. A black hole's gravity field is so intense that not even light can escape its surface, and time would stand still there.

This shows us, says Wheeler, who gave black holes their name, that time is a measuring tool, not an absolute flow or a substance.

Without an event, there is no time. This means, Wheeler believes, that time may be a secondary feature of nature, not a basic one.

But we are only talking about the physics of time here, says Wheeler. As much as anybody else, Einstein recognized that the mind's perception of time is a more subtle matter.

This kind of time of our bodies and minds has origins deep in a primordial past long before a set of gears on the wall told us when to go to bed.

Keeping Track of Time

Time is absolute, Isaac Newton declared in 1687. It flows equably without relation to anything external. That's obvious, you say, rushing to your next appointment. Physicists, however, have discovered that time is intimately tied to motion and space itself. Our image of time as a river eventually runs dry.

Albert Einstein shattered our notions about time in 1905 with his theory of special relativity. The motion of the observers affects the measurement of time intervals. Two years later, the mathematician Hermann Minkowski proposed a new geometry that added time to the three dimensions of space. This coordinate system, space-time, caught on as an efficient way to simplify Einstein's formulas.

Have you ever been at a train station and noticed the train next to you as it begins to move? It's odd, disorienting. Is it moving or are you? You do not know until you see a third reference point, like the platform. That's relative motion. In a similar way, time is relative. But there is no ultimate platform. We do not notice the differences because they are infinitesimally small. The relativity of time becomes significant only at great speeds, like those achieved in particle accelerators that produce velocities near that of light. Physicists verify special relativity daily; making it one of physics' most widely confirmed theories.

The idea is simple, but its implications are flabbergasting. It means, for example, that rapidly moving clocks tick more slowly than clocks at rest. A clock aboard a spaceship traveling at 87 percent the speed of light [inset] would tick only half as fast as a clock on earth. While such speeds are beyond present space technology, atomic clocks sent into orbit have recorded smaller differences repeatedly.

Odd indeed! says Princeton physicist John Wheeler photographed in his office as if receding into a black hole, a term he coined for collapsing stars that crunch not only matter but also the space around it, bringing times there to an end. Time cannot be an ultimate category in the description of nature, he declares. Before and after do not rule everywhere. A pioneer in quantum theory, at home measuring time by billionths of a second or by billions of years, Wheeler tests the edge of our understanding. We will first understand how simple the universe is, when we recognize how strange it is.

One way to imagine space-time is with a cone of light, each panel representing space at a different moment. The tip of the cone may be any point, say, earth at one instant. Events can be divided into those whose light has had time to reach us—those within our cone and those about which we still have no knowledge. As earth moves through time from left to right, our cone widens on each panel of space like a spreading flashlight beam, sweeping events into our present (i.e., our now). We do not see a star explode as a supernova until thousands of years later, when its light has reached us to announce the event.

So time is relative, changeable. Can it be reversed? No! The second law of thermodynamics, which states that those isolated systems move from order to disorder, unequivocally rules that out. Humpty-Dumpty won't ever put himself back together again.

Travel in Time

Time travel has been a popular science-fiction theme since H. G. Wells wrote his celebrated novel *The Time Machine* in 1895. But can it really be done? Is it possible to build a machine that would transport a human being into the past or future?

For decades, time travel lay beyond the outside edge of creditable science. In recent years, however, the topic has become something of a cottage industry among theoretical physicists. The encouragement has been partly holiday distraction; time travel is fun to think about. But this research has a serious side too. Comprehension of the relation between cause and effect is a key part of attempts to construct a unified theory of physics. If unrestricted time travel were possible, even in principle, the nature of such a unified theory could be drastically affected.

Our best understanding of time comes from Einstein's theories of relativity. Prior to these theories, time was widely regarded as absolute and universal, the same for everyone no matter what their physical circumstances were. In his special theory of relativity, Einstein proposed that the measured interval between two events depends on how the observer is moving. Crucially, two observers who move differently will experience different durations between the same two events.

The effect is often described using the twin paradox. Suppose that Sally and Sam are twins. Sally boards a rocket ship and travels at high speed to a nearby star, turns around, and flies back to earth, while Sam stays at home. For Sally, the duration of the journey might be, say one year, but when she returns and steps out of the spaceship, she finds that ten years have elapsed on earth. Her brother is now nine years older than she is. Sally and Sam are no longer the same age, despite the fact that they were born on the same day. This example illustrates a limited type of time travel. In effect, Sally has leaped nine years into earth's future.

Time Lag

No doubt I have gone way off the subject in most of the illustrations but to let the readers know the subject in depth, it was expedient to discuss some details of the time domain to discern the basic guideline of time in a most discriminating way. The journey of Prophet Muhammad [PBUH] to the indefinite cosmic order could possibly be travel back into time through the passages (wormholes) between different strata of the universe. For the journey back in time with a speed greater than the speed of light (thirty billion times the speed of light as discussed later in this chapter, through the escalator-type passages (70:3)) can easily be perceived, if we consider the very early moments when the universe took its stride and really expanded far faster than the speed of light as you learned in "The Perfect Creation."

I'm confident that my readers will now perceive the journey of Prophet Muhammad [PBUH] into the indeterminate cosmic order after reading this chapter more carefully.

The Prophet's journey of Me'raaj has baffled quite a few, and nobody could affirm, as to how it could have happened. I'm giving scientific details in the light of Qur'anic affirmations.

The angels and Spirit ascent unto Him in a day
The sort whereof is fifty thousand years a day
(Al-Maarij 70:4)

It's Allah Who,
Created the earth and heavenly *mall*
That's in eons six *in all*
And all between the infinite *sway in pace*
And settled on Throne *adorned in place*
You've none to keep or interpose *in glance*

Other than Lord hither *in stance*
Wouldn't you then caution *in trance*
He Commands all *the term in sway*
Of the heavens and earth *set in array*
All affairs at conclusion trend *in pace*
To The Lord Almighty *in Grace*
In a Day of tally *in trace*
Years thousand of your count *in place*
(Al-Sajdah 32:4–5)

For what is time?

How did Prophet Muhammad [PBUH] travel all the way in person with the angel Gabriel,, as it was not an illusion or fantasy or only a spiritual perception, for otherwise, there would not have been any need of appropriating this incident in the Holy Scripture. The whole incident took place in few moments of time when we refer to psychological time.

The understanding of wormhole theory gives a clear concept of such occurrences to be easily perceived today. Scientific fictions and facts are coming close to our discernment and deliberation of the universe as ordained in the Holy Scripture. How could one perceive travel in the time domain without even a fraction of moment passing on this earth? Perhaps this doggerel mentioned in *A Brief History of Time* by Stephen Hawking depicts it most befittingly.

There was a young lady of White
Who traveled much faster than light
She departed one day,
In relative way
And arrived on the previous night

Let us cite another example that will probably make things much easier to understand.

Say "A" is traveling in a train with seven compartments. The compartment closer to the engine is Sunday, the next one Monday, and the last is Saturday. "A" leaves the train in the "Friday" compartment with a speed much faster than the speed of light in the opposite direction and the reaches the train from in front of it (like a moving wormhole.) "A" is likely to catch the first "Sunday" compartment much earlier than the "Friday" compartment. Consider all such moves in the whole cosmic sway where every pin to comet is on the move with a speed relative to one another, close to the brim of a black hole, and the time is static. So traveling in the time domain is not foreign to our understanding if we take all these variables into account.

Scientists believe that large wormholes might exist naturally in deep space, a relic of the big bang. Otherwise, it is conceivable that the next generation of particle accelerators will be able to create subatomic wormholes.[29]

As detailed in the text, the Qur'an affirms the existence of these wormholes. If we can somehow prove that Prophet Muhammad [PBUH] traveled much faster than the speed of light *(thirty billion times the speed of light)* through wormhole-like passages (23:17 and 70:3) through different strata of skies and came back through moving wormholes (51:7), we can scientifically prove the cosmic journey of "Me'raaj."

Alpha Centauri is twenty million million miles away from the earth. Thus, one imagines or creates a wormhole that would lead from the vicinity of the solar system, static as compared to the earth, to Alpha Centauri. The distance through the wormhole might be only a few million miles. This would allow the news of the happenings on earth to arrive well before time; in such case, one would have to travel back to earth from Alpha Centauri through another moving wormhole.

Ordinary matter gives space-time a positive curvature, like the surface of the sphere. To allow travel into the past, space-time must have a negative curvature like the surface of a saddle. So the wormholes between two regions of space-time would make it possible to travel faster than light into the past or future.

Another way of discernment could possibly be explained in this pretence as described earlier through *spirituality*. For all that we consider in this context and perceive that time is not one for all domains, there was a time before the creation of the universe that we term the state of timelessness or nihility. We may name it time "F," i.e., pertaining to nihility or *Fanaa* or staying in the interminable arrow of time. When the sprawl of creation took its stride, the time also started its journey. We may call it time "B"; we may also call it servility, *because it was subsequent to creation* or "Baqaa time."

The discernment of these two (i.e., time pertaining to nihility and in subsequence servility) is perceptible but only when the earthly pot of the body melts into the soul and loses all its identity into nihility or the interminable arrow, and that's when you concentrate on the heart and slowly ruminate the Holy Name "Allah." Soon, you'll feel your body melting into soul and soul becoming a part of the whole. That's the state of mind when the blood supply to the left parietal lobe is gone. Some scientists affirm that there's only the divine source of nourishment during those moments of deep meditation. In such moments, you sway in the cosmic array like the wind whispering in

29 *Scientific American*, September 2002.

play. This flitting and fleeting illumination or edification is gone when we totter and stumble back to our run-of-the-mill frame of mind with our brains obsessed with the conventional earthly seductive possessions. And when this earthly pot once again accomplishes its identity, the turn of time takes its course in tine of the term *Baqaa* or servility, for it's conditional to creation. That's what we are concerned to account for in our day-to-day life without encumbrance of duality in mind.

This time (Baqaa or servility) has three notions of interpretation.

The thermodynamic arrow of time is to follow a definite path ever since the creation of time and the universe, whereas the cosmological arrow of time will be reversed if ever the universe starts contracting. But at the moment, we are really concerned with the psychological arrow of time in our day-to-day life, for which we apprise notions of past, present, and future, which we may call "yesterday," "today," and "tomorrow." Now we turn toward Qur'anic assertions in this regard. After creating the skies, the Lord created passages between the skies, where angels are abiding the dictum in dictate of the Lord Almighty, as stated by Hazarat Ali, the prophet's first cousin, in his first address in "*Nehj ul Balagha.*" Indeed, he was referring to the wormholes. Now let us bear in mind certain Qur'anic assertions that affirm the speed of light, besides other cosmic affairs, and also the speed of the angels traveling through different passages like "wormholes" in the cosmic stride.

And We,
Created over you seven ways *in cosmic sway*
We're not oblivious of "Our" creation *in array* (23:17)

These are probably seven routine passages for the angels to move toward the skies or seven different kinds of wormholes (i.e., static, escalator, spinning, and those jumping straight from past to future, future to past, past to present, and future to present).

A discipline of Lord *in prime*
The Lord of all tracts in trail *to climb*
The angels and Spirits ascent unto Him in a day
The sort whereof is fifty thousand years a day (70:3–4)

These elevator-type passages are for the rapid ascent of angels toward the heavens.

Vow be to the passages *(in skies)* swinging *in trail* (51:07)

The word used for such passages means "changing in position." How nicely it affirms "the spinning and moving wormholes" through the different strata of the multiverses.

If you carefully concentrate on the text of the verse (70:3–4), it clearly indicates the speed of the angels climbing through the passages in the skies (details given in the text).

Speed of Light and Lunar Orbital Motion

Fourteen centuries ago, the Qur'an was directed from the Lord Almighty to all humanity through Prophet Muhammad [PBUH], who lived in the Arabian Peninsula. The Arab people even now use the lunar calendar in their calculation of time.

The Qur'an addressed them in the only language they could understand without defying their seemliness. The Lord Almighty asserts in the Qur'an:

He created sun grandeur *in glow*
And the moon He set to gleam *in flow*
And held a determined term *in stride*
That you may discern the years *in count*
Lord had all this source, a truth *in adore*
He details trivia in trends *for some in lore*
For what they'd concern in score (10:5)

The lunar year is twelve months; the month is defined recently as the time of one revolution of the moon in its orbit around the earth. The Lord Almighty hints at such an orbit in the Qur'an.

He's The Lord!
Who created night and the day *in call*
Besides, gleam of moon and glitter of sol
They bob and drift in each ellipse *in mall* (21:33)

Here, an essential scientific fact is clearly stated, namely, the existence of the earth's sun and the moon's orbit; a reference is also made to the traveling of these celestial bodies in space with their own motion! A new concept had therefore been established in the Qur'an hundreds of years before it was discovered by modern science. Today, the concept of the lunar year is widely spread, and as we know, the moon is our nearest neighbor in space and a companion to our planet. It is often said that the earth and moon form a twin planet.

As the moon orbits around the earth, the change in the relative positions of the moon, earth, and sun cause the moon to show its phases. The time between consecutive new moons is 29.53 days and is called the syndic month. During this time, however, the earth and, consequently, the moon's orbit has traveled some way around the sun, so the position of the moon against the background of stars is different. The time for the moon to return to the same position in the sky as viewed from earth is called the sidereal month (27.32 days), which represents the actual real net time of one revolution in the moon's orbit. This orbit is almost circular, having an average radius of 384,264 kilometers.

Referring to the Qur'anic verse (10:5), we observe that it discriminates between the apparent syndic period for knowing the number of years and the real sidereal period for reckoning in scientific calculations. These two systems of measuring time are now given in the textbooks of astronomy as indicated in the table.

Table: Lunar Month and Terrestrial Day

Period	Sidereal	Syndic
Lunar Month = T	27.321661 days = 55.71986 hours	29.53059 days
Terrestrial day = t	23 h, 56 min 4.0906 sec or 86,164.0906 sec	24 hours = 86,400 sec

The purpose of the proposition is to determine the value of the greatest speed mentioned in the following relativistic Qur'anic verses. In these verses, the sidereal system should be used for both the lunar month and the terrestrial day, as an accurately measured period (with respect to a distant, apparently fixed star).

A New Relation in the Earth-Moon System

The length of the moon's orbit, L, and the time, t, of one terrestrial day are correlated in a marvelous Qur'anic verse which describes a universal constant velocity of a certain cosmic affair as follows.[30]

---

30 A day is equal to one thousand years in stance.

He Commands all *the term in sway*
Of the heavens and earth *set in array*
All at conclusion affairs trend *in pace*
To The Lord Almighty *in Grace*
In a Day of tally *in trace*
Years thousand of your count *in place*
In a Day of your count years thousand in stance (Al Sajdah 32:5)

The Qur'anic expression "of your reckoning" leaves no doubt as to our understanding of the year as the lunar year. The verse begins with a reference to a certain "cosmic affair," which the Lord Almighty creates and commands. This affair travels permanently through the whole multiverse between different strata of the heavens and the earth so speedily that it crosses in one day a maximum distance in space equivalent to that which the moon passes during one thousand lunar years (i.e., during 12,000 sidereal months). The question that now arises is: what could this cosmic affair be?

And what is its greatest velocity as expressed in this Qur'anic equation? To answer this question, we turn to the Qur'anic verse that has been understood in terms of the following equation.

The distance crossed in a vacuum by the universal cosmic affair in one sidereal day is equal to the length of twelve thousand revolutions of the moon around the earth.

$$Ct = 12000\ L \tag{1}$$

Where:

C is the velocity of the cosmic affair;

T is the time interval of one terrestrial sidereal day, defined as the time of one rotation of the earth about its axis relative to the stars (i.e., 23 hours, 56 minutes, 4.0906 seconds equals 86,164.0906 seconds);

And L is the inertial distance, which the moon covers in revolution around the earth during one sidereal month.

L is the net length of the moon's orbit due to its own geocentric motion, without the interference of its spiral motion caused by the earth's revolution around the sun (i.e., the lunar orbit length excluding the effect of the solar gravitational field on the measured value).

Let V be the measured average orbital velocity of the moon deduced from the average radius, R, of the lunar geocentric orbit, measured from an orbiting earth during its heliocentric motion.

$$V = 2\ Pi\ R/T \tag{2}$$

Substituting:

R = 384264 km and T = 655.71986 hr (the sidereal lunar month)

V= (2 × 3.1416 × 384264)/655.71986 = 3682.07 km/hr

This value is given in all the textbooks of astronomy and is accepted by NASA.

Let θ be the angle traveled by the earth-moon system around the sun during one sidereal month of period 27.321661 days. We can calculate θ if we take into consideration the period (365.25636 days) of one heliocentric revolution (one year) of the earth-moon system.

$$\theta = 27.321661 * 360/365.25636 = 26, 92848$$

Thus θ is a characteristic constant of this system depending on uniform periods of the month and the year. Since the presence of the sun changes the geometrical properties of space and time, we must screen out its gravitational effect on the earth-moon system. According to the validity condition of the second postulate of spatial relativity, we must only consider the lunar geocentric motion without the heliocentric motion of the earth-moon system.

Thus, a velocity component $V_0 = V \cos \theta$ representing the net orbital velocity of the moon is introduced for calculating the net length, L, of the lunar orbit assuming a stationary earth.

$$L = V \cos (\theta) T \qquad (3)$$

From equation (1) and (3), we get a new Qur'anic relation for the earth-moon system:

$$Ct = 12000 V \cos (\theta) T \qquad (4)$$

$$C = 12000 V \cos (\theta) T/t \qquad (5)$$

Substituting the sidereal values of the periods t and T from table (2), the NASA value of the measured orbital lunar velocity V = 3682.07 km/hr, and the calculated value of cos θ = cos 26.92848 = 0.89157, we get the velocity of the cosmic affair from equation (5), as expressed in the Holy Qur'an.

C= 12000 × 3682.07 × 0.89157 × 655.71986/86164.0906

C= 29,9792.5 km/s

Referring to the international value of C = 29,9792.458 km/s, we find an extremely marvelous agreement. Thus, we conclude that the cosmic affair mentioned in the previous Qur'anic verse is identical to light and all similar cosmic affairs traveling in a vacuum with this maximum speed, such as all types of electromagnetic waves propagating between the heavens and the earth, the expected gravitational waves spreading all over the universe, and all particles traveling in this cosmic greatest speed, such as neutrinos. It is very interesting to mention here the second Qur'anic verse that hints at the same relativistic Qur'anic equation in the earth-moon system. The Lord Almighty asserts: "A day in the sight of Thy Lord is like a thousand years of your reckoning" (22:47).

The interpretation of these verses in the light of scientific discernment determines a fascinating order to comprehend the speed of the angels in the cosmic glide.

The Speed of the Ordinary Angels[31]

A day is equal to years thousand in stance
He Commands all *the term in sway*
Of the heavens and earth *set in array*
All at conclusion affairs trend *in pace*
To The Lord Almighty *in Grace*
In a Day of tally *in trace*
Years thousand of your count *in place*
In a Day of your count years thousand in stance
(Al Sajida 32:5)

The angels and Spirit ascent unto Him in a day
The sort whereof is fifty thousand years a day
(Al Maarij 70:4)

Just consider the order of the day in 32:5 is mentioned to be a thousands of your count, and in 70:4, it asserts fifty thousand years in count. Could it be a day equals fifty million times the speed of light (1000 x 50,000 = 50,000,000) as we have discussed in the text?

The Speed of Special Angels of the Lord

All Acclaim in Adulation for Lord *in adore*
Who contrived *out of Nihility in score*
The heavens and the earth *in place*
Who made the angels *courier in space*

With fin to fly *thither in glide*

---

31   An angel ascends to the Lord Almighty in a day of fifty thousand years.

Wings in two or three or four pairs *to slide*
He appends to contrive to spread *in array*

As He intends to trend *in display*
For Lord has power over all *in sway*
(Al Fatr 35:1)

His Almighty asserts that if an angel or a spirit has to reach Him from earth, it would take a day of fifty thousand years of count (not of our count) where the day, as affirmed earlier, is a day of one thousand years of our count. This clearly shows that there are messengers of the Lord, whose speed is fifty million times the speed of light (1000 x 50,000 = 50,000,000). Then there are verses clearly indicating that angels may have two, three, or four pairs of wings, quite likely referring to their relation with the speed (of the messengers of Lord) of fifty million times the speed of light. Now consider all the means of communication of the Lord Almighty through certain passages like wormholes, with a speed two, three, and four times the fifty million times the speed of light (i.e., one hundred, one hundred and fifty, or two hundred million times the speed of light), fifty to two hundred million times the speed of light.

The speed of the cosmic sprawl is 186,000 miles per second of our count for the multiverses. Can how long it would continue not be perceived by a man like of today?

With the foregoing discussion, I would like to sum up the details once again to clearly understand the wrapping up of time and space.

The Speed of the Archangel Gabriel

This affirms that the distances in the cosmic sway are far beyond our comprehension, and reaching such places to establish the dictum of the Lord Almighty definitely requires a speed and passages also far beyond our discernment. It is affirmed in *Hadidh* that the number of wings of the Angel Gabriel are six hundred (i.e., his speed is six hundred times the speed of an ordinary angel or 600 x 50,000,000 = 30,000,000,000 (i.e., 30 billion times the speed of light) through the escalator-type passages *(Maarij)*. And so it affirms the Prophet's journey of Mee'raaj, as he was escorted by Archangel Gabriel, at a speed far beyond our discernment to comprehend; when he returned, the latch was still swinging.

In Surah *Al Maarij* Verse 3, the passages mentioned as "Maarij" are actually the escalator-type passages. Consider the actual speed of travel through these passages when the speed of Archangel Gabriel is thirty billion times the speed of light. If the speed of the escalators is also something like that, you can deduce from the above narration how the Prophet Muhammad [PBUH] traveled with a speed thirty billion times the speed of light with Archangel Gabriel through the passages (70:3–4) in the different strata of the multiverses and the skies and back through special passages, *Hubbuk*, moving like a whirlwind (moving wormholes), wrapping time and space and getting the holy Prophet back a in time (well actually in his past) that coincided with his time of departure from the place. When the Lord Almighty describes these passages, He soon affirms that Your Lord was not quite oblivious of the nature of His creation or what He intended for the organization of the whole cosmic sway and particularly for the administration of the cosmic order. Because we actually cannot comprehend how after spending that much time, the Prophet could be back in the blink of an eye that is actually one-hundredth of a second. But I presume he was a bit early so he was driven slowly while back in time when he could perceive the caravan moving toward Makkah, and he predicted that they'd reach it at a particular time here in the city. And he was back through the *Hubbuk* (moving wormholes) passages (51:07) while the latch was still swinging.

In the Holy Qur'an, the Lord Almighty described three types of passages with three different names: The *Tareeq* (Al Moumainoon 17) are the seven routine passages for the scheduled assignments for the angels probably with a basic speed of fifty million times the speed of light, and the Lord Almighty asserts in this Surah that He was not oblivious of the plan of creation. There are special escalator-type passages called *Maarij* (Al Maarij 3, 4) for the angels, having a speed of one hundred to two hundred times the speed of light. While passing through such passages, the speed of the angels could be far beyond our discernment. And finally, the *Hubbuk* passages (Al Zariat 7) are for the return journey and are changing their position. (They are whirlwind-like moving passages spinning at their axes far beyond the speed of light, wrapping *time and space* and getting the person/angels/spirits back in time.) The void between the clusters of galaxies of four different types in the cosmic order might be providing an infinitely long cylindrical passage spinning on its axis that would let the person travel through such passages and visit his own past by dragging light and squeezing space and time into the loop.

Similarly, if we look at the journey of the Prophet Muhammad [PBUH], we see it was actually a journey back in time when he was coming back to earth through the moving wormholes (Al-Hubbuk). After leading the prayers of all the prophets, going to the indeterminate cosmic sway, visiting all that which the Lord Almighty wished him to observe, and then coming through the moving wormholes that virtually squeezed and wrapped time and space and that actually coincided exactly with the time he left the place, he was abiding before leaving for the sacred journey of Me'raaj.

In science fiction, wormholes are often called star gates and they offer a shortcut between two widely separated points in space. One jumps through a wormhole as mentioned in (Al Maarij 70:1–4) and comes out moments later on the other side of the galaxy. Wormholes naturally fit into the general theory of relativity, whereby gravity also wraps not only time but also space. I have tried to learn the philosophy of gravitational force in this journey that could possibly be yet another way to squeeze time and space, but perhaps we have to work more on the Holy Scripture to comprehend its wisdom.

People often cannot reconcile themselves with the speed Prophet Muhammad [PBUH] traveled in the cosmic sway during Mee'raaj, but have you ever thought of your travel in the cosmic order while abiding on Earth?

We on earth are spinning around its axis with a speed of 1,670 kilometers per hour and then with the planet around its orbit (around the sun) at a speed of 108,000 kilometers per hour. And so with that as a part of the solar system around the Milky Way Galaxy at the speed of 720,000 kilometers per hour and then with the Milky Way swaying with a speed of 950,000 kilometers per hour in its universe. And the universe is spinning in the multiverse with an unknown speed, and the multiverse is swaying with an unknown speed in the strata of parallel universes. The parallel universes are spinning around with an unknown speed in the cosmic order and then all of it is speeding away with a speed of 300,000 kilometers per second from the core of the big bang or *Kun: Fa Ya Koon*, and we don't even feel dizzy traveling with such a stupendous speed in the cosmic order.

Today's scientific trends affirm that perhaps in the quite near future, man shall be able to create atomic wormholes between different strata of the universes and also acquire a speed far greater than the speed of light. He would probably be able to travel toward the faraway galactic order. But there is a catch in this man-managed journey by future scientists, because after a definite limit in space, the cosmic rays will be so intense that the space shuttle would need six hundred tons of water to elude the effects of cosmic rays (as it is not even possible for an astronaut to land on Mars, for there is no such shield to deflect the torment of cosmic rays), and it is not possible for the spacecraft to carry that much water. This is an interesting subject too. I'll make it convenient to explain this sometime later in an appropriate place.

For decades, time travel lay beyond the edge of creditable science. In recent years, however, the topic has become something of a very common subject among theoretical physicists. The encouragement has been partly holiday distraction; time travel is fun to think about. But this research has a serious side too. Comprehension of the relationship between cause and effect is a key part of attempts to construct a unified theory of physics. If unrestricted time travel were possible, even in principle, the nature of such a unified theory could be drastically affected. So man shall be able to accomplish such marvels (i.e., to travel to the far distant universe and come back in a wink).

I am confident with the foregoing discussion the reader will be able to understand the cosmic journey of Prophet Muhammad PBUH that indeed was travel back in time.

To summarize once again: While traveling toward the heavens, Prophet Muhammad PBUH was traveling in his future as we do in our routine, but this travel was with a speed that's far beyond our cognition (thirty billion times the speed of light) through the escalator-type (Al Maarij) of passages that might have doubled the ultimate speed. But when he was coming back, it was basically a travel back in time (i.e., into his own past) through the passages (Al Hubbuk) which were spinning beyond the speed of light and also changing their position like whirlwinds and that could wind up time and space. I would like to add a word for my readers that using the speed of light is one way to wind up space and time and gravitation is another. I've just affirmed the travel of Prophet Muhammad PBUH in the light of wormhole theory.

The gravitational element would have been around as long as the prophet's journey was through the cosmic order sweep with billions and trillions of cosmic bodies in the stellar sprawl around, but once he was beyond the cosmic order, the gravitational element was no longer there, as there is a void beyond the limits of the cosmic order that's limited by the lower skies. There is a point of concern in this context that spinning wormholes with speeds greater than that of light could possibly also evade the implementation of gravitational force in the cosmic order as long as stellar bodies are around.

A word about the gravitational element as to how it influences time: If we have a watch in the basement and another in the attic, the one in the attic runs faster than the one in basement as the element of gravitation on the earth is more when it is closer to the core of the earth. Can you comprehend the distance he traveled? Indeed, you cannot!

Our universe was billions to trillions of kilometers apart in first few moments of the big bang, and then it has been expanding at the speed of around three hundred thousand kilometers per second ever since, for fifteen billion light-years; and mind you, each light-year is six trillion miles (if our grand universe expanded just one meter per second, it would double its size, and if it expanded six trillion miles a second, imagine how much its size would be). And the limit of its expanse is the lowest sky. How far afar must it expand to reach that limit of cosmic order? The cosmic sway is beyond the lowest skies, where there are another six skies, each most probably with the same distance of nihility of the big bang to the first or the lower skies, when the expanding universe will experience a big smash, resulting in a series of big crunches eventuating in a singularity, forming a seedling for the new creation (details in "The Fate of the Universe").

Scientists affirm the existence of wormhole passages as a relic of the big bang, and the Qur'an confirms the existence of such passages (23:17; 51:07; 70:3–4). Scientists also contend that in the future, we shall be able to produce atomic wormholes in different strata of the universe.

As mentioned, speed is one way to wrap up time and space and gravitation is another. The spinning, moving wormholes (Al Hubbuk), probably moving with the speed of light, could also elude the gravitational influence of the stellar sprawl.

His Almighty asserts that if an angel or a spirit has to reach Him from earth, it would take a day of fifty thousand years of count (not of our count) where the day, as affirmed earlier is a day of one thousand years of our count. This clearly shows that there are messengers of the Lord, whose speed is fifty million (1000 x 50,000) times the speed of light. Then there are verses clearly indicating that angels may have two, three, or four pairs of wings, quite likely referring to their relation with the speed *(of the messengers of the Lord)* of fifty million times the speed of light. Now consider all the means of communication of the Lord Almighty through certain passages like wormholes, with a speed two, three, and four times the fifty-million-times-the-speed-of-light speed (i.e., fifty, one hundred and fifty, or two hundred million times the speed of light). The speed of Archangel Gabriel is thirty billion times the speed of light as already affirmed. Prophet Muhammad [PBUH] traveled toward the heavens with a speed of thirty billion times the speed of light through Al Maarij and came back into his own past through *Hubbuk*, the spinning passages wrapping up time and space.

In Hadith, it is affirmed that Archangel Gabriel has six hundred wings (allowing him a speed thirty billion times the speed of light). And the Prophet [PBUH] accompanied Archangel Gabriel through Al Maarij-like passages while going and coming back into his past through spirally swinging passages of Al Hubbuk and reaching the location at the time of his departure.

And We,
Created over you seven ways *in cosmic sway*
We're not oblivious of "Our" creation *in array*
(Al Moumainoon 23:17)

A discipline of Lord *in prime*
    The Lord of all tracts in trail *to climb*
    The angels and Spirits ascent unto Him in a day
    The sort whereof is fifty thousand years a day
    (Al Maarij 70:3–4)

    Vow be to the passages *(in skies)* swinging *in trail*
    (Al Zariat, "The Winnowing Winds" 51:07)

The word used for such passages is changing in position. How nicely it affirms "the spinning and moving wormholes" through different strata of the multiverses and beyond for a rapid swing into the future or instant retreat into the past—a journey back in time.

    He Commands all *the term in sway*
    Of the heavens and earth *set in array*
    All at conclusion affairs trend *in pace*
    To The Lord Almighty *in Grace*
    In a Day of tally *in trace*
    Years thousand of your count *in place*
    In a Day of your count years thousand in stance
    (Al Sajida 32:5)

A diagrammatic appearance of the Prophet's [PBUH] journey follows.

The Prophet's ^{PBUH} Journey of Me'raaj

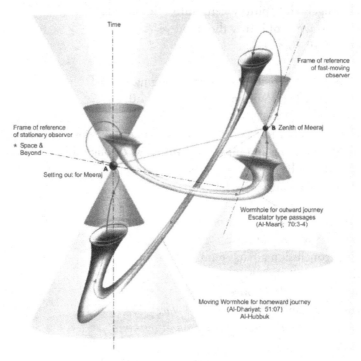

* **Space & Beyond:**

Space or Cosmic Order (Our domain of expansion of the universe is the lowest skies (Al-Saffat 37:6))
Beyond in Cosmic Sway with six skies (With no gravitational element)

Modified from Brief History of Time by Stephen Hawking

The angels and Spirit ascent unto Him in a day
The sort whereof is fifty thousand years a day
(Al Maarij 70:4)

All Acclaim in Adulation for Lord *in adore*
Who contrived *out of Nihility in score*
The heavens and earth *in place*
Who made the angels *courier in space*
With fin to fly *thither in glide*
Wings in two, or three, or four pairs *to slide*
He appends to contrive to create *in array*
As He intends to trend *in display*
For Lord has power over all *in sway*
(Al Malaika or Al Fatir 35:1)

Seas That Do Not Mix

He's let free two sinuous seas in obtrude
But a fence *(mid them)* doesn't let to intrude
(Al-Rahman 55:19–20)

In the verse stated above, it is indicated that two bodies of water meet each other yet do not mix together since there is a barrier preventing it.

How could a man of fourteen centuries back think of all those intricate ocean currents shown today by the most advanced research?

Modern research has in recent times encountered that in the places where two contrasting seas meet with divergent properties, there is a barrier between them. This barrier divides the two seas so that the stream of water flowing in the sea has its own temperature, salinity, and density.

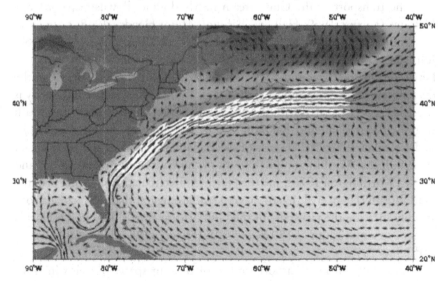

The **Gulf Stream** as represented by the Mariano Global Surface Velocity Analysis *(MGSVA)*. The Gulf Stream is the western boundary current of the North Atlantic subtropical gyre. The Gulf Stream transports a significant amount of warm water *(heat)* toward the North Pole. The averaging of velocity data from a meandering current produces a wide mean picture of the flow. The core of the Gulf Stream current is about 90 km wide and has peak velocities of greater than 2 m/s *(5 knots)*.

Beginning in the Caribbean and ending in the northern North Atlantic, the Gulf Stream system is one of the world's most intensely studied current systems. This extensive western boundary current plays an important role in the poleward transfer of heat and salt and serves to warm the European subcontinent. The Gulf Stream begins upstream of Cape Hatters, where the Florida current ceases to follow the continental shelf. The position of the stream, as it leaves the coast, changes throughout the year. In the fall, it shifts north, while in the winter and early spring, it shifts south (Auer 1987; Kelly and Gille 1990; Frankignoul et al. 2001). Compared with the width of the current (about 100–200 km), the range of this variation (30–40 km) is relatively small (Hogg and Johns 1995). However, recent studies by Mariano et al. (2002) suggest that the meridional range of the annual variation in the stream's path may be closer to one hundred kilometers. Other characteristics of the current are more variable. Significant changes in its transport, meandering, and structure can be observed through many time scales as it travels northeast.

The transport of the Gulf Stream nearly doubles downstream of Cape Hatteras (Knauss 1969; Hall and Fofonoff 1993; Hendry 1988; Leaman et al. 1989) at a rate of eight Sv every one hundred kilometers (Knauss 1969; Johns et al. 1995). It appears that the downstream increase in transport between Cape Hatteras and 55°W is mostly due to increased velocities in the deep waters of the Gulf Stream (Johns et al. 1995). This increase in velocity is thought to be associated with deep recirculation cells found north and south of the current (Hall and Fofonoff 1993). Examples of these recirculations include small recirculations east of the Bahamas (Olson et al. 1984; Lee et al. 1990), the Worthington Gyre south of the Gulf Stream between 55° and 75°W (Worthington 1976), and the Northern Recirculation Gyre north of the Gulf Stream (Hogg et al. 1986). Recent studies suggest that the recirculations steadily increase the transport in the Gulf Stream from 30 Sv in the Florida current to a maximum of 150 Sv at 55°W (Hendry 1982; Hogg 1992; Hogg and Johns 1995).

The Gulf Stream transport varies not only in space, but also in time. According to Geosat altimetry results, the current transports a maximum amount of water in the fall and a minimum in the spring, in phase with the north-south shifts of its position (Kelly and Gille 1990; Zlotnicki 1991; Kelly 1991; Hogg and Johns 1995). Rossby and Rago (1985) and Fu et al. (1987)

obtained similar results when they looked at sea-level differences across the stream. All of these studies found that the Gulf Stream has a marked seasonal variability, with peak-to-peak amplitude in sea surface height of ten to fifteen centimeters. The fluctuation is mostly confined to the upper two to three hundred meters of the water column and is a result of seasonal heating and expansion of the surface waters (Hogg and Johns 1995). Height differences so small, if assumed to decay linearly to zero at three hundred meters, would only result in annual transport fluctuations of about 1.5 Sv (Hogg and Johns 1995).

Interestingly, the variations in transport of the deep waters in the current appear to be almost opposite in phase to the surface waters, and their magnitude is more significant (Hogg and Johns 1995). As Worthington (1976) suggested, the maximum transport occurs in the spring, and the amplitude of the annual cycle is as large as 5 to 8.5 Sv (Manning and Watts 1989; Sato and Rossby 1992; Hogg and Johns 1995). The mechanism Worthington proposed was extensive convection south of the Gulf Stream in winter due to the atmospheric cooling of surface waters. This causes the thermocline to deepen and the baroclinic transport to increase (Fu et al. 1987). Although this idea has been controversial, alternate hypotheses have not adequately explained observations (Hogg and Johns 1995).

Like transport, the meandering of the Gulf Stream intensifies downstream of Cape Hatteras, reaching a maximum near 65°W. Meanders often pinch off from the current to form Gulf Stream rings. On average, the stream sheds twenty-two warm-core rings and thirty-five cold-core rings per year (Hogg and Johns 1995).

Once it reaches the Grand Banks, the structure of the Gulf Stream changes from a single, meandering front to multiple, branching fronts (Krauss 1986; Johns et al. 1995). Early oceanographic papers on the North Atlantic (Iselin 1936; Fuglister 1951a, 1951b; Sverdrup et al. 1942) mention the branching, but due to sparse data in this area, the branch points were considered largely theoretical until confirmed by Mann (1967). Mann (1967) showed two branches at 38°30, N 44°W.

The region of the Gulf Stream's branch point is highly dynamic and subject to rapid change. The high degree of mesoscale activity, along with rapid changes in the major surface currents, make this a very difficult region to study. Part of this variability arises from the high amount of eddy activity. Eddy kinetic energy along both the Gulf Stream and the North Atlantic current is at peak values here (Richardson 1983). There is also the presence of elongated, high-pressure cells along the offshore side of the North Atlantic current (Worthington 1976; Clarke et al. 1980; Baranov and Ginkul 1984; Krauss et al. 1987). These pressure cells may be linked to outbursts of

Labrador current water from the Grand Banks (Krauss et al. 1987) that lead to extensive mixing at the end of the Gulf Stream.

Similarly, another example is the water of the Mediterranean Sea, which is warm, saline, and less dense as compared to water of the Atlantic Ocean. When the Mediterranean Sea enters the Atlantic over the Gibraltar Sill, it moves several hundred kilometers into the Atlantic at a depth of about one thousand meters with its own warm, saline, and less-dense characteristics. Although there are colossal ocean sprays, forcible tidal flows, and the rise and fall of ocean currents in these seas, they do not mix or transgress this barrier.

The human eye cannot see the difference between the two seas that meet. Rather, they appear to us as one homogeneous sea. This information has been discovered only recently using advanced equipment to measure temperatures, salinity, density, oxygen, etc., whereas the Holy Qur'an clearly mentioned this more than fourteen centuries ago.

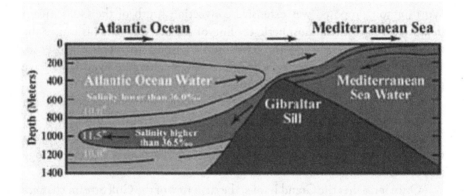

When the sea is mentioned in the Holy Qur'an, it is elucidated that there are two waters, which flow together, but there is a barrier that carries through between these two indeterminately. How could the Prophet have known this fact and conveyed it, except with the knowledge endowed by His Almighty Allah? Besides mentioning the details of these two waters, His Almighty's bestowals of the sea world have been enunciated. The pearl is just a citation of the variety of beautiful gems that we can gather from the depth of the sea; we also cherish the splendor and beauty of the coral reefs with the picturesque elegance in and around the depth of the sea world.

How could one imagine the awe-inspiring dazzle and display, elegance and enchantment, allure and attraction, splendor and seductiveness, and the pulchritude of the coral islands in the depth of the blues fourteen hundred years before?

Generally, when two oceans meet one another, their waters mingle, and the ratio of their salinity and temperatures reach an equilibrium. Yet, this is not the case with the Mediterranean Sea and the Atlantic Ocean or the Red Sea and the Indian Ocean. Although said oceans visually mix with each other, their water does not mingle due to a barrier in between them. This barrier is the force known as the "surface tension."

Freshwater Currents in the Sea

And Lord endowed a sway to aside
Two of the seas that stem in slide

One is delectable, luscious in taste
Other one salted and astringent in waste

But there's shawl mid them in slide

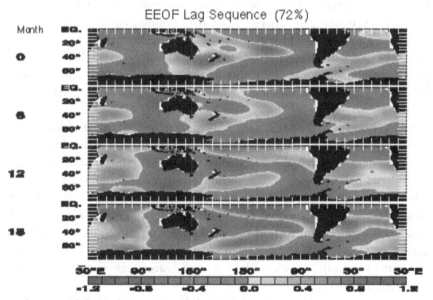

ENSO-Scale SST Anomalies

EEOF Lag Sequence (72%)

A deterrent defying their mix in glide (25:53)

Southern hemisphere SST anomalies were mapped every six months for a period of four years. This sequence is derived from observations made from 1982 to 1995 through empirical orthogonal function (EOF) analysis.

A newly discovered feature of the ocean circulation around Antarctica is the Antarctic Circumpolar Wave (ACW). This wave travels westward *against* the massive circumpolar current, in which it is embedded. The result is that the ACW travels eastward around Antarctica, but more slowly than the current, circling the globe each eight to nine years. The ACW has a *wave number* of two; there are two large regions of relatively warm water, each three to six thousand kilometers across, separated by two equally huge patches of cold water. The amplitude of the ACW is highest between 50° and 60° S.. It is not clear how these waves are triggered and maintained; the likely factors are the strong westerly winds in the region, the bottom topography, and the meridional temperature gradient in the upper ocean. There may be a connection with the El Niño Southern Oscillation, but it appears weak at best.

The ACW clearly affects the overlying atmosphere, in particular, the temperature and winds over the southern seas, but also the weather of the three southern continents bordering these seas. A warm region implies higher surface pressures and a tendency for long-wave ridging in the upper troposphere, resulting in drier-than-normal weather, especially just east of the ridge. In 1998, a cold region passed south of Tasmania. A warm pool should be to the south of Tasmania in 2000. A cold region implies a stronger meridional temperature gradient and therefore a stronger jet stream and more frontal activity. This implies more winter rain along the southern fringes of Australia.

The structure of the ACW suggests a four- to five-year cycle of rainfall. In coastal regions of the Australia Bight, and as far as the Australian Alps, there is some evidence of a four-year cycle in the annual rainfall, and the ACW cold phases correspond with the above-normal precipitation. In Southwest Australia, droughts recur every three to twelve years; the spectral variation shows a weak peak at a period of around four years. The ACW alternation may be more important than El Niño's in governing rainfall on the southern fringes of Australia. In New Zealand also temperatures and precipitation amounts in autumn and winter have a weak four- to six-year periodicity in sync with the ACW.

Thus precipitation onto Australia is affected by a changing combination of the ACW to the south, El Niño events to the east, and also the Indian Ocean Dipole (IOD) to the west. There are other variations in the North Atlantic and North Pacific, but they are too remote to have any effect.

The IOD is related to the northwest cloud bands (i.e., rain-producing disturbances that stretch across Australia from northwest to southeast). They are the chief cause of rain in the center of the country. The phenomenon involves warm water around Indonesia and New Guinea (especially in La Niña years), with colder water in the middle of the Indian Ocean, west of Australia.

A schematic display of the surface currents (solid curves) and deep currents (dashed curves) of the North Atlantic follows. The color of the curves depicts their approximate temperatures.

Credit: Jack Cook, Woods Hole Oceanographic Institution

Qur'anic Philosophy

Numerals and the Numerical System

When the Qur'an was revealed fourteen centuries ago, the number system known today did not exist. An alphabetic system was utilized whereby the letters of the Arabic, Hebrew, Aramaic, Greek, and Roman alphabets were used as numerals. The Roman numeral system (I, V, X, C, etc.) is still used extensively today. The number assigned to each letter is its "geometrical value."

Nineteen embraces the first numeral (1) and the last numeral (9), as if to proclaim Allah's attribute in the Qur'an (57:3) as the "first" and the "last."

"He is the First and the Last, and the Outward as well as the Inward; and is established on the throne of His Almighty."

Nineteen looks the same in Semitic and European languages. The components, (1) and (9), are the only numerals that look the same in these languages.

The word *Allah* (Allah) occurs in the Qur'an 2,698 times, and this number equals 19 x 142.

The sum of the verse numbers wherever the word *Allah* is found comes to 118,123 or 19 x 6,217.

The sum of all the occurrences of the word *Allah* in all the verses whose numbers are multiples of 19 (i.e., verses 19, 38, 57, 76, etc.) is 133, or 19 x 7.

The sum of all the occurrences of the word *Allah* in all the verses whose numbers are *not* multiples of 19 comes to 117,990, or 19 x 6,210.

The Surahs whose number of verses is divisible by 19 are Surahs 47, 82, 87, and 96. The word *Allah* occurs in these Surahs 27, 1, 1, and 1 times, respectively. By adding these sure numbers, plus the occurrences of the word *Allah*, the total is 342, or 19 x 18.

From the first set of Qur'anic initials (A. L. M. of Surah 2) to the last Crank initial (N. of Surah 68), the number of occurrences of the word *Allah* is 2,641, or 19 x 139.

Outside the initialed section of the Qur'an (Surah 1 on one side, and Surahs 69 through 114 on the other), the word *Allah* occurs 57 times, or 19 x3.

The Qur'anic message is that "Allah is 'One.'" The word for *one* (*Wahid*) occurs in the Qur'an twenty-five times, six of them do not refer to Allah, and the ones referring to Allah are precisely nineteen.

The number of occurrences of the word *Allah* from the beginning of the Qur'an to the end of Surah 9 (9:127) is 1,273, or 19 x 67.

The Surah number (9), plus its verses (127), plus the word *Allah* in Surah 9 (168), gives a total of 304, or 19x16.

The word *Allah* occurs in eighty-five Surahs; the sum of every Surah number, plus the number of the last verse with the word *Allah* equals 3,910 + 5,191= 9,101, or 19 x 479.

Take the eighty-five Surahs where the word *Allah* occurs. Add the number of every Surah, plus the number of verses from the first to the last verse where the word *Allah* occurs, and you get 3,910 + 4,260 = 8,170, or 19 x 430.

That figurative stamp of nineteen is secured on all its creation, as we'll encounter this figure in the holy text of the Qur'an, in chemistry, in our bodies, and in the whole cosmic order.

That's to affirm and conform that there couldn't be any change in the Scripture; for otherwise, it would divulge itself. Nineteen is the geometrical value of the word *one* in all the scriptural languages: Aramaic, Hebrew, and Arabic (please refer to the insert concerning the definition of geometrical value). The number 19, therefore, proclaims the First Commandment in all the scriptures: that there is only one Allah.

> Hear O Israel the Lord our Allah is one Lord and thou shalt love the Lord thy Allah with all thine heart, and with all thy soul, and with all thy might. (Deuteronomy 6:4–5)

> And Jesus answered him.
> The first of all the commandments is: Hear, O Israel; The Lord our God is one Lord:
> (Mark 12:29)

> Hear, O Israel; The Lord our Allah is one Lord
> And your Allah is one Allah: there is no Allah but He, most Gracious, most Merciful (2:163)

Hebrew	Arabic	Value
V	W	6
A	A	1
H	H	8
D	D	4
		19

As shown in the table above, the Aramaic, Hebrew, and Arabic alphabets used to double as numerals in accordance with a universally established system. The Hebrew word for one is *Vahd* (pronounced V-Ahad). In Arabic, the word for one is *Wad* (pronounced Wahid).

The Qur'anic dominant message is that there is only "one Allah." The word *one* occurs in the Qur'an twenty-five times. Six of these occurrences do not refer to Allah (one kind of food, one door, etc.). The remaining nineteen occurrences refer to Allah.

On a more celestial level, the earth, sun, and moon become aligned in the same relative position every nineteen years.

Halley's comet, a profound heavenly phenomenon, visits our solar system once every seventy-six years, which is 19 x 4.

Allah's stamp upon each of us is manifested in the medical fact that the human body has 209 bones, or 19 x 11.

Langman's Medical Embryology, by T. W. Sadler, is used as a textbook in most medical schools in the United States. On page 88 of the fifth edition, we read the following statement: "In general the length of pregnancy for a full term fetus is considered to be 280 days or 40 weeks after the onset of the last menstruation, or more accurately, 266 days or 38 weeks after fertilization." The numbers 266 and 38 are both multiples of 19 (19 x 14 and 19 x 2 respectively).

Surah Al Hadid (Iron)

الحديد Number 57 in the Qur'an

Iron (Fe) 57 is one of four stable isotopes.

Isotope	Half-Life
Fe-52	8.3 hours

Fe-54	Stable
Fe-55	2.7 years
Fe-56	Stable
Fe-57	Stable
Fe-58	Stable
Fe-59	54.5
Fe-60	1,500,000.0 years

Iron has four naturally occurring stable isotopes: ^{54}Fe, ^{56}Fe, ^{57}Fe, and ^{58}Fe. There are twenty-nine verses inside Surah 57.

Relation to Chemical Science: 2,957
Is the third ionization energy of Iron?

1st Ionization Energy	759.3 kJ/mol
2nd Ionization Energy	1,561 kJ/mol
3rd Ionization Energy	2,957 kJ/mol

In Arabic, iron is called *Hadiidh*. And the numerical value of *Hadid* is 26 (Ha + Dal + Ya + Dal = 8 + 4 + 10 + 4 = 26).

The atomic number of iron is 26.

There are 26 electrons in iron.

Iron *(Hadid)* is Surah 57. The numerical value of *Hadid* is 26, and 57 minus 26 is 31. The number of neutrons in Fe^{57} is 31.

Iso	NA	Half-life	DM	DE MeV	sDP
^{54}Fe	5.8 %	Fe is stable with 28 neutrons			
^{55}Fe	{syn.}	2.73 y	∈ cap-ture	0.231	^{55}Mn
^{56}Fe	91.72 %	Fe is stable with 30 neutrons			
^{57}Fe	2.2 %	Fe is stable with 31 neutrons			
^{58}Fe	0.28 %	Fe is stable with 32 neutrons			
^{59}Fe	{syn.}	44.503 d	B	1.565	^{59}Co
^{60}Fe	{syn.}	1.5E^6 y	β$^-$	3.978	^{60}Co

The word *iron* is found in verse number 25 in Surah 57.

The total number of verses in Surah 57 is 29.

The rest of it is 29 minus 25 which equals 4.

The number of energy levels in iron (Fe) is 4.

The number of stable isotopes of iron (Fe) is 4.

Iron has four naturally occurring stable isotopes: ^{54}Fe, ^{56}Fe, ^{57}Fe, and ^{58}Fe.

Remember that in Surah 57, there are 574 words in total.

Say that 57 is a Surah number and one of four stable isotopes and there are four energy levels in iron (Fe).

Letters (with *Hamza*) in Surah 57 is in total: 2,505 letters.

2505 – 574 = 1931

The number 19 is the figurative stamp of Al-Qur'an, Islam, and the universe.

The number of neutrons for Fe^{57} is 31.

The words in Surah 57 are in total 574.

The atomic mass average is 55.847.

55,847,574 = 19 x 2939346.0000

The melting point is 1808 K, 1535°C, 2795°F

574 1808 1535 2795 = 19 x 30220

575 042913305.0000

Boiling Point: 3023 K, 2750°C, 4982°F

3023 + 2750 + 4982 = 10755

1808 + 1535 + 2795 = 6138

The letters *(with Hamza)* in Surah 57 are in total: 2505.

10755 2505 6138 = 19 x 56606581902.0000

The boiling point (3023 K) minus the melting point (1808 K)

3023 2505 1808 = 19 x 15911844832.0000

574 words and 2505 letters in Surah 57

Boiling point 2750 C – melting point 1535 C

574 2505 2750 1535 = 19 x 30223711973765.0000

The four order numbers found by Dr. Peter Plichta (4, 26, and 3) play an interesting role also in the Qur'an in relation to its verses and to the number 19. The total sum of the verses of the first nineteen chapters is 2346, taking into consideration that Surah 9 has only 127 verses as proved in appendix 24 of the Authorized English translation of the Qur'an.

In the Qur'an, there are a total of 6234 numbered verses (counting the total verses of Surah 9 as 127 verses).

Dr. Peter Plichta discovered the reason that the eighty-one stable elements of chemistry must be divided into 4 x 19 and five separate elements. Nothing is responsible for it other than the universal nineteen code that the Lord Almighty set into these elements.

The number 81 is the complement of the number 19 (100-19 = 81). Nature and its chemical structure are mathematically organized.

He calculated that altogether, there are 243 isotopes or variations of elements. In other words, all natural existing stable chemical elements possess together 243 variations of elements. Dr. Peter Plichta was then interested in the relation of the fifty-seven double or multiple isotopes to the total number of isotopes (243). He found out that 243:57 = 4.263!

The relation of the 243 element variations to the fifty-seven elements, with which double or multiple variations occur, is indeed identical, as a sequence of numbers to the four meta-elements of his table. It is the same number that determines the relation of the eighty-one elements to their order number of 19.

This means that the elements 4, 2, 6, and 3 had been, therefore, separated in their order system from the remaining four characteristic classes deliberately and not at all by any chance.

This calculation becomes more astonishing, as there are 3 x 19 elements and 3 x 81 (243) isotopes (or additional neutron variations).

Who could have imagined a few decades ago that everything around us resembles an enormous computer that is well programmed and connected with finely regulated administration?

Wan Najm i Izza Hawwa
وَالنَّجمِ إذَاهَوٰى

In the very first verse of 53 Surah Al Najm, the Lord Almighty avows a star. In almost all the translations of the Holy Qur'an, the translation of the above text is: "Vow to the star that's setting in stride"

And later, in verse 49, the Lord Almighty asserts that he's Lord of Sirius, a star, so immense in qualities.

Al Najm (The Star) (53:1–14)
Vow to the star that's shifting in stance
Your friend isn't dissuaded or lost in trance
Nor does he deem to invoke on desire
Nothing but sent down to him for Vision to inspire

He's taught by one Mighty with Astral in Demand
Gifted with force of Sapience in Elegant Command

While he was in best cuff and glib of limit to diverge
Then he trends intimately next and nigh to converge

He's at a Ted of but two bows span in sway
So did Lord inspired His Savant to convey

The Prophet's heart lied not in sway
Will you dispute him, what he saw to convey

For indeed he saw him at a second dip and slide
Aside 'Astral O Esteemed Sidra none can pass in aside
Nigh to an Elegant Blissful Garden to abide

When! Super O Supreme Sidra awning a mystical shawl
His ken and view shared or skewed not, or getting to slant

For indeed he saw Great Symbols of His Peerless Lord (Sidra: Lote Tree)

By the star when it sets down: (changes its original position or shifting its stance)

But I didn't feel comfortable with this translation. I asked quite a few scholars for the other meaning of the text, because the following verses of the Holy Scripture clearly elucidate that this star is not an ordinary star in the cosmic order but has a very special property assigned with special duty like that Prophet Muhammad ᴾᴮᵁᴴ affirmed hither in vale.

Could it be? *"Shifting its original stance or position."*

I felt comfortable when I was told of this meaning of the text given in the stance and stanza of the Holy Scripture, for in the following verse, His Almighty asserts that your friend is not off his mind or dissuaded from the true path of the discipline. He had been amongst you for quite sometime enjoying a most dignified status and you found him to be "truthful" and "trustworthy." As to why he has, all of a sudden, turned toward some teachings that had never ever been asserted or affirmed before that stance, as to why he's defying your *Laat, Munaat, and Uzzaa* and proclaiming a new discipline, Islam.

He was there in the glorious ascent of Mee'raaj and alluring the bliss of the Almighty; at another moment, people were throwing trash on him, in the streets of Makkah, and in Taif, people were pelting him with stones.

"He is not irresponsible or gone crazy (*i.e.,* "... *letting him change his original most dignified status"*).

In the next few verses, His Almighty refers to His special messenger angel, Gabriel, who was assigned to pass the word of the Qur'an to Prophet Muhammad ᴾᴮᵁᴴ.

The messenger was very special among all the angels, who fell from his original exalted status down to earth to pass the word of the Lord Almighty to His savant.

In this context, consider the qualities of such a star that the Lord Almighty is referring to in this script.

Edwin Hubble set the stage for today's studies of galaxy formation when he discovered that the Milky Way was not alone. In the predawn hours of October 6, 1923, at the Mount Wilson Observatory in California, he photographed a fuzzy, spiral-shaped clump of stars known as M31, or Andromeda, which most astronomers assumed was part of the Milky Way. He soon realized that within the clump, he had found a tiny jewel, a star known as a Cepheid variable, whereas the Lord Almighty attributes the name

"Sirius" in the same Surah, verse 49, to this star of immense qualities. This type of star has a wonderful property. Its brightness waxes and wanes like clockwork, and the longer it takes to vary, the greater is the star's intrinsic brightness. That means the star can be used to measure cosmic distances.

This special star mentioned in verse 49, this Surah, *Cepheid* or *Sirius* is assigned as a gem and jewel of the cosmic order. It stays bright for quite sometime and then dwindles down from its original status of brightness to dimness. It stays in that order for quite sometime and then returns to its original status. This order of change in position or falling from the original status helps the cosmologists find the distances between different stars and galaxies. This notion helps to solve many riddles in the cosmic sway.

So, as this star is asserted as the gem and jewel of the cosmic order, Prophet Muhammad [PBUH] is the gem and jewel of humanity and Archangel Gabriel is the gem and jewel of the angels. Before closing the discussion, I would like to pen a few words in this context. The Lord Almighty enumerates innumerable qualities of "Cepheid" or "Sirius." There is a word for the future cosmologist to look into the other qualities of this star that could possibly prove a milestone in cosmic research.

Supersymmetry

Uncovering the "Al Meezan" Discipline of True Divine Measure or Supersymmetry: The Order of Measure

> Raised the heavens and set its confines
> That you may not transgress its defines
> Have *order of measure*[32] as in the cosmic role
> The earth He designated for the living soul   (Al Rahman)

The natural world around us abounds with the order of measure or symmetry "Al Meezan," order of measure (i.e., regularity and harmony, uniformity and balance, equilibrium and proportion approximate symmetries). The bilateral symmetry of most animals, the rotational symmetry of the sun, the fivefold symmetry of many starfish, and the manifold symmetries of fruit and flowers. Symmetry or the order of measure becomes so commonplace it takes something as extraordinary as a snowflake to awaken our awe.

The early verses of Surah Rahman refer to the creation of mankind, the galactic adoration with the sun, moon, and stars, and different cosmic orders. His Almighty refers to the strict discipline ordained in the creation of the universe and its various disciplines as just elucidated to forewarn man to appropriate such subjection in his conventional life as He has adduced from all things, from the tiniest particle-like atom to the incomprehensible cosmic order. This does not mean that the subjugation should only be left to the routine measure of the commodities, but rather a discipline of performance and rapprochement, disposition and demeanor, endowment and approximation should be venerated in all spheres of life. Everyone should observe a rightful injunction of discipline in communication and negotiation to redeem the legitimate command of discipline of His Almighty as in the creation of the universe and life. The pictures referring to the creation of the universe and the very early stages of the creation of a human fetus in the mother's womb ordain an undistorted discipline of measure and order of rule governing the whole. Before concluding this, I would like to give details of

---

32 *Al Meezan*, or the order of discipline

one of the most fascinating orders of discipline and veracities of measure in the divine order for a living being in the ecosystem.

Particle physics is replete with symmetries; in particular, the fundamental forces are dictated by symmetries called gauge symmetries. Specify the gauge group and the interaction strength and essentially all the behavior of the force is determined. For instance, electromagnetism involves a gauge symmetry group called U (1), which is the symmetry of rotations of a circle in a plane.

Much of fundamental physics, it turns out, amounts to uncovering other kinds of *Al Meezan* that characterize the universe. Einstein's theory of special relativity, for example, is a theory of the symmetries of empty space and time, which are governed by the Poincare group. (Groups are the mathematical structures that describe symmetries.) Effects, such as length contraction and time dilation, which flatten fast-moving clocks and make them run slow, are operations of the symmetry group, similar to rotating your point of view in space, but with time, as part of the rotation, you encounter a similar situation.

Conservation of the electric charge is a consequence of the U (1) symmetry. As proved by mathematician Emmy Noether in 1915, whenever the symmetry appears in mechanics, there is also a conservation law. The theorem works for both classical and quantum mechanics and tells us, for instance, that the law of conservation of energy follows from symmetry with respect to translations in time. That is, energy is conserved because the equations of motion yesterday are the same as those today. The conservation of momentum (symmetry under translation in space) and angular momentum (symmetry under rotations) are similar.

Finally, take the very definition of a particle in quantum field theory; this direct linkage of symmetry to the most basic structure of matter and force is what requires electrons and other particles to have an intrinsic quantity of angular momentum known as spin. A particle's mass is also a symmetry-related label.

Compared to the symmetries that govern the universe, snowflakes start to seem quite terrestrial.

A definite order of measures is a remarkable symmetry. In elementary particle physics, it interchanges particles of completely dissimilar types, the kind called fermions, such as electrons, protons, and neutrons, which make up the material world, and those called bosons (such as photons), which generate the forces of nature. Fermions are inherently the individualists and loners of the quantum particle world; no two fermions ever occupy the same quantum state. Their aversion to close company is strong enough to hold up a neutron star against collapse even when the crushing weight of gravity has overcome every other force of nature. Bosons, in contrast, are convivial copycats and readily gather in identical states. Every boson in a particular state encourages more of its species to emulate it. Under the right conditions, bosons form regimented armies of clones, such as the photons in a laser beam or the atoms in superfluid helium 4.

Yet somehow in the mirror of supersymmetry, standoffish fermions look magically like sociable bosons, and vice versa.

At least that is the theory elementary particle theorists have studied that holds the key to the next major advance in our understanding of the fundamental particles and forces.

In the 1980s, nuclear theorists proposed that super-violent collisions were not necessarily the only way to see supersymmetry; they predicted that a different form of supersymmetry could exist in certain atomic nuclei. Here, too, the symmetry relates what in physics are quite dissimilar objects: nuclei with even numbers of protons and neutrons and those with odd numbers.

Symmetries play major roles throughout physics, the basis of our understanding of the whole cosmic order. All ordinary symmetries respect the distinction between bosons and fermions. Supersymmetry theories incorporate powerful mathematical properties that interchange bosons and fermions. Such theories may be crucial for deeply understanding particle physics, but experimenters have not yet detected the supersymmetry of elementary particles.

In atomic nuclei, protons and neutrons each form pairs that behave like composite bosons. Nuclei thereby form four distinct classes (even-even, even-odd, odd-even, and odd-odd) depending on whether the protons and neutrons can each completely pair off. Physicists predicted that a variant of supersymmetry should relate a magic square of four nuclei of these types. Experimenters have now confirmed that prediction.

Supersymmetry (Strict Order of Measure) in Particle Physics

Symmetries form the foundation of the standard model. Electrons and electron neutrinos, for example, are related by symmetry, which also relates "up quarks" to "down quarks." A different manifestation of the same symmetry associates Z and W particles. Gluons are all related by a color symmetry, which also relates different colors of quarks. All these symmetries relate fermions to fermions and bosons to bosons.

This elementary particle supersymmetry is also intimately related to the symmetries of space-time that underlie Einstein's theory of special relativity. That is, supersymmetry extends those symmetries. The supersymmetry of nuclei is fundamentally different because it does not have that connection to space-time. The common ground between these two applications of supersymmetry in physics is that they both rely on super algebra.

The Order of Discipline in the Atmosphere

Every drop of water in the top one hundred meters of the ocean contains thousands of free-floating microscopic flora called phytoplankton. These single-celled organisms including diatoms and other algae inhabit three-quarters of the earth's surface, and yet they account for less than 1 percent of the six hundred billion metric tons of carbon contained within its phytosynthetic biomass. But being small does not stop this virtually invisible forest from making a bold mark on the planet's most critical natural cycles.

Arguably one of the most consequential activities of marine phytoplankton is their influence on the climate. Until recently, however, few researchers appreciated the degree to which these diminutive ocean dwellers can draw the greenhouse gas carbon dioxide (CO_2) out of the atmosphere and store it in the deep sea. New satellite observations and extensive oceanographic research projects are finally revealing how sensitive these organisms are to changes in global temperatures, ocean circulation, and nutrient availability.

Exploring how human activities can alter phytoplankton's impact on the planet's carbon cycle is crucial for predicting the long-term ecological balancing effects of such actions.

Climate Regulators

Evincing Ecological Balance and the Discipline of Measure

The rapid life cycles of marine phytoplankton transfer heat-trapping carbon dioxide (CO_2) from the atmosphere and upper ocean to the deep sea, where the gas remains sequestered until currents return it to the surface hundreds of years later.

If all of the world's marine phytoplankton were to die today, the concentration of CO_2 in the atmosphere would rise by two hundred parts per million or 35 percent in a matter of centuries.

Adding certain nutrients to the ocean surface can dramatically enhance the growth of phytoplankton and thus their uptake of CO_2 via photosynthesis.

The creation of the sun and moon are cited as very special favors with special citation of all their celestial movements in a perfect order.

The stars and the trees all set to adore

He has lifted the sky that looks so azure
Nicely ordained their magnitude in place
That you may not transgress in pace
But observe each of your living subjugation
Lawfully to the discipline of its perpetuation
Thoroughly, as you perceive in cosmic array
Strictly measure observed by the nature to obey (Al Rahman)

Stars and Trees Beseech His Adulation. Who could have known this fact except His Almighty?

Today, modern research shows that plants can communicate with each other. Ilya Raskin, a botanist at Rutgers University, shows how he and his colleagues demonstrated this in an experiment. Dozens of tobacco plants, picked because of their potent chemical response to a particular virus, were placed in two airtight chambers. Tubes carried air between the chambers. The scientists injected the plants in one chamber with the virus. Within two days, those infected emitted a volatile chemical into the air, stimulating the plants in the second chamber to produce chemicals in their leaves that protected them against the virus. This experiment followed the model that guides most scientific research today: develop hypotheses, run tests, and produce data that other researchers can confirm or challenge by conducting similar experiments. Until recently, botanists did not understand chemicals like those produced by the tobacco plants. But now it is known that plants produce chemicals that defend them against disease and also help them propagate. Knowledge about such chemicals could lead to the elaboration of inured plants and to changes in our basic understanding of how they function. "But there is still a huge amount going on in plants that we do not understand," Ruskin said. Such vast gaps in our knowledge exist in virtually all branches of science.

Likewise, Kathy Sawyer shows in *New Light on the Universe* that most of the mass that fills the universe has yet to be located. Now an expanding universe and the big bang theory are cornerstones of cosmology, the part of astronomy that studies the origins of the universe and its time-space relationships. Advances in genetics and astronomy are driven by the number-crunching capabilities of faster computers and by improved imaging techniques that make microscopes and telescopes more powerful. Such tools enable scientists to see things they have never seen before or even considered possible. Genetic researchers can examine objects that are only a millionth of an inch in diameter, while astronomers can see galaxies perhaps eleven billion light-years away. It is easy to forget how revolutionary modern science really is. Just a few hundred years ago, in the sixteenth and seventeenth centuries, most Europeans thought that the sun revolved around the earth and the four elements—air, fire, water, and earth—created and defined all life. Scholars mostly parroted what they had learned from classical writers like Aristotle, who believed, among other things, that the earth was enclosed by celestial spheres where nothing ever changed and everything was always perfect. Then pioneers such as Galileo Galilee and Isaac Newton demonstrated that experimentation and analysis could best explain the nature of the world. Why did not the scientific revolution (a phrase that did not come into popular usage until the mid-twentieth century) take place much earlier? Ancient Greek mathematicians and astronomers had calculated the circumference of the earth, charted the stars, and figured the distance to the moon. By AD 1100, Chinese scholars had developed a seismograph, a magnetic compass, and the concept of infinite empty space. Why did not the scientific revolution occur in either of those places? Among the best guesses so far is that not until the sixteenth century did European scientists begin to embrace quantification, the use of mathematics to measure the results of experiments.

One of the most significant effects of the scientific revolution has been population growth. Until modern science brought sewer systems and immunization in the nineteenth century, about half of all children died before age five. By the end of the nineteenth century, childhood death rates had fallen and human population began to surge. With advances in medicine, the population continues growing and further challenging our ability to live in ordained discipline and harmony "the order of measure" with nature.

Will scientific progress continue? Or will science reach some limit like the Pillars of Hercules, the classical and medieval symbol for what lies at the edge of the known? On these gates, according to legend, was written, *"Ne plus ultra,"* meaning "No further." The Pillars of Hercules for modern science may become moral and spiritual. Scientists and society will have to decide how much to change the genetic structures of plants and animals and whether to fiddle with the very genes that make us human. In the meantime, the achievements and challenges of modern science propel us further into the unknown. But the Qur'an clearly enunciates in many places and invites the attention of the men of wisdom to scrutinize the details of the cosmic order and our living planet, this blue pearl of the universe, and it will open new perspectives of exploration, study, and scrutiny to affirm more ratiocinative assertions, before the modern scientific evolution.

Raised the cosmos and fixed *to sustain*
That you may not transgress *its domain*:
(Al Rahman 7)

The universal space contains all the laws of the universe (inertia, gravity, quantum mechanics, biogenetics, electromagnetic emission, the atomic laws, evolution, and whatnot). Every cubic centimeter of space from one end of the universe to the other is filled with a definite law that makes the universe and everything in it work. These natural laws in turn created space and determined the size of the universe. Where the laws end, the universe ends—but it still continues to grow at the speed of light.

If the laws only extended outward, in all directions, just one meter, this would be the size of the universe. There would be no space beyond this sphere of influence. It could not extend one bit further. The laws of universal space precisely determine and control all actions and interactions of matter and energy, within the universe, from the tiniest space between the subatomic particles to the vast expanse of the universe. The laws of the Almighty created universal space; without its laws, the universe would not exist.

Energy is nothing without matter to push around. Matter has no mass without energy. Together, under the absolute rule of the laws of space, they create this complex, dynamic universe we live in. Even if there were no matter or energy in universal space, it would still exist as long as divine laws existed, although it would be rather pointless.

I cannot bring myself to believe that all these exquisite, impeccable, tangled, and all-pervading laws of nature just happened to come into being without some infinitely wise and all-powerful reality creating them. I am talking about natural laws of the universe, and there is the all-powerful reality, His Almighty Allah, behind all these philosophies of mankind, other living beings, and the cosmic order.

The universe is finite with regard to size and time. Where the influence of the law of universal space does not hold, the universe also ends. Beyond the laws of universal space, neither matter nor energy can remain, nor can the smallest fraction of measurement. Is there an ultimate barrier, the boundary of the universe? *The lower sky is the limit.* His Almighty proclaims, "I am the owner of the entire sweep and span of the vistas," to which there is no end. The universe began when His Almighty created its laws, perhaps as long as a trillion light-years ago.

The laws of space govern everything within the universe. They do not go on forever, nor do they gradually weaken and dissipate. They are either completely in force, or they do not exist at all. Where the laws do not apply, neither energy nor matter can exist; therefore, there is no space. The boundary of the universe is not a wall; it is simply where the laws of the universe end (details in "The Fate of the Universe").

The universe is shaped like a hollow sphere with nature's laws governing and unifying everything within the sphere. The laws of nature create space, as we know it. Outside the sphere, beyond the boundary of the universe, nothing can exist. It is completely devoid of all energy and matter. Beyond the boundary, the laws of universal space do not exist; therefore, nothing can exist, not even the space itself.

Stars and planets could not form since there would be no mass or gravity to hold them together. A light ray could not travel in this region because there are no laws to guide it. There would be no possible way to determine if this region ended just beyond our reach or extended out to infinity.

In the text, His Almighty, soon after elucidating His discipline of cosmic order that He has organized so ubiquitously in a fascinating discipline of measure, advises man to observe the same in his daily routine and not to dissuade the veracity of the true order of measure.

Extremophiles

The question rose repeatedly, ad nauseam, in my mind as to how one would endure the extreme temperatures of Hell. Recent studies reveal very fascinating discoveries in this direction.

They thrive on boiling heat, freezing cold, radiation, and toxic chemicals, and they have triggered a revolution in biology.

This is the abyss, which the convicts had defied
In feral simmering water, they linger to abide
(Al Rahman 43, 44)

It's hard to conceive of a more unfavorable place on earth than the hydrothermal outlets that pop up on the ocean floor. These rifts and slits in the sea's undersurface disgorge water superheated by rising magma to as high as 400° and are adulterated with toxic materials, such as hydrogen sulfide, cadmium, arsenic, and lead. Yet notwithstanding these virulent surroundings, life not only perseveres but also prospers in the form of communities of microbes that thrive on the poison and multiply in temperatures that could hard-boil an egg.

The frozen continent of Antarctica is almost equivalently pestilent, but at the other end of the temperature scale. Penetrate into the ice cap a kilometer, then another, and you reach, senselessness, a body of water known as Lake Vostok that approximates Lake Ontario in size. While scientists haven't yet worked with a drill into the lake itself, they have plucked up samples of frozen lake water clinging to the bottom of the ice cap that accommodate unambiguously the indication of microbial DNA. Although it floats near the freezing point, cut off from light and outside nutrients, Lake Vostok abounds with microorganisms. "Nobody," marvels John Priscu, a Montana State University microbiologist, who has studied the samples, "thought there could be any life down there."

Unprecedented as these conclusions might once have seemed, they have become almost commonplace. In the past few months alone, researchers have extracted colonies of microbes that thrive at 58°C in an underground hot spring in Idaho and found others eating into volcanic rock 366 meters beneath the seafloor. Over the past few years, in fact, scientists have been finding life in all sorts of places where biology textbooks say it should not exist. Microorganisms are thriving in thermal springs in Yellowstone National Park and in pristine veins of water 3 kilometers underground in South Africa. They are living in solid rock at the bottom of deep mines. They are growing in brine pools five times saltier than the ocean, in tiny pockets of liquid embedded in sea ice and in places with toxic levels of heavy metals, acids, and even radiation.

Taken one at a time, these creatures formally known as extremophiles, or lovers of extreme environments, are fascinating curiosities. Collectively, they have triggered a scientific revolution, forcing researchers to rethink biology's most basic assumptions about how life began.

Extremophiles also represent a biotech bonanza, pumping out unique substances that could be invaluable in all sorts of industrial and medical applications. Polymerase chain reactions (PCR), for example, the DNA-augmenting methods used most famously in the O. J. Simpson assassination litigation, takes advantage of an enzyme manufactured by Yellowstone extremophiles.

But the consequences of these microbes goes to a much greater extent. While some extremophiles are bacteria, some are so different from any other single-celled organism that scientists have created a new biological kingdom, called Archaea (from archaic), to accommodate them. As the name suggests, Archaea may be similar to the very first organism that populated the earth billions of years ago. The implication is that life on our planet may first have arisen, not in a warm tidal pool as Darwin and others theorized, but under conditions of sulfurous, searing heat.

Finally, there is a cosmic dimension to these bugs. So called exobiologists and astrobiologists, who speculate about life beyond earth, have long assumed that liquid water is a minimum requirement for existence. But if that water can range from frigid to boiling and if burial underground is not a problem, then it's not crazy to think that life exists in the permafrost beneath the surface of Mars, or in the ice-capped ocean that may encircle Jupiter's moon Europa, or in the seas that may exist on Saturn's moon Titan. Indeed, NASA considers extremophiles so relevant to its search for life in the universe that in 1997, it created the Astrobiology Institute at its Ames Research Center near San Francisco, which is devoted in part to the study of these peculiar organisms.

And indeed, life began to turn up just about everywhere scientists looked. Geologists had been arguing since the 1920s, in fact, that chemical contaminants found in crude oil suggested that some sort of life was thriving underground. They were not taken seriously until the 1980s, though, when Department of Energy scientists realized that if subsurface microbes really did exist, they might play a key role in regulating the purity of groundwater. So they began digging boreholes at DOE sites in South Carolina and Washington State.

Sure enough, they found bugs living more than 460 meters down, cut off, like their ocean vent cousins, from any conceivable contact with the surface. No one knows how deep the biosphere extends, but Tullis Onstott, a geologist at Princeton, has followed the trail three kilometers straight down. He began exploring South African gold mines in 1998, and so far, he and his international colleagues have pulled out scores of heat-tolerant, hydrogen-eating bugs from subsurface water.

"It's also clear that there are plenty of surprises left," says Priscu. "In the '70s, when I first got interested in this field, many colleagues called claims of life in extreme environments 'hand waving.'" Since then, he and the other extremologists have found life inside glaciers, at the bottom of mines, in searing heat, freezing cold, crushing pressure, and lethal toxicity. And that is after exploring only a tiny fraction of the planet. What they have discovered so far has transformed biology. What they will find next is anybody's guess.

What the Bugs Can Do for Us:

The discovery that life can thrive under horrific conditions is a major scientific advance. But it could also turn out to be hugely profitable. Extremophiles survive by manufacturing all sorts of novel molecules. Some digest harsh chemicals; some protect DNA against destruction by radiation; some stave off searing heat or freezing cold. Entrepreneurs are racing to turn these molecules into products, just as was done in the 1980s with *Thermus aquaticus*, the Yellowstone bug exploited in the PCR technique widely used today to analyze DNA.

San Diego-based Diversa Corp. is one of the most active prospectors. The company has searched for useful microbes at geothermal and hydrothermal vents, in acidic soils and alkaline springs, in marine sediments at industrial sites, and all over Antarctica, among other places. Eventually, says Diversa CEO Jay Short, they want to sample every portion of the globe. Any profits would be shared with the country of origin.

The company already has several extremophile-derived products on the market and plans to launch five more this year. One is an enzyme from a deep ocean vent bacterium that improves the synthesis of high-fructose corn syrup (used as a sweetener in soft drinks). Another will be used in genetic research. Yet another will make animal feed more nutritious.

Diversa has fourteen more products in the pipeline that it hopes could be used for everything from manufacturing pulp and paper to processing food, generating biofuel, and synthesizing drugs. While most of the activity thus far has been focused on the enzymes the microbes churn out, the bugs themselves are also being eyed for commercial exploitation.

And this is just one company. Extremophiles have already rewritten biology textbooks; they may soon be rewriting profit statements as well.

His Almighty adorned the sky with innumerable multiverses with galaxies, and each galaxy is studded with billions of stars. The earth abounds with phylum and granum, fauna and flora, with fascinating floral wreaths and the filigree of trees of diverse sets, sorts, and species.

Just consider the supreme unifying force and the systemically organized way of the universe with a definite law governing the whole of the cosmic order.

It is important to keep in mind, however, that the exquisite diversity in our mitochondrial code that allows us to trace these events is a classic exception that proves the rule. In most of the rest of our genes, 99.9 percent of them, every human being alive is exactly the same. Moreover, most of the variations in the remaining one-tenth of a percent do not bunch up into geographic regions or racial groups but instead are spread around the globe. Put another way, the snips and snippets of code that taken together make one person unique are scattered about in other unique genomes all over the world, binding all of us in a splendid tangle of interrelationship.

Genomically speaking, even bacteria are our cousins in code. The last and most powerful secret revealed by our genes, in fact, is the indisputable unity of everything alive.

From this message we conclude that the men with u nforgivable deeds shall be abididng in the most unfortunate places and forced to thrive on the most toxic foods in the extreme temperatures of Hell but also shall be able to communicate and be able to perform certain errands as well.

For Those Who Fear Facing His Almighty Lord

How would you cherish the beauty of the whole until you strive to reach the subliminal image of the whole? And that is only possible when you scarify the part of your whole (i.e. sleep) to adore the bounty of the Lord, His Almighty's resplendent excellence and elegance, illustriousness and ingeniousness. The quintessence of sacramental rites is the divine speech for which we behold the beauty. The divine names revealed imply a divine presence, which becomes operative to the extent that the name takes possession of the mind that supplicates it. Man cannot concentrate or focus on the "infinite" itself.

When the distinctive favored name is recited, where the form of the name has assimilated very intellective prominence, the divine essence of the name evinces fortuitously, for this revered form escorts to nothing outside itself. It has no assertive and assured consanguinity but with its essence, and in conclusion, its confines are glowing in that nature. Thus melding with the divine name complements union with His Almighty. Since His Almighty has made us in His own image, we should be able to discern Him in the depths of our minds instead of staring into the void or starting with metaphysical abstractions or other verbal distinctions. The moment we listen to the phrase, "His Almighty is Light, Sublime, Inspiring, Imposing, Majestic, Exalted, Virtuous, and Truth," we are vanquished in the beauty of it.

When a man has always made a routine the utterance of His Almighty's blessed name, "Allah," whose company is he keeping? The proximity is that of Allah, but at times, the fleshly stipulations of the body supervene, and one gets inadvertently indulged in misappropriation, but in determination to strive for His vindication, he seeks His Almighty's forgiveness with regret and remorse, compunction and contrition, submissiveness and subservience because nobody can avoid the fleshly demands of the body like sensual regalements and glutinous flavor. Exoneration is His favored gesture, if we sincerely beg His favor at each moment of our sustenance. And when you especially aspire to sustain and succor the company with the benison, blessing, and benefaction of His Almighty, the late hours of the night is the best time to converse with Him directly without any encumbrance and transitional reference. Sit comfortably on the prayer rug after ablution or on any immaculate place. Look toward your heart and start reciting the most venerated name "Allah" as you exhale. After a few moments, you will experience an echo from the core of your heart that will couple you in your beatified monologue. After a few minutes of true meditation, the vistas of the whole will start opening up, and you will feel an enchantment, elation, and exaltation, calmness and composure, appeasement and affiliation never experienced before in life. At that moment, have a sincere desire in the niche and kernel of your inaccessible self without interrupting the dazzling utterance. Be convinced that you will be blessed with your cherished aspiration if it is in your finest consequence, because His Almighty has created us a part of the whole and not as an unconstrained being. And to appropriate in the whole, one has to be comfortable as part of the whole. Figuratively speaking, if everybody enters upon demanding to thaw the highest point, how could that be possible, but to aspire for, wish and want for something before His Almighty is not proscribed.

When we actually discern the ecstasy through vision while recounting the Holy Name, we instinctively feel that His Almighty Allah can bestow us the significance and consequence, eminence and prominence of our lives. This evanescent and fleeting illumination or edification is gone when we totter and stumble back to our run-of-the-mill frame of mind with our brains obsessed with the conventional earthly seductive femme fatale and possessions. Try as we might, the same pacification and peacefulness, the same moment of inarticulate and reticent aspiration cannot be accomplished.

Yes! The bliss of solitude, the inner murmur of fortitude, and the vision of gratitude can only be cherished and perceived with persistence, patience, and perseverance in obeisance with His Almighty.

All things that participate in anything, which is common to them all, move toward that which is of the same kind with themselves. Everything that is earthly turns toward the earth, everything that is liquid flows together, and everything that is of an aerial kind does the same, so that they require something to keep them in bits and pieces and the utilization of energy.

Correspondingly, then, everything that partakes in the common reasonable nature moves in like manner toward that which is of the same kind with itself. The ultimate objective of all reasoned doctrine is to live conformably to nature, both a man's own nature and the nature of the universe. Prophet Mohammed ᴾᴮᵁᴴ ordained living according to nature in the light, track, and trail of true faith. If we look at history, we find what the Greek philosophers meant when they spoke in a style and guise of eloquence, not imprecise or inconclusive, but distinct, unbiased, and undistorted.

Mankind has a mortal or earthly, brainy and virtuous disposition appropriate for determined application, and on the whole, man accomplishes these uses during his stay before he leaves this vale. So the community carries through to luxuriate. The social state is evidently the natural state of man, the state for which his nature implements him, and a community surrounded by incalculable aberrations still survives. And conceivably, we may say that the narrative of the former and our current enlightenment gives us a rational confidence that its disorderliness will dwindle and that sequence of its executive regulation may be aggrandized and resolutely instituted.

We cannot envision how the command of the cosmos is continued. We cannot even visualize how our own vivacity from day to day is held up, nor how we accomplish the most sophisticated activities of the body, nor how we develop and conceive and course, although we understand many of the basic factors. The fundamental nature tries to gain the mortal perception when we behold on every side the divine endowments from a speck to the vast expanse of the universe, and instinctively, we proclaim the benevolence and beneficence, magnanimity and munificence of His Almighty.

Which of the favors, you may deny of your Most
Exalted O Elevated Lord?
Blessed Be Thy Name, O Great Grand O Glorious Lord
(Al Rahman)

Faith and the Physical Being

For virtue only of all human things
Takes her reward not from the hands of others
Virtue herself rewards the toil of virtue
(Unknown Greek poet wrote long ago)

The Holy Scriptures are not the only mathematically composed creations of the Lord Almighty where the number nineteen is the common denominator as discussed in detail in the preceding chapters. It is overwhelming when Galileo made his eminent statement: "Mathematics is the language with which God created the universe."

A plethora of scientific findings have now shown that the number nineteen symbolizes God's signature upon His particular innovation in the cosmic order. This divine stamp appears throughout the universe identifying God's work in much the same manner as the signatures of Michelangelo and Picasso identify their works. For example:

The sun, the moon, and the earth become aligned in the same relative positions once every nineteen years.

1. Halley's Comet, a greatly reflective heavenly phenomenon, visits our solar system every seventy-six years (19 x 4).
2. The Lord Almighty's stamp on you and me is discernible in the fact that the human body contains 209 bones (19 x 11).
3. *Langman's Medical Embryology*, by T. W. Sadler, is used as a textbook in most of the medical schools in the USA. On page 88 of the fifth edition, we read the following statement: "In general, the length of pregnancy for a full term fetus is considered to be 280 days or 40 weeks after onset of the last menstruation, or more accurately, 266 days or 38 weeks after fertilization." The numbers 266 and 38 are both multiples of nineteen.

A complex mathematical code, far beyond the ability of human discernment, has been revealed that's deeply insinuated in the stance and stanza of the Holy Scripture; like an ancient time capsule, it stayed veiled until our knowledge got fairly advanced, enough to decode its niceties. Computers deciphered this code.

The discovery of mathematically coded scripture assures us that the verses, words, letters, and all parameters of the original scripture were written down in accordance with an intricate pattern that is clearly superhuman.

The first discovery of this mathematical composition was in the eleventh century by Rabbi Judah the Pious. In a book entitled *Studies in Jewish Mysticism*,[33] Joseph Dan writes that Rabbi Judah and his disciples developed a theory that the words and letters of the various prayers are not accidental, nor are they only vehicles for their literal meaning. Their order, especially their numbers, reflect a mystical harmony, a sacred divine rhythm. This mystical harmony can be discovered in historical events, directed by the Lord Almighty; in nature, especially in the miraculous occurrences directly influenced by divine powers; and first and foremost, in the Bible. According to Rabbi Judah and the Ashkenazi Hasidic school in general, there can be nothing accidental in the Bible, not even the forms of letters, the punctuation, the vocalization, or especially the numerical structures as in the number of certain letters, consonants, or vowels in a certain verse; the number of words from the same root; the number and variety of divine names in a certain period; the absence of one or more letters from a chapter; and many other elements of the Scriptures besides their content.

Nine centuries after Rabbi Judah stated these elements of the code, the computer has demonstrated each of them. The original scripture was mathematically composed in a way that encodes and guards every single one of its parameters. If the scripture were to be tampered with, the code would be broken.

Joseph Dan writes that Rabbi Judah was critical of the French and British Jews when they altered the morning prayer by adding a few words.[34] Rabbi Judah pointed out that such an addition destroyed the numerical structure of the prayer and rendered it utterly nullified. He maintained that it is the "numerical combination," rather than the "meaning" of the words that influenced the needed contact between the worshipper and the Lord Almighty.

The people (Jews) in France made it a custom to add in the morning prayer, the words, *"Ashrei temimei derekh"* (meaning "Blessed are those who walk the righteous way"), and the rabbi wrote that they were completely and utterly wrong. It is all gross falsehood, because there are only nineteen times that the Holy Name is mentioned (in that portion of the morning prayer) ...

33 Association for Jewish Studies, 1982, p. 91.
34 Ibid., 88.

and similarly, you find the word "Elohim" nineteen times in the text of Ve-'elleh shemot ... Similarly, you find that Israel is called "sons" nineteen times, and there are many other examples. All these sets of nineteen are intricately intertwined, and they contain many secrets and esoteric meanings, which are contained in more than eight large volumes. Therefore, anyone who has the fear of the Lord Almighty in him will not listen to the words of the Frenchmen who add the verse, *"Ashrei temimei derekh,"* and blessed are the righteous who walk in the paths of God's Torah, for according to their additions, the Holy Name is mentioned twenty times, and this is a great mistake.

Furthermore, in this section, there are 152 words (19 x 8), but if you add, *"Ashrei temimei derekh,"* there are 158 words. This is nonsense, for it is a great and hidden secret why there should be 152 words ... but it cannot be explained in a short treatise ... In order to understand this religious phenomenon, we have to take the basic contention of this treatise exactly as it is stated: every addition or omission of a word, or even of a single letter, from the Sacred text of the prayers destroys the religious meaning of the prayer as a whole and is to be regarded as a grave sin. A sin could result in eternal demise from the truth, for him who commits it.[35]

The Lord Almighty as such, that is to say, Allah, envisaged, not as He manifested Himself in a specific way at a certain time, away in time or place of history and in as much as He is what He is and also as He originates and divulges by Himself. The Lord Almighty is also shaping an authenticity, materialization, and reintegration, whereas man is theoretical proposition, excellent discernment, and free choice. Man thus appears a preference as a dual repository made for the perfect faith, as religion comes to fill that repository primarily with the precision of the perfection and secondarily with the law—or the actuality and law.

The former is complementary to the discernment and subsequent to the choice.

The faith is indomitable to exterminate skepticism and vacillation and to have firm determination with no consternation. The notion of fortitude does not do away with the idea of independence of choice. Human supremacy, however, is appropriate in the sense that it is somewhat immaculate and well accomplished. Man is an a priori choice. Obviously, the discernment is not contradicted, but it is taken into attention only as an appearance of choice in the realm of the truth of intelligence.

Imagine an effulgent and sparkling summer sky and suppose simple people who stare at it, looking into it as their dream of the afterworld. Now assume that it were conceivable to convey these simple people into the

35 Ibid., 88–89.

caliginous, unlit, and frosty bottomless pit of the galaxies and nebulae with their awesome and stunning stillness. In this abyss, all too many of them would lose their faith, and this is exactly what eventuates as an outcome of neoteric science, both to the educated and to the immolation of popularization. Most men do not know, and if they could know it, why should they be called on to believe it?

Is this blue sky, a utopian deception, a visual blooper postulated by the sight of an extraterrestrial void, however, a convincing and cogent portraiture of the divine marvel of origin dappled with silver-gilt clouds overwhelming the shimmering and glimmering innumerable galaxies of stars? To remain devoted to our element of actuality, we may not be forfeited or transgressed by our deceptive approach with satisfactory action to the purpose in an incontestable intellect. It is the true sense of discernment that transforms the confidence of the simple and does rejuvenate the attainable to the immaculate understanding. But it is also an inquest in conformity to the instantaneous attribute of semblance of the bottomless pit of ubiquitous demonstration of this cosmic array whose confines indefinitely elude our ordinary experience. Finally, the extraterrestrial space conformably casts back concern to our ultimate demise—death—because the *soul* or the *efflux* is neither ours nor within our control.

There is progressive transformation from the geocentric to the heliocentric worldview. We are endeavoring hard to find a new synthesis of science and spirit because there is a point of prudence outside the inconsistency of deception, but with truth in the faith, life can be put back together again. Spiritually, however, the center is there, where the sight is. Stand on a height and view the horizon. The unprecedented expansion of the horizon cleanses the doors of the perception of our creation and that of the universe. Anyone who has had an experience of mystery knows that there is a dimension of the universe that is not that which is available to his senses. We live in the recognition of something there, which is much greater than the human dimension.

The outward prominence of our mortal invulnerability into a precipitous space and an incomprehensible mysterious world can only be rationalized in a numinous sense, since we must have a taste of death *as a spiritual being* before we die. What we would chiefly call to someone's attention here is the refutation of assuming the bare actuality of unbiased significance. Science maintains the capability and the claim to contort fables and religion, and it is thus some kind of higher experience, which is smothering the truth besides edifying the world. I have tried to touch at this point the spiritual or sensory order of the divine presence with two manifestations: the intelligence within us, which is the core of true discernment, and the cognition of His Almighty's manifestations displayed around us in a most fascinating order and accord.

Human sovereignty in decision making is appropriate in the sense that it is somewhat perfect. Man is the a priori choice; obviously, the discernment is not disregarded. It is taken into attention only as an appearance of choice; man is choice, and in man, choice is discernment. When something goes wrong with the choice, discernment is also contorted, in the reasoning that in no way could it set the choice to right. Therefore, heavenly interference is imperative, the sacrament, the meditation.

Certainly, there can be real judgment while one is taking a wrong course not intentionally but out of his wrong perception of the events, so the discernment is assimilated with cowardly and spineless decisions. Being nothing in itself, it needs the guidance of the soul. But in any case, we must not lose sight of what discernment is in itself, nor give credence to the work composed of stupid mistakes that could be the turnout of hearty or even better discernment. Discernment au fond constitutes a temperament of trustworthiness. Now, the accomplished innocence of discernment could be the outlandish aspect of negligence or distrust. Some will say that science has long since shown the divergence of the revelations, which arise, as some would reason, from our ingrained yearning as bashful and discontented discernment.

All this is the imperative part of the agile brainy competence to discern and perceive to whom these convictions and preferences give eminence. What is death? And the fact is if a man looks at the philosophy of death himself by the distillation capability and deliberates into the details bouncing back from this diverging world, he finds a concrete and lucid answer to this big query. All things, which present to the imagination, man will then consider it to be nothing else than an operation of His Almighty. This, however, is not only an operation of nature, but it is also a thing that is conducive to the purpose of nature. To observe, too, how man comes near to the deity and what part of man is so disposed.

If you then seek the truth in discernment, you will not seek to gain a victory by every possible means, and when you have found truth, you need not cower or fear being crushed. What frivolous talk is this? How can I any longer set assertion to the right standard of conduct or faith, if I am not content with being what I am, but am all aflutter about what I am supposed to be?

The Almighty has made all things in the world, nay, the world itself, free from encumbrances and immaculate and its parts for the use of the whole. No other living being is accomplished of comprehending His administration thereof, but the reasonable being, man, possesses endowments for the deliberation of all these things—not only that he is himself a part, but what part he is and how it meets that the parts should give place to the whole.

A man should have an object or purpose in life that he may direct all his energies to it—of course, a good object. He, who has not one object or purpose of life, cannot be one and the same all through his life.

Faith and Science

The cleavage of science and faith is one of the signifying substances of our contemporaries. Some reflective thinkers give credence to the belief that their coherence is conceivable and obligatory while others assert that the two are immanently unlike. Both sides have implemented much syllogism, but very frequently the issue has been confounded on wrong premises where one is reminded of Charles F. Kettering saying, "Beware of logic. It is an organized way of going wrong with confidence." The problem is so consequential and compelling that the minds of the vulnerable younger generation cry for a response that could comfort their troubled subliminal egos.

Whitehead has very rightly pointed out:

> When we consider what faith is for mankind and what science is, it is no exaggeration to say that the future course of history depends upon the decision of this generation and the relations between them.

(For details, see "Faith in the Unseen.")
Only those ideas that integrate vitally can evolve into faith. Many regard faith as the substantial innards of informative development—the only deportment and route of development open to man—and believe that they cannot be imposed by force, but it is possible to encourage and promote them by helping one faith with the furtherance of another. Whitehead also postulated that there is a consistent requirement of communication between our faith and our enlightenment of actuality. According to him, faith is a condensation or combination of contemplation, rectitude, and edification into an arrangement of a motif.

This motif, which invariably to specific grade is effective or sufficient and tends to issue in action of some sort thus giving a directional set to personality" and deciding an individual's general attitude or approach to life. So faith can gain subsistence to grow only if intellectual, scientific, artistic, practical, and moral ideas are integrated biologically as virtual parts of an organic whole.

On the other hand, they degenerate if one set of ideas constantly corrodes the other. It is, therefore, simply impossible to have two types of beliefs at one and the same time.

Now the refinements, diplomacy, poise, grace, and savoir faire are also gone; they just exchange kisses. The cultural attrition of a society epitomized in "two cultures" is a cause of great concern. Human culture, like organisms and societies, depends for its survival on their internal integration, an integration that can be achieved only to the extent that science remains meaningful to the living experience of man. No wonder, therefore, that scientists stress the need of integrating into our thinking and acting the full range of human wisdom, so that the philosophers, the social scientists, the writers, and the natural scientists are all intellectual brethren under the skin.

But in this age of ours, institutionalized science has stood up against institutionalized religion as a rival establishing its own sacred buildings, its monasteries, its esoteric language, its priests and acolytes, even its incantations and mummies. Thus science has become a metaphysical mother, a superhuman thing and a huge entity which has an independent existence of its own in which modern man believes in much the same way as his ancestors used to believe in religion. It has gradually spread its roots in all that we do and think and all that we feel, and we cannot tear them out; if we do, we would endanger our civilization.

One of the basic premises, gone very deep into common religious thinking, which is responsible for the dichotomy of religion and science, is the popular notion of "blind faith." It is said that faith begins where reason ends, and faith has nothing to do with reason. According to this view, faith in the unseen cannot but be "blind." The contention of "blind faith" leads one to the inference that the name of God has no pertinence to the discernible and the avowed. This assumption has done incalculable harm and has provided strong grounds for scientists to presume that faith is a white flag of acquiescence to the unascertained. Faith is just another name for man's gratification and serenity with incognizance, which interdicts the inquisitiveness of the mind and stunts kismet to all-scientific investigation and struggle. They also argue that since revelation issues from a region that is wholly inaccessible to man, the object of faith is something that is absurd to reason. But today, recent investigations are coming through to confirm the very existence of "Allah," "God," or "Bhagwan." Thus human reason (science) and divine reason (religion) do touch at this point.

Huxley's assertion, "If events are due to natural causes, they are not due to supernatural causes," is rooted in the same reason.

"The principle of a personal God," says Albert Einstein, "can always take refuge in those domains in which scientific knowledge has not been able to set foot." He calls this behavior on the part of the representatives of religion not only unworthy but also fatal By enthroning God in the unknowable, as if He despised the light of human knowledge, we assign Him an extremely vulnerable position in the universe so that the ever-expanding frontiers of scientific discoveries correspondingly push Him further and still further back into the ever-retreating unexplored parts of nature. No wonder, therefore, that the Russian space scientists on their first entry into space happily declared that there is "no" God in the universe. How may we hope to keep the flame of faith aglow if faith is just a sort of refuge in the nescience or naiveté conforming religion with seclusion and incognizance?

Another erroneous assumption on which religion pursues to constitute its excellence and preference over science is by way of its emphasis on the scientific discoveries of today. The religious main characters are obsessed with devising proclamations that science will never be able to accomplish this or do that, as these lie only within the proficiency of the "intangible," (i.e., God). Man is a changing phenomenon in the realm of science. Ever-increasing additions to his knowledge give him more and more power over nature, thus making him more and more "supra-natural" every day. Science has been consistently breaking its limitations and restoring the ground from underneath the erroneously rationalized religious beliefs. Even the strongest walls built by men of religion for the protection of their concept of God—narrowed by their own limited imaginations—are being demolished one by one as science marches victoriously in its progression. Had the imagination of the religious people been continuously broadened by new insights of science, which it perpetually provides to man through new discoveries, the idea of God would have been correspondingly widened.

Faith is an act of the intellect assenting to divine truth at the command of the will moved by the grace of God. That is to say, whereas in knowledge, the intellect is moved to assent by the object itself, known either directly or by demonstrative reasoning, in faith, the reasoning is moved to assent through an act of true discernment; for otherwise, it turns involuntarily to one side rather than to the other.

Philosophy of the Inner Mind

The beginning of philosophy is to know the condition of one's own mind. If a man recognizes that this is in a weak state, he will not then want to apply it to questions of the greatest moment. As it is, men who are not fit to swallow even a morsel buy whole treatises and try to devour them. Accordingly, they either vomit them up again or suffer from indigestion, from whence come gripping, fluxing, and fevers, whereas they should have stopped to consider their capacity.

Such are the impressions of the few, of whom I speak. And further, they apply themselves solely to considering and examining the great assembly before they depart. Well, they are derided by the multitude. So are the onlookers, by the traders; aye, and if the beasts had any sense, they would deride those who thought much of anything but fodder.

Thus, I would like to be initiated and employed, so that I may say to the Almighty, "Have I in any way transgressed Your commands? Have I in any way perverted the faculties, the senses, and the natural principles that You determined for me? Have I ever held You responsible or found lapse with Your administration? When it was Your good pleasure, I fell sick, and so did other men, but my will consented. Because it was Thy pleasure, I became poor, but my heart rejoiced. With Your blessing, I continue to live; I will live as one who is free and noble, as You would like me to behave. For You have made me free from hindrance, for what appears to me as a matter of lash or thrash. No power in the state was mine, because You would not; such power I never desired! Have You ever seen me of more doleful countenance on that account? Have I not ever drawn nigh unto You with cheerful look, waiting upon Your commands, attentive to Your signals? Now as I depart from the great assembly of men and put all my faith in You, wouldn't You bestow me the blissful smile? But have You no further need of me? I thank You, for up to this hour, I stayed for Your sake and none other's, and now in obedience to Thee, I depart. I go. I give Thee all thanks that You have deemed me worthy to take part with You in this assembly, to behold Your works, to comprehend this Your administration. Such is the subject of my thoughts, my pen, my study, when death overtakes me."

Conviction in Faith

Faith, the acceptance of truth or virtue, should be sincere, that is to say, it should be contemplative, for it is one thing to embrace an idea of nature— whether true or false, seasoned or innocent, virtuous or shrewd—because one has some material and sentimental interest in it and quite another to acknowledge it because one knows or believes it to be true, insinuated in the profundity of human nature.

Comprehensive elucidation of spirituality's assertive consequence on health is not so significant; similarly, we do not conceive or discern the implement of many drugs. We discriminate, from observing cause and effect, that they work. Likewise, we can see the effects of a person's spiritual consciousness on his outcome, so why not use that? It's like the placebo effect. Why did it work? Faith! It's a very potent and cogent power.

If medicine takes the position that devoutness and piety is healthful, it does not indicate that being sick or failing to redeem full health is a product of erroneous reverence. We are not here to abide indeterminately. We all have to die from one or the other reason. Indeed, even doctors who include spirituality in their medicine bag concede that it is crucial to use faith only as an accessory to medical care and only if the patient is open to talking about his or her beliefs. But at times, even in very serious situations when the doctors showed their out-and-out disappointment, supernatural occurrences of faith show up.

Ethical conduct is the action that's consistent with faith or with the principle grounded in belief. Faith in human excellence or importance will ascertain the attribute of the association between doctors and their patients and of the health care that the state furnishes for its people. Faith about the eminence or value of each human life will ascertain the skilled limits of a doctor's obligation in risky and ticklish areas of practice, from reproductive medicine to critical care. The faith that each human life has supreme eminence necessitates a scrupulous, steadfast, or unblemished obligation to sustain it in all state of affairs, heedless of other deliberations.

Faith, however, that there is a strong presumption in favor of each human life will entail a prima facie duty to save life, but leave the doctor with the discretion, and often the duty, to change the management, in the patient's interest, from listless prolongation to palliative terminal care. There are those who hold the despotic view in relation to the beginning of life in embryology, for instance, fetal medicine and neonatal care and those who profess it for the prolongation of life at the end, but not all are consistent in applying it to both. In recent decades, tension between these beliefs has cherished conscientious argument, as new understanding and technical proficiency have opened new possibilities for medical intervention and new options for patients.

I stress the importance of comprehending restitution to the numinous way in faith. The more mutated or devious and secluded from faith we are, the more we are distressed, aggrieved, and irked. Stress and faith are thus intimately associated with each other, when the tribulation, torment, disease, distress, agony, and alarm take over you and instinctively you call on your inner self, "the faith," to shepherd you along the way, to assuage and pacify your vulnerable impulsive instincts. "You feel shelter in the realm of faith."

The vicissitudes of discrimination between righteous and wrong, conscientious and sinister, scrupulous and flagitious, ethical and vulgar, virtuous and wicked, decorous and abominable, or the day and night are the signs for those who think. This nature is faith—the fount of religion and the very source of nature—whom we bore witness at the time of creation, His Almighty.

Faith has also done wonders even in ordinary, routine life. A pastoral group was traveling in the desert during the month of Ramadan. It was a hot summer day. The blistering, scorching heat was unbearable. Their tongues were woolly, dry, and stuck to their throats as they were fasting. The burning midday sun compelled them to wait under the paltry shadow of a desert tree. They thought for a while. How could it be possible to travel in the burning sand dunes in this unendurable heat while fasting? The saintly person who ushered the contingent asked them, "Recite the appellations of His Almighty zestfully while sitting under the tree and observe how they perceive." Surprisingly, all of them felt rejuvenated and restored, their throats were moist as if they had had refreshing and soothing drinks. They started once again in the scorching desert's searing heat and reached their destination well before time. During the whole course, they kept on reciting the venerated name of His Almighty.

Another startling event took place when this group was traveling in the high mountain tracks and had to spend a night in a modest, cold, quite frosty, and grubby dwelling. At night, they were all pestered and stung by mosquitoes and bugs. They could not get a wink of sleep. The next morning, Professor Noor asked the group leader, "How can it be possible to stay for a month when we are not in a position to possess the agony of one night?"

The group leader advised a common prayer before retiring to bed each evening. The professor said that they never experienced the torment of bugs or mosquitoes from then on.

Truth in Faith

Faith has a "conviction," and true conviction has the real "perception."

When His Almighty declares, "I am close to you and witness to all your deeds and know regardless it is in the obscure corner of your hearts or in the profundity of your *conscious or unconscious* mind," Allah Almighty declares, "Just supplicate and implore and I will bestow you whatever is in your finest expediency" (2:186).

I have an alarm clock set to buzz for late-night prayers. There is a recording of a cuckoo, the amusing "Coo, coo!" before the call for prayers. Once I wished in the veer of my core for a while if it was possible to hear the factual melodious "Coo, coo!" at this hour of the night. The next night, when I got up, I listened to the mellifluous and euphonic intonation of a cuckoo as if it was perched on the window of my bedroom. I contemplated for prayers without even comprehending my previous night's mental conception of the aspiration of giving ear to this enchanting phonation. As soon as the idea of my desire entered my mind, the "Coo, coo!" seized.

In the Qur'an it is clearly said:

For what you discern *candid in lore*
Or in the intimate veer *of core*
I care and concern each *bit in score* (3:29)

Faith—Precept of Christianity

"Take pleasure in one thing and and be fully devoted to it, in passing from one social act to another social act, thinking of God." Again, "Love mankind; follow God." It is the characteristic of the rational soul for a man to love his neighbor. Antoninus teaches in various passages the forgiveness of injuries, and we know that he also practiced what he taught. Bishop Butler remarks, "This Divine precept to forgive injuries and to love our enemies, though to be met with in Gentile moralists, yet is in a peculiar sense a precept of Christianity, as our Savior has insisted more upon it than on any other single virtue." The practice of this precept is the most difficult of all virtues. Antoninus often enforces it and gives us aid toward following it. When we are injured, we feel anger and resentment, and the feeling is natural, just, and useful for the conservation of society.

The core of the Christian faith lies in the belief in the fatherhood of God, the divinity of Christ the Messiah, and the morality of charity, love, and divine mercy. Justification by faith means faith in Christ, whose essential revelation is that God is merciful and forgives the sinner, who truly repents and strives to live a life of Christian morality.

Religion is entirely and exclusively the consequence of a decently good heart, it emanates completely from the wish of the good heart that the good in the world should triumph over the evil. God has not only sowed in men's minds that seed of religion of which we have spoken but revealed Himself and daily disclosures of Himself in the whole workmanship of the universe. As a consequence, men cannot open their eyes without being compelled to see Him. At various times, Calvin called the universe at large a book, a mirror, and a theater for the display of God's attributes, preeminently for the display of His goodness to us but also of His glory, wisdom, power, and justice. In the course of expounding this view that God can be known through his works, Calvin explicitly opposed the view that God can be known by speculation concerning His essence. It is by nourishing his sense of divinity and his conscience, with the contemplation of God's works, that man can in principle, arrive at the knowledge of God.

Sin! It was Calvin's persistent teaching, however, that in fact no one does come to know God in the manner described above. The positive demands placed on all men by God's internal and external revelation are rejected, and this rejection results in an endless series of spurious faiths. This resistance to God's demands is what Calvin identified as sin. Thus, sin is not primarily ignorance about God, although such ignorance, or blindness, as Calvin often called it, will always be a consequence. Rather, Calvin viewed sin as an active, volitional contrariety to God, as an emphatic disavowal to acknowledge His stipulations of adoration and compliance and as a conscious emotional distance from Him. Its fundamental distinguishing traits is obdurateness, and its root is ordinarily arrogance and amour propre.

Hinduism

This contrast between religion and faith becomes even more acute when with the Absolute is equated with a supernatural unity. Here, there is a striking parallel between Indian monism and the thought of F. H. Bradley. Some Hindu scriptures (notably the Bhagavad-Gita) describe God as a personal being, the Lord of the universe, whose "grace" *(parasada)* requires the "loving devotion" *(bhakti)* of his worshipers. The Gita is especially significant. Through the discernment in the eleventh chapter, it declares that Krishna *(the incarnate God, the friend of Arjuna)* is "more to be prized even than Brahman." But Sankara, following the non-dualistic strain in the Upanishads, they hold that the sole reality is the impersonal Absolute (Brahman) with which the soul is numerically identical. Personal faith in the Absolute belongs to the sphere of illusion *(maya)*. They are forms under which the One appears to benighted minds. Likewise, F. H. Bradley held that since reality is non-relational, a personal God is "but an aspect and that must mean but an appearance, of the Absolute."

Nirvana in Hinduism and Buddhism

Nirvana is a term used primarily to refer to the state of release or salvation in Buddhism. It is also one among a number of words used in the Hindu tradition (the most common of which is *moksa*) for the corresponding states in the various systems of Hindu mythology. In modern usage, *nirvana* almost always refers to Buddhist nirvana. The word is Sanskrit *(nirvan)*; its Pali version, as found in the Theravadan canon (the scriptures of the Buddhism of Ceylon, Burma, and parts of Southeast Asia) is *nibbana*.

Literally, nirvana means the "going out" or "extinguishing" of a flame. The imagery here is related to the Buddhist doctrine of rebirth and karma. An individual's series of lives is compared to the lighting of successive lamps, one lamp from another. The state of nirvana is achieved when the saint *(arhant)*, by uprooting craving, eliminates the fuel on which the flames feed, thereby achieving a state in which he will be no more reborn. The destruction of craving is typically attained by treading the "Eightfold Path," which includes not merely ethical self-training but also and importantly the techniques of yoga[36] or contemplative mysticism. Through the attainment of higher states of consciousness, the saint gains serenity and insight into the nature of reality, the ultimate true "faith."

Faith inside Islam

For nearly 1,400 years, Islam, even though sequestered in dissident groups, has concluded to be a concentrating and unifying faith for people reaching from the Atlantic to the Indian Ocean and beyond. Originating in the 1500s, Western dominion, which consummated in establishing colonies, abraded once magnificent Muslim sovereignty and shriveled the predominance of Islam. After the ratiocination of the Ottoman Supremacy succeeding World War I and the dissolution of European colonial authorities subsequent to World War II, Muslim nations embraced Western convictions and other dogmas. Their bureaucracy and political systems often endorsed by the West are exploiting and domineering.

Muslims perused their faith for solutions, indicating an Islamic renaissance. Westerners often call these appearances "fundamentalism" and take for granted they are against Western civilization. However, not all Islamists, who range from moderate to militant, hold up austere access to their religion, the ubiquitous certitude of Islamic law.

The word itself, *Islam*, is an Arabic word meaning "submission to God," with its code of behavior resolutely planted in Salaam (i.e., peace and serenity). That may show up as a stupefaction to numerous non-Muslims, whose discernment of the faith has been tampered with by terrorists, many from the Middle East, whose unspeakable acts in the name of Islam have been accursed far and wide.

---

36 Surprisingly, different notions of yoga are in the Muslims' five daily prayers. If someone accomplishes regular prayers in the true sense, as recommended in Sunnah, it is the true practice of yoga and meditation.

Reconciliation is the essential quality of Islam, with reference to the sanctification of life, is the foundation of Islamic faith, and of all great faiths.

Like Judaism and Christianity, Islam traces its lineage to the prophet Abraham, whom God (Allah in Arabic) made promises that became the endowment of the three faiths. Muslims esteem the Hebrew prophets, including Moses, and regard the Old and New Testaments as an indispensable part of their belief. They dissent with Christians about the divinity of Jesus but respect him as an eminently respectable emissary from Almighty God. The concluding ambassador of faith is Prophet Muhammad [PBUH].

The Qur'an is the only book that is memorized by hundreds and thousands of people, and there has been no mutation or shift in the original script. The Qur'an is a true manifestation of faith and discipline and a code of ethics; besides that, it enunciates a downright and comprehensive way of life.

God restrains us from religious compulsion but guided Muhammad [PBUH] to proclaim his true faith among the people of his region—no insignificant assignment, given the iniquitous, villainous, depraved, sinful, and debauched tribal armed conflict and idol worship rampant in seventh-century Makkah, much of it focused on the Ka'aba. This cube-shaped shrine was used for pagan rituals to honor a pantheon of deities. Muhammad [PBUH] and his followers were ridiculed and violently attacked for their belief in a single, unseen Allah.

After a decade of tyranny and torture, Muhammad [PBUH] and his retinue moved to Medinah, a city some two hundred miles from Makkah, where the Prophet inspired more believers and in due time came to command the town. After several years, he with an insignificant army of the allegiants repossessed Makkah, took the city, destroyed the idols of the Ka'aba, and rededicated it to the God of Abraham. From that time to this, pilgrims have revered the Ka'aba as the holiest mosque in Islam. Many reproduce the Prophet's journey to Makkah in the annual hajj, or pilgrimage, which attracts more than three million Muslims from all over the world to circle the Holy Ka'aba in the footsteps of Abraham [AS] and Muhammad [PBUH]. The benevolence, forbearance, absolution, tenderness, reverence, piety, graces, and mercy of the religion are manifest at that occasion. The Prophet [PBUH] could have taken vengeance for his torments and tribulations, afflictions and agonies when he seized Makkah, but instead, he condoned and absolved all disbelievers whosoever entered the great mosque or the house of his uncle.

One of the Five Pillars of Islam (along with fasting in the holy month of Ramadan, five daily prayers, benevolence, and asseveration of faith), the Hajj is obligatory of all who can manage it at least once in a lifetime.

For most of the world's 1.3 billion Muslims, Islam is not a political system. It's a manner of life, a code of ethics, firmly established on perceiving the world through the eyes of faith.

Reason and Revelation

"Islam gave me something that was lacking in my life," says Jennifer Calvo of Washington DC. Calvo is twenty-eight. She looks as if she just stepped out of a painting by Botticelli, with her aquiline features and striking blue eyes set off by a white headscarf tucked neatly into her full-length robe. Calvo was raised Catholic and works as a registered nurse.

"I used to get so depressed trying to conform to our crazy culture and its image of what a woman should be," she said, "the emphasis we put on looking good—the hair, the makeup, the clothes, and our hunger for material wealth. It left me feeling empty all the time."

Two years ago, as people have done for 1,400 years, Jennifer became a Muslim by simply declaring the words: "There is no god but Allah, and Muhammad ᴾᴮᵁᴴ is His prophet. There is no god but Allah, and Muhammad is His Messenger."

"Everything is so much simpler now," she said. "It's just me and Allah. For the first time in my life, I am at peace."

I asked Peter how he embraced Islam. He said, "My father is a priest in London, and I often attended the church rituals with him. One day, my father performed the wedding of two gays. I asked my father, 'How come you are performing such a rite, whether the religion acknowledges such a sacrament or not.'

"My father said, 'It is the rule of the state and not observance of the religion.'

"'But, Father! You are here in the House of the Lord for the consequence of religion.' I had no alternative but to avert my face towards veracity, righteousness, and perfection that I ultimately discovered in Islam."

These days, the Muslims' aspect of purgation cleansing and purification is recommended and backed by environmental control agencies to avoid water pollution caused by the indiscriminate use of toilet paper.

A laundryman turned Muslim in London because he beheld that the trousers of Muslims were not defiled or foul but those of others were really invidious and abominable. "I loved the idea to stay pure, unsoiled, tidy, and immaculate and hence acclaimed Islam."

Certainty in Faith

The Lord Almighty is both the "Manifest" (the "Known") and the "Hidden" (the Unknown). In fact, God would not be God if He could be fully known, and God would not be God if He could not be known at all.

The Holy Qur'an exhorts man to toil ceaselessly to meet Him (84:6), and man in turn determines to reach Him and be with Him (1:4).

He prays to God to show him the right path (1:5) (i.e., a path that passes straight through this concrete material world and does not detour in it).

The modern mind with its habits of concrete thinking demands exactly such a concrete living experience of God. While inviting attention to some of the natural phenomena of the material world, the Holy Qur'an proclaims in unambiguous words: "This is Allah! Where are you then led astray?" (6:96).

Faith in the Almighty

According to the Holy Qur'an, all natural phenomena are "signs of God," indicating the activity of His mind, urging its readers to observe minutely and ponder deeply these phenomena. The intent of the Holy Qur'an is to keep a close contact with the behavior of "reality." Man will sharpen his inner perception for a deeper vision of the truth. It is the intellectual capture of that power over the concrete that makes it possible for the comprehension of the man to interpret the wisdom of the concrete. Science based on the observation of sense data is thus a necessary preparation for man to see God and is thus a sort of prayer.

Numerous scientists have endorsed this view that scientific activity is a sort of religious activity. Iqbal assigns prayer as "... an essential correlative to the observance of nature. Beneath nature's surface beauties, there is a deeper beauty, whose contemplation offers most profound satisfactions. Science is rooted in the will to truth. With will to truth, it stands or falls. Lower the standard slightly, and science becomes diseased at the core. The will to truth, pure and unadulterated, is among the essential conditions of its existence."

Albert Einstein, too, is of the opinion that those who have the aspiration toward truth and understanding can only create science. This source of feeling, however, springs from the sphere of religion. I call it the intuitive perception of faith.

Another wrong premise on which some religious thinkers see the separation of religion from science is the idea that they come from and belong to different parts of the mind and are different kinds of mental activities. They say that the facts of religion can be comprehended only through intuitive perception, love, wonder, and appreciation, while the facts of science are learned through observation, sensory perception, intellectual effort, reasoning, and understanding. But the human mind never works in such severally isolated compartments as if it were divided into separate departments of thinking, feeling, and willing. No type of mental activity can ever be imprisoned into its own confines to the absolute exclusion of others; rather, they frequently walk and talk with one another. Thus, there is no such thing as pure thought or pure feeling or pure intuition. The world cannot be divided into classes like thinkers and feelers even though there are philosophers and scientists, poets and mystics.

On the one hand, there have been great scientists like Galvan, Perkins, Roentgen, and Fleming who made their great discoveries under the flashes of intuition, which came to them spontaneously. Still there were a number of scientists like Lecomte du Nuoy, Teilhard de Chardin, Edmund W. Sinnot, and Heisenberg, who had intuitive perceptions during their thinking over physical problems.

On the other hand, even great prophets having direct communion with God would at times beseech to ask Him, "My Lord, show me how You give life to the dead," Abraham[sws]. Or "My Lord, show me Yourself, so that I may gaze on Thee," Moses[sws]. And "My Lord, give me the knowledge of things as indeed they really are," Muhammad[PBUH]. Thus, the realms of religion and science, though clearly marked off from one another outwardly, have very strong reciprocal relationships and mutual dependencies inwardly, admitting of no departmental isolations in the human mind.

A noted scientist, R. G. H. Sill, has gone to the extent of saying, "The sense of perception is the discernment of the Perfect. It is immaculate veraciousness and no knowledge is conceivable under different ambient factors typifying its transformation into either:

i.   Intuitive perception
ii. The knowledge of sagacious enlightenment, the science"

However, a deep tactility of real learning at the root of all enlightenment in the scientific knowledge makes one see God in the atom.

Iqbal[37] hits upon the same point when he says:

---

37 A poet laureate of the East

These are all but the stages of seeker of truth in trust
Honored with the knowledge of all the names in Just
Stage of meditation, scanning through time and space
The stage of recitation:
All praises unto Thee O Lord Mightiest in Grace

Faith is the belief in revealed truths. Ultimately, the object of faith is the Lord Almighty Himself. The revealed truth is stringently conferred in the philosophy. Thus, to have faith means to believe the articles of faith symbolized in the basic confirmations of the religion.

It was July 28, 1980. I implored my ecclesiastic spiritual parson to evince my rightful course so that I could behold the purpose of my being in this world. After a couple of days, he came to my hospital office and secured the door. He took my hand in his grasp and advised me to recite certain divine names. He advised me to undertake the discipline of regular prayers. After a few days, I experienced a cardiac irregularity. The treatment was of no effect. These influences used to be quite profound, particularly when I was in bed. I was constrained to sit in a chair and read or remain prostrate the whole night. The symptoms reduced and even disappeared whenever I planned a medical checkup in the USA and appeared again when the schedule was relinquished. This situation continued until late December 1980. I once again adjured my numinous parson for guidance. He advised me to recite particular verses before retiring to bed. It was December 25, midnight, when I felt a sudden irregularity of the heart, and then it stopped. A monitor revealed runs of multifocal premature ventricular contractions followed by ventricular fibrillations eventuating in cardiac arrest. Instantaneously, a flash of intuition conducted me to an unimpeded limpid perception. I gave a great thump on my chest and threw myself out of bed. I removed the synthetic pajamas that I was wearing. My heart had revived, but it stayed irregular for a while. Gradually, it became regular.

Because of this occurrence, I contemplated that Almighty Allah was an unfeigned perception generated by the brain, and the brain itself has been wired to experience "the reality of the Almighty Lord."

These are rare experiences, requiring an almost total sweep of the briefing area of more conventional spiritual experiences, when allegiants "relinquish themselves" in prayer or perceive a notion of unity during a religious rite. Their research suggests that all these feelings can be founded not in emotional or wishful thinking, but probably by the genetically arranged wiring of the brain.

That's why religion flourishes in an age of reason. You cannot simply take the Lord Almighty out of existence, because religious feelings take root more from experience than from thought. They are born in a moment of spiritual connection, as real to the brain as any perception of ordinary physical reality.

All the amazement, presentation, supernatural occurrences, oddities, displays, and marvels around us are fortuitous. No Almighty handmade billions and billions of astral bodies. Are they all tearjerkers or mere quips, cracks, or witticisms? No force holds them in their poised equilibrium. How could the earth have grown fruit and vegetation from time inconceivable to sustain the life of all living beings without any source and power behind it? Is the fascination of the filum and granum, the fauna and flora, and the filigree of awe-inspiring resplendent landscapes stretched to eternity all a fluke or windfall?

Your temperament is squandered like the sharp edges of the concrete that pulled off the fuzz when you looked around the marvelous stunners of the natural setting. The electromagnetic pull of the earth and all the terrestrial bodies giving them a definite course in the boundless inconceivable universe, how could all that be just incidental? The rain, the storm, the day and night, the change of weather, the expanse of land from below to the vertex with diversified arrangements and distinctive surroundings, how could all that be altogether unintentional?

You take a moment to savor the sun's warmth on your face. Your baby holds out her arms to be picked up, and the trust in her smile brings tears to your eyes. But scientists now think that the positive moods these moments generate can have a subtle yet telling effect on your health.

Obedience in Faith

He is a happy man who has been wise enough to do this when he was young and had the opportunities. A man cannot always be so wise in his youth to encourage himself to do it when he can and not to let life slip away before he has begun. He who can propose to himself good and virtuous ends in life and be true to them cannot fail to live conformably to his own interest and the ubiquitous well-being, for in the attributes of effects, they are one.

For at the worst, if you don't turn to the Lord, you'll endure evil in fortune. But if you turn to His Almighty, Who in reality is the fate and fortune of all, He can endow His blessings for your ills and evils.

As Muslims, we assert that the Lord Almighty determines the time and place of death, but how we reach that destiny is definitely in our hands. For the Lord Almighty has ordained a discipline of life as to how to lead a numinous life with good health or turn to an outlandish life with ill health.

How could one die with a blissful smile on his face when one passes from this insubstantial and temporal, mundane life?

But how is that possible?

How could one achieve the perception and knowledge of creation of this grand universe?

Why are we created or brought to this earthly living?

What we shall have to do in this carnal living?

Whether we shall be able to achieve the cherished goal of our life and then beg before His Almighty with extreme humble prostration and plead His forgiveness that "To our most sincere efforts we did strive to abide the discipline whatever Your Almighty had ordained for us, we don't know with certainty, if we could ever succeed in it.

We have been insinuated with our genetic proscenium to perceive the discernment between the equitable and depraved, virtuous and vile, righteous and wrong, principled and flagitious, immaculate and abominable, tractable and perverse, or exceptional and nefarious, for these are all deeply ingrained in human nature. The discrimination of scrupulous or sinister is extremely dyed-in-the-wool in the human mind. Who shepherds the freshly fertilized cell to grow into a full-blown infant, and who teaches him to cry soon after coming to this vacuous and delusive world, to expand his lungs, and who shows the way to scream when famished? How can we stack up the life of one who dedicates his whole life for the alleviation of misery and agony of others, as did Mother Teresa, against one concerned in the massacres of hundreds and thousands of inculpable and humble people, besides the splintering, snapping, and sundering of human resources, like Hitler?

If there is no God, there should be no reparations for living a villainous life nor assertions of contentment in living a virtuous and disciplined life, because Mother Teresa and Hitler shall be conferred alike. And if there is a God, the well-deserved life spent by Mother Teresa will assuredly be prized. For otherwise, Teresa and Hitler will be equal. If there is a God, presumably, the justice for good and bad has to be there. Those who have faith and belief and have earned their glorified living dedicatedly, at least, have an edge over those who did not believe in God and who lived an outlandish, eccentric, erratic, droll, and queer life. This life of ours is just like spending a few moments in a transit lounge, where our conduct has to be ascertained in each discipline of life. If our conduct and attitude is admonishing with insalubrious comportment, we will be deserted and left forlorn and destitute. Then why not behave in a befitting manner in this transit lounge of earthly living to have confirmation of the everlasting world to come after demise.

Death is a snooze so deep
That makes a man to screech
Though a third of the life is passed in sleep

Why fear death? It is the most beautiful adventure in life.

Is death the last sleep? No, it is the last, final awakening (Prophet Mohammad[PBUH]).

That is the road we all have to take over the bridge of sighs in eternity (Danish).

Therefore, we must not concede to depravity before we concede to the ephemeral end of this carnal life at the cost of everlasting, enchanting, and captivating life, because there has to be justice for our conduct whether virtuous or vile.

What shall be done to the man who has never had the wit to be idle during his whole life, but has been careless of what the many care about: wealth and family interests, affluence, resources, profusion, property, and possessions? He did not go where he could do no good to mankind, but where he could do the greatest good privately to everyone and seek virtue and wisdom before he watched his sequestered approaches, and this would be the order that he observes in all his actions. What shall be done to such a one?

There had been no deception but sincerity of cause and faith.

"We are never deceived; we deceive ourselves" (Goth).

"One is easily fooled by that which one loves."

"You can fool some of the people all the time, and all the people some of the time, but you cannot fool all the people all the time" (Abraham Lincoln).

Islam Is a Faith of Natural Temperament and Attributes

Dial 20010911—a hankering awed silence?

Could it be the retaliation of the injustice done to a certain community? This was not a religious fanatic act but an act of vengeance shaking the peace and economy of the whole world. The perseverance, fortitude, and patience were not discernable. Why cannot we resolve our issues in a peaceful manner? The philosophy of Jihad is not to kill the innocents. Islam is a religion of peace, tranquility, nimbleness, and submissiveness. This never teaches aggressive retaliation. The Muslims' code of ethics as prescribed in the Qur'an and Sunnah teaches reconciliation and pacification, not hostilities or skirmishes.

The Qur'an very clearly declares:

For if some inclined to kill a man in pace
It would be of course a plan in state
As if killing of all the humanity in place
If one was to save a life of a man
It's like saving (the life) all humanity in plan_(5:32)

Look at Prophet Mohammad ᴾᴮᵁᴴ when he set foot in Makkah after vanquishing and subduing the city. He absolves all vindictiveness, retribution, malevolence, and vengeance he suffered at their end but instead bestows sanctuary and protection to all those who entered (the Great Mosque in Makkah) Haram Pak, without malice aforethought of their faith. He could have retaliated and squashed all the Quryesh, who had tormented, plagued, revoked, and distressed him after the declaration of the new faith.

The Muslims themselves should abide by the code of conduct and set an example for others to follow.

In the Qur'an, the Lord Almighty dictates us to be compassionate with one another and to live a scrupulous life. These conceptions are not just out, assuredly; the Qur'an substantiates innumerable illustrations of the discipline previously revealed in the earlier Scriptures. In numerous approaches, God's directive in the Qur'an vehemently lays down to entertain others in a more appropriate manner than they treat you.

Faith and the Physician

Accepting is seeing. If science could open a door by exhibiting that faith has worked in other cases, people might try themselves with firm conviction. They'll feel more energetic, have less chest pain, and begin to feel a sense of inner reconciliation or hearty feeling, and in due time, life becomes more entertaining, enchanting, enduring, and consequential for them. In science, we believe what we measure, so we can show cholesterol, blood pressure changes, and angiographic changes—the condition of the heart and its blood vessels.

Doctors and patients, however, need to fulfill to value the discipline of faith in the treatment of disease. Clergy-doctor teams introduce all the diversified faiths: Judaic, Buddhist, Islamic, Hindu, Roman Catholic, and Protestant. Students establish that some religious beliefs help in healing, when drugs are given with a pat of the conviction of faith. They are enlightened about how to bring a spiritual history and a medical history together, identifying a patient's belief in a non-menacing way. And they learn to hit and pat the religious approach, like hospital clergy, if a patient's condition desires it so.

We do need to know the mind of the patient beyond his physical condition. A patient's mind and life make a physical difference in the outcome of disease. Fears have unwanted effects on the body's well-being. The feelings and the mind of the patient do influence the process of healing. We must admit we are treating a whole person and not a disease.

Religion and medicine are deeply related, and we are seeing it time and again. It is not just organized religion giving some exemplary strength; it is the spirituality that indeed gives our life a meaning. The connection between spirit and body may be age-old, but as healing became a science, Western practitioners moved away from spirituality and religious faith. Now the patient's demand, coupled with scientific studies correlating faith with good health, is slowly converting a skeptical medical community. Scientific journals and many new books are taking up the subject. Doctors are attending conferences on faith healing in increasing numbers.

It is faith that gives meaning to our lives.

1. Long healthy life: Researchers found a seven-year difference in life expectancy between those who never attended religious services and those who attend more than once in a week (from a nationwide study of twenty-one thousand people from 1987 to 1995).
2. Well Esteemed: People who have strong religious beliefs have fewer health problems and function better than the non-religious (Jeff Levin, author of *God, Faith, and Health*).
3. Sickness: In 1997, an Indian study conducted among Hindus showed that those who prayed regularly were 70 percent less likely to have Ischemic Heart Disease.
4. Recovery: After open heart surgery, those who prayed and showed strong faith in His Almighty had three times the chance of being alive, than patients who found no comfort in religion (from a 1995 Dartmouth Medical School study).
5. Blood Pressure: A significant protective effect against high blood pressure was found among those who considered religion an important factor in their life (in a 1989 study of Caucasian men in Evans County, Georgia, by Duke researchers).
6. Mental Health: Regular prayers and meditation are found to release endorphins, soothing catecholamine, which alleviates depression and anxiety (from a 1999 Duke University study of nearly four thousand adults).

7. Stress: Humans under psychosocial and psychological stress experience raised blood pressure and increased heart and breathing rates, straining the body and lowering immunity. Regular prayer and meditation work wonders that pass a state of mental peace and tranquility of the mind, body, and soul (Herbert Benson of Harvard Medical School, author of *The Relaxation Response*).

Medicine and the Discipline of Faith

Professor Noor Ahmad Noor was representing the government of Pakistan in a Tokyo medical congress held in 1986. It was a ten-day schedule. Peers in his profession in different fields of medicine covered about ten thousand dissertations.

One day, the propositions about (various disciplines known in "Islam") different incredible medical attitudes were discussed with reference to Islamic disciplines. One of the papers discussed the results of eating food in a sitting or standing position. They affirmed that it was "settled upon" taking meals in a sitting posture, because in a standing posture, eating is not natural and invariably leads to gastrointestinal disturbances and peptic ulcers.

Secondly, they considered the attitude or position while urinating. It was affirmed that for subjects who customarily urinated in a sitting position, the rate of occurrence of benign hypertrophy of the prostate was less frequent. Similarly, some papers discussed and acclaimed that the incidence of constipation and subsequent hemorrhoids was more abundant when people used Western comfort seats when compared with those using Indian or Eastern Orthodox toilet seats.

The rate of occurrence of suicide or seppuku due to disappointment, anger at defeat, lack of fulfillment, and frustration are higher in Japan than the rest of the world. They established that the people who washed their hands and faces more repeatedly in a day, like the Muslims during ablution, had less frustration and were not repressed, and the incidence of suicide was minimal.

Regarding the Muslims' way of ablution, it was pointed out that using toilet paper increased the incidence of pilonidal sinus. Recent studies also indicate that it is a prime source of water pollution.

Mostly, the non-Muslims presented the papers referring to examples from the whole of the world. Professor Noor deliberated; the Muslims knew all the ethics of eating, drinking, ablutions, passing water, and defecation for more than fourteen hundred years, because all these notions of right and wrong are prescribed by our Holy Prophet Muhammad [PBUH].

Barring some exclusion, Western civilization has embraced the principles of Islam; that's the truth in the fundamental philosophy of faith ordained in all religions. The Muslims of the modern world have developed the stylish culture of the Western society, essentially with all its social ills, without even bothering to look at their cultural heritage, discipline of life, and code of ethics.

Faith is nothing but the truth of discipline that is deeply insinuated in the veer of our core, the seat of intelligence; it is determined to escort us in our daily course of life. I assure you cannot be dissuaded if ever you're stranded in confusion and you steal a while and ask your inner self to shepherd you in the perplexity of your daze; be sure you will never be deserted in a haze.

Faith Has a Healing Power

A rush of recent inquisitions is shaving the barrier between the house of God and fascinating medical explorations. Research has shown, for example, that people who attend religious services more than once a week live, on average, seven years longer than those who do not.

In ancient Egypt and Greece, temples erected to Asclepius, the Greek god of medicine, were often near such springs and festivals in his honor that have been located as far apart as Ancyra in Asia Minor and Agrigentum in Sicily. The cult was introduced in Rome to relieve a plague in 293 BC.

In Christianity, faith healing is exemplified especially in the miraculous cures wrought by Jesus (forty healings are recorded) and by his Apostles. The early church later sanctioned faith healing through such practices as anointing and the imposition of hands. Faith healing has also been associated with the antirecessionary miracles of saints.

During the nineteenth and twentieth centuries, faith healing often motivated pilgrimages and healing services in many Christian denominations. The apparent healing gifts of individuals have also attracted wide attentions, like Leslie Weather Head, a Methodist pastor and theologian; Harry Edwards, a spiritualist, in England; and Elsie Salmon, the wife of a Methodist minister in South Africa.

There are many instances that can be quoted in this context.

A patient was stabbed in the heart, stomach, and spleen during a domestic dispute. After seven operations, he was released from the hospital, the large wound in his stomach covered by a skin graft. The injury still had not healed a year later, so in December 1999, he came to Georgetown for a surgery, which finally closed his stomach. A first-year student conducting the interviews, nervously asked, "How did you find your source of strength?"

He said that there was something beyond the excellent medical care he received that he credited for his life. It was the Almighty Lord.

Professor Noor was principal in a medical school and also head of the department of medicine in 1981, when he suffered severe joint pains, which gradually became so excruciating and crippling that he was almost unable to get out of bed. He invariably used to accompany a group for preaching. When he could not attend the proceedings for quite some time, he was advised by one of the priestly persons of the group to recite a verse from the Qur'an; 21:87.

Dr Noor practiced that and was relieved of his excruciating pain, and ever since, he has not suffered any pain. In a like manner, Professor Noor's wife experienced severe joint pains, which were not responding to routine medical treatment for more than four months. Professor Noor said, "I repeatedly asked my wife to beseech and recite the same Qur'anic verses, but she always shrugged her shoulders in dissension." Once a good lady came to see her and advised her to entreat the Almighty and recite Surah Ẏa Śin. It was the sixth month of her crippling ailment, and by that time, she was totally exhausted. She initiated reciting the Surah intently, and exceptionally, she perceived excellent relief in her stifling joint pains in a couple of days. That was some time in 1982. She has never had the pains again.

In 1996, Joe Semmes, then an emergency-room doctor at Arlington Hospital in Virginia, was told he had pancreatic cancer and had a 50 percent five-year survival rate, recalls Semmes, now fifty-one and the father of four.

He admits that concepts such as balance and energy once made him roll his eyes. But when his wife, a practical businesswoman, asked people to pray for him, he did not argue. Not only was it harmless, but he had recently read about using meditation or contemplative prayer to calm the mind. "Despite debate on the issue, there is evidence in the literature that stress impairs the immune system. I thought whatever I can do to help my immune system is okay with me."

The day before Joe's exploratory surgery, his wife asked for a healing rite at her church. "All these people put their hands on me and sang hymns," he says. "It was incredible, the power of this community."

Semmes's tumor, wrapped around vital blood vessels, could not be cured by surgery. But radiation and thirty-six weeks of chemotherapy helped shrink it, and Semmes asked surgeons to try to remove it. In January 1998, an eleven-hour surgery excised the tumor.

Today, five years after his initial diagnosis, Joe Semmes shows no active evidence of disease and says he has "good energy," though the surgery removed most of his pancreas.

Early in his career, in the 1980s, Internist Matthews began to sense that his patients wanted something from him beyond a physical diagnosis and treatment; some of his patients, knowing of his strong faith, wanted him to pray with them.

"I did not have any models, my inclusion of spirituality in the doctor-patient relationship evolved by listening to the patients and paying attention and finding people having complete certitude in their faith." The son of a village doctor and medical scholar and the grandson of a missionary, Matthews practices internal medicine, but when taking patients' medical histories, he often asks the degree of their religious belief.

"It's as if he has a deeper range of support," says one of Dr. Matthews's patients, a biotech consultant chronically ill with an autoimmune condition.

At forty-seven, he had undergone surgery to replace an aortic valve; he also had Crohn's disease identified in his intestinal tract and lived with arthritis in his joints. Coming to terms with his degenerative, life-threatening illness had not been easy. He said he navigated the past six years by becoming more spiritual. Matthews will occasionally write Scripture references for him on his prescription pad and refer him to spiritual resources.

"There's a certain magic to it," said the patient, whose condition stabilized. Despite recent setbacks, he maintained, "My faith brings me to a point of balance where I do not feel that my illness is a burden."

One of a bank's senior, executives intended to accompany a pastoral care group for forty days. Since he was a heart patient, he came to seek my advice. His EKG and echocardiographic changes showed extensive anterior wall myocardial damage. His heart was quite enlarged. He used to be out of breath after walking a couple of yards. I advised him to take strict bed rest and to have regular medication. But he asked me to suggest some medicine that he could use during his journey. He was quite adamant to go. I was constrained to suggest to him certain medicines. He came to see me after about two months, when once again, he was intending to go for preaching with another group. I was surprised to observe that his EKG and X-ray reports showed spectacular improvement. I was taken off guard when he showed me the medicines that he had never used.

There are innumerable instances of faith healing. The mode of action of faith and firm conviction has yet to be ascertained, but seeing the cause and effect of the disease process, one has no alternative but to believe. It's because today most of the patients demand spiritual support for their illness.

We have case reports giving the fascinating results of faith. Maulana Aslam was suffering from chronic renal failure. There were no facilities for dialysis close to the village where he lived. He would supplicate his visitors to recite the opening Surah Al-Fatihah of the Qur'an on a tumbler full of water. He would drink only that water and lived for quite a few years, which no medical professional could understand, as his renal parameters remained stable till the time of his death.

Doctor's Approach toward the Patient and not the Disease

The medical establishment may be embracing spirituality because they themselves could use something to believe in. Physicians are called to a service, to put patients' good above our own. That's a very spiritual calling. But with managed care and making medicine a business, we are uncertain about giving up that significance of determination.

The doctor himself can be good medicine when to an alcoholic, an obese person, or a smoker he does not straight away condemn drinking or smoking but writes instead on his instruction slip and says, "Issue—drinking, potbelly, or smoking? Do you not think it's a problem?"

A good doctor should listen to the patient intently and address what he is feeling. A patient wants his doctor to know what he is about and certainly it makes a big difference to patients in a life-or-death situation. The patient must be aware that his doctors know what they are about and what they believe in and that they care about him. That probably makes a difference not only in the process of their care, but very likely in the outcome of their care. But in most of the situations, a patient is "a unique individual."

Mr. Abbasi was advised he needed a coronary bypass surgery in 1981 because of his unstable angina. He consulted me when a surge of adrenaline flashed across his face. A few soothing and consoling gestures with a pat of reassurance and a few words of advice were enough to build a new confidence in him. I advised him to wear cotton garments and use cotton bed linen, avoid smoking, drink lot of water, and take regular walks. I told him to pray and trust His Almighty and go ahead with his routine with full zest and self-reliance. He responded well to this unconventional treatment for unstable angina, and it was only after fifteen more years that he had his coronary bypass surgery done in 1996 when his unstable angina appeared again and did not respond to medical treatment.

Well people are different one from another; that's actually what makes a difference or fun in medicine. It is not so much their bodies that are different, it is that their minds are different. So in such a case, the physician has to focus hard on what we ought to, on what their minds are about and how that communicates with the rest of them. What does a good doctor do in connection with the sense of right and wrong in his patient's mind that could support him in getting better? First of all, a proficient doctor lends an ear to his patient, another poises and invokes his/her psyche and bestows assured and explicit recommendations aside from pertinent medication. All terminally sick patients responded excellently well.

Carcinoma in the Gall Bladder

A patient showed up with a recent history of severe jaundice with early signs of upper gastrointestinal symptoms. It was well advanced cancer of the gall bladder, confirmed clinically, that was implicating the liver and the upper small gut and stomach. We expressed our concern and explained the possible failure of the surgical intervention. He was thirty-one years old. He said with determined certitude, "Please go ahead. God Almighty will take care."

Despite all vigilant care, the growth could not be removed completely.

The surgeon told me that the patient was not going to make it, and most probably, he would die before the stitches were out. When I entered his room, the patient perceived a sense of disapprobation on my face. Before I could say something, he said, "Please, Doctor! You go ahead. I am not going to die."

Willy-nilly, I started helter-skelter low doses of cytotoxic medicines, alone and in combination, without a proper therapeutic schedule. It was sometime in the mid-seventies; the patient is still alive. Once I asked him what his source of confidence was. He just raised his finger toward the sky.

Carcinoma in the Breast

A fifty-seven-year-old lady, in 1977, was diagnosed with Stage-IV intra-ductal "fungating" adenoma carcinoma of the breast. The growth was well advanced, and she was refused surgery and radiotherapy. The patient was very poor, and she could not afford combination chemotherapy. She was given shots of cyclophosfamide along with a supportive herbal medicine. The assurance from the doctor was the only source of inspiration that enlivened and energized her to trust in faith. She prayed earnestly and begged forgiveness besides praying for her health. Her son always held congregations in the mosque for prayers.

The improvement was quite fascinating, and she carried through until 2004 when she died of CHD.

All who were brought back to health were made whole through their will-power and faith and not with the medicines alone. But in certain patients with type A behavior patterns, the response may not be completely gratifying.

There are scientific studies showing the reversal of serious heart diseases through the blending of medication, stress reduction, exercise, group therapy, a balanced diet, and well-disciplined faith. The principal purpose of the study was to ascertain whether arterial obstructions could begin to invert in a year. Until recent times, it was sustained that clogged arteries were going to get worse over time, so that the best you could do was to slow down the course or if the arteries were very badly clogged, do bypass surgery without really affecting the process itself. The study showed that in 82 percent of the patients who went through the program, the arteries actually became less blocked and the blood flow to the heart improved as a result. Chest pain also diminished markedly—by 91 percent in fact. But 53 percent of the control group actually got worse. No doubt the test group included highly motivated people, who were most ambitious. Those patients really wanted to make a change, and their will to do so was profound, but about 50 percent of the people recorded in the group were eager to associate the schedule even before the invasive diagnostic studies. These were the patients who never knew whether the program was going to help them or not. Scientists say, "Here is what we did, what we found, and here is how you can do it, if you want to." The new tests are very accurate and very reproducible. Many of the patients switched over in such a conforming and meaningful manner, as deliberated by the approved statistical methods, that the probability of the difference between the groups being due to a random chance was very small.

In my own practice, I never tell people, "You have to observe this diet. You have to come through this program, and you have to meditate." Because even more than feeling healthy, I think we want to stay unfettered and free. And you cannot feel free or open if someone is persuading you to do something, even if it is evidently for your personal care.

That goes back to Adam and Eve, when God said, "Do not eat this." We saw how effectual that was, and that was His Almighty talking.

We find faith ("Faith in the Unseen") also plays quite a substantial role in medical science, besides having a pivotal role in biology and physics, where science often provides a fundamental challenge to traditional religious thinking.

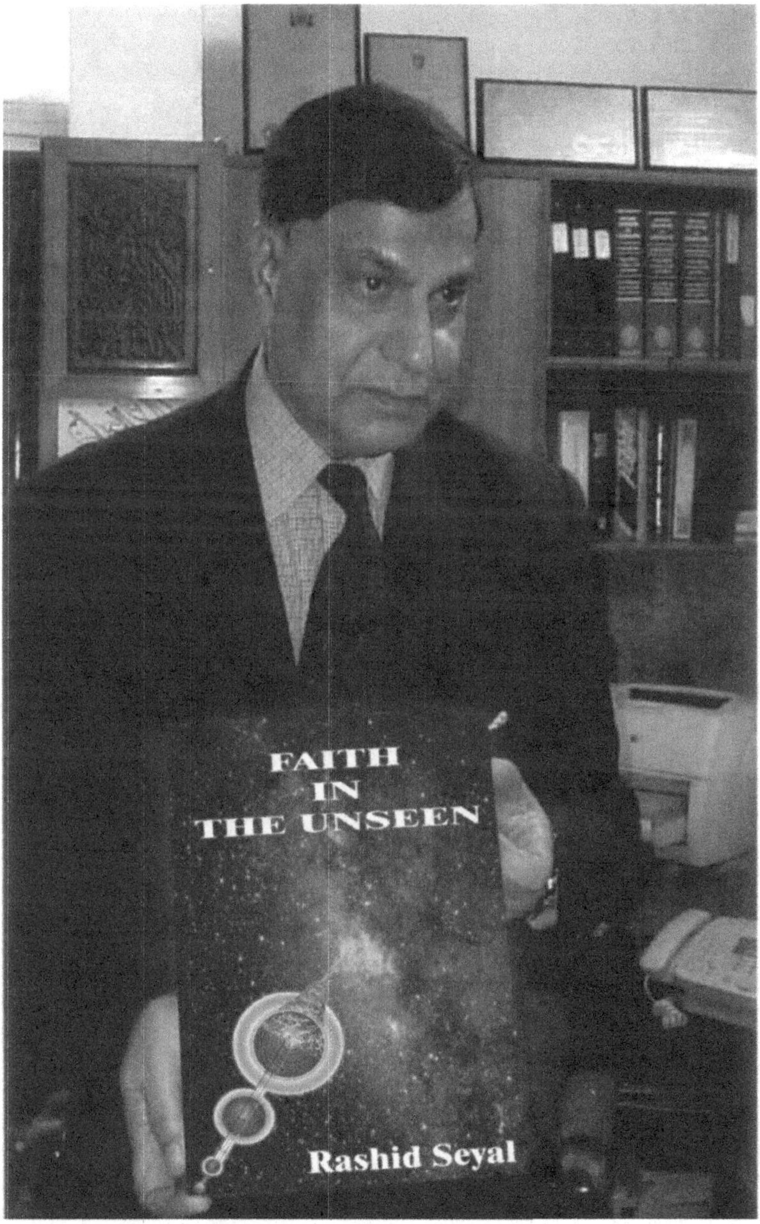
FAITH
IN
THE UNSEEN
Rashid Seyal

About the Author

Dr. M. A. Rashid Seyal is a seasoned cardiologist and an accomplished author. He has written many books including:

Garments and Human Health
Smart Living
Perception of Faith in Stress
Coronary Risk New Perspective (Recommended by the American College of Physicians)
Enigma of Sudden Cardiac Death
Living with the Heart (in press)

His work on Qur'anic poetry and philosophical interpretation in the light of modern-day science has given a new direction for understanding the Holy Scripture. He has already written three books on the subject including:

Divine Philosophy and Modern Day Science
Poetic Stance of the Holy Qur'an (Surah 1 through 114) *with Philosophical and Scientific Discernment*
Faith in the Scientific Philosophy of Religion
Morning Prayers
Glorious Qur'an in Poetic Stance, with Urdu Translation, English Poetry, and Scientific Assertions, in four volumes

Dr Seyal gives a detailed elucidation of faith in the unseen, faith in the hereafter, perfection in the creation, the fate of the grand universe, the philosophy of life, why the creation could not have taken place without a "creator," divine perception of time, travel back in time, and many other interesting topics that are detailed and affirmed in the Holy Qur'an.

These topics are touched with meticulous care in the light of the Holy Scripture, particularly the topics of faith in the unseen, divine perception of time, and the fate of the universe, in addition to the idea that the Adam of science and Adam of the Qur'an are one not two. He asserts if ever man should have sought guidance from the Holy Book regarding different notions of scientific concern earlier on, he would not have been loitering on the clue and code of such ideas as the roundness of the Earth and the motion of the earth, sun, and moon, along with many other topics affirmed scientifically today, which were already elucidated in the text of the Holy Book.

Bibliography

The substance affirmed in this book is derived from computer research and the pursuit of scientific information based on conceptual data tips and facts from the medical news and communications printed in well-known and specialized publications like *Reader's Digest*, *Time* magazine, and *National Geographic* and scientific magazines like *Scientific American* and is also embraced by authenticated and reconsidered correspondence. It is also based on my exclusive experience of forty-five years in my occupation, besides particular learning and probe to ensure many scholastic information bases exuberant in the scientific field as in *A brief History of Time* by Stephen hawking. It was not conceivable for me not to assert a small part of the published material on the subject from various sources in this book.

Arberry, A.J. *Sufism: An Account of the Mystics of Islam*. London, 1950.

Armstrong, Karen. *A History of God: The 4,000-Year Quest of Judaism, Christianity, and Islam*.

Bakhtiar, L. *Sufi Expression of the Mystics Quest*. London, 1979.

Bension, Ariel. *The Zohar in the Muslim and Christian Spain*. London, 1932.

Blumenthal, David. *Understanding Jewish Mysticism*. New York, 1978.

Butler, Dom Cuthbert. *Western Mysticism, the Teaching of Saints Augustine, Gregory and Bernard on Contemplation and the Contemplative Life, Neglected Chapters in the History of Religion*. 2nd ed. London, 1927.

Chittick, William C. *The Sufi Path of Love: The Spiritual Teaching of Rumi*. Albany, 1983.

Corbin, Henri, *Avicenna and the Visionary Recital*. Translated by W. Trask. Princeton, 1960.

——*Creative Imagination in the Sufism of Ibn Arabi*. Translated by W. Trask. London, 1970.

Encyclopaedia Britannica, 5:366:1a.

Encyclopaedia Britannica, 7:1008:1a.

Encyclopaedia Britannica, 15:846.

Encyclopaedia Britannica, 16:333:2b.

Encyclopaedia Britannica, 21:188.

Encyclopaedia Britannica, 22:985:2b.
Encyclopaedia Britannica, 26:593:1b.
Encyclopaedia Britannica, 26:596:1a.
Encyclopaedia Britannica, 26:985:2b.
Encyclopaedia Britannica, 26:987:b.